CONTENDING GLOBAL APARTHEID

Studies in Critical Social Sciences Book Series

Haymarket Books is proud to be working with Brill Academic Publishers (www.brill.nl) to republish the *Studies in Critical Social Sciences* book series in paperback editions. This peer-reviewed book series offers insights into our current reality by exploring the content and consequences of power relationships under capitalism, and by considering the spaces of opposition and resistance to these changes that have been defining our new age. Our full catalog of *SCSS* volumes can be viewed at https://www.haymarketbooks .org/series_collections/4-studies-in-critical-social-sciences.

CONTENDING
GLOBAL APARTHEID

Transversal Solidarities and Politics of Possibility

EDITED BY
MARTIN BAK JØRGENSEN
AND CARL-ULRIK SCHIERUP

Haymarket Books
Chicago, IL

First published in 2022 by Brill Academic Publishers, The Netherlands
© 2022 Koninklijke Brill NV, Leiden, The Netherlands

Published in paperback in 2023 by
Haymarket Books
P.O. Box 180165
Chicago, IL 60618
773-583-7884
www.haymarketbooks.org

ISBN: 979-8-88890-013-0

Distributed to the trade in the US through Consortium Book Sales and
Distribution (www.cbsd.com) and internationally through Ingram Publisher
Services International (www.ingramcontent.com).

This book was published with the generous support of Lannan Foundation,
Wallace Action Fund, and the Marguerite Casey Foundation.

Special discounts are available for bulk purchases by organizations and
institutions. Please call 773-583-7884 or email info@haymarketbooks.org for more
information.

Cover design by Jamie Kerry and Ragina Johnson.

Printed in the United States.

Library of Congress Cataloging-in-Publication data is available.

Contents

Preface

This book crowns another fruitful collaboration of the two editors. The book springs from our work and publication of a special issue in *Critical Sociology* on "Transversal Solidarities and the City", appearing in December 2020. Some of the discussions leading to that special issue go back to a seminar that took place in Aalborg, Denmark November 2018 under the heading "Seeing like a city". Invited guests discussed urban politics and social struggles with a special focus on the scale of the city. The discussions were characterized by an optimism identified among urban social movement actors and progressive municipalities. After publishing the special issue, we decided to expand the perspective in terms of geographical scale and invited contributors working in other parts of the world than Europe and North America. Hence, we include chapters from South Africa, Kenya, Chile, Mexico, and Latin America more broadly.

Four years after the workshop in Aalborg the world has not become a better place for migrants. The pandemic, still defining mobility and protection in parts of the world, has accentuated processes of precarization and made living conditions more difficult, especially for migrants. Likewise, the long summer of migration has turned into autumn, but thousands of refugees remain stuck in detention camps across Europe while new walls and barbed wire fences are being constructed as part of ongoing and new geopolitical struggles. Echoing the South African history of apartheid, a racialized world order and hyper-exploitative labor market, long imminent, is reproduced and exacerbated by the corrupted fusion of a crisis ridden financial capitalism with an extreme neoconservative nationalism. Confronted with this state of Global Apartheid, the book is informed by the idea that an alternative globality could sprout from transversal solidarities emerging in cities, municipalities, and urban neighborhoods, engendering imaginaries for social transformation. The essays in this volume take a critical investigative approach to solidarity in their discussion of migration and race-relations on a variety of scales. They interrogate the rise and potentials of a progressive socio-geographic emplacement of urban movements, including potentials of movements habitually judged reactionary or opportunistic. Discussing the experience of sanctuary or solidary cities in different parts of the world, they indicate that urban politics of solidarity can make a difference on a larger scale, as networks of regional or global scale connect progressive cities and provide grids for the sharing of experience with inclusive politics of transversal solidarity.

Acknowledgements

We are grateful for the support of David Fasenfest for the opportunity to publish this book in the Brill Series on *Studies in Critical Social Science* and for his encouragement during the process. We also thank the contributing authors in this book for their effort to enrich the perspectives on the issue at stake. Both the ones who contributed to the special issue and submitted updated versions for this volume, and the ones who contributed with new material.

Figures and Tables

Figures

Tables

Notes on Contributors

Aleksandra Ålund

is sociologist, professor emerita at REMESO, The Institute for Research on Migration, Ethnicity and Society at Linköping University. She has published widely in Swedish, English, and other languages on international migration and ethnicity, identity, culture, gender, youth and social movements. She has conducted several projects on, among other: working life, education, gender, employment strategies and social networks, immigrant associations, new ethnicities, cultural production, urban segregation, social exclusion/inclusion, and civic activism. Her present research (2014–2021) is focused on Urban Justice Movements and Global Activism for Migrant Rights. Among her recent publications is *Reimagineering the Nation. Essays on Swedish Society* (2017).

Ilker Ataç

is a Professor of Political Science at the Department of Social Welfare in the University of Applied Sciences Fulda in Germany. Before, he has taught at the University of Vienna and at the Institute for Migration Research and Intercultural Studies, University of Osnabrück. His research focuses on migration and social policy, social movements, civil society, citizenship studies and urban politics. He is on the editorial board of the journal *Movements*. His work has appeared in international academic journals including *Citizenship Studies, Ethnic and Racial Studies, Journal of Immigrant and Refugee Studies* and *Social Movement Studies*. He is the co-editor of the special Issue on Social Policies as a Tool of Migration Control (*Journal of Immigrant and Refugee Studies*, 2019, with S. Rosenberger).

Martin Bak Jørgensen

is Professor in Processes of Migration at DEMOS at the Department for Culture and Learning, Aalborg University, Denmark. He works within the fields of sociology, political sociology and political science. He has published the books *Politics of Dissent* (Peter Lang, 2015), *Solidarity Without Borders: Gramscian perspectives on migration and civil society alliances* (Pluto Press, 2016), and *Solidarity and the 'Refugee Crisis' in Europe* (Palgrave, 2019), all co-authored with Óscar García Agustín. He has published articles in the journals: *Internal Migration Review, Critical Sociology, Journal of International Migration and Integration* and *British Journal of International Politics*.

Harald Bauder

is a Professor in the Department of Geography and Environmental Studies and the Graduate Program in Immigration and Settlement Studies at X University in Toronto. He is the principal investigator of the international project "Urban Sanctuary, Migrant Solidarity and Hospitality in Global Perspective." His books include *From Sovereignty to Solidarity: Rethinking Human Mobility* (Routledge, forthcoming), *Migration Borders Freedom* (Routledge 2016, open access), *Immigration Dialectic: Imagining Community, Economy, and Nation* (University of Toronto Press, 2012), and *Labor Movement: How Migration Regulates Labor Markets* (Oxford University Press, 2006).

Iriann Freemantle

is an Associate Researcher with the African Centre for Migration & Society (ACMS) at Wits University in Johannesburg. Over the past decade, Iriann has worked extensively on migration policy and xenophobia in South Africa. More recently, Iriann's work focuses on the governance of mobility in Africa. Together with Loren Landau, she currently works on a book on the spatial and temporal dimensions of European involvement in regulating African migration.

Christophe Foultier

is a lecturer at Södertörn University. He has a master's degree in urban planning and a PhD in International Migration and Ethnicity. His PhD thesis, *Regimes of Hospitality: Urban Citizenship between Participation and Securitization—The Case of the Multiethnic French Banlieue*, analyzes how urban strategies generate intersecting processes of participation and security. With an international research profile, he participated in 50 studies in Sweden and France on social policy, housing and urban governance.

Óscar García Agustín

is Professor at the Department for Culture and Learning, Aalborg University, Denmark. He is research director of the research group DEMOS. His research interests include work on populism, cosmopolitanism, international relations and solidarity. He has published the books: *Solidarity Without Borders: Gramscian perspectives on migration and civil society alliances* (Pluto Press, 2016) and *Solidarity and the 'Refugee Crisis' in Europe* (Palgrave, 2019) both co-authored with Martin Bak Jørgensen, *Podemos and the New Political Cycle. Left-Wing Populism and Anti-Establishment Politics* co-edited with Marco Briziarelli (Palgrave Macmillan, 2018), and *Left-Wing Populism: The Politics of the People* (Emerald Group Publishing, 2020).

Shannon Gleeson
is Professor of Labor Relations, Law, and History at the Cornell ILR School. Her books include *Precarious Claims: The Promise and Failure of Workplace Protections in the United States* (University of California Press, 2016) and *Conflicting Commitments: The Politics of Enforcing Immigrant Worker Rights in San Jose and Houston* (Cornell University Press, 2012).

Margaret Godoy
holds a BA in Sociocultural Anthropology, University of Toronto, a Graduate Diploma in Public Policy & Program Evaluation, Carleton University, and recently completed her MA in Immigration & Settlement Studies, Ryerson University (2020). Her Major Research Paper examined the role of civil society actors in engaging with municipal policies and practices of migrant solidarity in the Santiago Metropolitan Region of Chile during the COVID-19 pandemic. Working in English, French, and Spanish, her recent professional experience spans international development project management and policy analysis within the context of refugee resettlement.

Els de Graauw
is Associate Professor of Political Science at Baruch College and the Graduate Center, the City University of New York. She conducts research on immigration, civil society organizations, urban politics, government bureaucracies, and public policy, with a focus on understanding how governmental and nongovernmental organizations build institutional capacity for immigrant integration and representation. She is the author of *Making Immigrant Rights Real: Nonprofits and the Politics of Integration in San Francisco* (Cornell University Press, 2016).

Ilhan Kellecioglu
is a political scientist, research assistant at Uppsala University, the Institute for Housing and Urban Research. He graduated in 2017 with a master's thesis on NGO participation in local politics in Husby, Stockholm. He has researched and written about popular education, urban planning, and citizen dialogues. His present research 2020–2021 is focused on Urban Housing and Urban Justice Movements in Sweden.

Loren B. Landau
is Professor of Migration and Development at the University of Oxford and Research Professor at the University of the Witwatersrand's African Centre for Migration & Society. His interdisciplinary scholarship explores mobility,

multi-scale governance, and the transformation of socio-political community across the global south. Publications include, *Forging African Communities: Mobility, Integration, and Belonging* (Palgrave, 2018); *I Want to Go Home Forever: Stories of Becoming and Belonging in South Africa's Great Metropolis* (Wits Press, 2018). As chair of the Consortium for Refugees and Migrants in South Africa (2004–2012) he served on the South African Immigration Advisory Board. He is now a member of the Academy of Science of South Africa.

Jorge Morales Cardiel
is a fellowship postdoctoral at the Institute for Migration Research and Intercultural Studies (IMIS) in the University of Osnabruck, Germany. He holds a master's degree in international migration at the University of Coruña, Spain. And graduated at the Universidad Autónoma de Zacatecas, Mexico with the PhD thesis *Crisis humanitaria de las migraciones centroamericanas en tránsito por México. Migración forzada y geopolítica del capital* (Humanitarian crisis of Central American migrations in transit through Mexico. Forced migration and geopolitics of capital). He possesses large experience in fieldwork entailing volunteering in migrant shelters, as a methodological strategy, throughout Mexico, focusing lately on cross-border studies.

Janet Munakamwe
is a Visiting Senior Lecturer at the Wits Mining Institute- Centre for Sustainability in Mining & Industry (CSMI). She is also affiliated to the African Centre for Migration & Society (ACMS) and Alumnus of the Global Labour University (GLU) Master's Program. She possesses vast experience spanning multiple and varied scholarly interests ranging from labor, migration, gender, extractives and development. Aside academia, Janet is a community activist scholar and has a proven track record working with trade unions, community-based organizations (CBOs), migrant-rights organizations (MROs), and non-governmental organizations (NGOs).

Kim Rygiel
is Associate Professor of Political Science and research associate with Laurier's International Migration Research Centre at Wilfrid Laurier University, Canada. Her research focuses on border security, migration and citizenship politics within North America and Europe. She is author of *Globalizing Citizenship* (UBC Press, 2010) and co-author (with S. Ilcan and F. Baban) of *The Precarious Lives of Syrians: Migration, Citizenship and Temporary Protection in Turkey* (McGill-Queen's 2021) and co-editor (with F. Baban) of *Fostering Pluralism through Solidarity Activism in Europe: Everyday Encounters with Newcomers*

(Palgrave, 2020) and (with P. Nyers) *Citizenship, Migrant Activism, and the Politics of Movement* (Routledge, 2012). She is Co-Chief Editor of and has published in *Citizenship Studies*, and in journals such as *American Quarterly, European Journal of Social Theory* and *Ethics and Global Politics*.

Ana Santamarina
is a PhD candidate in the Department of Human Geography in the University of Glasgow (UK). She holds a Degree in Political Science and Law by the Complutense University of Madrid and a Master of Research in Human Geography by the University of Glasgow. Her research focuses on migrant solidarity politics in the urban space, and it is funded by the Urban Studies Foundation. She is also interested in anti-fascist politics and the spaces of populism.

Carl-Ulrik Schierup
is professor emeritus at The Institute for Research on Migration, Ethnicity and Society (REMESO), Linköping University, Sweden. He has researched on international migration and ethnic relations, globalization, nationalism, multiculturalism, citizenship, and labor. His major current focus is on race and class, and subaltern struggles under conditions of neoliberal globalization and resurgent nationalism. Among Schierup's major works are the books *Migration, Precarity and Global Governance* (Oxford University Press, 2015), *Politics of Precarity* (Brill, 2017), and *Migration, Civil Society and Global Governance* (Routledge, 2019). He has published in journals like *Critical Sociology, Journal of Intercultural Studies, Ethnic and Racial Studies, Journal of Ethnic and Migration Studies, Race and Class*, and *Globalizations*.

Sarah Schilliger
is a senior researcher and lecturer at the Interdisciplinary Centre for Gender Studies, University of Bern. For her PhD project entitled 'Caring without Borders?' (2014, University of Basel), she ethnographically researched the working and living realities of Polish live-in care workers who take care of elderly people in Swiss private households. In 2017/18 she was a senior research fellow at the Institute for Migration Research and Intercultural Studies (IMIS), University of Osnabrück and at the Centre for Refugee Studies, York University in Toronto. Her current research focuses on (irregular) migration, (urban) citizenship, intersectional/transnational inequalities, un-/paid care work, infrastructures of solidarity and social movements.

   Maurice Stierl
is Lecturer in International Relations in the Department of Politics and
International Relations at the University of Sheffield. Before, he has taught at
the University of Warwick and the University of California, Davis. His research
focuses on migration struggles in contemporary Europe and (northern) Africa
and is broadly situated in the fields of *International Political Sociology*, *Political
Geography*, and *Migration, Citizenship and Border Studies*. His book *Migrant
Resistance in Contemporary* Europe was published by Routledge in 2019.

CHAPTER 1

Contending Global Apartheid

Transversal Solidarities and Politics of Possibility

Martin Bak Jørgensen and Carl-Ulrik Schierup

Introducing this volume on transversal solidarities we pursue a vision of politics of possibility contending border closure, precarization and social expulsion. The included essays explore, from variable methodological and theoretical perspectives, the emplacement of transversal solidarities with and by migrants and post-migrants in Western European, African, South and North American cities and local urban communities. They proceed from the idea that cities, municipalities, and urban neighborhoods may provide spaces across which an energizing transversal politics can develop. Cities may accommodate both a humanistic sensibility and a radical potential for social transformation (Finley 2017). The figure of the 'migrant' is pivotal here. A focus on transversal alliances of solidarity may illuminate "the centrality of the "migrant question" for thinking about democracy, collective subjects and citizenry" (Tazzioli 2020, 141).

This embodies, in other words, a plea for utopia in a crisis ridden 21st century. Our present state of the world corroborates with hindsight the worries of a deeply concerned Anthony B. Richmond (1994) outlined in his book Global Apartheid from 1994, on migration, refugees, racism and a discriminatory post-Cold War 'new world order'; the latter today more commonly designated by the floating signifier of 'globalization'. "[A]s apartheid in South Africa is gradually giving way to political reform", spelled Richmond (1994, 209), "the rest of the world appears to be moving in a different direction". However, he muses, just like South African Apartheid the mounting system of global apartheid is untenable (Richmond 1994): "all boundaries are permeable and borders can no longer be defended with walls, iron curtains, armed guards, or computer surveillance systems [...] [a] system of global apartheid is bound to fail".

A quarter of a century later Richmond's ominous scenario has indeed come to fruition in our present's predatory globalization, charging unequal development, dashing inequality, and a related plethora of forced mass migrations, married to a global apartheid of 'walled states' (Brown 2010) and exclusionary regimes of citizenship. Yet, no walls, except for the infamous Berlin one, have been tumbling down. Border fences are on the contrary multiplying, are built higher and increasingly mortal to climb, for example: the Royal Walls of Ceuta, the last stop for Sub-Saharan migrants fleeing poverty and deprivation in search of work or sanctuary in Europe; along Hungary's border towards Serbia Victor Orban's new iron curtain, symptomatic of post-Soviet societies gangrened by extreme nationalism; Donald Trump's 'great big beautiful wall' along the US border with Mexico, symbolic of a long standing illusion of American superiority.

Thus, the neoliberal assumed happy 'end of history'[1] opened a Pandora's Box of precarization and forced displacement. Its credo of market driven economic freedom and 'liberal democracy', supposedly to eventually engulf the world entire, was to be negated by a sweeping 'accumulation by dispossession' (Harvey 2004), dismantling social safety nets and sustainable livelihoods, setting 'free' a multimillion footloose, flexible and ultramobile 'surplus population'[2] at the disposal of transnational corporations across the former first, second and third worlds. It is a contemporary trajectory that brings into focus Rosa Luxemburg's (1951 [1913]) theory of capitalist crisis management by unremitting 'primitive accumulation', through financialization, structural adjustment and corporate land grabbing; a contemporary imperialism intersected with and developing in tandem with a predatory geopolitical scramble for global hegemony, masked as 'humanitarian intervention', using human rights to sell war (Bricmont 2006).

This combined structurally engrained political-economic and geopolitical scramble has caused forced migrations at a massive scale in the post-Cold War era, and it continues unabated. One example is the still ongoing so-called 'migrant caravans' (e.g. Sklaw 2018) – departing from depressed Central American states, fleeing structurally embedded precarity of livelihoods and institutionally entrenched violence, defying crackdowns by the Mexican national guard and trappings of criminal syndicates in their odyssey from Central America across Mexico in an unavailing attempt to seek asylum at the US border. Not to speak about Venezuela, choked by draconic sanctions from the US and the EU (Weisbrot and Sachs 2019), or the rise of forced migration driven by precarization of livelihoods following structural adjustment policies in several other Latin American countries. A grim feature of this great global transformation, has been mass expulsions of refugees from, among other, Rwanda and former Yugoslavia in the 1990s, in the wake of austere 'structural adjustment' programs, imperial intervention, civil war and 'ethnic cleansing'

---

1   Fukuyama (1992).
2   Referring to Marx (1976 [1885]) theory on a surplus population and a reserve army of labour related to the dynamics of the accumulation of capital.

(Storey 2001; Schierup 1999), followed in the 2000s by an exodus of biblical proportions from Afghanistan, Iraq and Syria; not to forget the human conse-quences of neoliberal restructuring, internecine warfare and environmental disaster across Sub Saharan Africa (e.g. Tobias 2012).

'Huddled masses' of the 21st century continue to drown in crossings over the Mediterranean by shaky boats or vanish in the graveyard of the Sonoran Desert. Electronic surveying systems are becoming more sophisticated, border guards multiplying and increasingly militarized. Methods for confining migrants in prison-like lockups, cramped ghettoes, or refouled to regimented homelands, are becoming more and more inventive, oppressive, and inhumane. Repellent detention lockups for adults and small children separated from their parents in minuscular iron cages (the US); so-called 'hotspots' for refugees aimed at return to Turkey, outsourced by wealthier European nations to the economi-cally depressed periphery of the EU. That is, less euphemistically, concentra-tion camps exhibiting appalling subhuman conditions of subsistence.[3] At the same junction, a much-hailed Global Compact for Safe, Orderly and Regular Migration (2018)[4] bypasses fundamental UN conventions on the rights of migrants. Major intergovernmental organizations (the UN, the World Bank, the IOM), propagate a securitized so-called circular migration (Cassarino 2013) as a technocratic win-win-win formula for the 'management of migration' (e.g. Schierup, et al. 2019); a position projecting pivotal institutional logics of the South African migration regime under Apartheid onto a global scale, albeit dressed in a benevolent language of 'human rights'.

Also seen from the perspective of the inner territories of the so-called 'Global North' – or more specifically the EU and the US – Richmond's scenario appears prophetic, in foretelling the state of crisis we are in today. He could, thus, record (Richmond 1994, 209) "an upsurge in racism, discrimination, intol-erance and xenophobia with neo-Nazi and other right-wing extremist groups gaining support"; urban riots revealing volatile interracial situations; a fateful backlash against immigration and "growing support for reactionary political parties"; populist cries for stricter immigration controls and curtailing the right to seek asylum; "confinement of refugees in isolated camps".

In truth, as noted by Massey (2005, 110 ff), an ostensible paradox of a doc-trinaire mobility of capital versus apardizing closure relating to human mobil-ity, appears politically logical; that is, in the greater scheme of neoliberal

---

3   At the time of writing this introduction coming into public spotlight through the arson set-ting the Moria camp on the Greek Island of Lesbos ablaze (Cossé 2020). See also the chapter by Agustín and Jørgensen in this issue.

4   Heavily criticized by a number of civil society coalitions (e.g. RSMMS 2018).

transformation and politics of precarization functioning to produce and manage unfree labor for hyper-exploitation to the avail of the higher end of the
wider asymmetric global power-geometrics. Or, as put caustically in a nutshell
by Bauder (2006, 22): Migrants "are valuable because they are vulnerable".
However, the 'migrant's' and the racialized Other's moral-political function
transpires as equally vital. It speaks to the post-political stalemate in North
Atlantic societies,[5] most obviously in the aftermath of the 2008 financial crisis and associated upheavals of a dispossessed precariat. As by fiat inflated
'problems' of immigration and race have become overwhelming themes of a
tendentially hegemonic neoconservative populism. They have come to function as floating signifiers, carrying the blame for a ripping social inequality
and precarity of labor, livelihoods, and citizenship, currently reaching a breaking point.

It is, returning to the rationale of the present volume, a present in which any
utopia of crafting munificent commensality and inclusive transversal solidarity may, paraphrasing Solnit (2010), appear a task of building 'paradise in Hell';
a contemporary reality, muses Munck, (2020, 8) of generalized crisis in which
"what has fundamentally changed is indeed astern, and there is no option of
returning to 'business as usual'". It poses the problem to social theory on how to
"imagine and to theorize [...] forms of collective political identity and agency
that might lead to the creation of new, ethical and democratic political institutions and forms of practice" (Gill 2000, 137), in increasingly 'illiberal' liberal
states (Guild, et al. 2009), trapped in a consensus-based 'post-politics' (Mouffe
2005) fixated on problems of 'migration' and the 'stranger within' as populist
substitutes for politics that have deserted visions of solidarity, equality and
social justice. It has led to a focus on 'civil society' as the 'last holdout' against
the 'economic tsunami' of neoliberal globalization (Burawoy 2006, 356), for
politics of 'emancipation' (Fraser 2013) and transversal solidarity beyond ethnic divides and national borders.

Possible openings have been conceived in terms of the development of
transformative global movements organizing along principles of a 'transversal
cosmopolitanism'; a new form of transnational practice "creating a common
ground [...] for progressive hybridization, and active political cooperation
among diverse identities and ideological visions [...] against existing capitalist social relations and structures of domination" (Hosseini, et al. 2016: 667).[6]

---

5 Most notably theorised by Mouffe (2005).
6 Elsewhere (Schierup, Likic Brboric, et al. 2019) we have pursued a critical analysis of strengths
   and weaknesses of one such grand movement for global transformation, tallying the idea of
   'transversal cosmopolitanism'.

Contrary, but conceivably complementary, to this grand vision for social transformation, it is an idea of grounding an alternative globality through a myriad of locally rooted politics of possibility that informs the present volume.

Revolving around these presuppositions the argument of the book proceeds through three main parts, each including several chapters. Part One, Transversal Solidarities and the Politics of Scale, discusses how solidarity can be conceptualized and provide an analytical vantage point in relation to transversality and the notion of scale. The literature on politics of solidarity has developed over the last decade. It offers a range of both empirical studies and theorizations. The concept of solidarity itself has been politicized and we see a criminalization of and a shrinking space for solidarity with migrants (della Porta and Steinhilper 2021). In this volume – and in Part One in particular – we expound the notion of transversal solidarity to capture a plurality of solidarities and to avoid dichotomies between in-group/out-group, national/international or society/institutions (Chapter 3 by Agustín & Jørgensen). Understanding solidarity in relation to scale is essential here, as it allows us to analyze manifestations of solidarity in connection with geographies of migration on a variety of scales. The chapters in this part seek both to conceptualize transversal solidarity and to offer empirical readings on the institutionalization of solidarity in cities. Two chapters discuss specifically trajectories of transversal solidarity formation between migrant organizations and labor unions intersecting with the wider institutional frameworks of individual cities.

Counterposed to this, the book's Part Two, Urban Emplacement: The Formation of a Heterogenous 'We', proceeds from the perspective of 'place' with the notion of 'emplacement' as conceptual centerpiece. This opens for alternative understandings of belonging, connectedness, and counterhegemonic politics. The chapters in this part of the book ranges from the comprehension of an everyday 'means of establishing rights to space in inhospitable places' (Chapter 6 by Landau & Freemantle) to examples of an open ended 'progressive' place building, actively contesting and opposing processes of a closed essentializing 'reactionary' place making (Massey 1991). Notwithstanding a gloomy global trajectory and exclusionary national ideopolitical configurations, we use the notion of urban emplacement, to denote an actual complexity of a social formation that includes territorial cum hierarchically ordered demarcation of the hole and in its parts, divisions and divided – in instantiations of place, subjected to intersecting spaces and scales of power, yet encompassing concrete localized potentials for social change, social justice, commoning and belonging.

The third part of the book locates politics of possibility, conveyed by notions such as sanctuary or solidary cities that exposes varying constellations between social movements, NGOs, and municipalities, exemplified by practices at various scales of institutionalization in cities across the Americas and Europe. The potential and ability to not only envision but also enact alternative imaginaries is an important aspect of solidarity (Agustín and Jørgensen 2019). Understanding radical alternatives has been a theme in urban studies for a long time and the city has been perceived as an open space of imagination. The chapters in this part reflect on the applicability of notions such as sanctuary policies and urban solidarity in different geographical contexts and discuss how solidarity is contested and enacted in civil society on the urban scale. Here, the city is as an analytical gaze for comprehending how alternative imaginaries of solidarity can develop, but not as *the* solution *per se*.

1 Transversal Solidarities and Politics of Scale

Central to the volume is, in consequence, an exploration of solidarity as transformative practice (cf. Featherstone 2012). It is a relational practice; it is contentious; it emerges strongly in moments or conjunctures (such as the economic crisis, the refugee crisis, the climate crisis and currently the health/Covid-19 crisis (see Fischer and Jørgensen 2021)); it is generative of political subjectivities and collective identities; it entails alliance-building among diverse actors; it is inventive of new imaginaries; it is situated in space and time and organized in multi-scalar relations; and it is linked in different ways to institutions (Agustín and Jørgensen 2019). Solidarity practices can connect different places or geographies and enable relations that go beyond national borders. Focusing on solidarities enables an analysis on how struggles are intersected across different categories, such as class, ethnicity, and gender, and create new commonalities (Herrera 2013). This understanding draws on Yuval-Davis' (1999, 1994) work on transversal politics. For her this requires the encompassment of difference by equality. She claims that differences are vital, but also that notions of difference should encompass, rather than replace, those of equality. This becomes an important point of departure when analyzing social justice struggles involving migrants and non-migrants.

   The book opens with two chapters offering theoretical perspectives on solidarity. In Chapter 2, Urban Solidarity: Perspectives of Migration and Refugee Accommodation and Inclusion, Harald Bauder investigates the concept of solidarity and related policies and practices central to urban initiatives throughout the global north in support of vulnerable migrants and refugees. In his contribution he untangles the notion of solidarity as a central category in philosophy and social science, carrying forth different perspectives with varying outcomes, as filtered through contemporary strategies of urban solidarity movements. Eurocities' Solidarity Cities network is an example of a top-down initiative involving mayors and municipal administrations that employ a solidarity framework. Other initiatives, such as Germany's solidarity city network, articulate a grassroots bottom-up approach to solidarity. In his contribution, Bauder unpacks various meanings of the concept of solidarity within urban migrant and refugee supporting initiatives and campaigns. Drawing on expert interviews with activists, community leaders, and municipal administrators and politicians in Berlin and Freiburg, Germany, and Zurich, Switzerland, he brings out contradictory ways in which urban solidarity is understood and practiced. While urban solidarity may appeal to a wide political spectrum and incorporate top-down policies and bottom-up practices and approaches, urban actors also embrace various terminologies, such as 'sanctuary city', 'solidarity city' or 'urban citizenship', in response to local circumstances and political strategies.

In comparison, Óscar García Agustín and Martin Bak Jørgensen in their contribution On Transversal Solidarity: An Approach to Migration and Multi-Scalar Solidarities (Chapter 3), focus on different varieties and implications of transversal politics and transversal solidarities. What maintains solidarity as transversal, they argue, is openness, dialogue, and collective shaping of commonalities, without excluding differences. They maintain that solidarity as contestative transversal openness shifts the focus to how activists of different backgrounds build a common ground in opposition to or in conflict with exclusionary positions. They offer a variable conceptualization of transversal solidarity relating to migration and migrants. It reflects different ways of practicing, organizing and articulating solidarity. The concept of 'transversal solidarity' is here related to three dimensions of solidarity practices 'from below' and the authors discuss how to bridge their respective dichotomies: an in-group, out-group dichotomy in terms of identity; a spatial dichotomy, in terms of separation of the local from the national and international; a dichotomy in terms of organization, related to an ostensible incompatibility of the civic and the institutional. These dichotomies are intersecting a typology of solidarity along three different scales (autonomous solidarity, civic solidarity, and institutional solidarity), with variable dynamics and degrees of institutionalization. This multi-layered typology is exemplified through an account of variable practices of transversal solidarity building, in Greece, the UK, Denmark, and Italy.

Space and locality are equally important when analyzing manifestations of transversal solidarities. Just as space relates to transversal politics in urban contexts, transversal solidarity is also linked to scale, as another central concept.

The contestation and struggles inquired into in several of the articles of this volume can be analyzed from the perspective of scale, traversing the local, the national, and the transnational.

Part One includes two further chapters that explore intersections between the urban space and scale, and the pivotal dynamics of transversality with a particular focus on the significance of labor unions. In their chapter, Labor Unions and Undocumented Immigrants: Local Perspectives on Transversal Solidarity During DACA and DAPA (Chapter 4) Els de Graauw and Shannon Gleeson elaborate on the complex constitution of transversality (see also de Graauw, et al. 2020; de Graauw and Vermeulen 2016) in challenging a disciminatory global migration regime and prevalent US politics of securitisation, dispossession and expulsion. But they also show how traversing power relations between city administrations, municipalities, labor unions, voluntary human rights organizations, and other actors vary from locality to locality. They point out that national labor unions in the United States have formally supported undocumented immigrants since 2000. However, drawing on interviews with union and immigrant rights leaders, they offer a locally grounded account, demonstrating how union solidarity with undocumented immigrants has varied notably across the country on the scale of the city. They find that San Francisco's progressive political context and dense infrastructure of immigrant organizations have enabled the city's historically powerful unions to build deep institutional solidarity with immigrant communities during the Deferred Action for Childhood Arrivals (2012) and Deferred Action for Parents of Americans (2014) programs. Meanwhile, Houston's politically divided context and much sparser infrastructure of immigrant organizations made it necessary for the city's historically weaker unions to build solidarity with immigrant communities through more disparate channels.

In her chapter Rethinking Solidarity in a Post-Migrant Labor Regime: The Case of Hospitality Work in Johannesburg, South Africa Janet Munakamwe likewise pursues transversal solidarity formation with a focus on the role and positionality of labor unions. However, while the US labor movements have in general developed an increasingly solidary approach to migrant workers, including undocumented migrants, the South African case stands out in contrast. Here a path of transversal community unionism once incorporating South African and cross border labor migrants in common struggles against apartheid and its discriminatory labor laws, has become reshaped into a paradoxical 'post-migrant labor regime' aligned with a mainstream international trade unionism but detached from organizing a new informal township precariat, including numerous informal cross border migrants. The example of Johannesburg demonstrates this ambiguity of a new ideopolitical hegemony.

It is associated with xenophobic attacks on the city's numerous migrant communities, and with labor unions partly complicit. But it also brings out positive visions for the formation of an including 'cosmopolitan city', and incipient union politics involving with a multiplicity of subjectivity formation among a fragmented urban precariat.

2   Urban Emplacement: The Formation of a Heterogenous 'We'

Scale is not indicative of hierarchies (from local to transnational) but emphasizes the connectivity of place-based struggles within politics of scale (Bauder 2019; MacKinnon 2010). Different practices of solidarity illustrate how varying spatialities (scale, place, networks, positionality and mobility) shape contentious politics (Fischer and Jørgensen 2021). Their dynamics channel the ways politics and power affect local places. It represents, a "multiplicity of transversal lines that connect agents of so many different types in terms of scales, but which are influencing each other, and generate dynamics of different magnitudes and different forms" (Bigo 2017, 25).

These dynamics underscore the complexity of the concept of 'place' as a 'concrete universal' in comparison with the abstractness of 'space' (Casey 2001). The power of 'place' consists in "gathering the lives and things, each with its own space and time, into one arena of common engagement" (Casey 2001, 16). In the context of an urban 'throwntogetherness' contingent on displacement, accumulation through dispossession and global migration this place-making, argues Massey, does not "require the constitution of a single hegemonic 'we'", but is formed through a heterogenous "myriad of practices of quotidian negotiation and contextation; practices [...] through which [...] constituent 'identities' are also themselves continually molded" (Massey 2005, 153–4; cf. Hansen 2019). Glick Schiller and Çağlar (2015, 5–6) frame these multifarious dynamics through the concept of *emplacement*, defined "as the relationship between the continuing restructuring of place within multiscalar networks of power and people's efforts, within the barriers and opportunities of a specific locality, to settle and build networks of connection". They counterpose theoretical meanings and methodological implications of the notion of emplacement to a dominant oppressive epistemology revolving around the prejudicial, distorting and ideologically loaded discursive notion of 'integration' that imposes and naturalizes "categories of racial, ethnic and religious difference, and their use in legitimating exclusion, criminalization and hyper-exploitation" (cf. Morrice 2019; Schierup 1993). Thus, the notion of emplacement opens for conceptions of belonging and connectedness alternative to those the institutional and legal

framework offer (Mbodj-Pouye 2016). It is thereby a pivotal concept in studies
of global migration, racialization and contestative social movements to be written into the alternative cognizance of what Casas-Cortes, et al. (2015) define as
'a new epistemic community' of cross-sectioned networks of migrants, activists and scholars emerging across cities of the world, attempting to confront
and go beyond canonized ideo-political paradigms.

The concept of emplacement denotes thus conceived a crucial intervention
for analyzing urban politics as they open for conceptualizing everyday politics
driven from 'below'. It invites framing an analysis of the complexity of mobilizing, organizing and claims-making that lie beyond the mandate of for instance
'sanctuary cities' and the limits of urban autonomy in the legal sense. Yet, it is
important to avoid any one-sided utopianism concerning politics of possibility
potentially embedded in the idea of 'emplacement'. Relating to this Massey's
(1991) distinction between 'reactionary' and 'progressive' place-making is
essential; an ambiguity of placemaking which is in varying ways reflected in
the four chapters included in this second part of the book.

Massey takes as vantage point that the velocity of socio-spatial disruption
and fragmentation, habitually referred to as 'time-space compression', has
given rise to a tendentially dominant, defensive, out of reach, nostalgia for the
restoration of 'heritage', extreme nationalism and antagonism towards perceived 'outsiders', to the degree that the seeking for a sense of place has come
to be seen as 'necessarily reactionary'. Against this she counterpoises an alternative understanding and practice of space, adequate to the age of time-space
compression; open, dynamic and outward looking, and attuned to transversal political struggles, allowing "a sense of place which is extraverted, which
includes a consciousness of its links with the wider world, which integrates in
a positive way the global and the local" (Massey 1991, 26).

Actually, existing practices of placemaking vary, innately, depending on their
positioning in intersecting multiscalar webs of power, and the conjointment,
collusion or collision of multifarious localized practices of emplacement,
including targeted activism and articulated social movements. There are a
wide variety of migrant struggles for livelihoods and placemaking without clear
leadership, ideology, or structured organization. The book's Chapter 6, Tactical
Cosmopolitanism as Urban Negotiation: Diversity Management 'From Beside',
by Loren Landau and Iriann Freemantle, communicates, in this vein, heterogenous practices in migrant struggles emerging from the harshness of livelihoods
and hostile xenophobic attitudes in the cities of Johannesburg and Nairobi; a
disparate multitude of actions undertaken by groups, fragmented by language,
religion, legal status, and mutual enmity. The authors develop the notion of
'tactical cosmopolitanism' in interrogating the modalities of coexistence in

some of the most rapidly transforming localities within these two highly ethnically heterogeneous and exceedingly unequal and class polarized African cities, magnets for a multitude of international and internal migrants. Rather than a coherent philosophy, tactical cosmopolitanism signifies a bricolage of rhetorical and mobilizational tools drawing on a diversity of more established discourses and value systems. It allows excluded outsiders to capitalize on cosmopolitanism's power without being bound by its responsibilities. By drawing attention to migrant motivations and the spatial scale at which they negotiate social recognition, the chapter provides a lens for understanding the socialities of coexistence in the thrown together, often informally governed spaces that comprise Africa's rapidly expanding urban peripheries. Moreover, the conceptualization of 'tactical cosmopolitanism' challenges the ethics and desired outcomes in terms of social cohesion that scholars of migration and diversity often presume ought to underlie conviviality in heterogeneous urban localities. As such, it is not a charter for a unified, counter-hegemonic movement that seeks to articulate an alternative order. But it serves as a pragmatic kit for a remarkable ability to swiftly amalgamate claims of disparate subaltern segments of the urban population according to current necessity.

Chapter 7, Yellow Vests in Metropolis: A Chance for Transversal Solidarity, by Christophe Foultier, focuses, in contrast with the preceding chapter, on a disorganized mayhem churned out by a furious movement of a marginalized, predominantly white, 'autochthonous' precariat, protesting against the debilitating consequences of an increasingly asocial neoliberal French political regime. It brings forth, at the same time, that an informal, utilitarian, and disjointed 'politics of the governed' (Chatterjee 2002) trading upon universalist schemes (in this case consecrated, supposedly universal, values of French 'citoyenneté') is not an attribution quintessential to Africa, or the so-called 'South', or to racialized migrant minorities. But it also demonstrates how a seemingly spontaneous and anarchic upheaval may turn into an increasingly articulated social movement producing transversal bonds reaching out in unsuspected directions (from the perspective of a dominant ideo-political hegemony). The chapter highlights how in Paris the Yellow Vests promoted a capacity for marginalized city dwellers to summit vivid gatherings and dialogues in unconventional places, like for example central roundabouts and, while subjected to a hegemonic injunction of accountability, exposed a need for establishing a progressive citizenship status based on direct participation. Arguably, the movement has occasionally generated ambivalent nationalist positions, yet also points of progressive convergence through reimagining citizenship and processes of urban emplacement in dialogue between a heterogenous 'white' French precariat in suburban areas and that of the racialized excluded in the so-called *quartiers populaires* of the French capital. This puts biased hegemonic stereotypes to shame that denigrates the movement in terms of a retrogressive prey for the potent French extreme right.

The following two chapters expose more clearly articulated ideopolitical positions and localized processes of urban emplacement in confrontation with the racializing neo-conservative specter haunting Europe.

Chapter 8, Forward through the Past? Reinventing the 'People's House' in Subaltern Stockholm, by Carl-Ulrik Schierup, Aleksandra Ålund and Ilhan Kellecioglu takes its point of departure in an urban justice movement initiated by young post-migrants in Sweden's disadvantaged metropolitan areas. Through the organization of popular education, protest rallies and involvement in local politics they re-emplace their local communities, defamed as no-go 'spaces of outsidership' in hegemonic media and political discourse, in terms of *The Place* (Orten). That is a cherished place of contestative organization and counterhegemonic identity, where the racialized urban subalterns can raise their backs in dignity.[7] Founded on links of transversal solidarity across ethno-cultural identities, confessional affiliations, and organizational confines of a wider Swedish civil society, and a global subaltern ecumene, the Stockholm based activist network Megafonen came to struggle, in continuity with this contestative trajectory, for re-establishing a legendary urban common, The People's House, with roots in the incipient Swedish working class of the late nineteenth century. The authors explore the ambiguous emplacement of this contemporary community center in one of metropolitan Stockholm's most disadvantaged neighborhoods, envisioned to promote civic education and the formation of critical political subjectivity and counter-hegemonic organization with capacity to contest urban segregation and a dashing race-class inequality. They discuss its convoluted conditioning exposed to processes of predatory financialization, new public management, the commodification and appropriation of crucial welfare institutions and interventions of large competing NGOs. This is related to the dominance of a racializing 'post-politics' across most of the nation's political spectrum, under pressure from an expansive xenophobic political party born out of the Swedish neo-Nazi movement.

In Chapter 9, The Spatial Politics of Far-Right Populism: VOX, Antifascism and Neighbourhood Solidarity in Madrid City, Ana Santamarina explores the spatial politics of the Spanish far-right party *vox*, which deepens the understanding of the emplacement of antifascist politics *versus* xenophobic populism. The chapter foregrounds the need for moving beyond nation-centered

---

7 Paraphrasing Serhhede, et al. (2019).

institutional and descriptive approaches, seen as typical for a proliferating literature on far-right politics. It shifts the focus to a scrutiny of quotidian grounds of far-right mobilizations and a co-constitutive relationship between 'institutional politics' and the 'politics of the street'. Focusing on Hortaleza – a peripheral working-class area in the outskirts of Madrid – Santamarina positions everyday politics at the core of xenophobic populisms which exploit urbanization of border regimes and situated social inequalities. Yet, in the same instance she discusses ways in which extreme right narratives and localized mobilization are being challenged by diversified neighborhood movements and their transversal antiracist politics of belonging. On this background the chapter emphasizes the centrality of the neighborhood, as the lived space of political socialization makes it a key scale for emplacement of sustainable antifascist politics.

3   Politics of Possibility and the City

Part Three of this volume interrogates how politics of possibility is articulated and practiced in the context of the city. The scalar relations and conditions of the city is the focus of a series of contributions from Europe, North and South America. Focusing scale to the city brings out a distinctive perspective and practical alternative.[8] Throughout the world, cities have responded to the disjuncture between exclusionary national migration and residence policies, and the need to be inclusive at the local scale (Bauder and Gonzalez 2018). Migrants and refugees may enter a given country in remote coastal areas or enter through the countryside or desert – but they move towards cities. As Barber (Barber 2013, xx) argues in *If Mayors Ruled the World*:

> The politics of the city have a very different character to the ideological politics of the nation. [They] are about making things work – you've got to pick up the garbage, you've to keep the hospitals open, it doesn't matter if the immigrants are legal or illegal – they have children who get sick and who have to go to school, they ride buses, they drive cars. If you asked a mayor, 'Do you think immigrants should be allowed in or not?' they'd say 'They are here'.

---

8   Parts of this section was developed as a position paper for the 8th World Social Forum on Migration in Mexico City, November 2018.

Cities must find a way to secure access, legal residency, social protection, cultural belonging, and physical presence of illegalized migrants (Agustín and Jørgensen 2019). This is not an easy task as national governments hold the right to issue visas, permits, residence, etc. Yet a new municipalist surge demonstrates that the municipality is becoming a strategically crucial site for the organization of transformative social change (Agustín 2020; Roth and Russell 2018). The nation state remains a significant force within the politics of migration but, as Darling and Bauder (2019, 2) argue, the presumption that the nation state is uniquely placed to respond to migration, overlooks other sites of activity, other scales of analysis, and other political possibilities. The city can be – and is – a strategic location for an emergent and active citizenship, and the urban scale is the central analytical point of orientation in many of the contributions to this volume.

In the US, Canada and the UK the 'Sanctuary City' has become the preferred label to capture the local level responses to exclusionary national policies. In the US, California, Colorado, Connecticut, Illinois, Massachusetts, New Jersey, New Mexico, New York, Oregon, Vermont and Washington are all Sanctuary States and they included 179 cities and counties identifying themselves as Sanctuary spaces as of November 2020.[9] In Canada, Toronto, Hamilton, London and Montreal have sanctuary city designations. Vancouver has adopted a policy of *Access to City Services without Fear for Residents with Uncertain or No Immigration Status*, taking action to support non-status migrants beyond the standard designation.[10] In the UK and Ireland more than one hundred cities identify as – 'City of Sanctuary'.[11] However, the scope of protection and commitment differs substantially. Basically, being a sanctuary city designates how these cities (covering both municipal authorities, public services, corporate organizations, and civil society) are defending those under imminent threat of exclusion by the State. Moreover, it designates how these cities are operationalizing the demand that municipal rights and services be extended to all through tools such as the 'city card' or 'Don't Ask, Don't Tell' (DADT) policies (Atakm 2019; Hudson 2019). As Sanctuary Cities do not offer absolute protection from federal or national immigration authorities, in the sense that they can nullify federal laws – illegalized migrants are still subject to possible detention and deportation in sanctuary cities – they are still committed to include all inhabitants regardless of status in the local community and strive for improving their lives (Bauder and Gonzalez 2018).

---

9   https://cis.org/Map-Sanctuary-Cities-Counties-and-States.
10   http://canadianlabour.ca/sanctuary-cities.
11   https://cityofsanctuary.org.

It has been an open discussion how we could best label this type of protection, services, and practices. We could rightly ask what's in a name? The origin of sanctuary has religious connotations and alludes to protection of persecuted religious minorities. Sanctuary has been connected to asylum in churches throughout Europe. There can still be links between the church and sanctuary policies, especially in the US where the church has had a crucial role in fostering the establishment of sanctuary places. For some scholars and political actors, the notion of 'sanctuary' still connotes a kind of pastoral relationship where the church or local authorities offer the dependent protection and sanctuary. Critics therefore see 'sanctuary' as describing a top-down relationship, which leaves little room for the engagement and voice of the illegalized migrants themselves. In other countries other terms have been preferred such as 'refuge cities', 'intercultural cities', 'cities of reception' or 'solidarity cities'. In any case, the notion of solidarity has implications, which depict illegalized migrants as co-habitants of the city and as co-producers of and within the city. Using the notion of 'solidarity city' thus evokes the idea of a bottom-up approach. Moreover, in contrast to the label of sanctuary city, a city of solidarity also includes critiques of the prevalence of a predatory political economy and signifies how cities attempt to assert control over their own affairs in the light of national and regional austerity, privatization, unfair migration policies and other types of repression (Bauder and Gonzalez 2018). The crucial point is here to understand and identify practices constituting local-level protection and allocation of rights.

The urban scale and the city here become an analytical point of departure and not a normative one. Purcell argues that scales "are socially constructed strategies to achieve particular ends. Therefore, any scale or scalar strategy can result in any outcome. Localization can lead to a more democratic city, or a less democratic one" (Purcell 2006, 1921–2). He further agues, that "as we discover, narrate, and invent new ideas about democracy and citizenship in cities, it is critical to avoid what I call the local trap, in which the local scale is assumed to be inherently more democratic than other scales" (Purcell 2006, 1921). Cities are not inherently progressive, and we follow the argument of Russell (2019, 1) who argues that: "Rather than essentializing cities as inherently progressive or democratic, the municipal is instead becoming framed as a 'strategic front' for developing a transformative politics of scale".

In his seminal work *Rebel Cities – From the right to the city to the urban revolution* Harvey (2012, 164) ends on an optimistic concerning social change to come:

Whose side will each of us, as individuals, come down on? Which street will we occupy? Only time will tell. But what we do know is that the time is now. The system is not only broken and exposed, but incapable of any response other than repression. So, we, the people, have no option but to struggle for the collective right to decide how the system shall be reconstructed, and in whose image.

The year Harvey's book was published, 2012, marked a moment of global uprisings. Inspired by the Arab Spring, the world witnessed protests in Iceland, the Portuguese *Geração à Rasca*, the Spanish *indignados*, the Greek anti-austerity protests, and the Occupy movement. On October 15, 2011, demonstrations were organized in 950 cities across 82 countries for change based on "dignity, direct democracy and proactivity" (Sanchéz 2011). A similar kind of tactics has later been used to mobilize solidarity with refugees during the 'long summer of migration' from 2015 and onwards. However, since the global protests in 2011 and the mobilization of refugee solidarity, it has also become clear that such mobilizations have not been enough to effect profound systemic change. As a German solidarity city activist Antje Dieterich (2017, 55–6) state with a certain cynicism: "The state has adapted to our tactics: demonstrations were simply allowed to move peacefully through the city, slowing down traffic here and there, but not leading to any real political change".

4   Who Is Right Here, Only Time Will Tell

How does politics of possibility play out in the context of the city in this volume? In Part 3 we include five chapters offering rather different perspectives. Chapter 10, Sanctuary and Solidarity Cities in the Global South: A Review of Latin America, written by Margaret Godoy and Harald Bauder, offers a critical reading of the applicability of concepts as urban sanctuary and solidarity in the context of Latin America. In this chapter, they argue that the literature on urban sanctuary and solidarity in the context of the Global North is robust and rapidly expanding. However, there remains a gap in the literature regarding how these concepts may apply to the Global South. To address this gap, Godoy and Bauder conduct a scoping review of academic and grey literature on urban sanctuary and solidarity policies and practices in Latin America. They focus on the connection between top-down urban policies and bottom-up grassroots initiatives and practices of solidarity and sanctuary pertaining to migrants and refugees. Their findings reveal that, in some contexts, the academic literature lags behind, in terms of in acknowledging the connection between top-down and bottom-up approaches.

The following Chapter (11), Solidarity Cities in Santiago de Chile and Civil Society Participation During COVID-19, also by Margaret Godoy and Harald Bauder, investigates how civil society activism has played important roles in engaging municipal policies and practices of solidarity in the Santiago Metropolitan Region of Chile during the COVID-19 pandemic. Here, they explore how a solidarity city can continue to enable participation for migrants in vulnerable situations and how civil society may facilitate the transformative potential of solidarity cities, in a context where mobility restrictions, due to physical distancing policies and the heightened controls of movement in public and private spaces, have been put in place. Semi-structured interviews with key informants and local experts, including local government officials, policy-makers, activists, NGO staff, and academic researchers, reveal the importance of horizontal relations at the local level, in particular relating to the participation of local civil society actors and their impact on municipalities' enactment of policies of solidarity and the ability to resist exclusionary national-level policies.

Chapter 12 takes us some 7,000 kilometers further north to Mexico City and the context of Mexico more broadly. In Nascent Solidarity and Community Emergency: Forced Migration and Accompaniment in Mexico Jorge Morales Cardiel investigates conditions for solidarity on the urban scale in the context of Mexico. The chapter scrutinizes prospects for the development of sanctuary cities in Mexico through a discussion of the concept of 'accompaniment' (acompañamiento), rooted in a Latin American trajectory of social Catholicism. It encapsulates solidarity and recognition of human rights with a potential impact on Mexican society and state. The author discusses, conveyed by the principle of accompaniment, efforts of civil society to involve the local population and governments at different levels, especially government in migrant receiving local communities. Thus, the process of accompaniment is seen by involved CSOs as a 'community emergency' facing violence by criminal syndicates and by the state. From this perspective the idea of the 'Sanctuary City' is pertinent to the analysis.

The following two chapters are situated in the European context. In Chapter 13, Building Transversal Solidarities in European Cities: Open Harbours, Safe Communities, Home, Kim Rygiel, Ilker Ataç and Maurice Stierl develop the notion of transversal solidarity through another multicase study. It unravels differential forms and meanings of the concept. The chapter focuses on transversal solidarities by and with migrants, rooted in cities. This includes the exploration of a CSO providing a home to migrant newcomers in Copenhagen, an activist organization in Vienna providing support for LGBTIQ migrants, and a transversal civic coalition in cooperation with the city of Palermo, striving to create open harbors and 'corridors of solidarity', from the Mediterranean Sea to cities throughout EUrope. These examples are situated in and across different urban spaces. Yet, they share a common grounding in building solidarity through spaces of encounters related to ideas of home, community, and harbor. They examine the linkage of spaces of encounter across political scales.

Vienna is also the focus of the final Chapter 14 of the book, Civil Society Organizations Engaged with Illegalized Migrants in Bern and Vienna: Co-production of Urban Citizenship, by Ilker Ataç and Sarah Schilliger. Here, they investigate the role of CSOs in the provision of inclusionary services as well as in forming advocacy coalitions for migrants with irregular status in the urban contexts of Bern and Vienna. Empirical data are drawn from two cities. The authors provide an analysis of the variety of CSOs which actively challenge policies of exclusion on the urban level. They thereby examine the political and social practices of CSOs in local welfare arrangements and their organizational structures, the way they build up solidarity relations, networks and alliances, and their relation to municipality and urban authorities. By focusing on varieties of practices and strategies of CSOs, they shed light on civil society's crucial role concerning the construction of an urban infrastructure of solidarity. This, furthermore, contributes to a more nuanced conceptualization of urban citizenship which goes beyond the dichotomous distinction between urban citizenship practices 'from above' (by municipal governments) versus 'from below' (by social movements and civil society initiatives) and show how local welfare arrangements for irregular migrants are co-produced and negotiated by a variety of actors within urban settings.

References

Agustín, Ó. G. (2020). New municipalism as space for solidarity. *Soundings*, 74, 54–67.

Agustín, Ó. G., and M. B. Jørgensen (2019). *Solidarity and the 'Refugee Crisis' in Europe.* Cham: Springer.

Atakm, I. (2019). Toronto's sanctuary city policy: rationale and barriers. In Darling, J. and H. Bauder (eds.) *Sanctuary cities and urban struggles: Rescaling migration, citizenship, and rights.* Manchester: Manchester University Press, 105–30.

Barber, B. R. (2013). *If mayors ruled the world: Dysfunctional nations, rising cities.* New Haven, CT & London: Yale University Press.

Bauder, H. (2006). *Labor Movement: How Migration Regulates Labor.* Oxford: Oxford University Press.

Bauder, H. (2019). Migrant solidarities and the politics of place. *Progress in Human Geography*, 44 (6), 1066–80.

Bauder, H., and D. A. Gonzalez (2018). Municipal responses to 'illegality': Urban sanctuary across national contexts. *Social Inclusion*, 6 (1), 124–34.

Bigo, D. (2017). International political sociology: Rethinking the international through dynamics of power. In Basaran, T., et al. (eds.) *International political sociology: Transversal lines.* Abingdon & New York, NY: Routledge, 24–48.

Bricmont, J. (2006). *Humanitarian Imperialism. Using Human Rights to Sell War.* New York, NY: Monthly Review Press.

Brown, W. (2010). *Walled States, Waning Sovereignty.* New York, NY: Zone Books.

Burawoy, M. (2006). *Public Sociology vs. the Market,* Public address. No., Berkeley (CA): University of California.

Casas-Cortes, M., S. Cobarrubias, N. De Genova, G. Garelli, G. Grappi, C. Heller, S. Hess, B. Kasparek, S. Mezzadra, B. Neilson, I. Peano, L. Pezzani, J. Pickles, F. Rahola, L. Riedner, S. Scheel, and M. Tazzioli (2015). New keywords: migration and borders. *Cultural Studies*, 29 (1), 55–87.

Casey, E. (2001). Between Geography and Philosophy: What Does It Mean to Be in the Place-World? *Annals of the Association of American Geographers*, 91 (4), 683–93.

Cassarino, J.-P. (2013). The Drive for Securitized Temporariness. In Triandafyllidou, A. (ed.) *Circular Migration between Europe and its Neighbourhood: Choice or Necessity?* Oxford: Oxford Scholarship Oline.

Chatterjee, P. (2002). *The Politics of the Governed.* New York (NY): Columbia University Press.

Cossé, E. (2020). Greece's Moria Camp Fire: What's Next?, https://www.hrw.org/news/2020/09/12/greeces-moria-camp-fire-whats-next.

Darling, J., and H. Bauder (2019). *Sanctuary cities and urban struggles: Rescaling migration, citizenship, and rights.* Manchester: Manchester University Press.

de Graauw, E., and F. Vermeulen (2016). Cities and the politics of immigrant integration: a comparison of Berlin, Amsterdam, New York City, and San Francisco. *Journal of Ethnic and Migration Studies*, 42 (6), 989–1012.

de Graauw, E., S. Gleeson and X. Bada (2020). Local context and labour-community immigrant rights coalitions: a comparison of San Francisco, Chicago, and Houston. *Journal of Ethnic and Migration Studies*, 46 (4), 728–46.

della Porta, D. and E. Steinhilper (eds. 2021). *Contentious Migrant Solidarity: Shrinking Spaces and Civil Society Contestation.* London: Routledge.

Dieterich, A. (2017). The Promise of Solidarity Cities. *ROAR #6* (Summer), 48–59.

Featherstone, D. (2012). *Solidarity: Hidden Histories and Geographies of Internationalism.* London: Zed Books.

Finley, E. (2017). The new municipal movements. *ROAR* #6 (Summer), 14–23.

Fischer, L., and M. B. Jørgensen (2021). "We are here to stay" vs. "Europe's best hotel": Hamburg and Athens as geographies of solidarity. *Antipode*, 53 (4), 1062–82.

Fraser, N. (2013). A triple movement? Parsing the politics of crisis after Polanyi? *New Left Review*, 81 (May), 119–32.

Fukuyama, F. (1992). *The End of History and the Last Man.* London: Penguin.

Gill, S. (2000). Toward a Postmodern Prince? The Battle in Seattle as a Moment in the New Politics of Globalisation. *Millenium: Journal of International Studies*, 29, 131–40.

Glick-Schiller, N., and A. Çağlar (2015). A multiscalar perspective on cities and migration. A comment on the symposium. *Sociologica* (2), 1–9.

Guild, E., K. Groenendijk, and S. Carrera (2009). *Illiberal Liberal States. Immigration, Citizenship and Integration in the EU.* Farnham: Ashgate.

Hansen, C. (2019). *Solidarity in Diversity: Activism as a Pathway of Migrant Emplacement in Malmö.* Malmö: Holmbergs.

Harvey, D. (2004). The new 'imperialism': Accumulation by dispossession. *Socialist Register*, 40, 63–87.

Harvey, D. (2012). *Rebel Cities.* London: Verso.

Herrera, G. (2013). Gender and international migration: Contributions and cross-fertilizations. *Annual Review of Sociology*, 39, 471–89.

Hosseini, H., B. K. Gills, and J. Goodman (2016). Toward transversal cosmopolitanism: Understanding alternative praxes in the global field of transformative movements. *Globalizations*, 14 (5), 667–84.

Hudson, G. (2019). City of Hope, City of Fear: Sanctuary and Security in Toronto, Canada. In Darling, Jonathan and Harald Bauder (eds.) *Sanctuary cities and urban struggles: Rescaling migration, citizenship, and rights.* Manchester: Manchester University Press, 77–104.

Luxemburg, R. (1951 [1913]). *The Accumulation of Capital.* London: Routledge and Kegan Paul Ltd.

MacKinnon, D. (2010). Reconstructing scale: Towards a new scalar politics. *Progress in human geography*, 35 (1), 21–36.

Marx, K. (1976 [1885]). *Capital: A Critique of Political Economy.* Harmondsworth: Penguin Books.

Massey, D. (1991). A global sense of place. *Marxism Today* (June), 24–29.

Massey, D. (2005). *For Space.* London, Thousand Oaks CA, New Dehli: Sage.

Mbodj-Pouye, A. (2016). Fixed abodes: Urban emplacement, bureaucratic requirements, and the politics of belonging among West African migrants in Paris. *American Ethnologist*, 43 (2), 295–310.

Morrice, L. (2019). Abyssal lines and cartographies of exclusion in migration and education: towards a reimagining. *International Journal of Lifelong Education*, 38 (1), 20–33.

Mouffe, C. (2005). *On the Political.* London: Routledge.

Munck, R. (2020). Pandemia en la era del neoliberalismo: Covid-19 y más allá en América Latina. *Izquierda: teoría y praxis* (1, July 2020), 6–13.

Purcell, M. (2006). Urban democracy and the local trap. *Urban Studies*, 43 (11), 1921–41.

Richmond, A. H. (1994). *Global Apartheid: Refugees, Racism, and the New World Order.* Toronto and New York, NY, and Oxford: Oxford University Press.

Roth, L., and B. Russell (2018). Translocal Solidarity and the New Municipalism. *ROAR* #8, (Autumn), 80–93.

RSMMS (2018). 'Position du Réseau Syndical Migration Méditerranéennes-Subsahariennes (RSMMS) sur le "Pacte mondial pour des migration sûres, ordonnées et régulières"' (Ed, RSMMS) Les organisations syndicalles membres du RSMMS.

Russell, B. (2019). Beyond the local trap: New municipalism and the rise of the fearless cities. *Antipode*, 51 (3), 989–1010.

Sanchéz, J. L. (2011). October 15th: Dreaming of a "new global citizen power", Take the Square, Available online at: https://takethesquare.net/2011/10/13/october-15th-dreaming-of-a-%e2%80%9cnew-global-citizen-power%e2%80%9d/.

Schierup, C.-U. (1993). *På kulturens slagmark: mindretal og størretal taler om Danmark.* Esbjerg: Southern Jutland University Press.

Schierup, C.-U. (ed. 1999). *Scramble for the Balkans: Nationalism, Globalism, and the Political Economy of Reconstruction.* Houndsmill: MacMillan.

Schierup, C. U., R. D. Wise, S. Rother, and A. Ålund (2019). Postscript. The Global Compact for Migration: what road from Marrakech? In Schierup, C. U., et al. (eds.) *Migration, Civil Society and Global Governance.* London: Routledge, 156–64.

Sernhede, O., R. León Rosales, and J. Söderman (2019). *'När betongen rätar sin rygg'. Ortenrörelsen och folkbildningens renässans.* Gothenburg: Daidalos.

Sklaw, S. (2018). American policy is responsible for the migrant caravan *The Washington Post.* October 29.

Solnit, R. (2010). *A Paradise Built in Hell.* Penguin.

Storey, A. (2001). Structural adjustment, state power and genocide: the World Bank & Rwanda. *Review of Africain Political Economy*, 89, 365–85.

Tazzioli, M. (2020). What is Left of Migrants' Spaces? Transversal Alliances and the Temporality of Solidarity. *Political Anthropological Research on International Social Sciences (PARISS)*, 1 (1), 137–61.

Tobias, S. (2012). Neoliberal globalization and the politics of migration in Sub-Saharan Africa. *Journal of International and Global Studies*, 4 (1), 1–16.

Weisbrot, M., and J. Sachs (2019). *Economic Sanctions as Collective Punishment: The Case of Venezuela.* No.: CEPR – Centre for Economic and Policy Research.

Yuval-Davis, N. (1994). Women, ethnicity and empowerment. *Feminism & Psychology*, 4 (1), 179–97.

Yuval-Davis, N. (1999). What is 'transversal politics'. *Soundings* (12), 94–98.

CHAPTER 2

Urban Solidarity

Perspectives of Migration and Refugee Accommodation and Inclusion

Harald Bauder

Throughout the global north, restrictive immigration policies are denying many migrants and refugees access to services and security.[1]

In response to these national policies, urban communities have developed municipal policies and engage in local practices of inclusion that seek to enable migrants and refugees to participate in urban social and political life. Although different labels, such as sanctuary city, solidarity city, city of refuge, etc. are used to describe such policies and practices (Ataç, et al. 2020; Bauder and Gonzalez 2018; Darling and Bauder 2019), the concept of solidarity has been central in the scholarly framing of such urban approaches (Agustín and Jørgensen 2016; Christoph and Kron 2019; Heimann, et al. 2019).

In this paper, I empirically examine the concept of solidarity and its application in the context of urban initiatives and local campaigns that aim to accommodate migrants and refugees. The paper thus contributes to a fast-growing literature on migrant and refugee solidarity (Agustín and Jørgensen 2016, 2019; Oosterlynck, et al. 2016; Stierl 2019), which has recently demonstrated the ambiguity and multidimensional nature of the concept of solidarity (Bauder and Juffs 2020). This paper therefore seeks to offer clarity regarding the way in which urban actors understand the concept and apply it in their initiatives and campaigns.

Below, I first review the literature to develop a set of research questions that I pursue in this paper. Then I discuss the methods involving expert interviews in Berlin and Freiburg im Beisgau in Germany and Zurich in Switzerland. Thereafter I present the results of the analysis of these interviews in the context of interpretations of the concept of solidarity and its application in the urban initiatives and campaigns. I end with a conclusion that discusses the findings in light of the literature.

---

1 An earlier version of this work has been published as an article in *Critical Sociology*: Bauder, H. (2020). Urban solidarity: Perspectives of migration and refugee accommodation and inclusion. *Critical Sociology*, 0896920520936332.

1   Literature Review

Over the last decade, the concept of solidarity has received a considerable amount of attention in the literature related to migration and refugees
(Agustín and Jørgensen 2016, 2019; Bauder 2020; Bauder and Juffs 2020; Rygiel
2011; Stierl 2016). Within this literature, however, there is no consensus how
solidarity should be defined. As a result, it has been framed in reference to various philosophical departure points. On the one hand, the concept has usually
been grounded in a Eurocentric philosophical Enlightenment tradition. On
the other hand, within this overarching tradition, solidarity has been following
multiple distinct lines of reasoning (Bauder and Juffs 2020). For example, it
has been approached from a Hobbesian perspective of self-interest, suggesting
that acting in solidarity is a rational choice that serves the common interest of
a community of people or a community of states such as the European Union
(Greenhill 2016; Ventrella 2015). Another common perspective of solidarity
can be traced to the philosophy of David Hume and suggests that solidarity
is driven by compassion that guides free will and the capacity to act. This perspective has connected solidarity with migrants and refugees to humanitarianism and hospitality (Chouliaraki and Stolic 2017; Musarò and Parmiggiani
2017). A further perspective references solidarity in a Kantian perspective of
universal practical reason according to which solidarity with migrants and refugees is inspired by human equality and the responsibility towards upholding
human and other universal rights (Bado 2016; Siebold 2017). Finally, solidarity
has been framed in a Hegelian-Marxian perspective that stresses liberation
from oppression in the form of the political inclusion and economic participation of migrants and refugees (Baban and Rygiel 2017; Campbell 2016).

Rather than relying on scholarly perspectives of solidarity and thus the interpretation of the concept by researchers (Bauder and Juffs 2020), the empirical
investigation in this paper examines interpretations of the concept of solidarity among various urban actors involved in migrant and refugee accommodation. The first research question therefore is: *What perspectives of solidarity do
these actors embrace?* Answering this question is important because different
perspectives of solidarity entail different motivations and political aims for
urban policies and practices supporting migrants and refugees.

The literature stresses that solidarity connects circumstances and activities in different places, often crossing international boundaries (Agustín and
Jørgensen 2016; Bauder 2020; Featherstone 2012). For example, solidarity activities address economic interdependencies between the global north and south
and connect corresponding global labor struggles (Allard, et al. 2013; Raynolds
and Bennett 2015). In a context of migration and refugees, practices of

solidarity can also be associated with mobility itself and in this way transcend territorial and place-based logics (Papadopoulos and Tsianos 2013; Stierl 2016). Yet, migrant and refugee solidarities are also place-bound, for example, when they emerge in detention camps (Rygiel 2011) or when activists support activities that occur in particular locations (Kelliher 2018; Oosterlynck, et al. 2016).

Of particular interest is how the concept of solidarity translates to the urban scale. In different parts of the world, urban solidarity initiatives and movements have supported local migrants and refugees (Bauder 2019; Bauder and Gonzalez 2018; Darling and Bauder 2019). These initiatives and movements, however, are embedded in rather different regional geopolitical situations, national legal regimes, local discourses of migration, and other place-particular circumstances. In addition, they pursue different political aims and localized strategies. As a consequence, urban solidarity policies and practices are highly diverse and lack a common terminology. In Canada, the USA, and the UK many urban initiatives have adopted the label 'sanctuary city' (Bauder 2017; Darling 2010). In other parts of the world, such as Latin America and Continental Europe, the term 'solidarity cities' has been popular (Koellner 2019). The 2004 Mexico Plan of Action established the *Ciudades Solidarias* ('Cities of Solidarity') network of more than 50 cities, which promotes municipal migrant and refugee integration in collaboration with UNHCR (Varoli 2010). Latin American cities, however, also endorse other labels. For example, Quilicura (Chile) calls itself a 'community of reception' (Bauder and Gonzalez 2018; Correa, et al. 2014). In Europe, the organization Eurocities established the 'Solidarity City' network in 2016, which works with the European Commission on "the management of the refugee crisis" (Solidarity Cities n.d.). Another label used in Europe is 'city of refuge' (Bauder and Gonzalez 2018; Christoph and Kron 2019). Despite the use of different labels, a discernible urban solidarity approach exists across local and national contexts.

In the context of urban approaches to migrant and refugee accommodation, recent research has pointed out the patriarchal and charitable relations between migrants and refugees and their urban 'hosts' (Bagelman 2016; Houston and Morse 2017). Urban practices of solidarity may have in common that they are seeking to address such asymmetrical relationships (Nyers 2010; Walia 2013). Another characteristic of the urban solidarity approach may be that it creates a forum in which formal policy actors, such as the mayors and municipal administrations that are participating in top-down networks such as Latin America's *Ciudades Solidarias* or Solidarity Cities in Europe, can interact with grassroots activists in pursuit of common strategic aims (Bauder and Gonzalez 2018; Christoph and Kron 2019). A second research question therefore is: *What does urban solidarity entail for actors in different cities who are involved in migrant and refugee accommodation?*

Although there may be a common solidarity approach in terms of the over-arching motivations and goals to urban migrant and refugee accommodation, various labels and terminologies are being used to describe corresponding urban efforts and campaigns. A final research question therefore is: *Why do actors in different cities endorse various labels to describe urban policies and practices that pursue similar aims of migrant and refugee accommodation?* Addressing this question is important because understanding the motivations and arguments to use particular terminology will provide insights into the nuances and possible limitations of an urban solidarity approach.

2   Methodology

The results presented below derive from a larger project on urban sanctuary and solidarity policies and practices in Germany and the German-speaking part of Switzerland. Empirical case studies involved Freiburg im Breisgau and Berlin in Germany and Zurich in Switzerland (Kößler 2013; Schwenken 2008). In these cities, urban initiatives exist to accommodate vulnerable migrants and refugees, especially those without status or with precarious status (Freiburger Forum aktiv gegen Ausgrenzung 2016; Morawek 2019; Neumann 2019). Yet, local solidarity initiatives that are embedded in particular national and regional migration legislative frameworks, geopolitical situations, and migra-tion discourses. Scholars have pointed out the infeasibility of US-style urban 'sanctuary' policies to protect illegalized migrants and refugees in Germany due to federal legislation requiring municipalities to register and report all residents (Scherr and Hofmann 2016). Although some activists started to explicitly use the term 'sanctuary city' (*Zufluchts-Stadt*) in local campaigns (Freiburger Forum aktiv gegen Ausgrenzung 2016), the term 'solidarity city' has become popular recently. In Zurich, the term 'urban citizenship' is com-monly used in reference to local solidarity initiatives and practices (Morawek and Krenn 2017).

Between fall 2018 and spring 2019, I conducted 10 semi-structured expert interviews in each city. The experts included local activists, NGO staff, members of the municipal governance body, and municipal officials and administrators, including at the local police. I used the same interview guide in all three cit-ies but shaped the interview according to local circumstances. The interviews were conducted, transcribed, and analyzed in German; the quotes presented below are my translation. The interview transcripts were analyzed initially using priory coding involving codes derived from the literature. Subsequent axial coding permitted linking the data from the different codes and cities. A set of questions in the interview guide asked participants to reflect on the concept of 'solidarity'. To stimulate further discussion related to this concept, I probed the participants whether and why this concept is important, what solidarity means in the context of a participant's activities, and whom solidarity includes. The answers to these questions and the ensuing conversation form the basis of the below discussion.

3   Findings

In this section, I examine perspectives of the concept of solidarity among the combined sample of participants in the three cities. Then, I explore how solidarity applies to the urban scale. Thereafter, I focus on each city to investigate the use and application of various concepts related to urban migrant and refugee accommodation.

3.1   *Perspectives of Solidarity*
As expected, the interviews revealed the ambiguity of the concept of solidarity. On the one hand, solidarity has universal appeal. An activist from Berlin explains that their campaign may have been inspired by the North American sanctuary-city movement but they nevertheless embrace the term solidarity rather than sanctuary: "solidarity is understandable everywhere". On the other hand, the participants are keenly aware of the complexity of the concept. A staff member at an NGO in Berlin says that solidarity "can be seen in very different contexts in relation to very different solidarity practices; some of them are articulating demands and some are simply practical in concrete terms". An activist from Zurich further remarks:

> Solidarity is a concept that is now slowly being discussed a little bit; but for a long time it was not en vogue in this asylum-rights movement. It has a quite charitable origin; some people have rights and privileges and others don't. And solidarity is then just that, one helps the other. But ... the universalist concept of solidarity, which is still unresolved, [addresses] the relationship between us in Europe and all the others in the world and how can rights be shared. Well, almost ... a global citizenship, how do we get there. And ... this concept of solidarity has not been clarified at all.

This participant is skeptical of the solidarity concept and, as I will later show, it has not played a defining role in the local campaign in Zurich to accommodate vulnerable migrants and refugees.

Corresponding to the literature (Bauder and Juffs 2020), participants embraced various perspectives of solidarity. The first perspective relates to solidarity as *self-interest* in liberating ones' community from oppression. An activist from Berlin explains that the idea of solidarity in their campaign "originates from solidarity among workers. So really to say: Okay ... basically our problem is a repressive structure and we respond by standing together to help each other; so actually an ego-driven community". Another Berlin-based activist elaborates:

> I would define solidarity as relating to each other based on common interests. As opposed to charity; not charity but to develop a sense of common interests and thereby develop positions for action. And these common interests are primarily city-related and with the people who are here, but not only. ... For me, solidarity is really a common process of transformation in this country or in the cities of this country.

The perspective of self-interest emphasizes not only material gain but also stresses a *common* interest in shaping society.

A second perspective suggests that *human compassion* motivates people to act in solidarity. This perspective was endorsed by the police force. A high-ranking police officer in Freiburg says:

> Here at the police force ... [in] our work, above all, there is proportionality, law and order, what we do, we do on a legal basis and in the course of proportionality of each individual event or activity ... here solidarity is not an external topic, but solidarity is part of it when you look at humanity or proportionality, it is of course always immanent. ... For example, the situation can be that a patrol sees a person early in the morning at three o'clock and the patrol has the impression that the person could be in a helpless state. Now you have to help these people. ... As police we have the obligation to do something. Before somebody freezes to death in the winter because they have no roof over his head, then the police will put this person somewhere where they are warm. ... Of course, it includes [assessing] who is this person and what is the status of the person.

Solidarity as an act of compassion, in this case, relates to a migrant or refugee's physical well-being but not their denial of status or social exclusion. In fact, other respondents have difficulties to include the police in their solidarity efforts, as an activist from Berlin explains:

> The police are the physically repressive arm of the state and therefore I find it incredibly difficult to find a solidary approach here and my experience with the Berlin police is also not that there is a great interest in anti-racist work (laughs). To put it carefully, they are simply appalling racists.

Surprisingly, participants beyond the police did not discuss the perspective of solidarity as an act of compassion.

Participants in all three cities embrace the perspective of solidarity as relating to access to *rights*, especially *human rights*. An activist from Berlin says:

> This is ... the basic idea of solidarity [at my organization] ... everyone should have a right to medical care. This [idea] is already 20 years old at [organization] in Berlin and emerged ..., as the rights of legal refugees were restricted in the medical sector and as it became clear, even then, that there are more and more illegalized people.

Participants in Zurich framed solidarity in reference to human rights. A municipal administrator says:

> From the side of the municipality ... we're trying to find an approach to the topic [of including *sans papiers*] ... based on solidarity and on basic and human rights. Put simply, this means that there is no human right to receive a residence permit, but there are human rights to receive education and health, as well as access to justice.

In Freiburg, a grassroots activist explains their interpretation of 'solidarity' in this way:

> I personally assume that no human being is better or worse in any way. So you can't make anybody smaller or bigger either because ... they were born here or because they came here. ... Every human being has in principle only one life and in this life they need all rights, so to speak, to fulfil themselves. ... And in this context there is solidarity, for me that means ... that everyone gets the same rights. In terms of voting rights, co-determination in the community, and so on. Where one lives, one must be able to participate and so on. So for me that is solidarity.

This participant sees solidarity not only in terms of equal rights for all but also possessing the ability to participate in the community. This viewpoint overlaps with the final perspective of solidarity that was discernible in the interviews.

Several participants framed solidarity in reference to social and *political participation and democracy*. A staff person at a Berlin-based foundation remarks that "the concept of solidarity ... is not only about specific groups, but about practices of solidarity and thus potentially something like a class-based political perspective". This participant elaborates:

> There is a wide range of people who just want to help and [people participating in] political debates who say, let's build another city and not just who gets what rights, but how we engage in politics together. So not only for whom, but also with whom. ... That's what's so exciting about this term, that I believe it can be extended in this way, and potentially can be extended further and further. From help more and more towards practical solidarity and then towards debates about what kind of city we want to live in.

A member of Berlin's House of Representatives (*Abgeordnetenhaus*) suggests that solidarity is not something that is restricted to migrants or refugees as recipients, but rather something that penetrates society as a whole:

> Well, the concept of solidarity basically encompasses everything that is a matter of organizing social cohesion and facilitating the most possible equal participation in social life. First, we have a lot of homeless people in Berlin. ... A large proportion of them are EU citizens. Many of them have been recruited into exploitative working conditions where accommodation was included and if they complain about exploitation they not only lose their jobs but also their accommodation. That's a huge problem and ... they're generally not entitled to benefits. ... Many of the people who are homeless also have addiction problems. ... You don't solve an addiction problem by getting people out. ... For me this is also the concept of solidarity: creating ways back into society. And that also means taking care of the individual.

For this participant, solidarity expands beyond politics narrowly focused on migrants and refugees, and instead encompasses a wider societal political spectrum.

3.2 *Urban Solidarity*

The interviews showed how the urban scale imbeds relationships of solidarity in personal interactions of daily life. A Berlin-based activist juxtaposes these relationships with a disembodied view of solidarity framed in nationalistic terms: "What can't be, for me there can be no solidarity between institutions, also not between nations. At some point, there was this solidarity of nations or junk (*Kram*) like that". Another Berlin-based activist explains that the solidarity city instead focusses on locally embodied relationships

> because in the cities the real life actually takes place with [interactions] among the people themselves. I think that is why there is more solidarity, because the mayors simply have to be in much more direct contact with the people who live there, and the local people who are also the ones who live together with the people who migrate here.

For this participant, the urban scale connects the political leadership (i.e. mayors) with the experiences of local residents who interact daily with migrants and refugees.

Participants discussed the relationship between top-down and bottom-up approaches that are reflected in solidarity cities initiatives and practices. Several participants suggested that the political pressure emanates primarily from the bottom. An activist says:

> we are trying to solve the problem more from below and say: "Okay, the workers in the respective institutions, the nurses, the caretakers, the teachers" [we] approach the issue through them, instead of saying: "From above comes the Senate, here is now a new instruction, hopefully it works". [We] rather try to generate the idea of a city of solidarity from below.

An administrator at a Berlin-based NGO affirms that the local government "is pressured (*gedrückt*)" from below to meet grassroots demands. Another activist notes:

> What is important … is that we succeed in influencing the [Berlin] Senate. And we have also … talked to churches – they are not really considered the [political] Left (laughs) – in Germany at least. What comes from above, in the form of changes in the law, is something that is potentially more sustainable. Because such a law is fixed and then there are certain resources that can be allocated to it and things like that. But

> I believe that if we really want good regulations, then pressure must come from below.

Other respondents see more interaction and convergence between bottom-up and top-down urban-scale solidarity efforts. A staff member at a Berlin-based foundation remarks:

> In the best case, ... it's like a ping pong game – this is how I imagine it sometimes. The city declares itself to be a solidarity city and, in this way, becomes a target for the grassroots initiatives, as it offers a greater area of attack in the sense of making demands on the city. And in the best-case scenario, this [situation] develops into a joint dialogue in relation to certain topics: what can be improved, and how can the city be advanced in certain areas?

While many participants agree that grassroots efforts play an essential role in solidarity city initiatives, many also believe that being a solidarity city entails interaction and collaboration with the city administration and government. This interaction and collaboration blur the distinction between bottom-up and top-down approaches (Bauder and Gonzalez 2018).

Some Berlin-based participants also remark how 'solidarity city' potentially appeals to a wide political spectrum. An activist and organizer comments:

> It's not about who is ideologically committed to this concept [solidarity city], but rather what is the idea behind it and what kind of practices exist in the city that relate to it. ... I don't think it's so important that we erect a political front, but rather ... to simply say: okay, there are things, especially with all this heterogeneity, with diverse motives, that we need to bundle [our efforts] and say, yes, this is happening here, this is a city of solidarity.

A staff person at a foundation affirms this encompassing nature of the concept of solidarity city: "the nice thing about the term, I think, is that it is applicable to a diverse terrain (*geländegängig*)". A Berlin-based organizer observes that solidarity has appeal beyond the political left, which historically has laid claim to the term: "you used to be classically left-wing in the past, today you tend to become a member of a solidarity initiative and maybe ideologically you are not left-wing either". The downside of a relatively flexible and widely applicable definition is that the term 'solidarity city' may lack clarity. A consultant at a political foundation observes that "in Europe, it is long not defined what a solidarity city is". The following section therefore examines terminologies in the three urban contexts.

3.3   Berlin: A Solidarity City for All

Berlin has a long tradition of activism, which solidified around solidarity practices that bridge ethnic communities and supporting refugees starting in 2013 (Dietrich 2019). In the fall of 2015, *Solidarische Stadt Berlin* (Solidarity City Berlin) was founded and, at the point of the interview, included the organizations *MedioBüro*, *respect!*, *Kampagne Bürgerinnenasyl*, *Interventionistische Linke*, and *Oficina Precaria*. Since late 2016, Berlin has been governed by a left red-green-red coalition sympathetic to such initiatives. In December 2018, Berlin's governing party, *Die Linke*, committed to the slogan "Solidarische Stadt Berlin," and in January 2019 Berlin officially joined the European network Solidarity Cities (Dietrich 2019; Neumann 2019). At the time of writing, Berlin's Commissioner of the Senate for Integration and Migration is posting the first permanent position to coordinate Berlin's membership in the Solidarity Cities network.

In Berlin, the term 'solidarity city' has received significant attention in local activism and politics. While urban solidarity initiatives there have their origin in the protection and accommodation of vulnerable migrants and refugees, the idea of the solidarity city encompasses a larger population. Dietrich (2019) writes: solidarity city is about "an improvement for all Berliners, or rather all Berliners in precarious life situations". She uses the example of care, which should be accessible to all people regardless of "whether they are German citizens, intra-European migrants, illegal immigrants, people with toleration (*Duldung*) or in asylum proceedings" (Dietrich 2019, 61, my translation). When Berlin's *Die Linke* started using the term "solidarische Stadt Berlin," it also had in mind that it would address the needs of all people living in Berlin (Neumann 2019, 23–24). A participant and high-ranking politician corroborates this view:

> For us, *Die Linke*, it's actually the term [solidarity city] that frames our politics. This is the *leitmotif* of city politics here in Berlin. At the last party congress, we passed a motion precisely on the concept of the city of solidarity, Berlin as Solidarity City, where we again reiterated: What does it mean for housing, which is one of the most burning problems here in the city; what does it mean for education; what does it mean for health; what does it mean for refugees, but not only; what does it mean for workers; what does it mean for single parents?

Other interview participants in Berlin are aware of this party-political strategy. An activist observes that *Die Linke* ...

> and the more institutional actors have adopted [the concept] for the time being, because it sounds good, 'Solidarity City,' where you say: "Ah okay, there are different questions, and one is the question of housing, the other is work, and the third is residence status." And at the very least, there will be equal treatment, equal rights.

A consultant at a political foundation explains that there is a strong political movement promoting affordable housing in Berlin, which also advocates for migrants and refugees lacking access to affordable housing. This movement is "loosely connected to the sanctuary-city movement". This participant sees political potential in the solidarity city idea: "let's say we want a kind of urban cohabitation that is more democratic and we also see the democratic deficits for other groups. Homeless, precarious people, etc. and not only for the illegalized refugees and migrants". A Berlin-based activist argues that an important aspect of the solidarity city is to provide "access to social rights", including health and education for all.

Several participants linked the solidarity city concept to other political concepts, such as democratization and 'right to the city'. An activist argues that a solidarity city entails "to demand a city for all. An extensive democratization, beyond the specific group of migrants, a democratization for all". Another activist notes that their group in Berlin seeks to

> put these 'right to city' and Solidarity City ideas together. Last year and this year, we have done this through conferences, which focus on the right to city but which [transformed] a little bit to a solidarity city conference. To bring together exactly these themes: housing, city, politics under a solidarity city.

In Berlin, the concept of solidarity city has garnered significant support from grassroots initiatives and parts of local government and administration. The appeal of this concept, however, is not universal, as the case of Zurich illustrates.

3.4 *Zurich: Migrant and Refugee Inclusion through Urban Citizenship*
Like Berlin, Zurich is an official member of Eurocities' Solidarity Cities network. Since the early 2000s, civil-society organizations, such as *Sans Papiers-Anlaufstelle Zürich* (SPAZ), *Colectivo Sin Papeles*, and *Meditrina* have focused on

offering medical, social, and legal advice and services to non-status migrants living in Zurich (Morawek 2019). A consultant at a local NGO recalls a catalytic project that was launched in the fall of 2015:

> There was a project "The whole world in Zurich" (*Die ganze Welt in Zürich*) ... in an art gallery ... where they wanted to talk about urban citizenship models in Zurich. ... We then formed three working groups. One group set itself the goal of discussing and promoting the cultural participation of migrant women, one group the goal of freedom from discrimination, and the [third] group the goal of security of residency.

In the wake of this arts project, the book *Urban Citizenship* (Krenn and Morawek 2017) was published. In addition, the association *Züri City Card* was founded to promote a municipal identification card available to all residents, including *sans-papiers*. In 2018, city parliament (*Gemeinderat*) decided to introduce a municipal identification card and instructed the city government (*Stadtrat*) – both of which are controlled by left-leaning parties – with its implementation by 2020 (Morawek 2019).

Many participants from the sample in Zurich do not use the labels sanctuary or solidarity city but rather spoke of 'urban citizenship' (they adopt the English term). The reason for using this terminology lies in the origin and history of the local campaign. A member of city parliament believes that the publication of the book *Urban Citizenship* "has certainly something to do with" entrenching this term in the local campaign. An artist-activist affirms:

> Our project was not called that from the beginning, but the publication was called that and the publication came out two years later. ... The project was actually titled "the whole world in Zurich – concrete interventions in Swiss migration policy," so in a way we played on a different keyboard.

In addition to the publication of this book, the concept of urban citizenship has conceptual appeal for the campaign. The same artist-activist elaborates that the concept of urban citizenship permits engaging in "an academic debate, in the social sciences and urban sociology". This participant further explains that the campaign seeks to connect to

> a debate that understands citizenship more as a process of democratization, that is much more intersectional, that does not only aim at *sans-papiers* as the primary objects of this debate, but also at the post-migrant society, that also looks at which dimensions of citizenship occur in a

post-migrant society. [This debate] has separated itself a bit from this very charitable care for people without a valid residence permit.

This participant elaborates that urban citizenship addresses "various aspects of citizenship or of a certain form of subject-formation (*Subjektwerdung*) by those who, so to speak, were not necessarily considered to be part of the Swiss national body". Other participants comment on the personal appeal of the concept of urban citizenship. A participant explains:

> For me personally, I am a second generation [foreign national], so I am naturalized Swiss, but I also have a [foreign] passport and the urban citizenship idea was very enriching for me personally, because I don't feel personally as Swiss, but as a Zuricher ... That's why it was also very personal for me, that's why I believe that [urban citizenship] can also be understood in a broader sense than just the *sans-papiers* and the topic of refugees.

This participant acknowledges that urban citizenship encompasses the wider local population but also differentiates between urban solidarity and urban citizenship:

> We have identified very much with the idea of the urban citizenship, that everyone who lives here also equally belongs to Zurich society, whether with or without a passport. I think that was already very much our focus. ... For me personally there are many other marginalized struggles [to whom the term solidarity applies], low-income people, the right to cheap housing, the right to the city. To me all this belongs under the guise of solidarity in the city. But in our campaign we have a strong focus on *sans-papiers*.

This participant interprets urban citizenship as more narrowly focused on the local belonging of migrants and refugees as opposed to urban solidarity, which includes non-migrant populations in precarious circumstances. A staff person at a local NGO affirms this viewpoint:

> When one speaks of a solidarity city, then it is also about participation, shaping something together. And [our campaign] is taking a step backwards because it is actually about ensuring access to justice for people and initiating fundamental rights cases ... There is first a need for work that takes a step backwards and says, yes, it is about very basic rights that

are being violated and people have no access before we can talk about something like participation.

By framing the campaign in more narrow terms, the conception of urban citizenship differs from the solidarity city the way it is used in Berlin as encompassing migrant and non-migrant groups in precarious situations.

Similar to Berlin, however, there is considerable interaction and collaboration between grassroots activists and the city administration in Zurich. In fact, some activists supporting local urban citizenship initiatives are also members of city parliament. A member of city parliament who has long been involved in urban citizenship initiatives explains that "we are already strongly networked with political parties and the parliament". This respondent elaborates that "we also had the advantage that we've had a city governed on the left or tended to have a left-wing government, the executive as well as the legislature. I think these factors were decisive that it was so easy for us to penetrate politics or institutional policy". Another activist adds that "direct exchange does exist in certain areas" with the city administration. This exchange is facilitated by Zurich's membership in Eurocities' Solidarity City network:

> We tried to use precisely this interface between civil society and, let's say, decision-makers, policy-makers. ... We have tried to use this interface again and again by asking the Office for Integration Support (*Stelle für Integrationsförderung*), well what is going on at Solidarity City, i.e. on the EU level? And we have also tried again and again to stay in contact and to extend invitations to talk.

The connection between Zurich's official membership in the Solidarity Cities network and grassroots efforts under the banner of urban citizenship illustrates that the two concepts are treated not as mutually exclusive but complementary.

3.5   *Freiburg: Contesting Terminologies*

Freiburg's city council has been dominated by left-leaning parties. In 2012, it passed a resolution to support foreign Roma threatened by deportation. Although it recently declared that Freiburg would accept refugees in distress in the Mediterranean Sea, it has not offered official support to the local solidarity city campaign (Bauder and Gonzalez 2018). Grassroots efforts in support of vulnerable migrants and refugees in Freiburg bundle in a particular location, the 'Rasthaus,' which is a housing complex that hosts organizations such as *medinetz*, *Südbadisches Aktionsbündnis gegen Abschiebung*, and *aktion Beiberecht* (Rasthaus n.d.).

Although there is an active Solidarity City campaign (https://www.freibur ger-forum.net/solidarity-city/) in Freiburg, there has been less clarity among activists, politicians, and supporters regarding the terminology that should be applied to local migrant and refugee accommodation. A city councilor who has been very supportive of the idea of urban migrant and refugee inclusion acknowledges:

> I have come to realize that 'sanctuary cities' is no longer the up-to-date concept in Germany ... but rather 'solidarity city,' although I must hon- estly admit that I may never quite understand the difference ... I think it really has to do with legal frameworks, but I am not quite sure about that now.

An activist participant critiques the solidarity city idea for its ridged territo- riality, suggesting that "one must be careful that the solidarity does not end at the city limits". Rather, this participant proposed that solidarity transcends municipal boundaries and that the term solidarity city is too limited to capture effective solidarity practices. A volunteer at a local ethnic minority associa- tion (*Verein*) rejects the term solidarity city outright: "It's a term that somehow comes from white people. 'Solidarity city' (derogatory), yes that's ... something neo-colonial, ... I know the people who make solidarity cities". Echoing existing critique of sanctuary cities (Bagelman 2016; Houston and Lawrence-Weilmann 2016), this participant problematizes the imbalance in respect to access to resources and political influence between those who endorse the concept of solidarity city and the recipients who are denied agency in shaping the circum- stances in which they live.

The lack of agreement on terminology was also fueled by an ongoing debate at the time I conducted the interviews about whether Freiburg should join the country-wide *Seebrücke* (sea bridge) initiative, calling on the national govern- ment to permit cities to directly accept refugees rescued in the Mediterranean Sea or who are currently located in EU-border countries. In the context of this debate, the concept of safe harbor (*sicherer Hafen*) was also applied to the accommodation of vulnerable migrants and refugees who had already arrived in Freiburg. An activist explains:

> It is already difficult with solidarity city, the term is well known, but has never developed this piercing impact (*Durchschlagskraft*) that the term safe harbor now has, and I do not know exactly how to bring them

together later. ... Personally, I would be more in favor of replacing 'solidarity city' with something of its own, maybe it's not safe harbor either, but a new concept may emerge.

Although 'solidarity city' has been used in major campaigns and on banners at display at demonstrations and festivals, there seems to be no consensus about which term should frame local policies and practices.

4 Conclusion

The case studies in Berlin, Freiburg, and Zurich show that urban actors concerned with the local accommodation of migrants and refugees interpret the concept of solidarity from a variety of perspectives. These perspectives include self- and common-interests, human compassion, access to universal rights, and political participation and democratization. This finding affirms the treatment of the concept of solidarity in the scholarly literature, which offers similar perspectives (Bauder and Juffs 2020). This paper provides evidence that not only scholars but also urban actors such as activists, NGO staff, municipal politicians and administrators assume these diverse perspectives of solidarity. This finding also indicates that urban initiatives and movements that seek to accommodate migrants and refugees are grounded in diverse motivations and do not follow a single script of solidarity. Rather, diverse perspectives of solidarity reflecting different interests and motivations converge in these cities.

At the urban scale, the idea of solidarity appeals to a wider political spectrum and, in this way, may open the possibility for urban policies and practices that transcend the political left, which may traditionally have laid claim to the concept of solidarity. In addition, urban solidarity can be embraced by grassroots initiatives as well as municipal administrators and local government representatives. Corresponding urban solidarity practices and policies thus possess the capacity to connect bottom-up and top-down efforts to accommodate migrants and refugees (Bauder and Gonzalez 2018).

The findings, however, also show that terminology revolving around urban solidarity is contested. In Berlin, many urban actors are embracing the term 'solidarity city' in the context of an urban vision that is inclusive of and offers justice for not only migrants and refugees but other vulnerable groups who may be non-migrants and citizens. The participants from Zurich have a different vision to which they apply the concept of urban citizenship. This terminology reflects a narrower focus on the local political inclusion of illegalized migrants and refugees. In Freiburg, participants have expressed skepticism of urban solidarity but apparently lack a consensus on the terminology they should endorse.

The findings illustrate that the terminology around urban solidarity is locally contingent. In each city, the use of particular terminology is subject to debate and a matter of strategic choice, which respond to a wide range of local and national circumstances, including local political configurations, national legal and administrative frameworks, local and national migration and refugee discourses, etc. While in cities like Barcelona, New York, or Montreal, mayors have assumed key roles in driving urban solidarity initiatives, the findings in this paper highlight the importance of other actors. In Berlin, the election of a left government coalition allowed the language of solidarity city, which had circulated mainly among activist groups, to enter the official policy debate. In Zurich, a particular arts project and the publication of a book have shaped the use of the concept urban citizenship. In Freiburg, the lack of consensus around terminology may also reflect the lack of clear political or civil-society leadership that consolidates public debate around the issue. Despite the common overarching urban struggles for migrant and refugee accommodation and inclusion, local politics and key urban actors are critical in shaping the way the local debate unfolds and which urban solidarity policies and practices are put on the political agenda.

Acknowledgements

I thank Timo Weisser, Janine Schmittgen and Laura Richter for research assistance, and Bernd Kortmann and Britta Küst for hosting me at FRIAS. This research received funding from the EU's Horizon 2020 research and innovation program under the Marie Skłodowska-Curie grant agreement No 754340 and a SSHRC Insight Grant No. 435-2018-0845.

References

Agustín Ó.G., and M.B. Jørgensen (2016). *Solidarity Without Borders: Gramscian Perspectives on Migration and Civil Society Alliances*. London, UK: Pluto Press.

Agustín Ó.G., and M.B. Jørgensen (2019). *Solidarity and the 'Refugee Crisis' in Europe*. Cham, Switzerland: Springer.

Allard J., C. Davidson, and J.A. Matthae (2013). *Solidarity Economy: Building Alternatives for People and Planet : Papers and Reports from the 2007 US Social Forum*. Chicago, IL: ChangeMaker Publications.

Ataç, I., T. Schütze, and V. Reitter (2020). "Local responses in restrictive national policy contexts: welfare provisions for non-removed rejected asylum seekers in Amsterdam, Stockholm and Vienna". *Ethnic and Racial Studies* 43(16). Routledge: 115–134. DOI: 10.1080/01419870.2020.1723671.

Baban, F., and K. Rygiel (2017). "Living with others: fostering radical cosmopolitanism through citizenship politics in Berlin". *Ethics & Global Politics* 10(1). Routledge: 98–116. DOI: 10.1080/16544951.2017.1391650.

Bado, A.B. (2016). "Assessing Advocacies for Forcibly Displaced People: A Comprehensive Approach". *Journal of International Migration and Integration* 17(2): 593–603. DOI: 10.1007/s12134-015-0413-5.

Bagelman, J.J. (2016). *Sanctuary City: A Suspended State.* New York: Palgrave Macmillan. Available at: https://books.google.ca/books?id=uv7MCwAAQBAJ&printsec=fro ntcover&dq=jennifer+bagelman&hl=en&sa=X&ved=0ahUKEwipztDkpYToAhXBc 98KHYJlCiIQ6AEILjAB#v=onepage&q=jennifer%20bagelman&f=false (accessed 5 March 2020).

Bauder, H. (2017). "Sanctuary Cities: Policies and Practices in International Perspective". *International Migration* 55(2): 174–187. DOI: 10.1111/imig.12308.

Bauder, H. (2019). "Urban Sanctuary and Solidarity in a Global Context: How Does Africa Contribute to the Debate?" In: *MIASA Working Papers on Migration, Mobility, and Forced Displacement*, Accra, Ghana, 2019. MIASA. Available at: https://www .ug.edu.gh/mias-africa/miasa-working-papers-migration-mobility-and-forced -displacement (accessed 8 March 2020).

Bauder, H. (2020). "Migrant solidarities and the politics of place". *Progress in Human Geography.* Available at: https://journals.sagepub.com/doi/10.1177/0309132519876 324 (accessed 7 March 2020).

Bauder, H., and D.A. Gonzalez (2018). "Municipal Responses to 'Illegality': Urban Sanctuary across National Contexts". *Social Inclusion* 6(1): 124–134. DOI: 10.17645/ si.v6i1.1273.

Bauder, H., and L. Juffs (2020). "'Solidarity' in the migration and refugee literature: analysis of a concept". *Journal of Ethnic and Migration Studies* 46(1): 46–65. DOI: 10.1080/ 1369183X.2019.1627862.

Campbell, S. (2016). "Everyday recomposition: Precarity and socialization in Thailand's migrant workforce". *American Ethnologist* 43(2): 258–269. DOI: 10.1111/amet.12303.

Chouliaraki, L., and T. Stolic (2017). "Rethinking media responsibility in the refugee 'crisis': a visual typology of European news". *Media, Culture & Society* 39(8). SAGE Publications Ltd: 1162–1177. DOI: 10.1177/0163443717726163.

Christoph, W., and S. Kron (eds.) (2019). *Solidarity Cities in Europe: Charity or Pathways to Citizenship – A New Urban Policy Approach.* Berlin: Rosa Luxemburg Stiftung. Available at: https://www.rosalux.de/en/publication/id/40039/ (accessed 8 March 2020).

Correa, L., S. Correa, and T. Novoa (2014). *Plan de Acogida y Reconocimiento de Migrantes y Refugiados de la Comuna de Quilicura*. 1st ed. Santiago, Chile: Municipalidad de Quilicura.

Darling, J. (2010). "A city of sanctuary: the relational re-imagining of Sheffield's asylum politics". *Transactions of the Institute of British Geographers* 35(1). [Royal Geographical Society (with the Institute of British Geographers), Wiley]: 125–140.

Darling, J., and H. Bauder (eds.) (2019). *Sanctuary Cities and Urban Struggles: Rescaling Migration, Citizenship, and Rights*. Manchester, UK: Manchester University Press. Available at: https://manchesteruniversitypress.co.uk/9781526134912 (accessed 8 March 2020).

Dietrich, A. (2019). *Solidarity Cities: Lokale Strategien Gegen Rassismus Und Neoliberalismus*. Münster: Unrast Verlag.

Featherstone, D. (2012). *Solidarity: Hidden Histories and Geographies of Internationalism*. London: Z Books. Available at: https://www.press.uchicago.edu/ucp/books/book/distributed/S/bo20852295.html (accessed 8 March 2020).

Freiburger Forum aktiv gegen Ausgrenzung (2016). Freiburg – Eine Zufluchts-Stadt! Pamphlet unavailable online.

Greenhill, K.M. (2016). "Open Arms Behind Barred Doors: Fear, Hypocrisy and Policy Schizophrenia in the European Migration Crisis". *European Law Journal* 22(3): 317–332. DOI: 10.1111/eulj.12179.

Heimann, C., S. Müller, H. Schammann, et al. (2019). "Challenging the Nation-State from within: The Emergence of Transmunicipal Solidarity in the Course of the EU Refugee Controversy". *Social Inclusion* 7(2). 2: 208–218. DOI: 10.17645/si.v7i2.1994.

Houston, S., and O. Lawrence-Weilmann (2016). "The Model Migrant and Multiculturalism: Analyzig Neoliberal Logics in US Sanctuary Legislation". In: Bauder, H., and Matheis, C. (eds.) *Migration Policy and Practice: Interventions and Solution*. New York: Palgrave Macmillan. Available at: https://books.google.ca/books?id=npKkCgAAQBAJ&pg=PT6&dq=Bauder+Matheis&hl=en&sa=X&ved=0ahUKEwjQr-vUpoToAhWict8KHU3WA5kQ6AEIKDAA#v=onepage&q=Bauder%20Matheis&f=false (accessed 5 March 2020).

Houston, S.D., and C. Morse (2017). "The Ordinary and Extraordinary: Producing Migrant Inclusion and Exclusion in US Sanctuary Movements". *Studies in Social Justice* 11(1). 1: 27–47. DOI: 10.26522/ssj.v11i1.1081.

Kelliher, D. (2018). "Historicising geographies of solidarity". *Geography Compass* 12(9): e12399. DOI: 10.1111/gec3.12399.

Koellner, F. (2019). *Refugee Integration in Solidarity Cities in Latin America & the EU: A regional comparative analysis*. Saarbrücken: AV Akademikerverlag. Available at: https://www.bookdepository.com/Refugee-Integration-Solidarity-Cities-Latin-America-EU-Francy-Koellner/9786202218801.

Kößler, M. (2013). *Aufenthaltsrechtliche Illegalität – Beratungshandbuch 2013*. Berlin/Freiburg: Caritas, Rotes Kreuz.

Krenn, M., and K. Morawek (eds.) (2017). *Urban Citizenship – Democratising Democracy*. Vienna: Verlag für Moderne Kunst. Available at: http://www.martinkrenn.net/?p=2341 (accessed 5 March 2020).

Morawek, K. (2019). "Städtische Bürgerschaft und der kommunale Personalausweis". In: Christoph, W., and Kron, S. (eds.) *Städtische Solidarische Städte in Europa*. Berlin: Rosa-Luxemburg Stiftung., pp. 37–54. Available at: https://www.rosalux.de/fileadmin/rls_uploads/pdfs/sonst_publikationen/Broschur_SolidarischeStaedte.pdf.

Morawek, K., and M. Krenn (eds.) (2017). *Urban Citizenship Democratising Democracy*. Vienna: Verlag für Moderne Kunst.

Musarò, P., and P. Parmiggiani (2017). "Beyond black and white: the role of media in portraying and policing migration and asylum in Italy". *International Review of Sociology* 27(2). Routledge: 241–260. DOI: 10.1080/03906701.2017.1329034.

Neumann, M. (2019). "Baustelle solidarische Stadt: Berlins Landesregierung und linke Bewegungen forcieren soziale Rechte für Migrant*innen". In: Christoph, W., and Kron, S. (eds.) *Solidarische Städte in Europa: Urbane Politik Zwischen Charity Und Citizenship*. Berlin: Rosa-Luxemburg Stiftung., pp. 17–34. Available at: https://www.rosalux.de/publikation/id/40039/solidarische-staedte-in-europa/.

Nyers, P. (2010). "No One is Illegal Between City and Nation". *Studies in Social Justice* 4(2). 2: 127–143. DOI: 10.26522/ssj.v4i2.998.

Oosterlynck, S., M. Loopmans, N. Schuermans, et al. (2016). "Putting flesh to the bone: looking for solidarity in diversity, here and now". *Ethnic and Racial Studies* 39(5). Routledge: 764–782. DOI: 10.1080/01419870.2015.1080380.

Papadopoulos, D., and V.S. Tsianos (2013). "After citizenship: autonomy of migration, organisational ontology and mobile commons". *Citizenship Studies* 17(2). Routledge: 178–196. DOI: 10.1080/13621025.2013.780736.

Rasthaus (n.d.). Available at: https://www.rasthaus-freiburg.org/ (accessed 15 May 2020).

Raynolds, L.T., and E.A. Bennett (2015). *Handbook of Research on Fair Trade*. Cheltenham: Edward Elgar. Available at: https://www.e-elgar.com/shop/gbp/handbook-of-research-on-fair-trade-9781783474615.html (accessed 8 March 2020).

Rygiel, K. (2011). "Bordering solidarities: migrant activism and the politics of movement and camps at Calais". *Citizenship Studies* 15(1). Routledge: 1–19. DOI: 10.1080/13621025.2011.534911.

Scherr, A., and R. Hofmann (2016). "Sanctuary Cities: Eine Perspektive für deutsche Kommunalpolitik?" *Kritische Justiz* 49(1): 86–97. DOI: 10.5771/0023-4834-2016-1-86.

Schwenken, H. (ed.) (2008). *Leben in der Illegalität: ein Dossier*. Flüchtlingsrat 2008,2=123. Berlin: Heinrich-Böll-Stiftung.

Siebold, A. (2017). "Open borders as an act of solidarity among peoples, between states or with migrants: changing applications of solidarity within the Schengen process".

European Review of History: Revue européenne d'histoire 24(6). Routledge: 991–1006. DOI: 10.1080/13507486.2017.1345862.

Solidarity Cities (n.d.). Available at: https://solidaritycities.eu/about (accessed 8 March 2020).

Stierl, M. (2016). "Contestations in death – the role of grief in migration struggles". *Citizenship Studies* 20(2). Routledge: 173–191. DOI: 10.1080/13621025.2015.1132571.

Stierl, M. (2019). *Migrant Resistance in Contemporary Europe*. Abingdon: Routledge. Available at: https://www.routledge.com/Migrant-Resistance-in-Contemporary -Europe-1st-Edition/Stierl/p/book/9781138576230 (accessed 11 March 2020).

Varoli, F. (2010). "Ciudades Solidarias: la integración local en Latinoamérica". *Migraciones Forzadas Revista* 34: 44–46.

Ventrella, M. (2015). "Recognising Effective Legal Protection to People Smuggled at Sea, by Reviewing the EU Legal Framework on Human Trafficking and Solidarity between Member States". *Social Inclusion* 3(1). 1: 76–87. DOI: 10.17645/si.v3i1.170.

Walia, H. (2013). *Undoing Border Imperialism*. Oakland, CA: AK Press.

CHAPTER 3

On Transversal Solidarity
An Approach to Migration and Multi-scalar Solidarities

Óscar García Agustín and Martin Bak Jørgensen

The fire in Moria refugee camp, the largest one in Europe, in September 2020 was both a tragic human incident and a dramatic episode of the failing European Union refugee policy.[1] The camp, sited in Lesvos (Greece), was known as a 'living hell' due to the scarcity of water, food and electricity, the cases of sexual violence, and the image of children playing amongst rubbish (Hitchings-Hales 2020a). Although the camp was originally intended to accommodate 3,000 people, nearly 13,000, including 4,000 children, were left without shelter when it burned down. Besides, the camp was locked down due to a COVID-19 outbreak, which made conditions even worse and 35 were already tested positive before the fires. Greece, due to its location as EU border, has become an increasingly toxic point of contention. On the other hand, the emphasis on speeding up the asylum process does not contribute to a safe, fair and just system in which the right to asylum is guaranteed (Bird 2020). The Moria refugee camp was a testimony to the failure of this policy model; a reality of border containment through overcrowded camps and refoulement, but also a humanitarian failure since 7,500 people who were not relocated or moved to other camps were compelled to live in 'Moira 2.0', a temporary field of tents with limited access to water and sanitation (Hitchings-Hales 2000b). The political leaders quickly adopted a rhetoric of 'solidarity' in response to the humanitarian crisis, like Greek Prime Minister Kyriakos Mitsotakis claiming that "Europe must move from words of solidarity to acts of solidarity. We must place the migration crisis at the heart of our discussions and be much more concrete" (Tidey 2020). Germany and France encouraged other European countries to take responsibility and host unaccompanied minors who lived in the Moria camp. However, the measure was limited to children and not extended to all the refugees, and the number of relocated children is far from impressive, as some countries refused to provide shelter. As an alternative response, protestors in many cities

---

1 An earlier version of this work has been published as an article in *Critical Sociology*: Agustín, Ó. G., & Jørgensen, M. B. (2020). On Transversal Solidarity: An Approach to Migration and Multi-Scalar Solidarities. Critical Sociology, 0896920520980053.

demanded a more just refugee system and some municipalities offered to receive more refugees. These actions which expressed what we consider real acts of solidarity show the necessity of changing the approach to a solidary refugee policy which was already promoted by civil society in 2015.

The European Commission reacted promptly to the Morio case by announcing the *New Pact on Asylum and Migration*. The impetus on 'solidarity and responsibility', already drawn up in the Commission's response in 2015, should be concretized through specific mechanisms of solidarity. It implies an acknowledgement to search for a model not based on imposing quotas on member states (Chadwick and Monella 2020) and a critique of "solidarity *à-la-carte*", as labelled by former European Commission President Jean-Claude Juncker instead of solidarity as a two-way street. "There are times in which member states may expect to receive support, and times in which they, in turn, should stand ready to contribute" (Juncker in Heath 2017). Despite the intentions, the Pact entails a continuity with the previous EU strategy by maintaining the focus on border externalization, detention and deportation. What is new then? The 'mandatory solidarity', meaning the 'balance between solidarity and responsibility', implies that Member States have to show solidarity but not through quotas. Yet, the notion of 'mandatory' can be confusing here since the states are not obliged to relocate asylum seekers from the first country refugees reach. Solidarity can be shown by 'sponsoring returns' (JRS 2020). This mechanism was against the very idea of solidarity since it replaces relocation with sponsoring returns and thus leave the 'burden' of enforcing returns to the countries at the external borders. In addition, it is barely 'mandatory' because state members are not obliged to receive refugees and can opt for financing returns. It is difficult not to interpret the Pact as reinforcing 'solidarity *à-la-carte* dish' when states can decide if deporting, hosting, relocating or sponsoring returns. Rather than a balance between solidarity and responsibility, we are witnessing how the distribution of responsibility blurs any possibility of building migration and asylum politics grounded on the principle of solidarity. Not least, it can be argued that the new Pact could contribute to the uneven geographical development within the EU. Member States are expected to contribute according to GDP and population rather than their spending power. As a consequence, "if richer EU states do not act with the solidarity on which the pact relies, this flexibility will create a prisoner's dilemma that shifts responsibility for hosting migrants from the geographically disadvantaged to the economically disadvantaged", argues Kollek (2020). The economic divide is going to deepen existing uneven geographical divides regarding migration and asylum by privileging the capabilities of the richest countries and reducing only in part the pressure on frontline EU states.

Under these circumstances, the questions are: How to imagine an alternative European geography based on the principle of solidarity? And how to conceptualize solidarity to grasp the variety of existing solidarity practices which contribute to shape such an imagination? Our proposal consists of adopting a conceptualization of solidarity, which reflects the wave of solidarity from civil society as contesting the migration and asylum policies carried out by the EU and its Member States since 2015. The objective is consequently to offer a framework to analyze diverse forms of solidarity and their contribution to the relation between civil society and refugees. We define solidarity practices emerging from 2015 onwards in terms of 'transversal solidarity' in order to reflect their plurality and avoid dichotomies between in-group/out-group, national/international or society/institutions. We are not arguing that there are good or bad forms of solidarity but different manifestations which contribute (differently) to enable and connect geographies of solidarity within (and beyond) Europe. Together with a conceptualization of transversal solidarity, a typology of different models for organizing transversal solidarity is presented.

1   Transversal Solidarity

Solidarity is, without any doubt, a major force in transforming society and challenging migration and asylum policies from below. It is important, at the same time, to stress that solidarity can be promoted from different positions, like e.g. state or transnational corporations, but what is unique about solidarity from below is that it is produced through alternative and inclusive social and spatial practices and has the capability of generating new social bonds and expanding the space for participation. Furthermore, these forms of solidarity emerge in situations of contestation, as opposition to systems of domination and exclusion. We proceed in the following from a conceptualization of solidarity in terms of 'transversal solidarity' relating to three dimensions involved in solidarity practices from below and discuss how to bridge their respective dichotomies: *identity* and the related in-group and out-group dichotomy; *space*, in terms of the separation of the local from the national and international; *organization*, related to the incompatibility of the social and the institutional. We discuss how, by implementing the idea of 'transversal solidarity', it is possible to integrate these three dimensions without reproducing their inherent dichotomies.

The notion of transversal politics, as developed by Nira Yuval-Davis (1999), is framed as an alternative to cosmopolitan universalism, often exclusionary, and politics of identity, often suffering from 'essentialism'. From this perspective notions of solidarity as universalism or solidarity as based on sameness are problematic. The relevance of transversal politics consists of the encompassment of difference through equality. Referring to transversal feminist political movements, Yuval-Davis claims:

> The participants, while being engaged with 'others' belonging to different collectivities across borders and boundaries, act not as representatives of identity categories or groupings but rather as advocates, how they are reflectively engaged in 'rooting' and 'shifting' and how their strength lies in the construction of common epistemological understandings of particular political situations rather than of common political action (2011, 12).

Thinking of solidarity as relational, transversalism implies an openness beyond two or more groups (or individuals) which challenges pre-existing collective identities, but where the encounter (or dialogue) does not necessarily lead to a third collective identity. In other words, it allows social formations which are not limited to the divide between in-group and out-group inasmuch as identities can coexist as different and, at the same time, claim equality. The participants can maintain their identities while moving to other positions and forging a common ground. Thus, from this perspective, commonalities do not necessarily imply diminishing differences. Moreover, it does not imply that transversal solidarity is exempt from tensions as far as equal recognition and respect prevail. What maintains solidarity as transversal is the openness, the dialogue and the collective forging of commonalities without excluding differences. What is at stake here is not whether the voices of refugees are the ones to be listened to or if locals and nationals try to impose their views or idealize refugees. Solidarity as transversal openness shifts the focus to how activists, participants, refugees forge a common ground which is in opposition to or in conflict with exclusionary positions; whether derived from migration and asylum policies, or policies by local authorities, national governments or the EU. Hence, despite the importance of dialogue in shaping transversal solidarity, it is compatible with a contentious approach towards advocates and institutions considered responsible for devising exclusionary policies.

The application of transversalism to spatial relations aims to overcome the distinction and borders between local and transnational spaces, aiming to imagine commonalities in traversing and connecting different geographies. Schwiertz and Schwenken (2020, 414) highlight "how solidarity practices cross borders, boundaries and frontiers of supposedly well-defined social units". Although solidarity relations may be rooted in local practices, they can entail a transnational dimension, just as transnational practices are likewise rooted in diverse local practices. Featherstone (2013, 1408) refers to this idea in terms 'transnational solidarities', seen as "forms of connectivity that are forged through encounters that can exceed and refuse the obviousness of national spaces". Similarly, we conceive of transversal solidarities as multi-scalar connections between the local and the transnational. Transversality transgresses the dichotomy between local and transnational and adds new dynamics, which are not trapped by the predominant focus on national practices.

One important historical example of problems related to thinking solidarity is the defense of internationalism by the working class. As pointed out by Gago (2019), the leading principle of the First International (1864–76), The International Workingmen's Association was solidarity to counteract divisions of the working class manipulated by capital and state. Thus, solidarity meant unity of an international working class, blocking potential antagonisms based on difference. Besides assuming a homogenous working men's community, however, the First International neglected an actual plurality of spatial practices and struggles, opposing the power of capital. The point is, reflecting on dilemmas of solidarity making today, *not* to prevent national unity by claiming international unity or universalism but rather to encompass "what produces connection between trajectories, experiences and struggles which happen in diverse spaces" (Gago 2019, 206). Thus, to avoid homogenizing identities or abstractions which eradicate the importance of spaces and connecting geographies, transversal solidarity shifts the scope from achieving unity and universality to respect differences and advance the formation of commonalities; a cardinal principle in contending exclusionary politics, accounting for the emerging socio-spatial bonds developed by a plurality of activists in civil society, including migrants.

The third dichotomy we wish to overcome through implementing the notion of transversal solidarity is the one between social and institutional realms. Posing such a dichotomy requires a clarification. Also, institutions are constituted by the social, however, we make a distinction between the formalized and regularized realm set up by institutions established on the basis of political norms and guidelines and what we understand as the social realm. The latter here involves the possibility of an expansion and embedding of informal practices and solutions that can have a more inclusive nature than the pre-existing institutions. The social in this sense denotes the possibility for democratic transformation. The discussion on the institutional derives from the need for organizations, which guarantee stability and continuity to ongoing social struggles. The risk is quite clear: Pre-existing institutions can dismantle the potential of those social struggles and eliminate their emancipatory potential. The tension is accordingly derived from this dual need for change and continuity. We argue that transversalism is helpful in promoting an alternative understanding of 'institutions', when civil society generates its own institutions, on one hand, and, on the other hand, in how existing institutions can be opened to changes or influences by civil society. Despite their history and constraints, existing institutions (and the importance of not reducing institutions to only state institutions) may show openness and receptiveness in response to crises and particular conjunctures, while everyday solidarity practices may, in turn, shape new institutions from below. Both ways may inhabit a transversal dimension in which the social and the institutional are intertwined since institutions "are produced to constitute processes of recognition and collective acceptance, but also processes of creating social meaning in which those institutions make sense and can be accepted as having done so" (Agustín 2015, 9–10). Transversal solidarities, besides connecting difference identities and scales, connect institutions and social imaginaries (see Figure 3.1). Thus, social struggles gain organizational continuity and possibly impact on existing institutions; and the latter may be activated in new ways in confronting social and spatial struggles.

In our previous work, the book *Solidarity and the 'the Refugee Crisis' in Europe* (Agustín and Jørgensen 2019), we have argued that solidarity, in the conjuncture of the economic crisis and the long summer of migration, can contribute to developing the political opportunities available into alternatives. Based on Massey's idea of articulating conjunctures in distinctive and productive ways, Featherstone and Karaliotas (2018) highlight the importance of acknowledging the logics of the financial crisis of 2008 as well as its impact on different groups

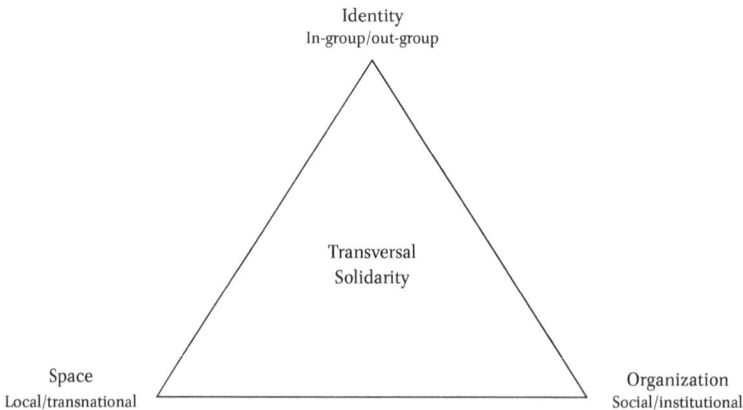

FIGURE 3.1   Conceptualizing transversal solidarity

to "envision articulations of solidarities/alternatives across differences in the context of the European crisis" (Featherstone and Karaliotas 2018, 294). The challenges posed are enormous: From the return of nationalism and xenophobia to the production and fragmentation of a multifarious precariat (Jørgensen 2016). However, the articulation of alternatives is already present in many of the responses to the crisis of CSOs movements, byself-organization, the shaping of new and the potential renewal of existing institutions. This solidarity is *inventive* in creating imaginaries, practices and institutions.

This is not withstanding pessimistic interpretations of the dynamics and outcome of crises. For example, Harvey argues that "crises are essential to the reproduction of capitalism. It is in the course of crises that the instabilities of capitalism are confronted, reshaped and re-engineered to create a new version of what capitalism is about" (Harvey 2014, ix). The so-called 'refugee crisis' is in truth entangled with the political economy of neoliberal globalization. Thus the 'refugee crisis' is not just about human flows, humanitarian concerns and securitization but part of a global economy where the migrant precariat is very functional in producing cheap exploitable labor. However, as we have seen in terms of responses to the financial crisis (to put it in short), we also see how a crisis can actually spur the development of new relations and solutions. Thus, by acknowledging that solidarities are 'inventive', that they produce new configurations of political relations, political subjectivities and spaces, we focus on the potentially transformative imaginations and practices they may produce.

Hence, solidarity is not a given; a position that opens up the possibility for reading the diversity of struggles and for analyzing the formation of alliances in civil society as constitutive, productive and basically political (Agustín and Jørgensen 2016). Solidarity is, thus conceived, contentious and as such a counter-hegemonic social and political mode of action which can unify diverse actors to come together to challenge existing institutions and governmental authorities "in order to promote and enact alternative imaginaries" (following Leitner, et al. 2008, 157). The potential and capacity to not only envision but to truly *enact* alternative imaginaries is another important aspect of solidarity and one, which is decisive for analyzing how solidarity actually responds to the European asylum and migration political geography.

All in all, transversal solidarity, understood as laid out above, will expand the sense of community (not restricting it to pre-existing 'chosen' ones), move beyond borders (without reproducing the logics of national borders), be produced from below (from understandings mostly at odds with that of mainstream politics or discursive abstractions by mainstream media). It is an understanding of solidarity straddling social and institutional arenas (without rejecting the impetus to transform institutions from within as well as from the 'outside').

2   Typology of Transversal Solidarities

In our earlier work (Agustín and Jørgensen 2019), we introduced a typology of solidarity of autonomous solidarity, civic solidarity and institutional solidarity, which reflects different ways of practicing, organizing and articulating solidarity (see Figure 3.2). Through this typology we showed how the 'crisis of solidarity' was rather a crisis of states or, in other terms, of institutionalized solidarity, i.e., the incapability of existing institutions to develop or support forms of solidarity, as demonstrated by the *New Pact on Asylum and Migration*. We do not see the categories in this typology as fixed or completely coherent. They are fluent and can be open to changes and even contradictions. In any case, they must not be seen as idealized forms of solidarity but rather as rooted in practices and the conjuncture provoked by the economic and 'refugee' crises. Taking a spatial approach, we consider the spaces of solidarity and the resulting ways of organizing, the (re)shaping of communities, relating to the state (and other institutions), and the kind of alternatives they produce. As argued above, solidarities are spatially produced. Thus, Arampatzi (2017, 2156) speaks of 'urban solidarity spaces' in terms of "spatial practices of solidarity and struggle that unfold at the territorial, social and economy levels, and aims to further understandings of how people and communities contest crises". Consequently, space represents one dimension of transversal solidarity. In line with this, Featherstone uses, critically, the term 'nationed geographies of crisis' to "suggest ways in which the nation is reasserted as the primary locus through which grievances are articulated and envisioned" (Featherstone 2015, 21). It is an articulation apt to generate exclusionary articulations of the nation; e.g. neoconservative alliances as supposed alternatives to neoliberalism. Seen from this perspective, trans-local solidarity networks, connecting local with regional or global geographies, involve encounters transcending national borders (Agustín 2017). They are essential in redrawing progressive cartographies, relating "to diverse internationalist trajectories and connections" (Featherstone and Karaliotas 2018, 299).

The follow-up question is to ask how these different manifestations of transversal solidarity can, in a variety of ways, contribute to enable and connect geographies of solidarity within (and beyond) Europe. Departing from there we develop, in the following our typology to investigate and analyze various types of transversal solidarity. First, we discuss transversal solidarity

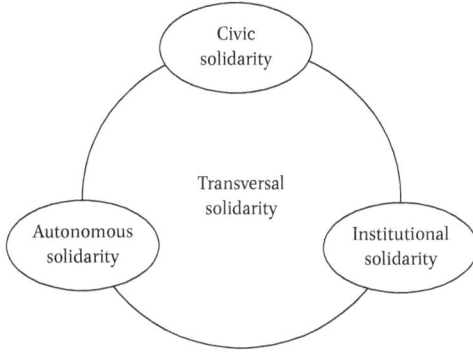

FIGURE 3.2   Typology of transversal forms of solidarity

as manifested through practices of autonomous solidarity exemplified by the case of City Plaza Refugee Accommodation Center in Athens and the Reclaim the Power organization in the UK. Second, we discuss transversal solidarity as manifested through practices of civic solidarity by looking at *Venligboerne*, the welcome refugees movement in Denmark. Third, we focus on 'institutional solidarity' exemplified by transversal practices of municipal solidarity.

2.1   *Autonomous Solidarity*

Autonomous solidarity implies relations and practices that are produced in self-organized (mainly urban) spaces. Based on our earlier work we investigate how autonomous solidarity can represent a particular way of organizing transversal solidarity. It is about solidarity based on horizontal participation such as direct democracy and assemblies, emphasizing equality if participation and influence among their members. Collaboration with state institutions and their so-called 'securitized humanism' (Mudu and Chattopadhyay 2017) is rejected, as well as the idea of supporting 'anyone in need' professed by many NGOs and other civil society actors (Dicker 2017). The principle of equality, which underlies this horizontal and participatory approach to solidarity, aims at undoing dichotomous categorizations and to define their members by 'doing', like encapsulated in the idea of 'activist citizens' (Isin 2009). The focus on self-organization moves beyond specific moments of mobilization in developing other forms of institutions, understood as the infrastructures through which autonomous solidarity materializes. Therefore, the principle of rejecting institutions, here refers to established institutions, since there is indeed a need for alternative institutions or 'social institutions'. The autonomous solidarity responds to what Graeber (2004) calls a 'theory of exodus', perceived as the most effective way of opposing capitalism and the liberal state (see further Agustín and Jørgensen 2019). It implicates that instead of taking on or challenging power, new forms of communities are created as a strategy to 'slip away from' power. Although autonomous solidarity is produced locally in the urban spaces, it can also 'scale up' (Kurasawa 2014) by connecting different anti-governmental modes of transnational politics and thus connect different political geographies. In concrete manifestations of autonomous solidarity, we also find the mentioned dimensions of transversalism; i.e. in terms of identity, space and organization.

One example of autonomous solidarity is the City Plaza Refugee Accommodation Center in Athens. The City Plaza Hotel was a self-organized housing project for homeless refugees in the center of Athens, which accommodated 400 people. This accommodation center evolved as a concrete practical response to the conditions of asylum seekers in Greece and to a perceive lack of responsibility by both the Greek state and the international community in a situation of escalating emergency in April 2016. Describing itself as 'the best hotel in Europe', the space was occupied as a direct response to the EU-Turkey deal at that time, with the goal of providing safe accommodation to transiting migrants trapped in Greece (European Council 2016). City Plaza became known for fostering an egalitarian environment of mutuality between migrants and Greek and international volunteers. At the same time, the project articulated a multi-scalar critique – against the European border regime, against the fascist encroachments on the Athenian center, and against the transformation of Syriza into both a manager of austerity and an organizer of a problematic NGOized and securitized response to refugees stranded in Greece (Refugee Accommodation and Solidarity Space City Plaza 2016; 2019).

The occupation of the hotel was not seen by the activists as the only solution to the 'refugee crisis' but as exemplary case demonstrating how solidarity work can provide alternatives; a 'micro-utopia' showing how the crisis could be dealt with. It offered a lived example that could be replicated elsewhere in Europe. The City Plaza Hotel case is thus an example of how a local initiative, involving a single urban site, can articulate the crisis of failed management, while presenting a new imaginary and a practical alternative. City Plaza can thus be read as example of one type of organizing transversal solidarity. In terms of identity the people who constituted the residents of City Plaza transgress the dichotomy of in-group and out-group. City Plaza used the notion of 'co-habitants' emphasizing even more than 'inhabitant' the collective solidarity creating its principled position. Solidarity is thus generative of the shared identity 'co-habitant' (Agustín and Jørgensen 2019). Stressing the commonalities constituting City Plaza is also what made it so strong.

City Plaza sees itself as part of a multitude of different solidarity practices and struggles that emerged since last year, which constitute a specific demand to the Greek state, against the detention of refugees in
despicable detention centers as well as against their isolation in monstrous camps; for the decent housing of refugees in the cities, ensuring
their access to health care, education and all social services. On the other
side City Plaza sees itself as part of the European and international solidarity movement which challenges the militarization of borders and
the externalization of asylum policies and which claims the freedom of
movement and the right to stay.

> Refugee Accommodation and Solidarity Space City Plaza 2016

The statement above by the Refugee Accommodation and Solidarity Space of
City Plaza is, as well, an illustration of transversal solidarity's spatial dimension. Although City Plaza was a very locally anchored and contextualized experience it transgresses the separation of the local and the international. It is
both at the same time. The struggles that took place within a particular neighborhood of Athens, is also a struggle opposing the exclusionary European asylum system.

Finally, City Plaza provided an example on how social structures can be built
from below. The center was shaped according to principles of self-organization
and autonomy, depending entirely on the voluntary political support and practical solidarity from within Greece and abroad (Refugee Accommodation and
Solidarity Space City Plaza 2016). City Plaza organized, without implicating
any irony, an online support campaign describing the hotel in terms of: "No
pool, no minibar, no room service, and nonetheless: The Best Hotel in Europe".
In a two year period, 385,000 warm meals were served by the kitchen group,
35,000 hours spent on security posts at the entrance and balconies of the hotel,
there were 13,560 hours of shifts at the reception and 18 tons of heating oil
was used in the boilers and radiators (Refugee Accommodation and Solidarity
Space City Plaza 2017), all depending on solidarity support, from the ground
up, and did not received any funding from NGOs, the state or the EU.

City Plaza was a reaction to the dramatic border spectacle of 2016 and the
stalemate of the EU asylum regime, including individual member states' reluctance to receive and accommodate, with the upshot of inhospitable detention
centers the conditions of which seemed to be devised to deter refugees from
crossing the borders. It is history that will most likely come to be replicated,
given the actual character of the EU's *New Pact on Asylum and Migration* and
the dubious "solidarity à-la-carte dish" it offers. City Plaza did not provide *the*
solution to the exclusionary policies of the EU border regime, as such, but it is

an example on how transversal solidarity can be articulated and point at alternatives. As stated by the organizing group of City Plaza:

> We do not, of course, believe that the problem can only be solved through squatting, as the provision of shelter is a fundamental obligation of the state and the local authorities; we do, however, believe that squats can act not only as a means for claiming rights but also as a factual exercising of rights precisely by those who are deprived of rights: the illegalized and excluded economic and political refugees.
>
> Refugee Accommodation and Solidarity Space City Plaza 2016

Another text launched by City Plaza and the solidarity network Welcome to Europe repeated this argument, claiming: "The squat cannot be the solution for all of this but a vivid example of how things can be better if each of us tries. It will not solve the European shame, but it can be an outcry of solidarity". It goes on arguing that it is not a solution for the ones remaining outside the walls of 'Fortress Europe', the ones stuck on the islands, in the so-called hot spots – but even for them "City Plaza is a symbol that it can be possible: Another, a welcoming Europe" (Welcome to Europe 2016). When those accommodated in City Plaza and other self-organized spaces risked being evicted in 2019, as a consequence of a new government coming into power, the organizing group decided to close down the space; a decision taken facing an intensified crackdown on self-organized spaces by the new conservative government (Nashed 2019), as well as the politically unacceptable alternative of institutionalization through NGOization, City Plaza decided not to accept any new guests (see Fischer & Jørgensen 2021).

Our second example is Reclaim the Power, a UK based direct action network fighting for social, environmental and economic justice. It aims at building "a broad based movement, working in solidarity with frontline communities to effectively confront environmentally destructive industries and the social and economic forces driving climate change" (Reclaim the Power 2019). In June 2019 it organized an action camp called 'Power Beyond Borders: against new gas and the hostile environment'. The action camp expands the struggle against the destruction of the environment with pro-migrant and anti-racist struggles. The camp took, symbolically, place in the shadow of Rye House power station in Hoddesdon, UK, where participants wanted to live as a community, to learn from each other and take action. The 500 participants later rallied under the slogan "No borders, no nations, no gas power stations!". The analysis of Reclaim the Power reads it is no coincidence that a climate action network is embarking on solidarity work with migrants and racialized groups. Here the focus is on commonalities and to establish an inclusive identity. Doing so, entails not to eradicate group identities but to create a space for transversal solidarity politics. Dealing with the climate crisis and its consequences implies a fair treatment of people who cross borders. There is no climate justice without justice for migrants, it is argued. Migrant collectives as All African Women's Group, Anti-Raids Network, End Deportations, Resist + Renew, North East London Migrant Action and more were part of the camp. The group claims that. "Bringing together activists to learn and skill up on climate and migrant justice was every bit as important as the actions that we took. With this camp, we have begun to take steps so that we can take effective action, in solidarity with activists on the sharpest end of the UK's racist treatment of migrants" (ibid.). This statement again reflects a transversal politics, which combines different geographies.

2.2   *Civic Solidarity*

Civic solidarity indicates ways of organizing produced as civil society initiatives to include refugees. It counts a vast number of manifestations and actors, such as NGOs, local communities and individuals. It is practiced by non-state civil society actors, but the degree of contention varies depending on the claims and strategies of each organization. Connected to our conceptualization of transversal solidarity, it relates first to identity and transgressing the construction of in-group and out-groups by emphasizing commonalities. Civic solidarity is "the sphere of fellow feeling, the we-ness that makes society into society" (Alexander 2006, 53). It is wider than the state as vehicle of protection of citizens (Scholz 2008, 27), and at the same time receptive to the idea that the vulnerabilities, which prevent people from participating in society on equal terms, must be eliminated. Thus, practices of civic solidarity combine the expansion of rights with the shaping of we-ness or sustaining "collaborative relations within and between different social groups, inasmuch as it [civic solidarity] represents individuals' *interests*" (Sammut 2011, 416).

   In terms of space, the 'long summer of migration' saw forms of civic solidarity multiply, in a situation when states were not capable of managing the crisis and offer refugees and asylum seekers means to become part of the national communities. Together with attempts to expand rights, the we-ness also is reshaped and expanded. In opposition to movements for fragmentation, i.e. exclusion of refugees, as those that are aimed exclusively towards nationals, civic solidarity also contributes to forging new alliances and collective identities in different kinds of spaces, from community kitchens to those who provide legal assistance. This opposition to state practices does not imply, as mentioned before, that civic solidarity is 'against the state' since there are different kinds of positions on it, from critical to trying to gain influence in policy-making. Different scales are combined from local communities to national (to have more visibility and influence) and transnational (to achieve global awareness and exchange practices). Likewise, this type of organizing points to attempts to combine the social and institutional – or to install the social in a reconfiguration of institutions. We will refer to the Danish welcome refugees movement *Venligboerne* as a case in point.

At the end of 2017, more than 100,000 people were active in refugee solidarity groups in Denmark (Toubøl 2019, 1203). Many if not most of these people joined local groups of the movement *Venligboerne* (literally 'friendly neighbors'). The *Venligbo* movement started up already in April 2013, with a local initiative to improve the wellbeing of residents in the small town of Hjørring in northern Jutland. During the 'refugee crisis', the movement grew as it switched its focus to welcoming the refugees arriving in Denmark. Initially the members of the loosely organized welcome refugees movement engaged in exactly welcoming arriving refugees. This kind of action illustrate, in various ways, forms of transversal solidarity. A statement of a central organizer of the solidarity network working from the central train station in Copenhagen published in a letter to *The Washington Post*, is indicative (see also, Agustín and Jørgensen 2019): "It was a political cause where we felt we for once could contribute. A cause where *we* could make a difference. We will never do something which goes against our conscience – even if the state demands it" (Samir in Róin 2016; our translation and our italics). The *we* here is important as it illustrates the emerging tranversal solidarity across ethnic and social divisions. Here Samir is also speaking as a post-immigrant coming from the Nørrebro area of Copenhagen, habitually stigmatized in terms of being an immigrant 'ghetto' (Agustín and Jørgensen 2019). At one and the same time a sense of we-ness is established (identity), which is anchored in a local community contesting what was considered inadequate actions by the Danish authorities (space), and new civil alliances are forged (organization). After the Danish authorities introduced legal restrictions for entering Denmark and de facto closed the border, the *Venligbo* movement started developing into a humanitarian service provider. The movement has a number of characteristics, which still exist. This include to provide various forms of practical assistance, such as legal aid, medical support, language training, job-seeking assistance, transportation, and to make available everyday donations. It creates broad alliances that include both experienced activist and people new to solidarity work. It makes visible the problems of the asylum-process and integration into Danish society, insisting on a humanitarian approach, different from the exclusivist approach taken by the state (Agustín and Jørgensen 2019).

Overall, the movement advocates for inclusive democracy, shaped through and by actors in civil society. The movement also highlights the commonalities between refugees and Danes, thus subverting a hegemonic discourse on refugees as dangerous, uncooperative, subversive or worse. It challenges the commonsense idea that 'we cannot learn something from them' (Jørgensen and Olsen 2020). From the beginning, the movement regarded itself as 'non-political', not only as an attempt to separate the movement from any party-political affiliation, but also to signify that the movement would not criticize government policies but rather provide practical solutions to problems. This position caused an internal conflict, as a growing number of local groups – especially in Copenhagen – wanted to take and overtly political stance *vis a vis* the state with less of a focus on humanitarianism. The 'political' fraction did not want to become service providers but rather to spur political change through political actions. This position leans towards a more autonomous form of solidarity. However, we also see a turn towards deepening institutional solidarity from below. Perhaps the opening of a political or politicized space has also spurred the development of a new phase of transnational engagement. It is an engagement that does not ignore the role and importance of the local but which connects different geographies in an attempt to influence and change the European border regime. Like in other European countries, the conditions in Greek hotspots, such as the Moria camp, has long been a focus for the Danish solidarity movement. As stated in the introduction, the lock-down caused by the COVID-19 pandemic in combination with the devastating fires in the Moria camp worsened conditions of refugees, trapped there, even more. The situation caused individual members of the solidarity movement of *Venligboerne* to initiate various initiatives in the Danish context, such as raising money for necessities, but also long-term projects like establishing educational and cultural facilities for migrants in Greece. Spurred by initiatives in other European cities that jointly offered to give unaccompanied minors from the camps asylum – thus circumventing the Dublin regulations – the *Venligbo* members started forging alliances with local city council members. The Danish government has repeatedly stated its opposition to receiving refugees from these camps. However, because of ongoing solidarity work by *Venligboerne* on the local level, at least seven Danish city councils have now joined the cities of Amersfoort, Amsterdam, Barcelona, Ghent, Groningen, Leipzig, Nuremberg, Tilburg and Utrecht, in a claim for being allowed to bring in children from Moria (Wandrup 2020). Although perhaps more a political posturing than of an action of substance by these cities – as they will require the formal approval of the Minister of Immigration and Integration to actually receive refugees – their hope is that bringing the issue to the European scale

will create pressure on the national scale, and by this facilitate practical solidarity on the local scale. In this way, different geographies are connected in a
transversal struggle. Here practices of civic solidarity intersect with practices
of institutional solidarity.

2.3   *Institutional Solidarity*

Institutional solidarity represents the formalization of different degrees of solidarity, which connects the civil society arena with institutional policy-arenas.
Institutional solidarity is usually related to how "members contribute both
because they are obliged to do so according to institutional arrangement and
because they expect to get something back if they are in a situation of need"
(Fenger and van Paridon 2012, 51). This conception of institutional solidarity as
rights and obligations or as systems based on anonymous or contractual forms
of solidarity (Arts, et al. 2001, 476) tends to refer specifically to the welfare state
as a form of mechanical solidarity. However, we prefer to use the term 'institutionalized solidarity' and maintain an open definition of 'institutional' in
which informal social relations and institutional norms can converge (Agustín
and Jørgensen 2019).

Conceiving, as argued above, institutional solidarity a produced by formalization of solidarity relations, implicates that there will be a constant tension
between potential political actions of solidarity and their regularization by
institutions. The key for defining institutional solidarity - in contrast with
institutionalized solidarity - is the capacity of enabling (infra)structures to
solidify solidarity and maintain, reproduce and foster connections civil society, including migrant and refugee organizations. This emphasizes an understanding of transversality rejecting the incompatibility of the social and the
institutional. It appears logical to see the local or the city as pivotal for the
shaping of institutional solidarity; that is, a scale where the relations (and
also the tensions) between institutions and civil society are tighter and less
distanced. The relation to the nation state (and its form of institutionalized
solidarity) is often conflictual since the aims and realities dealt with are different. At the same time instances of conflict between the local and the national
scales appears to explain, why and how the international scale is promoted in
order to retrieve transnational alternatives going beyond the opposition and
restrictions of states. The most prominent cases of institutional solidarity are
'sanctuary cities', mainly in the US and Canada but also in the UK, and the
re-municipalization or 'new municipalism' in Europe. To illustrate this type
of organizing practices we use the case on how municipalities within Europe
has challenged the European border and asylum regime and on how new

municipalism is promoting politics of solidarity at the local urban and the transnational scale.

The number of migrants dying in attempts to cross the Mediterranean Sea reached a peak in 2015, when 5,143 people were registered as drowned (Statista 2020). Numbers show a decline since 2015 but still counts 1,885 people dying in the attempt to reach Europe in 2019. European activists have sought to help migrants with safe crossing. Organizations like Sea-Watch, Jugend Rettet, SOS Mediterranée, Mission Lifeline, and others began chartering boats and small planes in an effort to rescue shipwrecked migrants and activist collectives as Alarm-Phone seeks to assist migrants with info and routes while at sea. The EU's increasing militarization of its maritime missions and the criminalization campaigns of European governments (especially receiving countries in Southern Europe) has intensified the activism and civic responses. At the same time – or very likely as a direct consequence of this development – we see some cities developing accommodating policies and offering protection in solidarity with the refugees. Palermo is one such example. "We cannot say today that Palermo respects the rights of migrants. Because we have no migrants in Palermo. If you ask how many migrants are in Palermo, then I do not answer 100,000 or 120,000, but none. If you are in Palermo, you are a Palermitan", exclaimed the Mayor of Palermo, Leoluca Orlando (quoted by Bauder 2019) in the aftermath of the European 'refugee crisis'. When Italy's interior minister, Matteo Salvini, got the parliament's support of his anti-immigrant decree in 2018 intended to make Italy more unwelcoming to migrants, Orlando refused to apply the decree in a stand that has become a prominent example of a widening grassroots and urban resistance to the hard line on immigration (Horowitz 2019).

Although cities are not progressive per default, challenges faced by cities in accommodating newcomers (migrants and refugees) require them to find ways to secure access to legal residency, social protection, cultural belonging and to accept the presence of illegalized migrants. This is a difficult task, as national governments hold the right to issue visas, permits, residence etc. – yet the new municipalist surge demonstrates that the municipality is becoming a strategically crucial site for the organization of transformative social change (Roth and Rusell 2018). This kind of solidarity is produced both spatially and organizationally. Indeed, a new municipalism emerged in the case of Spain from the attempt to strengthen hybrid (including political parties, social movements and activists) and local organizations responses to the crisis of legitimacy of traditional state-parties. Promoting progressive localism, the new municipalism has faced two challenges: the politicization of the local level, affecting the redefinition of community and the relationship between the public and the

private, and the enablement of new social imaginations capable of connecting
alternative geographies (Agustín 2020). The city emerges as the pivotal space
of transversal solidarities in addressing this dual challenge. On one hand, communities of solidarity are based on everyday socio-spatial practices and avoid
consciously to reproduce the divide between nationals and outsiders, while
idea of the 'commons' emerge strongly as a project to re-municipalize public
services. On the other hand, municipal initiatives are pursued in order to prove
that real change emerges from cities (and not only from the nation-state) and
that a new social imagination is resulting from connecting the cities' democratic practices at different scales.

Taking the case of Barcelona, which is emblematic in this context, two trajectories in developing institutional solidarity are important: the Barcelona's
Refuge City Plan and the Fearless Cities initiative. The former was launched
by the City Council in 2015 to give institutional form to already existing solidarity relations as response to the so-called 'refugee crisis' and to facilitate the
arrival and accommodation of refugees. The city was presented as the place to
deal with global issues and the City Council aimed to expand the institutional
scope of action, including civil society groups and activities, and to enhance
spaces of convergence between the local and the transnational. The goal of
the Plan was to create "a citizen space to channel urban solidarity and to set up
coordinated ways of participating in its application" (Barcelona Ciutat Refugi
n.d.). The mere idea of a city of refuge generates the imaginary of the city as
space of solidarity, in strong contrast to the position of the European Union
and its Member States. Although the original idea was to be prepared for a
humanitarian situation of emergence, the Plan was transforming itself due
to the existing realities faced by migrants and refugees as well as the changes
in the place of origin of the refugees. At the transnational scale, the launch
of Fearless Cities in June in 2017 represented an ambitious project to reclaim
the city as space of global politics of solidarity. The initiative of Fearless Cities
sustains that localism is necessary to promote transformative politics of scale
(Russell 2019). Ada Colau, major of Barcelona, framed new municipalism as
the main opposition to neoliberalism: "municipalism is a rising force that
seeks to transform fear into hope from the bottom up, and build that hope
together" (Colau 2018, 194). The idea of upscaling municipalism and moving
towards a global municipalism entails a clear transversal component since it
seeks to overcome dichotomist divisions between winners and losers, us versus them, and propose the creation of an international network to promote
human rights, environmental justice and feminism. One of the specific projects, The Fearless Cities map, elaborated by Barcelona en Comú in collaboration with other municipalities, represents visually the international scope

of municipalism as an alternative way of acting locally (through cooperation between civil society and institutions) and translocally (through the connection between municipalist practices).

At the Fearless Cities gathering, Debbie Bookchin stated, "municipalism is not about implementing progressive policies, but about returning power to ordinary people" (Roth 2019). This openness creates the space for transversal solidarity, but it does not imply that there are no tensions derived from undoing dichotomies (the balance between institutions and civil society participation or the articulation of scales). Transversalism is not a goal but a dialogic way of creating relations together. In this regard, new municipalism is exposed to contradictions, which reflect a complexity of relations from the state to local civil society.

3   Conclusion

Our intention with this article has been to develop a conceptualization of transversal solidarity, which we initiated in our previous work to grasp the solidarity practices and dynamics, particularly after the humanitarian crisis of 2015 in Europe. The idea of conceptualizing solidarity as transversal aims to overcome some of the problems related to solidarity and to elaborate a complex definition based on three dimensions (identity, space and organization). Importantly, this acknowledges that not all forms of solidarity are the same and it implies different actors, goals and practices.

Therefore, we work on a typology of forms of solidarity, autonomous, civic and institutional, which are transversal, although in different ways. Some examples were discussed relating to each category in order to illustrate how transversal solidarity works within each type, by focusing on their achievements as well as innate tensions and potential shortcomings. In Table 3.1 we present this comprehensive conceptualization of transversal solidarity, attending to variable types and dimensions.

As reflected in table 3.1, the different types of transversal solidarity differ in terms of identity, space and organization. This stands out, for instance, in the naming of their identity (activist citizens, cosmopolitan activism, grassroots institutions) as well as in the type of transversal identity (or common positioning) resulting from encounters and acting together (co-habitants, we-ness, institutions as rights and obligations). None of these identities preexisted solidarity relations and they are the consequence of finding a common ground where the plurality of identities coexists with the claim for equality. Regarding space, it remains clear that transversal solidarity is rooted locally and promotes

TABLE 3.1   Types and dimensions of transversal solidarity

Types	Dimensions		
	Identity	Space	Organization
Autonomous solidarity	Activist citizens, co-habitants	Occupied/ appropriated urban spaces, multi-scalar critique	Social institutions, direct democracy
Civic solidarity	Cosmopolitan activism, we-ness	Local communities, contesting the nation state	Self-organization, inclusive democracy, shaping civil alliances, policy oriented
Institutional solidarity	Grassroots institutions, institutions as rights and obligations	Institutional(izing) urban spaces, national and transnational networks	Municipal openness to civil society's cooperation, participatory democracy

a form of progressive localism. However, local relations and practices are different as are their way to connect other geographies and to promote politics of scale. The question of organization is controversial since it is connected with conventional modes of understanding democracy. While principles of autonomous solidarity rely on direct democracy and the formation of social institutions in confrontation with existing local and national institutions, civic solidarity is oriented towards developing civic practices and influencing policies through an inclusionary approach to democracy. Institutional solidarity is different, since it is not implying the way in which civil society influences institutions but rather how institutions can cooperate and include civil society in policymaking. Here, democracy is conceived mainly as being participatory and not limited to institutional or political actors.

   In conclusion, our hope is that this model can be useful for exploring recent and future experiences of solidarity. Complex conceptualizations of solidarity are needed to account for the manifestations coming from below to challenge a migration and asylum system, which so far has proved to be unjust and exclusionary. Transversal solidarities will continue to emerge in opposition to this.

References

Agustín, Ó.G. (2015). *Sociology of Discourse. From Institutions to Social Change.* Amsterdam: John Benjamins.

Agustín, Ó.G. (2017). "Dialogic Cosmopolitanism and the New Wave of Movements: From Local Rupture to Global Openness". *Globalizations*, 14(5): 700–713.

Agustín, Ó.G. (2020). "New municipalism as space for solidarity". *Soundings*, 74: 54–67.

Agustín, Ó.G., and M.B. Jørgensen (2019). *Solidarity and the 'refugee' crisis in Europe.* Cham: Palgrave.

Agustín, Ó.G., and M.B. Jørgensen (2016). *Solidarity without borders: Gramscian perspectives on migration and civil society alliances.* London: Pluto Press.

Alexander, J.A. (2006). *The Civil Sphere.* Oxford: Oxford University Press.

Arampatzi, A. (2017). "The spatiality of counter-austerity politics in Athens, Greece: Emergent 'urban solidarity spaces'". *Urban Studies*, 54(9): 2155–2171.

Arts, W., R. Muffles, and R. Ter Meulen (2001). "Epilogue: The Future of Solidaristic Health and Social Care in Europe". In Arts, W., Muffles, R., and Ter Meulen, R. (eds.) *Solidarity in Health and Social Care in Europe.* Dordrecht: Kluwer Academic Publishers: 463–477.

Barcelona Ciutat Refugi (n.d.). "Espacio ciudadano". *Ciutat Refugi.* Available at: https://ciutatrefugi.barcelona/es/espacio-ciudadano.

Bauder, H. (2019). "If you are in Palermo, you are a Palermitan" An interview with Mayor Leoluca Orlando. RCIS *Research Brief* No. 2019/1, April 2019.

Bird, G. (2020). "Fire destroys Moria refugee camp: another tragic wake-up call for the EU's asylum policy". *The Conversation*, September 10, 2020. Available at: https://theconversation.com/fire-destroys-moria-refugee-camp-another-tragic-wake-up-call-for-the-eus-asylum-policy-145899.

Chadwick, L., and L.M. Monella (2020). "What is the EU's new migration pact and how has it been received?". *Euronews*, October 8, 2020. Available at: https://www.euronews.com/2020/09/24/what-is-the-e-u-s-new-migration-pact-and-how-has-it-been-received.

Colau, A. (2018). "Convertir el miedo en esperanza". *Ciudades sin miedo. Guía del movimiento municipalista global.* Barcelona: Icaria.

Dicker, S. (2017). "Solidarity in the city: Platforms for refugee self-support in Thessaloniki". In Fiori, J., and Rigon, A. (eds.) *Making Lives: Refugee Self-Reliance and Humanitarian Action in Cities*. London: Humanitarian Affairs Team, Save the Children: 73–103.

European Council (2016). EU-Turkey statement, 18 March 2016. Available at: https://www.consilium.europa.eu/en/press/press-releases/2016/03/18/eu-turkey-statement/.

Featherstone, D. (2013). "Black internationalism, subaltern cosmopolitanism, and the spatial politics of antifascism". *Journal of the Association of American Geographers*, 103(6): 1406–1420.

Featherstone, D. (2015). "Thinking the crisis politically: lineages of resistance to neo-liberalism and the politics of the present conjuncture". *Space and Polity*, 19(1): 12–30.

Featherstone, D., and L. Karaliotas (2018). "Challenging the spatial politics of the European crisis: nationed narratives and trans-local solidarities in the post-crisis conjucture". *Cultural Studies*, 32(2): 286–307.

Fenger, M., & Paridon, K. v. (2012). "Towards a globalisation of solidarity". In *Reinventing Social Solidarity Across Europe*, edited by Marion Ellison. Bristol: The Policy Press: 49–70.

Fischer, L., and M.B. Jørgensen (2021). "'We are here to stay' vs. 'Europe's best hotel': Hamburg and Athens as geographies of solidarity". *Antipode*.

Gago, V. (2019). *La potencia feminista o el deseo de cambiarlo todo*. Madrid: Traficantes de Sueños.

Graeber, D. (2004). *Fragments of an anarchist anthropology*. Chicago, IL: Prickly Paradigm Press.

Harvey, D. (2014). *Seventeen Contradictions and the End of Capitalism*. London: Profile Books.

Heath, R. (2017). "Juncker slaps down Orbán over border funding request". *Politico*, September 9, 2017. Available at: https://www.politico.eu/blogs/playbook-plus/2017/09/juncker-slaps-orban-over-border-funding-request/.

Hitchings-Hales, J. (2020a). "A Fire has Decimated Europe's Largest Refugee Camp. Here's How You Can Help". *Global Citizen*, September 9, 2020. Available at: https://www.globalcitizen.org/en/content/moria-refugee-camp-lesbos-greece-fire-how-to-help/.

Hitchings-Hales, J. (2020b). "Refugees Who Escaped the Moria Fire Now Live in Even More Dire Conditions". *Global Citizen*, September 9, 2020. Available at: https://www.globalcitizen.org/en/content/moria-new-refugee-camp-fire-lesvos-greece/.

Horowitz, J. (2019). "Palermo Is Again a Migrant City, Shaped Now by Bangladeshis and Nigerians". *New York Times*, May 22, 2019. Available at: https://www.nytimes.com/2019/05/22/world/europe/italy-palermo-immigrants-salvino.html.

Isin, E.F. (2009). "Citizenship in flux: The figure of the activist citizen". *Subjectivity*, 29(1): 367–388.

JRS (2020). "New pact on asylum and migration: more (worrying) questions than answers". *JRS*, September 23, 2020. Available at: https://jrseurope.org/en/news/new-pact-on-asylum-and-migration-more-worrying-questions-than-answers/.

Jørgensen, M.B. (2016). "Precariat–what it is and isn't–towards an understanding of what it does". *Critical Sociology*, 42(7–8): 959–974.

Jørgensen, M.B. (2019). "A goat that is already dead is no longer afraid of knives": Refugee Mobilizations and Politics of (Necessary) Interference in Hamburg". *Ethnologia Europaea*, 49(1): 41–57.

Jørgensen, M.B., and D.R. Olsen (2020). "Civil society in times of crisis". In Hellström, A., Jørgensen, M.B., and Norocel, C.O. (eds.) *Nostalgia and Hope: Intersections between Politics of Culture, Welfare, and Migration*. Cham: IMISCOE Series Springer: 153–167.

Kollek, E. (2020). "Uncertain solidarity: Why Europe's new migration pact could fall apart". *ECFR*, September 29, 2019. Available at: https://ecfr.eu/article/commentary_uncertain_solidarity_why_europes_new_migration_pact_could_fall_a/.

Kurasawa, F. (2014). "An Alternative Transnational Public Sphere? On Anarchist Cosmopolitanism in Post-Westphalian Times". In Nash, K. (ed.) *Transnationalizing the Public Sphere*. Cambridge (UK): Polity: 79–97.

Leitner, H., E. Sheppard, and K.M. Sziarto (2008). "The spatialities of contentious politics". *Transactions of the Institute of British Geographers*, 33(2): 157–172.

Mudu, P., and S. Chattopadhyay (2017). "Migration, squatting and radical autonomy: conclusions". In Mudu, P., and Chattopadhyay, S. (eds.) *Migration, Squatting and Radical Autonomy*. London: Routledge: 285–287.

Nashed, M. (2019). "Greece's new war on refugees: clearing the squatters in Athens". *The Daily Dose*, 20 October 2019. Available at: https://www.ozy.com/around-the-world/greeces-latest-war-on-refugees-clearing-squats-in-an-athens-anarchist-hub/97219/.

Reclaim the Power (2019). "Power Beyond Borders: against new gas and the hostile environment". July 10, 2019. Available at: https://reclaimthepower.org.uk/actions/power-beyond-borders-2019/power-beyond-borders/.

Refugee Accommodation and Solidarity Space City Plaza (2016). "Support the City Plaza Refugee Accommodation and Solidarity Center in Athens, Greece". June 23, 2016. Available at: http://solidarity2refugees.gr/support-city-plaza-refugee-accommodation-solidarity-center-athens-greece/.

Refugee Accommodation and Solidarity Space City Plaza (2017). "Athens: Today City Plaza is one and half years old". October 21, 2017. Available at: https://en.squat.net/2017/10/21/athens-today-city-plaza-is-one-and-half-years-old/.

Refugee Accommodation and Solidarity Space City Plaza (2019). "39 μήνες City Plaza: Ολοκλήρωση ενός κύκλου, αρχής ενός νέου". Available at: https://best-hotel-in-europe.eu/el/.

Róin, P. (2016). "Da medborgere blev menneskesmuglere". *Information* May 13, 2016: 14, section 3. Available at: https://www.information.dk/mofo/medborgere-menneskes muglere.

Roth, L. (2019). "Which municipalism? Let's be choosy". *Open Democracy*, 2 January, 2019. Available at: https://www.opendemocracy.net/en/can-europe-make-it/which -municipalism-lets-be-choosy/.

Roth, L., and B. Russell (2018). "Translocal solidarity and the new municipalism". *Roar*, Autumn (8): 80–93.

Russell, R. (2019). "Beyond the Local Trap: New Municipalism and the Rise of the Fearless Cities". *Antipode* 1(3): 989–1010.

Sammut, G. (2011). "Civic Solidarity: the negotiation of identity in modern societies". *Papers on Social Representations*, 20: 410–424.

Scholz, S.J. (2008). *Political Solidarity*. Pennsylvania: The Pennsylvania State University Press.

Schwiertz, H., and H. Schwenken (2020). "Introduction: inclusive solidarity and citizenship along migratory routes in Europe and the Americas". *Citizenship Studies*, 24(4): 405–423.

Statista (2020). "Number of recorded deaths of migrants in the Mediterranean Sea from 2014 to 2020". Available at: https://www.statista.com/statistics/1082077/dea ths-of-migrants-in-the-mediterranean-sea/.

Tidey, A. (2020). "Moria camp fire: France and Germany urge EU states to welcome migrants". Euronews, 10 September, 2020. Available at: https://www.euronews .com/2020/09/10/moria-camp-fire-france-and-germany-urge-eu-states-to-welcome -migrants.

Toubøl, J. (2019). "From democratic participation to civic resistance: the loss of institutional trust as an outcome of activism in the refugee solidarity movement". *The British journal of sociology*, 70(4): 1198–1224.

Wandrup, F. (2020). "Politikere i nyt forslag: Helsingør skal have uledsagede børne-flygtninge". *Helsingør Dagblad*, 29 July, 2020. Available at: https://helsingordagb lad.dk/artikel/politikere-i-nyt-forslag-helsing%C3%B8r-skal-have-uledsagede -b%C3%B8rneflygtninge?fbclid=IwAR1SicKMQmcxpzho28OCyxM6yW_oJEqA FnFakuqVRfMnggkJ8KofRK90_Lk.

Welcome to Europe (2016). City Plaza Hotel Athens (Greece). Infomobile information with, about and for refugees in Greece. May 29, 2016. Available at: https://en.squat .net/2016/05/29/greece-city-plaza-hotel-athens/#more-17494.

Yuval-Davis, N. (1999). "What is 'transversal politics'?" *Soundings*, 12: 94–98.

Yuval-Davis, N. (2011). *Power, Intersectionality and the Politics of Belonging*. Institut for Kultur og Globale Studier, Aalborg Universitet. *FREIA's tekstserie* No. 75. Available at: https://doi.org/10.5278/freia.58024502.

CHAPTER 4

Labor Unions and Undocumented Immigrants
Local Perspectives on Transversal Solidarity during DACA and DAPA

Els de Graauw and Shannon Gleeson

In 2012, President Obama created the Deferred Action for Childhood Arrivals (DACA) program following prolonged congressional inaction on comprehensive immigration reform.[1] While achieving a path towards citizenship for at least some of the country's then nearly 12 million undocumented immigrants had been one of Obama's promised reforms, DACA would be his only success and the last major piece of inclusive immigration reform to date. DACA, which has provided temporary deportation relief and work authorization to nearly 800,000 young undocumented immigrants in the United States, was realized only following the tireless advocacy of diverse national and local coalitions that came together in solidarity with undocumented immigrants. In 2014, the Deferred Action for Parents of Americans and Lawful Permanent Residents (DAPA) program succeeded DACA and would have provided relief to an additional 4.5 million undocumented immigrants. DAPA was eventually struck down in court and never implemented.

In recent decades, organized labor has demonstrated several—often contested—forms of solidarity with immigrant rights. As unions now see immigrant rights as integral to the struggle of workers and their organizations, the DACA and DAPA programs offered them important opportunities to build solidarity with undocumented workers. One aspect of this shift has been to center immigrant rights as a core labor issue, a reversal from a long history of antagonistic stances towards immigrants (Fletcher and Gapasin 2008; Hamlin 2008). A second form of union solidarity has focused on coalition-building with non-union organizations, even outside the traditional scope of a labor organizing campaign (de Graauw 2016; Fine, et al. 2018). Third, union platforms increasingly rally for the entirety of working class individuals, many of whom are not union members and increasingly non-white and immigrant (Milkman 2020; Milkman and Ott 2014). This has also meant that unions have been more

---

1 An earlier version of this chapter was previously published as an article in *Critical Sociology* 47(6).

willing to take on new functions such as providing 'know your rights' trainings and legal aid to immigrant union and non-union members alike (Bacon 2018).

Other scholars have examined these new forms of transversal solidarity, especially in efforts to promote national immigrant rights policy campaigns to bring about new congressional laws or executive initiatives (e.g. Gonzales 2013; Nicholls 2013; Zepeda-Millán 2017). We know less, though, about their role in implementing key immigration victories such as DACA and DAPA and how unions' efforts to build transversal solidarity with immigrant communities through such implementation efforts might vary across local communities. Not only does organized labor have greater power in some places than others, but unions also deploy distinct strategies in different political and civic contexts (de Graauw, et al. 2020). Just as past research has shown that local context is consequential for when and how immigrant rights advocacy occurs (de Graauw and Vermeulen 2016), we argue that local context also matters for how unions go about building transversal solidarity such as through their role in implementing the DACA and DAPA programs.

Through a comparison of labor unions in San Francisco and Houston, this paper shows how local political and civic contexts matter for how unions have attempted to build solidarity with undocumented immigrants in the wake of DACA and DAPA. Labor unions in both San Francisco and Houston are publicly committed to advancing the rights of undocumented immigrants. San Francisco unions, however, have been historically powerful actors in local politics, and they operate in a local political and civic context that facilitates deep transversal solidarity building. This helps explain why they have played a significant and direct role in implementing the DACA and DAPA programs. Most notably, they developed their own center to offer immigration legal services to immigrant union members and their families. Houston unions, in contrast, are notably weaker political actors in a more moderate political context with fewer immigrant organizations. This has posed significant challenges to their ability to build lasting transversal solidarity, and as a result they have focused primarily on DACA and DAPA outreach, legal service referrals, and strategic media coverage. In both cities, local context has clearly determined the trajectory of union solidarity with undocumented immigrants.

1   U.S. Labor Unions and Solidarity with Undocumented Immigrants

The labor movement in the United States has had an uneven relationship with undocumented workers. Rampant xenophobia and anti-immigrant sentiment among leadership and rank-and-file union members are well doc-umented, stemming from racism, fears of labor competition, and an aversion to the challenges of organizing undocumented and other immigrant workers. Undocumented immigrants also cannot vote and thus play a secondary role in the political machine of the labor movement (Hamlin 2008). Yet unions at various points in history have been, and are now, central actors in the immi-grant rights movement (Burgoon, et al. 2010). Two decades after the American Federation of Labor-Congress of Industrial Organizations (AFL-CIO)—the biggest labor federation in the United States—declared solidarity with undoc-umented immigrants, unions today are vocal allies for immigration reform that includes a legalization path for undocumented immigrants (Jacobson and Geron 2008). While several unions such as those representing the build-ing trades are far more moderate, the AFL-CIO's solidarity with undocumented immigrants reflects a move away from the immigrant threat narrative and towards a critique of neoliberal policies that have degraded the labor condi-tions and rights of all workers in the United States (Milkman 2020).

Yet this new solidarity with undocumented immigrants, while a far cry from unions' hostile position in the mid-1980s and before, remains uneven. Some argue that the U.S. labor movement represents the inner establishment of reformist immigrant organizations (Gonzales 2013), while others highlight the central role of many 'immigrant unions' (Ness 2010) in recent mass mobili-zations, especially following a shift to 'social movement union strategies' that produced key union victories on the West Coast during the late 1990s and early 2000s (Zepeda-Millán 2017). This vocal grassroots support for undocumented immigrants laid the foundation for later national solidarity declarations and the heavy lobbying for comprehensive immigration reform. After years of con-gressional gridlock, and following a split in the U.S. labor movement around issues central to immigrant organizing, the AFL-CIO eventually endorsed a more narrow strategy that summoned President Obama to exercise discretion to create the DACA program (Nicholls 2013). Two years later, these same unions collaborated with major worker center alliances such as the National Day Labor Organizing Network (Sarmiento, et al. 2016) to advocate for the DAPA program, which the courts eventually blocked.

Scholarly accounts of labor unions' work on immigration often focus on the U.S. labor movement's national strategy. In reality, however, the AFL-CIO is comprised of dozens of state federations and thousands of central and regional labor councils, each with a distinct immigrant base and facing varied local con-ditions that shape their work. The same is true for the remaining Change to Win coalition members that broke away from the AFL-CIO starting in 2005.

For a more comprehensive understanding of unions' immigration advocacy, we therefore must look to the local contexts in which unions are organizing, forming coalitions, and serving their members, and not just the larger historical and structural determinants (Fine and Tichenor 2012a). Indeed, we know that local 'battlegrounds' shape union strategy (Turner and Cornfield 2007) and that local politics are increasingly relevant for immigrant life and organizing (e.g. Varsanyi 2010).

Local context is not simply a determining factor of union solidarity with immigrants, but likely also a strategy in itself. In their book *A New Deal: How Regional Activism Will Reshape the American Labor Movement*, Dean and Reynolds (2010) document the ways in which the labor movement has leveraged coalitions with community organizations to pursue a progressive agenda rooted in the local concerns of working people. This has inevitably included thinking through immigration not solely as a distant federal policy, but also a local reality that requires investments such as in organizing local protests to denounce anti-immigrant federal policies, efforts to coordinate and provide legal advice, and immigrant leadership training. The labor movement has built on these local investments to push for national reform, within the labor movement but also in Congress and the White House. In many ways, labor unions' engagement with the DACA and DAPA programs—the dimension of union solidarity with undocumented immigrants we focus on in this chapter — is an outgrowth of this local and regional activism in the labor movement.

This chapter shows how local context shapes unions' varying hand in implementing the DACA and DAPA programs. Indeed, unions' ability to build solidarity with undocumented workers importantly reflects the political opportunity structures they face (Meyer and Staggenborg 1996) and the broader ecology of civil society organizations in which they operate (Bada, et al. 2010). More specifically, in politically progressive places where local government officials have enacted pro-immigrant legislation, built municipal institutions designed to promote immigrant integration, and invested in immigrant services, unions can leverage these local government efforts to build solidarity with undocumented immigrants, opportunities that often are absent in places where local government officials are more tepid about or outright opposed to immigration. Similarly, in places with a lot of active immigrant organizations that have long been fighting for the rights of undocumented and other immigrants, unions have ready opportunities to collaborate with and learn from them as they develop their own solidarity strategies. Such opportunities for cross-organizational solidarity building are scarcer in places with relatively less developed infrastructures of immigrant organizations.

2   Methods and Data

2.1   *The DACA and DAPA Programs*

We examine union solidarity with undocumented immigrants through the lens of the 2012 DACA and 2014 DAPA programs, two of President Obama's executive actions that provide two-year and renewable deportation relief and work authorization to undocumented youth and the undocumented parents of U.S. citizen and legal permanent resident children, respectively. President Trump has repeatedly attacked the 2012 DACA program. Though in June 2020 the U.S. Supreme Court overturned Trump's 2017 decision to rescind the program and ordered the administration to resume processing new applications, the Trump administration refused to back down and began granting only one-year renewals. The 2014 DAPA program was first blocked in court in February 2015, a decision left in place by a split 4–4 U.S. Supreme Court decision in June 2016. The DAPA program never went into effect, but during the three months between the program's announcement in November 2014 and the initial court injunction in February 2015, community organizations, labor unions, and other immigrant allies worked to defeat the court challenge, issue legal advice, and ready immigrants to apply for DAPA in case the program would move forward.

There are various ways that unions could have responded to DACA and DAPA, given the labor movement's history of immigrant solidarity. At the very least, labor unions could simply inform their members and other undocumented immigrants of these programs, the benefits they could reap, and the risks they could face in applying. Given the relationships unions have built with immigrant advocates, they could also refer immigrants to community organizations for help in applying for DACA or DAPA. Taking an even further step, some unions could provide such support in-house, or make their staff, resources, and union halls available for DACA and DAPA information sessions and application workshops. Beyond direct service provision, labor unions could pressure local governments to invest in DACA and DAPA implementation. How unions engaged in transversal solidarity under DACA and DAPA ultimately depended on their specific characteristics and the local political and civic contexts in which they operated.

2.2   *Research Sites*

We explore how unions engaged with the DACA and DAPA programs in San Francisco (CA) and Houston (TX), two cities with very different political and civic contexts. As Table 4.1 also shows, these are two cities with large immigrant populations, though unions in these cities have developed distinct levels of political and economic clout.

TABLE 4.1   Local context in San Francisco and Houston, 2016

		San Francisco	Houston
Demographic context [a]	Total population	840,763	2,217,706
	Number of foreign-born (%)	295,417 (35)	632,743 (29)
	Number of foreign-born noncitizen (%)	115,186 (39)	454,336 (72)
	Number of undocumented [b]	49,000	412,000
Political context [c]	2012 Pres. vote: % Democrat	83	49
	2016 Pres. vote: % Democrat	86	54
Civic context	Reg. nonprofits/10,000 pop. [d]	76	38
	Percent Union members [e]	10.4	2.5

Notes:
a   All population data, unless otherwise noted, are city-level data from the 2015 American Community Survey, 5-year estimates. Percentages are rounded
b   Sources: Migration Policy Institute (2016a-b) for San Francisco County (San Francisco) and Harris County (Houston)
c   Election data are for San Francisco County (San Francisco) and Harris County (Houston). Percentages are rounded. Source: *Politico* (https://www.politico.com/mapdata-2016/2016 -election/results/map/president)
d   Number of registered nonprofits per 10,000 residents in 2016. Data are for San Francisco County (San Francisco) and Harris County (Houston). Sources: National Center for Charitable Statistics (http://nccs.urban.org/sites/all/nccs-archive/html/tablewiz/bmf.php) and 2015 American Community Survey, 5-year estimates
e   Percentage of private sector workers in the larger metro area who are union members. Source: 2016 Current Population Survey (http://www.unionstats.com)

San Francisco is the fourteenth largest city in the United States and home to about 840,000 residents, 35 percent of whom are foreign born, including an estimated 49,000 undocumented immigrants (MPI 2016a). San Francisco is at the leading edge of social, economic, and political change. The vast majority of San Franciscans have supported Democratic candidates in recent presidential elections, and most, if not all, local government officials have publicly declared support for protecting undocumented immigrants. Since the late 1990s, city officials have enacted ordinances addressing the language access, labor protections, health care, municipal identification, civic participation, and legal and due process rights for immigrants. San Francisco created the Office of Civic Engagement and Immigrant Affairs in 2008, which promotes immigrant integration initiatives and funds local immigrant organizations. Led by a politically influential central labor council, unions in San Francisco are vocal and polit-ically active (Voss and Sherman 2000). California labor protections surpass federal standards, and in 2000 San Francisco created its own Office of Labor Standards Enforcement to enforce even stronger local wage and labor laws. San Francisco has a thick and robust organizational landscape that some have called 'hyperpluralist' (Coyle 1988), and immigrant organizations are numer-ous and very active in local politics (de Graauw 2016).

Houston is the fourth largest city in the country, with about 2.2 million res-idents. Twenty-nine percent of Houstonians are foreign born, including an estimated 412,000 undocumented immigrants (MPI 2016b). The balance of power in Houston oscillates, though Democrats have gained ground in recent elections. Local immigration policies reflect the area's partisan divisions and the vocal advocacy of conservative and anti-immigrant lobbies. For much of the last decade, for example, the Harris County Sheriff's Office participated in a controversial 287(g) agreement, which permitted local law enforcement to collaborate with U.S. Immigration and Customs Enforcement. However, Mayor Sylvester Turner recently declared Houston a 'welcoming city' and dis-avowed Texas' 2017 anti-immigrant 'show me your papers' legislation. Overall, Houston officials have created fewer immigrant protections and benefits than their counterparts in San Francisco, and the city office dedicated to promot-ing immigrant integration is much smaller in scope and has been restructured and renamed twice since its creation in 2001. Located in a 'right-to-work' state that weakens labor power, union density in Houston is among the lowest in the country. The local labor federation in Houston recently reorganized as the Texas Gulf Coast Area Labor Federation in an attempt to consolidate regional power. Compared to San Francisco, Houston has a less developed and sparser infrastructure of civil society organizations with fewer (though a growing number of) immigrant organizations.

2.3   Data

We draw on 69 interviews conducted between 2012 and 2016 to examine unions' transversal solidarity with undocumented immigrants. We interviewed representatives of 11 different unions (5 in San Francisco and 6 in Houston) and leaders of 33 different immigrant organizations (16 in San Francisco and 17 in Houston) who often collaborate with unions. On several occasions, we interviewed more than one individual with the same union or immigrant organization, and we also conducted several follow-up interviews with the same respondent to take stock of changes over time. We queried both labor and immigrant rights leaders queried about their organization's responses to the DACA and DAPA programs, including how they had collaborated with other local stakeholders, and the challenges they faced along the way. We also interviewed four representatives of national labor unions, including the AFL-CIO, SEIU (Service Employees International Union), UNITE-HERE (Union of Needletrades, Industrial, and Textile Employees—Hotel Employees and Restaurant Employees Union), and UFCW (United Food and Commercial Workers Union), to help us contextualize the union-immigrant solidarity dynamics in San Francisco and Houston. We transcribed and systematically coded all interviews to find distinctive patterns and trends in union solidarity with undocumented immigrants. We complement our interview data with field observations at labor and community events, newspaper reports in local media, and documentary evidence from labor unions and immigrant organizations.

3   San Francisco Unions: Deep Solidarity with Undocumented
       Immigrants

San Francisco unions have built deep solidarity with undocumented immigrants during, and well before, DACA and DAPA. The San Francisco Labor Council (SFLC)—the countywide federation of local AFL-CIO unions— publicly acknowledged its common interests with all immigrant workers in 2006 (de Graauw 2016). Yet, several unions—notably HERE, SEIU, and UFCW— recognized as early as the 1970s the need to mobilize immigrant workers in efforts to revitalize the San Francisco labor movement (Voss and Sherman 2000). In fact, San Francisco unions helped lead the organizing responsible for the national AFL-CIO's changed stance on immigration (Zabin, et al. 2001). Since the late 1990s, unions with notable numbers of immigrant members have led local campaigns to improve the rights of immigrant and other low-wage workers, resulting in new local minimum wage, paid sick leave, and universal health care policies. They have also supported immigrant organizations in advocacy to secure language access protections, municipal ID cards, and some noncitizen voting rights (de Graauw 2016). In 2015, the SFLC and SEIU (the key union in the breakaway Change to Win Coalition) worked together to create the We Rise SF Labor Center for Immigrant Justice (We Rise Center hereafter) to provide legal services to immigrant union members and their families. To explain how and why San Francisco unions have advanced this transversal solidarity with immigrant communities, we must account for the local political and civic context in which they operate.

3.1   *Progressive City Government Facilitates Transversal Solidarity*

San Francisco's many progressive city officials have created policies, built municipal institutions, and allocated funding that made it possible for unions to build solidarity with immigrant communities. Among elected city officials are several individuals who came up in the labor and immigrant rights movements (e.g. former Supervisors Eric Mar and John Avalos, Supervisor Hillary Ronen, and former Mayor Ed Lee). They regularly engage with labor and immigrant rights leaders in crafting policies and initiatives that benefit the city's diverse immigrant communities. City officials have also developed municipal institutions that benefit vulnerable immigrants in San Francisco—notably the Immigrant Rights Commission (from 1997), the Office of Labor Standards Enforcement (from 2000), and the Office of Civic Engagement and Immigrant Affairs (from 2008). This has positioned the city as a prominent actor and convener in the immigrant and labor advocacy space. The city has also contracted with unions and immigrant organizations to provide municipal services to immigrants, at times providing opportunities for them to do so as a coalition. One key example has been the city-funded Rapid Response Network, created in 2007 to respond to the growing number of federal immigration raids targeting San Francisco businesses.[2]

In July 2015, Mayor Ed Lee provided support to SFLC and SEIU Local 87 (the Janitors Union) to open the We Rise Center. With funding from the Mayor's Office of Housing and Community Development, the Center provides critical legal and social services to union members and their families as they navigate DACA and other aspects of the increasingly fractured U.S. immigration system. SFLC and SEIU also received a DreamSF Fellow through the OCEIA-directed leadership development program that offers immigrant youth—including undocumented youth—hands-on experience in direct services, advocacy, and immigration law careers. This fellow conducted multilingual outreach around DACA and citizenship issues, work she continued as a full-time Center employee after her fellowship ended. This city support has helped facilitate the participation of SFLC and SEIU in monthly OCEIA meetings with other community organizations where DreamSF Fellows are placed, which has helped unions build solidarity with immigrants. In all, with the creation of the We Rise Center, San Francisco labor unions have doubled down on their commitment to build solidarity with immigrants. The calculus is clear, as a Center employee explained, because "as a movement, we are paralyzed if we can't unlock both

---

2   Interviews: 25 May 2016, 1 June 2016, 14 June 2016.

the activism and the potential leadership of this huge sector of our [immigrant] members".[3]

San Francisco's political progressivism provides labor unions valuable opportunities to strengthen and deepen their solidarity with immigrant communities, though the relationship between unions and various government officials and municipal institutions can be contentious. Unions often advocate for more than city officials are prepared to legislate or fund. This forces them to use their political and electoral heft at strategic moments, such as when they pushed for city funding for the We Rise Center after President Obama announced the DAPA program. This close relationship with city government also arguably makes it challenging to maintain the social movement unionism that San Francisco unions are famous for and that scholars argue is critical to revitalize the labor movement (e.g. Clawson 2003; Fantasia and Voss 2004). However, unions in San Francisco have the staying power—with robust workforce representation and notable political clout—that allows them to diversify their work. This includes developing and investing in a new center that focuses on providing legal services to undocumented and other immigrants.

3.2 Dense and Mature Infrastructure of Immigrant Organizations Compels Unions to Step Up

San Francisco's civic context has similarly enabled unions to advance transversal solidarity with immigrant communities, especially in recent years when community organizations have had to challenge a barrage of federal anti-immigrant policies. As an established gateway city that has long been a hotbed for social movements, San Francisco today has a dense and well-developed infrastructure of over 215 immigrant organizations (de Graauw 2016). These organizations have long provided essential services to immigrants and advocated on immigrants' behalf in local politics and beyond, well before unions took up the immigrant cause. This has created a very crowded and at times competitive immigrant advocacy space where unions must vie to carve out unique advocacy and service niches.

San Francisco unions have worked with immigrant organizations in successive campaigns since the late 1990s to advocate for local policies that support immigrants and other low-wage workers (de Graauw 2016). In these various campaigns, unions and immigrant organizations have had both the opportunities to lead and motivations to work together to influence local policy. Unions can draw on stable financial resources, large cadres of members who can be

---

3 Interview: 14 June 2016.

mobilized in the political process, and clout with city officials. Immigrant organizations, on the other hand, have deeper connections to immigrant communities that help unions build trust with and organize alongside immigrant workers. This is especially important to reach undocumented and limited English proficient workers (Fine 2006; Jayaraman and Ness 2005). Over time, San Francisco's rich infrastructure of immigrant organizations has provided unions with a variety of opportunities to join advocacy causes that enable them to build solidarity with immigrants and the organizations serving them.

Following the 9/11 terrorist attacks, unions started to reach out to immigrants by "giving out food", according to an SFLC employee.[4] "More and more immigrants were coming for assistance" following the announcement of President Obama's DACA and DAPA programs, he added, "and we figured we need to do something on a larger scale to be part of the movement".[5] This demand for increased immigration legal services incentivized SFLC and SEIU to set up the We Rise Center. The Center's creation built on unions' previous outreach around DACA and naturalization assistance, which included referrals to other community organizations that, according to the same SFLC employee, were largely not reaching union members.[6] "We wanted to put something together with brick and mortar", another SFLC employee commented, "so that people know that the labor movement is also going to start taking immigration on as one of the big issues that we have".[7] The Center, in other words, has provided unions the opportunity to grow and, in turn, immigrants the opportunity to gain information both about their legal case and the labor movement. These efforts have also signaled to the larger immigrant rights movement that organized labor in San Francisco is a committed partner, as well as to city officials that unions are relevant actors in reaching immigrant constituents.

In this dense hub of immigrant advocacy and support, San Francisco unions have been careful not to duplicate other efforts nor to create the impression that they are competing with immigrant organizations for city funding. "Our goal was to add to the pie, not to take it away", an SFLC employee assured.[8] Unions walked this fine line through working in coalition with immigrant organizations to identify their value-added approach to providing legal services. "We didn't want to be just a well-intentioned *notario* [often an unscrupulous legal service provider]", the same SFLC employee said, nor did they think it

---

4 Interview: 14 June 2016.
5 Interview: 14 June 2016.
6 Interview: 14 June 2016.
7 Interview: 14 June 2016.
8 Interview: 14 June 2016.

was effective to "organize big workshops where everyone only gets 15 minutes [with a lawyer]".[9] Instead, the We Rise Center has provided a case management approach in an environment where "at least 75% of union members have some complicated [immigration] case" that requires far more resources than straight-forward DACA and naturalization applications.[10] In the end, the Center's legal service model has focused on contracting with several experienced law firms to provide union members and their families initial screenings and the option to pursue further legal representation at a reduced, Center-negotiated rate. In the first six months of operation, the We Rise Center had helped about 150 immigrants obtain such comprehensive consultations.[11]

4   Houston Unions: Limited Solidarity with Undocumented Immigrants

Compared to San Francisco unions, on the whole, Houston labor unions were able to build only limited solidarity with undocumented immigrants in the wake of DACA and DAPA. Houston unions lack the staff, resources, and political clout to create independent support systems for immigrants. They also operate in a more tepid political climate for immigrant rights, and they have access to far fewer established immigrant organizations as possible collaborators and solidarity allies. This is not to say that Houston unions have stood on the side-lines in the wake of DACA and DAPA. Indeed, they have strategically leveraged relationships with allies in local government and the business community in advocating for inclusive immigration reform. Also, the Harris County AFL-CIO has helped to incubate local worker centers and support their work, such as in their historic policy campaign to end employer wage theft in 2013 (de Graauw and Gleeson 2017). In other words, Houston's political and civic context has meant that labor unions have had to adopt a different brand of transversal solidarity than their San Francisco counterparts.

4.1   *Moderate City Government Complicates Transversal Solidarity*
Unlike in progressive San Francisco, immigration has long been and continues to be a divisive issue in Houston's mixed political climate. Over the years, there have been several notable immigrant rights supporters on city council (e.g. for-mer Council Members Mike Laster and Ed Gonzalez), but the countervailing

---

9   Interview: 14 June 2016.
10   Interview: 14 June 2016.
11   Interview: 14 June 2016.

pressures of the region's pro-business and small government ethos and a vocal contingent of anti-immigrant forces (including former Council Members Orlando Sanchez and Helena Brown) have stopped Houston government from embracing the city's undocumented immigrants more fully. Labor and immigrant organizations have wielded limited power in this space. One labor organizer with a broad-based community organization working with Houston's diverse immigrant communities characterized power in Houston as being "wielded by a combination of multi-national corporations, largely oil and gas, finance, engineering, construction", with unions merely occupying the "third or fourth tier" of local power far behind these corporate giants.[12]

Despite this pro-business culture and hesitant position toward immigrant rights, Houston politicians have not entirely ignored the needs of its large foreign-born and undocumented population. Support from several immigrant-friendly, Democratic mayors and allied council members made possible the 2001 creation of the Mayor's Office of Immigrant and Refugee Affairs (MOIRA), later renamed the Office of New Americans and Immigrant Communities. This office provided funding for the creation of a day labor center in immigrant-dense southwest Houston, though this initiative was short lived because of controversy over the use of public funding to help undocumented workers. It also participated in the Justice and Equality in the Workplace Project, an immigrant worker rights initiative catalyzed by the local office of the federal Equal Employment Opportunity Commission and the Mexican Consulate. The Harris County AFL-CIO played a central role in each of these initiatives as it sought openings for advocating on behalf of the region's immigrant workforce.

While San Francisco unions' direct involvement in immigrant service provision helped garner funding from and increased legitimacy with local government, the stakes and resources were very different in Houston. When President Obama created DACA in 2012 and DAPA in 2014, Houston Mayors Annise Parker and Sylvester Turner publicly supported both programs and spoke out against both Texas Governor Greg Abbott's attacks on these initiatives (Singer 2015) and President Trump's repeated attacks on cities that support their undocumented residents (Shilcutt 2017). This mayoral support for DACA and DAPA notwithstanding, the city made no funding available for their implementation, and there have been no tangible opportunities for unions to work directly with local government on DACA and DAPA issues. This largely explains why unions instead have directed their immigrant solidarity efforts towards local immigrant organizations, albeit largely in a peripheral way.

---

12   Interview: 7 June 2012.

4.2 Unions Struggle to Collaborate Long-term with Immigrant Organizations

Unions' relatively passive response to DACA and DAPA can also be explained by the fact that Houston is "a huge city, and we only have a very small number of organizations", as described by the leader of a local worker center.[13] This has made sustained coalitional work around immigration issues difficult in Houston. To be sure, there have been a handful of immigrant rights coalitions over time, including the Catholic-led Hispanic Council of Organizations that supported amnesty for undocumented immigrants during the 1980s,[14] a local chapter of the state-wide Texas Immigrant Rights Coalition,[15] the direct-action oriented Houston United,[16] and the business-driven Americans for Immigration Reform convened by the local chamber of commerce and several high-profile immigration lawyers.[17] However, none of these coalitions operated for very long, and labor unions have not typically been prominently involved in them.[18] This has made it challenging for unions to build solidarity with undocumented immigrants in collaboration with other nongovernmental organizations pre-DACA.

Immigrant rights coalitions in Houston today often operate statewide, wearing multiple advocacy hats and motivated by the necessity to work in coalition and across partisan lines. Seeing a need for expanded immigration legal services and better service coordination among local providers, two local foundations—the Houston Endowment and the Simmons Foundation— seeded the creation of the Houston Immigration Legal Services Collaborative (HILSC) in 2013, after DACA was announced. The result today is an ethnically diverse set of about a dozen funded service providers, many also working with Houston's large population of resettled refugees. Conspicuously missing from this collaborative are Houston labor unions, which have no track record of sustained direct service provision. Unions have instead relied largely on referrals to HILSC service providers to connect immigrant union members to needed legal services.

These challenges notwithstanding, Houston unions have curated a particular approach to building solidarity with undocumented immigrants by working with local immigrant organizations in selected advocacy campaigns. For

---

13   Interview: 29 May 2012.
14   Interview: 4 June 2012.
15   Interview: 4 June 2012.
16   Interview: 4 March 2015.
17   Interview: 7 June 2012.
18   Interview: 1 April 2016.

example, the Harris County AFL-CIO has collaborated with the local chapter of United We Dream (UWD)—the largest immigrant youth-led organization in the country—in advocating against Texas' 2017 anti-immigrant 'show me your papers' legislation and in pressuring the Harris County Sheriff's Office to end their 287(g) program in 2017 (Flynn 2017). This alliance between the AFL-CIO and UWD represents unions' effort to remain relevant to a younger workforce (Tapia and Turner 2018), but also UWD's need to diversify its alliances in this city with a notably large and diverse immigrant population. "There is never going to be one organization that's going to service all of Houston", one UWD organizer explained, "you just can't do it; no amount of money would ensure that".[19] So, while the Harris County AFL-CIO did not hire their own lawyers or host their own DACA and DAPA workshops as unions in San Francisco have done, they have provided referrals to HILSC and advocated alongside undocumented immigrant-led organizations like UWD.[20]

Indeed, the statewide Texas AFL-CIO president sees Houston and the larger Texas Gulf Coast as part of a driver for "working very consciously with immigrant organizations".[21] Even after the Harris County AFL-CIO reorganized into the regional Texas Gulf Coast Area Labor Federation in 2015, its leadership viewed remaining connected to immigrant resources as key to remaining relevant to union members. "We can play that very important role [for immigration assistance] for some of our members and for the community as a whole", this leader explained, "and we want to figure out ways in which we can do that".[22] The Texas Gulf Coast Area Labor Federation has done so largely through resource referrals, an approach that is unsurprising given the lack of local government funding for immigrant services and foundations' general aversion to funding unions (Dean 2017).

To do more is tough for Houston-area unions, given persistent staffing and resource challenges. One organizer, for example, explained how few UNITE-HERE organizers there are in a state as large as Texas. "For these four cities [Austin, Dallas, Houston, and San Antonio], I think we have seven staff people right now".[23] Also, while the national AFL-CIO had funded training for organizers to help boost naturalization and voter turnout among immigrant members, this funding was not concentrated in Texas. "We don't actually have many resources at our local [and] we don't actually help with the actual [DACA and

---

19 Interview: 17 March 2015.
20 Interview: 10 March 2015.
21 Interview: 22 September 2016.
22 Interview: 29 July 2016.
23 Interview: 2 August 2016.

DAPA application] process", one SEIU Texas organizer explained, "but we can direct people to places that do". Additionally, her union regularly fields requests from local press such as the *Houston Chronicle* and ethnic media outlets like *Univision* and *Telemundo*. "The Spanish media definitely sees SEIU Texas as an immigrant rights organization, actually sometimes even more than a labor organization", she noted, adding that "they always know that we're reliable".[24] This public storytelling in a place that can be very hostile to undocumented immigrants is another way in which Houston unions have managed to build their own brand of solidarity with undocumented immigrants.

5   Conclusion

The U.S. labor movement has played an important role in shaping inclusive federal immigration policies in recent years, but the extent to which unions have subsequently helped immigrants to access key immigration benefits varies from place to place. In this article, we examined how U.S. labor unions have engaged with immigration policy implementation in efforts to build solidarity with immigrant communities. Specifically, we examined how unions in San Francisco and Houston—two immigrant-dense cities with notably different political and civic contexts—have engaged with the Obama administration's DACA and DAPA programs. We show that besides unions' history of political and economic power in a particular place, a city's political and civic context also determines how and how deeply unions are able to build transversal solidarity.

In San Francisco, long-standing political progressivism has enabled historically powerful unions to build deep solidarity with immigrant advocates and to eventually create the city-funded We Rise SF Labor Center for Immigrant Justice. San Francisco's rich infrastructure of immigrant organizations means that powerful unions face a very crowded and sometimes competitive arena that they must carefully navigate to determine their advocacy and service niches. Conversely, Houston's political context is far more ambivalent towards worker and immigrant rights and has granted unions fewer opportunities to build transversal solidarity. While the city has remained largely hands-off with regard to DACA and DAPA, private philanthropy has played a major role in funding and coordinating legal service providers in Houston. This has relegated Houston's historically weak unions to the backseat, where they focus largely on public education, service referrals, and strategic media coverage.

---

24   Interview: 5 March 2015.

These findings suggest that we need to look beyond the national immigration policies that diverse coalitions of immigrant advocates strive to enact, to consider also the local strategies that emerge to implement them. The organizations that advocate to create policies such as DACA and DAPA are not always the same ones that are active in their implementation (de Graauw 2016). In progressive jurisdictions like San Francisco, local governments played an important role in funding immigrant services and convening pro-immigrant organizations, which has in turn further facilitated union solidarity with immigrant communities. In more moderate cities like Houston, where local politicians are more ambivalent about immigrant rights, private funders wield relatively more influence, making it more challenging for unions to act in solidarity with immigrant communities. In such divergent contexts, advocates confront different (dis-)incentives for investing in immigration initiatives like DACA and DAPA. As social movement scholars track the evolution of immigration advocacy, we must therefore take care to distinguish the locally-determined dynamics of federal policy implementation.

A lot has been written about the U.S. labor movement's often complicated role in pushing for federal immigration reform, but our research argues that the national story does not necessarily determine the longer-term on-the-ground reality. Federated organizations like the AFL-CIO have set certain national priorities, but local central labor councils operate with notable autonomy, shaped importantly by the local context in which they operate. Local chapters of unions such as SEIU and UNITE-HERE also differ substantially based on their local industries and membership characteristics, as well as on where their national organizations invest staff and financial resources. Therefore, while the national labor movement has repeatedly declared solidarity with immigrants, the realization of these commitments depends on local unions' ability to engage in a range of advocacy and service activities as well as their ability to leverage the immigrant rights investments of different governmental actors and nongovernmental organizations.

Our research has shown that solidarity strategies are certainly not entirely supply-side driven. Understanding the motivations and goals that organizations have to build solidarity with immigrants is important. For unions, this includes a need to develop legitimacy with immigrant workers who are, or could one day be, union members. It also reflects unions' desire to remain relevant in progressive movements, especially as their membership wanes and organizing new members becomes increasingly more difficult. Unions' desire and ability to do more than negotiate collective bargaining agreements, however, depends on the availability of new resources and willing partners. In the case of DACA and DAPA, the federal government was completely absent, and only some local governments took up the charge to help immigrants take advantage of these programs. Private philanthropy has a long record of providing such implementation support, though rarely do they extend that to unions, and they certainly did not in Houston. As a result, while unions across the country may have similar desires to build solidarity with immigrant communities, the ways in which they can do so are far from uniform.

Our research offers insights into unions' solidarity strategies at a particular moment in time, when DACA and the promise of DAPA mobilized unions to deepen their solidarity with immigrant communities. Now that U.S. immigration policy nearly exclusively focuses on surveillance, detention, and deportation, immigrant allies are increasingly stretched thin, exactly at a time when it is ever more important for them to act collectively in defense of immigrant communities. What does union solidarity look like now that immigrant communities writ large are under attack and COVID-19-induced austerity measures threaten government and philanthropic funding to support immigrants? In moving forward and extending this research into the current period, it is important also to take seriously local realities for understanding patterns of transversal solidarity more broadly and to consider local contextual determinants of union solidarity efforts with immigrants more specifically.

Finally, the United States offers a unique context for understanding how labor unions build solidarity with immigrants and the organizations that advocate on their behalf. Unlike in Europe and beyond, where unions have sectoral bargaining (Fine and Tichenor 2012b), U.S. unions must build power worksite by worksite. Unions operating in any one of the 27 states with 'right-to-work' laws are even more constrained due to their inability to collect dues uniformly. Therefore, labor scholarship outside the United States can help shed light on how other national and local conditions shape union solidarity strategies. Important insights could be gleaned, for example, from union solidarity strategies in Canada where the federal government invests notably in immigrant integration (Bloemraad 2006) and provinces also have a hand in developing both labor and immigration policies (Gabriel and Macdonald 2011). In extending this research to other country contexts, scholars should remember that the extent and depth of unions' transversal solidarity are bound to differ also according to local context.

References

Bacon, D. (2018). "How unions help immigrants resist deportations". *American Prospect*, 13 February. Available (consulted 20 November 2020) at: https://prospect.org/labor/unions-help-immigrants-resist-deportations.

Bada, X., J. Fox, R. Donnelly, and A. Selee (2010). "Context matters: Latino immigrant civic engagement in nine U.S. cities". Available (consulted 20 November 2020) at: https://www.wilsoncenter.org/sites/default/files/media/documents/publication/Context%20Matters.pdf.

Bloemraad, I. (2006). *Becoming a Citizen: Incorporating Immigrants and Refugees in the United States and Canada*. Berkeley, CA: University of California Press.

Burgoon, B., J. Fine, W. Jacoby, and D. Tichenor (2010). "Immigration and the transformation of American unionism". *International Migration* 44(4): 933–973.

Clawson, D. (2003). *The Next Upsurge: Labor and the New Social Movements*. Ithaca, NY: Cornell University Press.

Coyle, D.J. (1988). "The Balkans by the Bay". *Public Interest* 91(Spring): 67–78.

Dean, A.B. (2017). "If foundations want to tackle inequality, labor must be a partner". *Stanford Social Innovation Review*, 29 March. Available (consulted 20 November 2020) at: https://ssir.org/articles/entry/if_foundations_want_to_tackle_inequality_labor_must_be_a_partner.

Dean, A.B., and D.B. Reynolds (2010). *A New Deal: How Regional Activism Will Reshape the American Labor Movement*. Ithaca, NY: Cornell University Press.

de Graauw, E. (2016). *Making Immigrant Rights Real: Nonprofits and the Politics of Integration in San Francisco*. Ithaca, NY: Cornell University Press.

de Graauw, E., and S. Gleeson (2017). "Context, coalitions and organizing: immigrant labor rights advocacy in San Francisco and Houston". In: Greenberg, M., and Lewis, P. (eds.), *The City Is the Factory: New Solidarities and Spatial Strategies in an Urban Age*. Ithaca, NY: Cornell University Press, 80–98.

de Graauw, E., S. Gleeson, and X. Bada (2020). "Local context and labour-community immigrant rights coalitions: a comparison of San Francisco, Chicago, and Houston". *Journal of Ethnic and Migration Studies* 46(4): 728–746.

de Graauw, E., and F. Vermeulen (2016). "Cities and the politics of immigrant integration: a comparison of Berlin, Amsterdam, New York City, and San Francisco". *Journal of Ethnic and Migration Studies* 42(6): 989–1012.

Fantasia, R., and K. Voss (2004). *Hard Work: Remaking the American Labor Movement*. Berkeley, CA: University of California Press.

Fine, J. (2006). *Worker Centers: Organizing Communities at the Edge of the Dream*. Ithaca, NY: Cornell University Press.

Fine, J., L. Burnham, K. Griffith, M. Ji, V. Narro, and S.C. Pitts (eds). (2018). *No One Size Fits All: Worker Organization, Policy, and Movement in a New Economic Age*. Champaign, IL: LERA Research Volume Series (distributed by ILR/Cornell University Press).

Fine, J., and D.J. Tichenor (2012a). "Solidarities and restrictions: labor and immigration policy in the United States". *The Forum* 10(1): 1–21.

Fine, J., and D.J. Tichenor (2012b). *An Enduring Dilemma: Immigration and Organized Labor in Western Europe and the United States*. Oxford: Oxford University Press.

Fletcher, B., and F. Gapasin (2008). *Solidarity Divided: The Crisis in Organized Labor and a New Path Toward Social Justice.* Berkeley, CA: University of California Press.

Flynn, M. (2017). "Undocumented community puts heat on Sheriff Gonzalez to cut controversial policy". *Houston Press*, 27 January. Available (consulted 20 November 2020) at: http://www.houstonpress.com/news/undocumented-community-puts-heat-on-sheriff-gonzalez-to-cut-controversial-policy-9146677.

Gabriel, C., and L. Macdonald (2011). "Citizenship at the margins: the Canadian seasonal agricultural worker program and civil society advocacy". *Politics & Policy* 39(1): 45–67.

Gonzales, A. (2013). *Reform Without Justice: Latino Migrant Politics and the Homeland Security State.* New York, NY: Oxford University Press.

Hamlin, R. (2008). "Immigrants at work: labor unions and non-citizen members". In: Ramakrishnan, S.K., and Bloemraad, I. (eds.), *Civic Hopes and Political Realities: Immigrants, Community Organizations, and Political Engagement.* New York: Russell Sage Foundation Press, 300–322.

Jacobson, R., and K. Geron (2008). "Unions and the politics of immigration". *Socialism and Democracy* 22(3): 105–122.

Jayaraman, S., and I. Ness (eds.) (2005). *The New Urban Immigrant Workforce: Innovative Models for Labor Organizing.* Armonk, NY: M.E. Sharpe.

Meyer, D.S., and S. Staggenborg (1996). "Movements, countermovements, and the structure of political opportunity". *American Journal of Sociology* 101(6): 1628–1660.

Milkman, R. (2020). *Immigrant Labor and the New Precariat.* Medford, MA: Polity Press.

Milkman, R., and E. Ott (2014). *New Labor in New York: Precarious Workers and the Future of the Labor Movement.* Ithaca, NY: Cornell University Press.

MPI, Migration Policy Institute. (2016a). "Profile of the unauthorized population: San Francisco County, CA". Available (consulted 20 November 2020) at: https://www.migrationpolicy.org/data/unauthorized-immigrant-population/county/6075.

MPI, Migration Policy Institute. (2016b). "Profile of the unauthorized population: Harris County, TX". Available (consulted 20 November 2020) at: https://www.migrationpolicy.org/data/unauthorized-immigrant-population/county/48201.

Ness, I. (2010). *Immigrants, Unions, and the New U.S. Labor Market.* Philadelphia, PA: Temple University Press.

Nicholls, W.J. (2013). *The DREAMers: How the Undocumented Youth Movement Transformed the Immigrant Rights Debate.* Stanford, CA: Stanford University Press.

Sarmiento, H., C. Tilly, E. de la Garza Toledo, and J.L. Gayosso Ramírez (2016). "The unexpected power of informal workers in the public square: a comparison of Mexican and US organizing models". *International Labor and Working Class History* 89: 131–152.

Shilcutt, K. (2017). "Mayor Sylvester Turner issues statement on immigration". *Houstonia Magazine*, 26 January. Available (consulted 20 November 2020) at: https://www .houstoniamag.com/news-and-city-life/2017/01/mayor-sylvester-turner-issues -statement-on-immigration.

Singer, A. (2015). *Metropolitan Immigrant Gateways Revisited, 2014*. Washington, D.C.: Brookings Institution.

Tapia, M., and L. Turner (2018). "Renewed activism for the labor movement: the urgency of young worker engagement". *Work and Occupations* 45(4): 391–419.

Turner, L., and D.B. Cornfield (2007). *Labor in the New Urban Battlegrounds: Local Solidarity in a Global Economy*. Ithaca, NY: ILR Press/Cornell University Press.

Varsanyi, M.W. (ed.) (2010). *Taking Local Control: Immigration Policy Activism in US Cities and States*. Stanford, CA: Stanford University Press.

Voss, K., and K. Sherman (2000). "Breaking the iron law of oligarchy: union revitalization in the American labor movement". *American Journal of Sociology* 106(2): 303–349.

Zabin, C., K. Quan, and L. Delp (2001). "Union organizing in California: challenges and opportunities". In: Ong, P., and Lincoln, J. (eds.) *The State of California Labor, 2001*. Los Angeles: UC Institute for Labor and Employment. Available (consulted 20 November 2020) at: https://escholarship.org/uc/ile_scl2001.

Zepeda-Millán, C. (2017). *Latino Mass Mobilization: Immigration, Racialization, and Activism*. New York, NY: Cambridge University Press.

CHAPTER 5

Rethinking Solidarity in a "Post-migrant Labor Regime"

The Case of Hospitality Work in Johannesburg, South Africa

Janet Munakamwe

South Africa has a long history of hosting labor migrants, not only from African countries but from across the globe. However, only few studies explicitly interrogate union responses to migrant labor historically, or today.[1] The canonized understanding of migrant labor in mainstream South African politics originates from the duality of the racial migrant labor system during colonial rule and under the apartheid regime (1948–95). Workers were then drawn from two sources: from across the southern African region and, during apartheid, from the former so-called 'tribal homelands' or 'Bantustans', encapsulated labor reserves within the borders of the republic of South Africa. Under apartheid, Black South Africans were converted into a migrant labor population through legal apparatus which confined social reproduction to the 'homelands', alienating them from citizenship in the republic of South Africa. Men domiciled in the 'Bantustans' were recruited as contracted workforce to South Africa's huge mining districts as 'foreign natives' (Neocosmos 2015) through an elaborate system of passes and work permits, combined with influx control and dual system of industrial relations that accorded limited rights of workplace–based residential rights, and political participation (Munakamwe 2018).

The migrant labor system allowed vast gains for the South African mining sector as social reproduction was sustained through subsistence farming undertaken by the unpaid work of women in 'homelands' of male migrant workers (Wolpe 1972; Arrighi 1973; Burawoy 1976; Fakier 2012). After independence, the feminization of migration has increased, while the contemporary migrant woman still is expected to play a double role as underpaid worker responsible for unpaid social reproduction (see Dodson 1998). The feminization of migration comes in tandem is with a conspicuous post-apartheid rise in clandestine migration from other parts of Africa, without state protection, and without any guarantee of employment after they cross into South Africa.

---

1 See, however, e.g. Schierup (2016).

This casts what the post 1995 democratic South Africa – distancing itself from apartheid's infamous migration system – dubbed the 'post-migrant labor regime', in a paradoxical light. It comes, moreover, together with a puzzling transformation of the strong South African labor movement, that had been one of the main forces in the long struggle against the apartheid regime (Munakamwe 2021): from a legendary community unionism under apartheid deeply involved with migrant workers and poor township dwellers, to a post-apartheid alignment with a mainstream international trade unionism but detached from the informal precariat (see Standing 2011) and migrant workers. The so-called 'post migrant labor regime' represents thus a euphemistic ideological label for an inconsistent political scheme which pretends to overcome the injustices of the old migrant labor system in an abstract and non-committed way. It is associated with democratically induced immigration and labor law reforms although in practice it appropriates copiously from the old system and, in certain respects, is more detrimental to workers as it embraces a proliferating precarization through encumbering so-called 'flexible contracts' and a rambling informalization of labor relations.

On this background, the present chapter provides an overview of this shift in South African labor market restructuring and migration, with particular focus on the hospitality sector, an important part of an expanding post-apartheid South African service economy. I discuss migration and politics of inclusion in the case of metropolitan Johannesburg. The city is one of the largest hosts to immigrants and refugees in the African continent, but is also associated with xenophobic attacks on migrant communities. I address the convoluted dynamics of the city's migration management, partly complicit in a conspicuous rise of xenophobia. Yet, the other side of the coin is emergent transversal solidarity formation traversing origin, ethnicity and newly emerging political subjectivities related to the broader economic, social, political, and legal contexts in a city struggling to provide everyday material needs and social services for its citizens. This duality encompasses, a politics for promoting the imaginary of migrants seen as contributing to "the rich tapestry of the cosmopolitan city", yet perceived to place "strain on employment levels, housing and public services", as expressed by a former Executive Mayor of Johannesburg.[2] This ambivalence is also somehow consistent with the stance of organized labor and in consequence contributes towards the sporadic xenophobic riots that have become a common feature in poor Black townships.

---

2   Quoted from Gotz and Landau (2004, 14).

As the chapter shows, central to unions' ambivalent position concerning organization of migrant workers are restrictive state-crafted migration laws at odds with South Africa's progressive labor law, coupled with pragmatic policies that trigger circular migration (Munakamwe 2021). This comes in tandem with increasing unemployment and the formation of a new fragmented township precariat in the wake of neoliberalism. Seen through this lens I argue that an adapted perception of the Gramscian (Gramsci 1971) notion of 'the subaltern', is essential for unravelling new identities subject to an ideopolitical hegemony that excludes subordinated social groups from democratic agency, and by this for understanding quandaries of and opportunities for union politics with a multiplicity of subjectivity formation among a fragmented precariat in South Africa's large multi-ethnic cities.

As I have argued in detail elsewhere (Munakamwe 2018) an updated Gramscian (Gramsci 1971) perspective on class solidarity is essential for comprehending the formation of transversal solidarities among the emerging precariat, the formation of new political subjectivities and a contingent ambivalent position among trade unions confronted with the challenge of organizing migrant workers in the neoliberal era. Gramsci' notions of 'the subaltern' and 'hegemony' provide heuristic value in explaining the relationship between economic, social and political transformation. The state emanates here not simply as a repressive force but gestated by mediating institutions that, through the agency of a composite civil society, organizes class, race, and gender relations into a consensual hegemony. In contrast with a dominant Marxist perspective presupposing class as the foundation for a united workforce Gramsci warned against neglecting heterogeneity. He, thus, emphasized the need for solidarity among the suppressed 'subaltern' – at his time, the centrality of an alliance of workers and peasants – yet also that unity and discipline cannot be mechanical or achieved by coercive means. However, while acknowledging Gramscian insights that emphasize the centrality of contending hegemonic power among workers, underpinned by overarching class alliances, it is important to consider that the contemporary class structure is inherently fragmented, with workplaces, economic sectors and urban economies marked by extreme job insecurity, casualization and hyper-exploitation. This is valid to the situation of large swaths of working people in general and particularly concerning immigrants. Against this background, it is critical to understand how actual solidarity has been mobilized (or not) between locals and migrants in non-standard employment; in effect, to ask whether the subaltern have been able to articulate common subjectivities and struggles and how these are met by trade unions.

The present chapter draws, empirically, from my doctoral thesis (Munakamwe 2018) for which I employed extensive desk research review, ethnography, direct observations, archival research, and in-depth interviews with migrant and non-migrant workers and with key players within the hospitality value chain.

1   Vicissitudes of the "Post-migrant Labor Regime"

Several draconian apartheid laws and policies were repealed followed by the adoption of a progressive South African Constitution in 1996. It soon transpired, however, that the new dispensation came about with empty promises and politicians could conveniently instrumentalize the presence of foreign nationals as scapegoat in their explanations for failing to fulfil socio-economic expectations (e.g. Schierup 2016). In view of the new post-apartheid hegemony, with the trade unions complicit, it is also not surprising that unions are ambivalent on their position to organize migrant workers. Union leadership became soon intricately linked to government positions as the former serves as a ladder to the latter and, in consequence, raising controversies concerning the migrant issue could be politically risky. In general, workers' power has diminished, as labor restructuring threatens job security, and a perceived threat regarding employment of migrant workers has become manifested in xenophobic riots.

South Africa is, indeed, extolled for possessing some of the most progressive labor laws including a pronounced social dialogue platform – the National Economic Development and Labor Council (NEDLAC) – and the country adopted a number of ILO core conventions, and complies with ILO's social dialogue and collective bargaining requirements. However, workplace restructuring and fragmentation is taking place in all sectors (Underthun and Jordhus-Ler 2015) as company owners (and their financiers) attempt to adjust to the current realities in the labor market; a result of imposed neo-liberal policies which were popularized by Bretton Woods institutions in the 1990s. Contingent with this, is a large share of the country's workers outside of standard employment involving precarious employment relations, casualization, and outsourcing coupled with an expanding informal economy. A poor de facto regulation of the labor market has permitted hiring of undocumented hyper-exploited migrants combined with wage dumping and extraordinarily poor working conditions in sectors where foreign nationals have a strong presence.

Restrictive bureaucratic conditions make it difficult to acquire work permits especially for those in possession of low skills. As a result, many are compelled to work without legal documentation and employers often prefer to hire undocumented migrants to undercut gazetted wages. Moreover, employers have the prerogative of monitoring migrant employees' work permits, which induces patronage as the latter attempt to enchant their bosses to avoid deportations. Where gaps are noted in national laws, legal recourse could be pursued through international human rights, equality laws, regional and ILO instruments. However, the challenge is that beneficiaries, in most cases are not cognizant of international human rights and labor instruments, which makes it difficult to seek recourse through that route.

In the context it appears symptomatic that South Africa has not ratified the key ILO convention on migrant labor, adopted in 1990, the International Convention on the Protection of all Migrant Workers and Members of their Families, including the undocumented, which covers a broad spectrum of security benefits and rights concerning freedom from employment discrimination, organization, and collective bargaining. All combined, the post-apartheid democratic government ineptly failed to develop a clear policy on migrant labor. Legislation on migration draws on the statutory Immigration Act of 2002, which is in many ways hostile towards migrant workers. Some bilateral agreements with neighboring states are still in place, much like they were initially crafted under apartheid. The democratic government, much like its predecessor, has crafted restrictive laws that bind the migrant worker in toxic ways. They limit contract workers from the option of becoming either permanent residents or full citizens of the country. Migrant workers are thus subjected to circular migration as they straddle between their countries of origin and South Africa in their efforts to avoid breaching provisions of the Immigration Act. Circular migrants are those who episodically come and work in South Africa temporarily and go back to their countries of origin. Policy gaps result in increasing precarity, low wages, and unchecked safety hazards for migrant workers and this antagonistic to the ILO decent work agenda (e.g. Musabayana 2014).

An increasingly restrictive trend relates also to refugees and asylum seekers, not least from the neighboring state of Zimbabwe, which significantly diminishes asylum and refugee rights as guaranteed in the South African Constitution as well as the International Covenant on Economic Social and Cultural Rights (ICESCR). This involves, as inscribed into White Paper on International Migration adopted in 2017, the blocking of political participation by refugees. A key shortcoming of the White Paper is its draconian approach to socio-economic rights of asylum seekers in which it clearly prohibits the right to work, study and free movement within the country. It forces refugees 'underground' for survival through precarious labor in the informal economy.

Following the adoption of neoliberal policies imposed on African countries by the Bretton Woods Institutions in the 90s, the 2000s witnessed a decline in centralized recruitment of foreign miners to the South African gold mines. This signified an end to migrant labor regime typical for the Apartheid era. At the same time there has been a steep rise in casualization, fixed term contracts, part-timing, subcontracting and informalization of employment. This became coupled with decline in private sector unionization, high rates of unemployment, persistent poverty, all coupled with migration flows, tied into irregular and temporary labor, with a politically and economically unstable Zimbabwe as a main source of irregular flows (e.g. Fine 2014a). Inequality, poverty and unemployment have moreover, been exacerbated due to repercussions of the Covid-19 pandemic (Fine 2014b).

Consequently, in the era of the so-called 'post-migrant labor regime' informal migration has, paradoxically, become pervasive and is characterized by clandestine mobility outside the purview of state-crafted regulatory frameworks. Those who migrate formally, are subjected to circular migration. Furthermore, while the post 1994 dispensation has paved way for free mobility, internal migrants from former homelands, are ironically caught in migrancy reminiscent of the apartheid period. This involves continued dependence on the rural hinterland to sustain social reproduction borne by women while male bread winners still depend on selling their labor in large cities such as Johannesburg. However, as I shall relate to in detail below, a shifting political economy has, at the same time, produced an increasing feminization of migrant labor. Generated by sectoral restructuration, a shift in migration patterns has taken place in the post-apartheid period. Compared to the past, when migrants were overwhelmingly male, a rapid feminization of the migrant labor force has taken place, with almost four in ten migrants being women in the 2000s. Parallel with this informal labor migration has become dominant with a remarkable decline in fixed contracted labor (see Crush 1997; DoL 2007; Simelane and Modisha 2008). This represents the flipside of the fall of the old migrant labor system (Simelane and Modisha 2008) precipitated by labor policies that emphasize recruitment of local labor (see Forrest 2013; Mujere 2015); a process which has not done away with the employment of migrant labor but squeezed it into clandestinity. This ultimately poses huge challenges to organizing strategies of unions.

1.1 *Fragmented Solidarity: Organized Labor and the New Precariat*

Central to the Gramscian theory of civil society and hegemony, introduced above, is the emphasis on solidarity formation among the 'subaltern', and from that position it is critical to understand the extent to which a fragmented contemporary precariat has been able to articulate common struggles. Civil society, and particularly trade unions, play a fundamental mediatory role as an arena for control through formation and dissemination of hegemony. It is a complex ideological terrain which presents the interests of the dominant group as the interests of all, but also harbors opportunities for transformation (e.g. Von Holdt 2002). However, phrasing hegemony in terms of 'democracy' expressing the will of the majority tends to relegate migrant issues to the periphery of the political process and labor struggles (Munakamwe 2018). In the process, workers in non-standard informal, casual and outsourced employment are marginalized based on their employment contracts, or lack of the same, which cannot sustain union subscriptions.

Exacerbating this quandary, the rhetoric of 'comradeship' has to some extent precluded mobilization, protests and revolts against the poor economic situation workers found themselves in again (Von Holdt 2002). Many trade union leaders such as the founding General Secretary of the National Union of Mineworkers, Cyril Ramaphosa and former shop stewards who led the mobilization and protests during apartheid occupied top government positions in the new dispensation (see von Holdt 2002), and the labor unions have become a key pillar for the sustainability of the post-1995 neoliberal hegemony. At the center of their 21st century dilemmas and labor organizing, argue Webster and Ludwig (2017, 165), is "a tension between the extent to which trade unions focus on immediate interests of their members against a broader commitment to the interests of working people". This has meant paying particular attention to policy reforms related to socio-economic 'bread and butter' issues of permanently employed core workers while neglecting issues of a new informal precariat, and in particular discriminatory policies that affect migrants such as the Immigration Act of 2002 and the White Paper on International migration.

Thus, the 21st century labor movement in South Africa has become alienated from its historical trajectory. Moreover, it is currently presented with the challenge of organizing in a very volatile environment that is characterized by labor deregulation, 'flexploitation', and hostile migration laws. The changing migration and recruitment trends have displaced the class struggle from the factory gates where the mass of workers was organized collectively (Seidman 1995), towards a fragmented territory of precarious employment contracts. Workplace restructuring and flexible employment contracts which are at the core of neoliberalism in the labor market promote competition while fragmenting worker solidarity (Webster, et al. 2008) and this has impacted on mobilization. Thus, migrant workers are marginally represented, and unions are ambivalent and slow in developing explicit policies to address issues and vulnerabilities associated with migrancy. This ambivalence demonstrates unions' failure to acknowledge the heterogeneous nature of the subaltern, thus paving the way for super-exploitation, undercutting of wages, xenophobia and fragmented solidarity. Similarly, circular and irregular migration does not only pose challenges to the governance and integration strategies for large cities like Johannesburg but also offers a scapegoat for legitimizing union ambivalence', concerning the organization of migrant workers, and thus functions to fragment worker solidarity.

Competition for jobs in the post-apartheid period has repeatedly resulted in xenophobic attacks by natives on migrants in poor urban townships (Munakamwe 2018). This stands out in contrast with the apartheid period, in which Black workers forged unity (Von Holdt 2002) regardless of nationality in their struggle to dismantle the apartheid system. A strong sense of solidarity existed among both local and migrant workers as their primary enemy was the capitalist apartheid system (see Allen 1992). There was a marked sense of solidarity between local and migrant workers who forged strong collectives (von Holdt 2002) in various economic sectors which culminated with the formation of the first black unions led by migrants (e.g. Nel and Rooyen 1993; Allen 1992). In her book, *Gold and Workers: A People's History of South Africa (1886 -1924)* Callinicos (2014), demonstrates how the history of mobilization trajectories among African miners (regardless of nationality) could be traced back to the African Mineworkers Union (AMWU) which was formed in the 1940s and "heroically managed to organize 80.000 Black miners, closed in compounds, to go on strike in 1946" (2014: iv). While all Black workers were then still denied the right to unionize, their defiance as a united force and solidarity based on common grievances most importantly the desire to move freely without passes, culminated in the dismantling of the apartheid system. Nonetheless, the euphoria brought about by the 1994 dispensation was soon translated into bigotry towards those from outside the borders, with an exclusivist nationalism centered on the privilege of citizenship pushing the racial issue into the background.

1.2   The Case of the Hospitality Sector

Following the downturn of apartheid's state-centered migration regime gravitating on the mining sector, new service-oriented sectors (construction, hospitality, finance) have moved into the foreground in a globalized South Africa scheme of capital accumulation; not least the hospitality sector which became one of the fastest growing sectors of the entire economy. This presents, as I have argued in detail elsewhere (Munakamwe 2018), opportunities to analyze how the emerging unregulated, 'post-migrant labor regime' has impacted union organizing strategies. It is, in the context, significant that the expansion of the hospitality sector has coincided with feminization, as younger women have come to constitute a large share of workers on the move. The hospitality sector is not only expanding but has stimulated employment in the economy and evolved as a key magnet attracting migrant workers to metropolitan Johannesburg and other large cities in the context of the post-migrant labor regime. The evolution of the sector presents challenges to debates and theories on labor, migration, gender dynamics and solidarity. It renders itself to individualistic and clandestine mobility and exposes the emergence of a fragmented and diminishing solidarity. This demonstrates the need for a new understanding of the emergent sectors that attract migrant workers and puts intricate questions on the table concerning political subjectivity, political mobilization and transversal solidarities amongst local and migrant workers. It highlights, as well, needs to analyze how the unregulated, post-migrant labor regime has shaped political subjectivities among trade unions. The sector is predominantly female and invokes the need for a gender analysis of union responses to migrant labor.

While employment in the mining sector has dwindled, hospitality is an example of a new emerging sector that attracts migrant workers despite the absence of any formal arrangements between sending and hosting countries as was the case with the migrant labor system to the mines and commercial farms. As such, many are undocumented and for those who are in possession of work permits, the lifespan of their work contracts is habitually benchmarked alongside the former. Historically, male migrants were recruited from diverse countries in the southern African region to work in the mines. In fact, the democratization of South Africa was a culmination of strong unity and solidarity forged among migrant miners who at that time included those from former homelands (internal migrants) and cross-border migrants from the region. Today, feminization of migration has paved the way for new gendered struggles and solidarities. This involves also contending stereotypes that perceive highly feminized sectors as non-receptive to unions and thus, unorganizable (Munakamwe 2008).

The case of the hospitality sector invites, accordingly, an in-depth analysis of how we should rethink migration today and how political subjectivities among both local and migrant workers change over time. That the hospitality sector has become a dominant recruiter of migrant labor in the post migrant labor regime dovetails with a general trend towards intensive use of temporary transnational migrant labor across the globe (Valiani 2012). A multifarious exploitation of temporary, clandestine and at times, undocumented migrants who are very often hired as casuals, with exceptionally precarious employment and working conditions, and without guaranteed wages evidently tends to undermine the power of unions.

The increased use of temporary migrant labor may be viewed as a more recent strategy of employers and states to shift power away from workers and unions following from the successes of worker and union power in both the global North and South circa 1950 to 1980. (Valiani 2012; Valiani 2013b). In fact, the hospitality industry in South Africa relies predominantly on migrant labor (see SWOP 2012; Jinnah and Cazarin 2014). It is recorded as an exploitative sector that leverage on flexible employment contracts and very low wages. Very often, workers engage in other economic activities to supplement their meagre wages or seek supplementary part-time jobs (see Alberti 2014). Informal employment relations are common (see Jinnah and Cazarin 2014). Casualization, outsourcing, stealthy labor broking, temporary employment contracts and high turn overs tend to undermine union organization, and the rate of unionization in the sector is, with exception of labor in agriculture, the lowest in South Africa (NALEDI 2005). Yet, migrants experience it as a niche industry to earn a living and remittances to send back for sustaining social reproduction in the communities of origin (see Jinnah and Cazarin 2014).

It is an exceedingly labor-intensive industry marked by irregular hours, low wages and a lack of job security. Employees, with the exception of people in senior and middle management, face poor working conditions, low wages and casualization, and the sector is segmented according to migration status, gender, reflected in differential employment contracts. Some migrant workers are highly qualified, but exposed to extreme deskilling (see Munakamwe 2018), in this increasingly informalized and precarious sector. It epitomizes, as such the flipside of the so-called post-migrant labor regime, characterized by economic restructuring, massive job losses and progressive marginalization of migrant miners (see Budlender 2013). For example, the annual report of the Labor Report Service (LRS 2012), documented that in the hospitality sector, workers operate under a high pressure of job insecurity with constant threats of retrenchments. According to a research by NALEDI (2005), more than 70% of workers in the sector are not covered by collective agreements or Bargaining Councils. This means that most workers in the industry are protected only by the sectoral determination (SD). Essentially, SD is the minimum wage and work conditions laid down by the Minister of Labor to protect workers in industries that are seen as particularly vulnerable to exploitation and where there is a very low level of representation by unions. Retrenchment threats make it difficult to push for financial benefits (wages) within the collective bargaining process (HSRC 2005). Hence, a few or no protests have occurred in this sector since the democratization of the country.

The excessive vulnerability and fragmented solidarity between local and foreign nationals has to some extent been blamed on the increased number of migrant workers in the sector, which is also seen to pose a challenge to organizing efforts by unions (LRS 2012: 22). Thus, migrant workers are described as "an easy target for management" like in the quotation from the LRS report below:

> [T]hey do not know their rights or are willing to give them up in order to keep their jobs. This vulnerability makes immigrants popular with management as they are cheaper and easier to control. On the other hand it sows divisions among workers who see immigrants as destroying the hard won gains for conditions that South Africans have fought for as well as making it more difficult for locals to get jobs. Where immigrants have joined unions, it is reported that South African workers are not always willing to join the union if they see that foreigners have joined it. (2012: 22).

In the process, however, conflicts in the hospitality sector lay bare the emergence of new political subjectivities in a post migrant labor regime, among nationals as well as migrants.

2 A Contorted World City Built by Migrants

Labor migration to Johannesburg could be traced back to early industrialization in the colonial era when diamonds were discovered in Kimberley and gold in the Witwatersrand (see Callinicos 2014). The development of the city is intricately linked to the apartheid legacy and its contract migrant labor system (predominantly male). In the 'post-migrant labor regime', it has become the major hub for young female migrants who seek an economic safety net in domestic services, retail, and hospitality.

Johannesburg came into existence before the nation state of South Africa, and migrant workers co-founded and developed the city. Thus, this beautiful city, popularly known as *Egoli*,[3] is the product of the work of both internal migrant labor from former 'homelands' and those from the entire southern Africa region. Today, the City of Johannesburg is home to a dynamic population of communities, tracing their background from within as well as outside the borders of the present republic of South Africa. Since the early 1990s,

3 Colloquial term derived from its association of large gold deposits.

a large number of people have migrated to the city from the country's rural areas, and a growing stream of international migrants have been seeking refuge, new economic opportunities, or both (Gotz and Landau 2004, 13).

Since the discovery of mineral deposits such as gold in South Africa in 1896, Johannesburg has been the primary destination for migrants from the southern African region (see Callinicos 2014) and continues to be so today. Migrant laborers were recruited in labor sending countries such as Malawi, Mozambique, Lesotho, and Botswana to work in the mines on the West Rand and East Rand regions of the City of Johannesburg. As the City became well established, migrants were also recruited to work as laborers, domiciled in central Johannesburg which by time became the site of struggles and the emplacement of solidarity directed against the brutal apartheid system. One of the migrant hostel sites in Johannesburg was subsequently developed into a Workers Museum, which documents migrant workers' trajectories, living and working conditions. Historically and in contemporary South Africa, the city holds an important position in the making and unmaking of solidarities. The historical dimension is well documented by numerous scholars. But it is important to interrogate the transition taking place in the post 1994 epoch, which coincided with the decline in recruitment of migrant miners and the emergence of the service and hospitality sector. The City's response to migrants exposes much about how it positions itself within the global village in its ambition to become a world-class city of the 'post migrant labor regime'.

However, tensions have been noted over the years triggered by a sharp decline in job opportunities in the manufacturing sector, which for many decades was a key source of employment. After 1994, migrants moving into South Africa, to seek a better life, employment, income opportunities, refuge and asylum have become an increasingly important source of hyper-exploited workers, who have often been met by animosity by the native precariat.

Johannesburg has, in tandem with this, come to be exposed at the epicenter of xenophobic attacks against migrants, taking off in poor Black communities such as Soweto, Hillbrow, Orange Farm, Alexandra and Diepsloot. In January 1995 armed gangs in Alexandra frog marched suspected 'illegal' foreign nationals to police stations in an attempt to purge migrants in a campaign dubbed '*Buyel'ekhaya*' which is a Nguni expression for '*go back home*' (Munakamwe 2020). In September 1998 a Mozambican and two Senegalese were thrown out of a train by a group returning from a rally that accused foreigners for unemployment, crime and spreading AIDS. In 2008 for example, at the core of the attacks were serious allegations concerning city officials who were involved in corruption in which foreign nationals were awarded government subsided housing, so-called RDP houses. The township of Alexandra in Johannesburg was the epicenter of the attacks. There is a strong perception that local government officials sell RDP houses to foreign nationals. In a context where housing is in heavy demand, conflict between locals and migrants is rampant.

In response, the city has been developing a long-term strategy to curb episodic and sporadic xenophobic attacks to integrate migrants, particularly those with critical skills required by the contemporary labor market. According to Gotz and Landau (2004):

> *Joburg 2030* and other official documents have already begun to outline strategies for recruiting and incorporating highly skilled migrants and foreign capital into the city's socio-economic networks. However, it is also increasingly evident that Johannesburg's leaders and citizens feel overwhelmed – if not threatened – by migration, and especially the movement of people from the rest of the continent (2004, 14).

As mentioned earlier, the City of Johannesburg strives to be a world class city and as such, seeks to minimize publicity related to xenophobia, if not to completely eradicate it. The City is a major hub for regional and international trade, and there is an awareness that investors may shun channeling capital to cities marked by rampant socio-economic insecurity and political instability. Thus, the leadership of the City has been involved in the development of robust programs to strategically reposition and rebrand its image.

2.1   *Rebranding Egoli: Emplacing Transversal Solidarity?*

In 2007, the metropolitan administration of the City of Johannesburg officially established the Migrant Help Desks as part of its long-term strategy to curb xenophobia and encourage social cohesion across all six regions under its jurisdiction. In the aftermath of the brutal 2008 xenophobic attacks, the Joburg Migrant Advisory Committee (JMAC), was officially launched on the 6th of October 2009. A multi-stakeholder panel, the Johannesburg Migrant Advisory Panel (JMAP) comprising representatives of the City departments, provincial and national government departments, international organizations, academia, various civil society role players, migrant-rights organizations, faith-based organizations, and small-enterprises was appointed to support the MHD; its mandate being to ensure migration issues are mainstreamed to promote 'social inclusive programs and initiatives within the City of Joburg'. Programming is issue-based and coordinated by working groups which report quarterly to the JMAC. The four working groups include the Health and Social Assistance (housing and shelter); Business and Economic (banking, street trading and by-laws); Education, Training and Labor including Safety

Justice and Immigration. However, trade unions are not represented in any of these fora.

The city also developed a Social Cohesion Program Implementation Plan to address fragmentation and exclusion from social services based on either socio-economic status, ethnicity or migration status. Today, the city collaborates with civil society organizations and conducts anti-xenophobia dialogues in communities aimed at educating and raising awareness on the role of migrants from historical and contemporary contexts. In 2011, the City was part of the multi-stakeholders coordinated by the Southern Africa Women's Institute for Migration Affairs (SAWIMA) to roll out social cohesion dialogues across the six regions. Other stakeholders included the African Diaspora Workers Network (ADWN), the South African Football Players Union (SAFPU), and the social movement Show Me Your Number (SMYN). The trade union, SAFPU organizes football players, and has been instrumental in reinforcing social cohesion and solidarity between locals and migrants, working closely with other civil society organizations, the City of Johannesburg, and Gauteng Provincial Legislature. SAFPU fully subscribes to the principle of international solidarity as many of its members at one point find themselves working abroad or traveling to other countries for matches. For many years, the union has been mobilizing its members to participate in anti-xenophobia campaigns and to act as peace ambassadors. Several soccer players have featured on local televisions and radio stations 'preaching' African unity and solidarity.

In the same spirit and according to the same principle, the Ubuntu multi-stakeholder collective hosted a seminal social cohesion match dubbed 'Ubuntu Derby' match, in which one South African Premier Soccer League (PSL) team, Pirates played against Dynamos, a leading PSL Team from Zimbabwe. This match brought together locals and cross-border migrants to share space in one of the best soccer fields sponsored by the City as part of the anti-xenophobia campaigns. This project aimed to promote social cohesion and peaceful integration between locals and foreign nationals in and around selected townships and also targeting infamous epicenters of xenophobic violence: Soweto, Hillbrow, Orange Farm, Alexandra and Diesploot.

Programs aimed at social cohesion were put in place by the local government in collaboration with civic organizations, and xenophobic attacks relatively subsided for a short while. However, in February 2017, fresh attacks on foreigners re-surfaced and fifteen houses belonging to foreign nationals were burnt down to ashes in what locals attributed to 'witch-hunting' for drug lords and pimps. The 2017 attacks were blamed on reckless utterances by the Johannesburg Mayor who in December 2016, labelled foreign nationals as criminals and as relegating the beautiful City to a 'jungle'. In response, to the Johannesburg Mayor's public statement and subsequent visit to a predominantly immigrant suburb in the southern part of the city on a 'witch-hunting' mission for drug lords and pimps, a group of South Africans based in the capital city, Pretoria, self-organized with the aim of 'driving out' all foreign nationals as they believed the latter were stealing their jobs. Having been sanctioned by authorities, they marched to the government buildings in Pretoria and handed a memorandum requesting the government to act on the issue of immigrants and threatened to take civilian action if their demands were ignored.

On the 27th of February 2019, the Cabinet of South Africa approved a National Action Plan to Combat Racism, Racial Discrimination, Xenophobia and Related Intolerance (NAP). The Department of Justice and Constitutional Development (DoJ and CD) launched the NAP on the 25th of March 2019 whose key ideal is to "reinforce the culture of human rights within the spirit of our Constitution and democracy".[4] However, as a somber shadow of the NAP launch, xenophobic attacks took place in Durban. Xenophobic attacks have, consequently, remained a common feature in South Africa, and particularly during national and local government elections as political candidates instrumentalize the issue of migration to vindicate or dismiss allegations related to poor service delivery, crime, and limited resource distribution. Furthermore, migrants are blamed for the high unemployment while unions remain complacent except for a few like the earlier mentioned SAFPU. Yet, current research from North America, championing the development of 'solidary cities' in defense of migrant rights, demonstrate that inclusionary cities need to understand complex transversal solidarities, underpinned by strong committed trade unions as a critical link.[5]

3   Solidarity "On Global Appeal"?

At the time of concluding this chapter (Summer 2021), none of the most influential unions have committed themselves sincerely to craft truly proficient policies, whether on national, regional or city level. They remain ambivalent on their position towards migrant labor although some have begun to embrace migrant workers stirred by an inducement to 'solidarity on global appeal'. It is a selective approach to organizing that demonstrates unions'

---

4   National Action Plan to Combat Racism, Racial Discrimination, Xenophobia and Related Intolerance (NAP). http://www.justice.gov.za/docs/other-docs/nap.htm.
5   See, for example, the chapter by de Graauw and Gleeson in this volume.

failure to acknowledge the heterogeneity among the post-apartheid South African precariat that paves the way for super-exploitation, wage dumping, and xenophobia.

On a different but related note, despite its rebranding efforts the metropolitan administration of the City of Johannesburg is somehow complacent in reproducing circular migrants through its by-laws that enforce immigration laws, while local authorities fail to develop strategies to document migrants (see Gotz and Landau 2004). Instead, the issue of 'migration' continues to be instrumentalized during local government elections, with the foreign presence in the land being blamed for poor service delivery, housing deficits and crime. In the post 1994 epoch, despite noble liberation rhetoric, the economy did not transform, neither was the wealth redistributed, with the result being deepened poverty and bigotry against foreign nationals. This was further exacerbated by utterances from the highest echelons of power, who looted the country dry, and then conveniently, and deceptively, shifted blame to migrants and in so doing created 'us' and 'them' among the urban poor in the city. In other words, migrants within the city continue to present a convenient scapegoat for the failure of government and corrupt politicians.

Nonetheless, over the years progressive civil society movements have played a very critical role in lobbying the metropolitan administration to integrate migrants. As mentioned earlier, the City of Johannesburg has established an exclusive Migrant Help Desk to support migrants in various ways and observes all international days related to migration such as Africa Day, Refugee Day, and International Migrants Day. The City subscribes to the spirit and letter of the national Constitution and as such, pledges its support to inclusive transversal solidarity formation although this is not clearly articulated in its policies. This could be a tactic to avoid 'shooting itself' in the foot given the constrained resources to provide infrastructure and social services indiscriminately (see Gotz and Landau 2004).

The union that organizes municipal workers, the South African Municipal Workers Union (SAMWU) which is also an affiliate of the Public Service International (PSI), has been advocating for peaceful integration of casual workers and migrants in the City and has since established a Migrant Help Desk as well. The PSI has been supporting its affiliates in different national contexts to organize and integrate migrants.

But in general, unions have continued to neglect workers who fall outside of standard employment and as a result, their rights are gradually diminishing along the decent work continuum (e.g. Buhlungu 2010). Particularly affected are migrant workers who contribute immensely to South Africa's sprawling urban economies, although they are deprived of their labor rights by state crafted migration policies and laws. While unions do acknowledge the vulnerability of those who fall outside standard employment, their organizing strategies are nevertheless guided by normative discourses of 'formality', negatively biased towards those working in the formal economy, and 'illegality' concerning migrants. On the one hand, unions sincerely acknowledge that migrant workers are vulnerable while on the other hand, they stereotype migrants as being passive and submissive to the dictates of capitalism by undercutting wages. Yet such 'acquiescence' may be seen as the very result of a representation gap by unions (see Webster 2008).

Nevertheless, a slight shift can be noted in terms of an emerging discourse that pays particular attention to migrant workers and in response to civil society supplications for social cohesion and the emergence of alternative worker organizations such as worker advice offices, public litigation organizations including migrant-rights organizations. Particularly noteworthy is that SACCAWU, The South African Commercial, Catering and Allied Workers Union, which among other represents hospitality workers is one of the few affiliates of the legendary Congress of South African Trade Unions (COSATU) that has committed itself to organize workers who fall outside of standard employment, such as casual, outsourcing, scheduling, short term contracts and temporary employment status (see LRS 2012; Hlatshwayo 2013). Moreover, SACCAWU stands out as an example of a proactive union relating positively to the quandary of migrant workers. However, while there is a high level of conscientization at national level, the opposite continues, seemingly to stand out concerning the union's shop stewards at shop floor level, who are still reluctant to embrace migrant workers (see LRS 2012).

As part of its strategy, SACCAWU set up an exclusive desk that runs campaigns such as anti-xenophobia and educational programs on international worker solidarity. Moreover, it supports its sister unions from within the SADC region such as Zimbabwe with material support such as office furniture, computers, stationery, and other as part of its strategy to promote union to union solidarity (Munakamwe 2018). Similarly, it aspires to promote worker to worker solidarity through the International Union Federation (IUF) which is a Global Union federation (GUF) that it is affiliated to. Moreover, the union is also well known for its progressive approaches to championing workers' rights. It is the first union in the country to win gender related demands for workers such as maternity protection and workplace childcare facilities.[6] In its endeavor to

---

6   Interview conducted by author with Patricia Nyman, SACCAWU Gender Co-ordinator, 05/05/2014. Union Head Office, Braamfontein, Johannesburg.

organize migrant workers, the union has established links with some migrant rights organizations and local worker advice offices, with the idea of supporting efforts to fight xenophobia in the workplace. In an interview, Mike Abrahams, the then spokesperson of the union declared the union's support towards organizing and uniting "all workers regardless of their country of origin" (quoted in Hlatshwayo 2013, 275).

While in principle the union has demonstrated a strong resolve to organize migrant workers in the hospitality sector, it still needs to clarify its position by developing clear policy to provide guidelines and organizing strategy. For instance, the recruitment form still requires one to provide the 'Green' identity card number. In an informal interview with the then National Organizer about the content matter of the recruitment form, he acknowledged that indeed it required review to accommodate passport holders (Munakamwe 2018). In its determination to organize migrant workers, the union is confronted by a plethora of challenges which include meagre financial resources and human resources. Quality organizing and service delivery requires ample resources which could be derived from workers subscriptions, the most reliable source of revenue for unions. Given the kind of flexible contracts in the sector coupled with a high turnover, prospects of achieving this goal might be futile. Aside, an attempt to reconcile local and migrant workers requires adequate human resources to render services to all members. Thus, while there, in principle, exists a strong political will and alliances to organize migrant workers, this endeavor still tends to be blocked by inadequacy of resources.

The other challenge is that of unrealistic expectations by migrant rights organizations (MROs) as allied partners. For example, in November 2016, I witnessed a situation whereby one of the MRO leaders called the National Organizer with the impression that a group of migrant workers were keen to join the union. The National Organizer abandoned his schedule for the day (of which one of such was a follow-up interview with me) with the hope to recruit new members. Unexpectedly, he landed himself in a hearing for one of the migrant workers in which he was left without choice but participate as an observer in the absence of an informed briefing. Subsequently, he advised the affected worker to postpone the case until such a date when the union had been fully informed and after she had formalized her relationship with the union to be allowed external representation in the internal hearing. This observation was such an enlightening moment as it revealed some of the underlying technicalities of forging alliances between traditional unions and MROs. Trade unions operate in a more formalized environment while MROs are often informal structures established out of emotions and limited with respect to service delivery to their members. Furthermore, MROs do not fall within the formal tripartite arrangement which is formally recognized at NEDLAC and in many ways are not eligible to represent workers in labor disputes.

A further 'technical challenge' is that of undocumented migrants. While the union is clear about embracing migrant workers, still it cannot be found operating outside of the country's laws (in the case of undocumented migrants) although there is room to assist and advice undocumented workers with labor disputes lodged at the Commission for Conciliation, Mediation and Arbitration (CCMA). Nevertheless, altogether, compared to other unions in South Africa, SACCAWU stands out as a good example. Significantly, migrant workers, and particularly those in vulnerable sectors, have become keener to join unions, which appears evident judging from interactions on social media platforms such as Facebook and WhatsApp (Munakamwe 2018).

This corroborates data gathered through participant observation and shadowing, which reveal that migrants are not docile as they have begun to self-organize. This includes self-representation in labor disputes underpinned by collegial support through social media networks, in particular WhatsApp and Facebook (see Ueno 2014). The current workforce in the hospitality sector comprises young female and male workers who are articulate in the use of digital technology and social media in their thirst to improve their everyday working conditions and livelihood. Considering this development, some trade unions have begun to open up their doors after realizing that not only are migrant workers keen to self-organize but also that local young workers who fall outside of unions are actively participating through social media platforms in a strong desire to belong and to be recognized.

Yet, the fact that, aside from the case of SACCAWU, trade unions in general are still reluctant to organize and represent workers who fall outside of standard employment. This has provoked the emergence of new forms of worker organizations outside the traditional union model. Thus, various alternative organizing models offer potential for mobilization of migrant workers and help to provide much needed legal representation and support for migrant workers. Emerging social movements, worker advice offices, migrant rights organizations, *pro bono* legal centers including private legal firms strive to cover the union representation gap by traversing a broader spectrum of issues beyond the workplace, including community challenges like xenophobia. However, while such models of representation may address social and legal needs, they tend to leave out exigencies such as wages and working conditions, which pertain to the collective bargaining process at the NEDLAC level.

Thus, there is a need for broad and composite alliances between, for example, trade unions and migrant-oriented advice offices, which could serve to invigorate trust in traditional national trade unions among immigrant workers

(Wilderman, et al. 2016). Such alliances could offer complementary strengths. For example, migrant-rights organizations could assist in identifying and mobilizing migrant workers while traditional trade unions could take up migrant specific needs and issues at the collective bargaining table, targeting specific employers and institutions as well as bringing added resources and capacity to organize and advocate for migrant workers' rights. In this way, complementing strengths and shortcomings of migrant oriented advice centers and collaboration with trade unions, would allow both sides to build greater power and unity for workers. In this context, the power of emerging social movements like *#outsourcingmustfall* (Phanyeko 2017) should not be under-estimated as these could be vehicles to unite all workers based on their status in the labor market as causals, outsourced and labor brokered, irrespective of nationality.

Drawing from the case of SACCAWU, GUFs have embarked on shaping trade union responses to migrant workers in positive ways despite resistance and challenges dependent on national contexts. There is thus an emerging potential for local unions in South Africa to organize migrant workers with the support of global labor federations. This may serve to ensure that all workers fully enjoy their universal labor rights and the fruits of democracy regardless of nationality or geo-political dynamics. Yet, for trade unions, the presence of many migrant workers in the labor market requires a shift from a 'national outlook' model (Ryan 2005), in organizing a fresh scope for labor mobilizing. In a way, going forward through the past, considering the challenges facing South African unions and the global unions at large, mobilizing migrant workers offers a platform for labor to organize across scales – locally, nationally, and transnationally, on a strategic basis in a way that departs from orthodox 'citizenship or local worker' approaches towards worker internationalism (Webster, et al. 2008).

4   Imagineering Transversal Solidarities

Focused through a Gramscian lens it is important to distinguish between economic class and political class (e.g. Boothman 2008) in understanding how migrant workers are integrally emasculated as they are deprived of both economic and political power. Clearly, the xenophobic attacks on migrants in South Africa experienced over the years point to the domination of precaritized local citizens as against their migrant counterparts. At the same time, the strategic reorientation of unions in the post-apartheid period has, as I have argued in the preceding, tended to prioritize 'international solidarity' traversing national borders (see Hlatshwayo 2017), while ignoring the precarious state of migrant workers who are already within the nation. This orientation encourages union-to union-solidarity while paying little attention to transversal solidarity between native and migrant workers (Munakamwe 2018).

This dovetails unwittingly with the neoliberal collusion of state and business that has devised new covert ways of ensuring maximization of profits by exploiting cheap, and often clandestine, migrant labor, embraced by the so-called 'post-migrant labor regime'. Thus, business exploits a continued position of dominance in the ensuing post-apartheid hegemony, to craft and instrumentalize migration laws and policies that reinforces intricate divisions among workers-based inclusion-exclusion into/from citizenship and which, in consequence, paves the way for xenophobic attacks. Unions, on their part, have, as detailed in the preceding, done little to organize migrant workers in the post-apartheid period and are also quick to criticize self-organizing among the migrant precariat. This reflects conflicting power relations, inequalities and citizenship biases among what Gramsci refers to as the 'subaltern'. Homogenizing struggles tends to overshadow the politics of difference. Thus, not least, the issue of 'race' remains a poorly analyzed category, pertinent to migration and labor in the post-apartheid 'Rainbow Nation'. It is, inherently, exploited politically as a fundamental dividing line traversing other social markers such as gender, income, and skill among a proliferating multitude of working poor.

Thus, the argument by Milkman (2006) that unions still tend to perceive immigrants as 'unorganizable' is indeed valid for an analysis of union strategies in post-apartheid South Africa; and this without in depth analysis of structural factors underlying precarity and clandestinity, and without self-introspecting their own strategies which may deter migrants from joining unions in favor of a preference for self-organizing or joining other alternative worker organizations (Munakamwe 2018). Yet, the advancement in information technology presents emerging opportunities and techniques for reaching out to all workers, using digital tools for political mobilization, and in particular related to migrants who, else, tend to be viewed as 'invisible' or 'unreachable' (Segatti and Munakamwe 2014). In the 21st century workers across the globe are increasingly connected through social media (see Ueno 2011; 2014). Most importantly, global union federations (GUFs) have started to play a critical role in worker-to- worker solidarity effected through social media. GUFs bring together workers and trade unions sector wise across the globe. They thus play an organizing role in ensuring that their affiliates, particularly in destination countries embrace migrant workers into their ranks. This has also started to embrace a more inclusive stance towards migrant labor. For instance, with the support of the global federation, International Union of Food, Agricultural, Hotel,

Restaurant, Catering, Tobacco and Allied Workers' Associations (IUF) the South African Commercial, Catering and Allied Workers Union (SACCAWU) has begun to organize migrant and casual workers in the hospitality sector. Yet, overall, migrant workers are still marginally represented as South African unions are ambivalent and slow in developing explicit policies to specifically address issues and vulnerabilities associated with the new post-apartheid migrancy, ideologically hinging on an orthodox Marxist Universalist approach that maintains the dogma of a homogenous working class (Munakamwe 2018).

The present has laid bare organizing strategies of unions which are still ambivalent coupled with blurry migration policies. Unions are caught up in conflicting views of how to respond to migrant labor and this quandary is further compounded by negative ramifications of the neoliberal policies that have resulted in debilitating workplace restructuring, labor market flexibility and deregulation. On the one hand there is the desire to preserve jobs for natives and to enforce immigration laws that are crafted by proponents of a discriminatory neoliberalism while, on the other hand, the aim is to seek legitimacy by responding to the dictates and principles of international solidarity (see Fine 2014a).

However, as I have related to in detail in the preceding, the largest union in the hospitality sector, SACCAWU has initiated organization of migrants, including casual and irregular workers, and this initiative is supported at global level through its global union federation. I have further discussed how self-organizing is taking place parallel to these breakaway union efforts. In their interface with migrant workers, unions need to understand discourses of agency and vulnerabilities which could facilitate or constrain organizing efforts. Most importantly, there is need to appreciate that while discourses of vulnerability tend to overshadow the agency of these workers, they are not passive, but may be demobilized by structurally embedded blockages, in particular institutional xenophobia manifested through migration laws and outright physical xenophobic violence (see Hayem 2013; Misago 2011, Munakamwe 2018). While xenophobic tendencies have been overtly elicited in the hospitality sector, this is subtle in the mining sector, where workers are more united based on historical ties forged during the struggles against apartheid (see Buhlungu and Bezuidenhout 2008).

The current workplace is constantly changing as a result of neoliberal policies and so is the workforce which has become increasingly precarious (see Standing 2011) regardless of nationality. Thus, unions need to move out of their comfort zone and further devise transformative strategies and demands on the collective bargaining table from a fixation on 'bread and butter' issues to non-traditional social and policy related demands such as those related to documentation of migrant workers who stand as their potential members. Unions in alliance with civil society and non-governmental organizations (Jinnah 2012), and reforming city administrations, could influence crafting of more tolerant and embracing migration laws and policies (see Crush 1995) to guarantee all who live and work in South Africa (regardless of origin and nationality) full access to the 'fruits of democracy' and universal rights as provided for in the Bill of Rights of the national Constitution (Coplan and Thoahlane 1995), including international labor conventions and human rights law. This includes eliminating barriers represented by national immigration laws that acquiesce and emasculate migrant workers power and agency. International labor instruments such as the ILO Migrant Workers Convention 143 and the wider international human rights framework provide alternative routes in recourse to justice and workers' rights as they are universally designed to serve all workers.

Partnerships between trade unions and local migrant-oriented advice offices, in line with those established in Johannesburg in efforts to curb xenophobia, could serve to not only restore confidence, but might invigorate trust in traditional national trade unions amongst immigrant workers (Wilderman, et al. 2016). In terms of alternative representation various models of association and representation have emerged which include social movements, worker advice offices, migrant-rights organizations, and *pro bono* legal centers, including private legal firms, which endeavor to close the representation gap and while addressing a broader spectrum of issues beyond the workplace, involving to community challenges like xenophobia. Similarly, the example of Johannesburg, proves that South African cities have realized the significant economic contribution of migrants and are thus making efforts to ensure smoother integration and social cohesion. Unions have been criticized for clinging to traditional ways of organizing, yet the workforce is dynamic, calling for unions to shift strategies and tactics to embrace migrant workers. As argued by Castel Branco (2015), unions are "sites of struggle between competing interests and visions, capable of shifting direction, strategies and tactics" (2015, 99). Indeed, unions are caught in a cross draft between the desire to comply with national laws designed to protect jobs for natives, and the wider mission and obligation of satisfying the principles of international worker solidarity. Thus, it appears reasonable to conclude that, as every sector of the economy is being forced to change due to global neoliberalism, it is equally important for trade unions to shift their demographic focus and traditional ways of organizing, whether on the local and city level, the national level, or transnationally.

Intriguingly, at the time of concluding this paper (August 2021), Jolidee Matongo the son of a migrant worker from Zimbabwe and a local Zulu mother from KwaZulu Natal was unopposed elected Mayor of the City of This brings a new promising dimension into the complex political drama of transversal solidarity versus xenophobic bigotry discussed in the preceding. Matongo was born, bred and educated in Soweto, Johannesburg. However, despite his citizenship acquired at birth and also based on his mother, his appointment triggered controversy and seditious xenophobic attacks on both mainstream and social media platforms. For those who grew up with him in Soweto and voted him as ward councilor (a pre-requisite for one to contest for the post) identify him as one of their 'own' while assemblages from other wards could not understand why 'a migrant would lead the largest commercial city in the country'. In response to media inquiries on the matter, Matongo clearly pointed out that he was a bona fide citizen and 'had never been to Zimbabwe' even though his father hailed from that country. Some political analysts were of the view that the appointment of a descendant of a migrant was a cosmetic' publicity grandstanding as the country was heading towards local government plebiscite in October, 2021. In other words, none of the parties in the Council were keen to second candidates or contest such a short-time framed political hence no contestations regarding particular social markers of interested runners. However, as if by fate, meeting an sudden death in a traffic accident by mid-September 2021, 'the migrant' was to serve for the shortest period of time in the history of this powerful political position.

References

Alberti, G. (2014). "Organizing Intersecting Identities: Trade Unions and Precarious Migrant Workers across the Atlantic". *Conference Paper: XVIII ISA World Congress of Sociology, July 2014.* Conference: XVIII ISA World Congress of Sociology.

Allen, V. (1992). *History of Black Mineworkers in South Africa: The techniques of resistance, 1871–1948.* I. Keighley: Moor Press.

Arrighi, G. (1973). "Labour Supplies in Historical Perspectives: A study of the Proletarianisation of the African Peasantry in Rhodesia" In Arrighi, G., and Soul, J.S. (1973) *Essays on the Political Economy of Africa. Journal of Development Studies*, 6, 197–234.

Boothman, D. (2008). "The sources for Gramsci's concept of hegemony". *Rethinking Marxism* 20.2 (2008): 201–215.

Budlender, D. (2013). "Improving the quality of available statistics on foreign labor in South Africa: Strategic recommendations". *MiWORC Report.* Johannesburg: University of the Witwatersrand.

Buhlungu, S. (2010). *A Paradox of Victory: COSATU and the Democratic Transformation in South Africa.* Pietermaritzburg: University of Kwazulu- Natal Press.

Buhlungu, S., and A. Bezuidenhout (2008). "Union solidarity under stress. The case of the national union of mineworkers in South Africa". *Labour Studies Journal, 33*(3), 262–287.

Burawoy, M. (1976). "The functions and reproduction of migrant labour: Comparative material from Southern Africa and the United States". *American Journal of Sociology,* 1050–1087.

Callinicos, L. (2014). "Gold and Workers 1886 - 1924". Online book. http://www.sahist ory.org.za/archive/gold-and-workers-1886-1924-luli-callinicos.

Castel–Branco, C.N. (2015). "Economics and Development Research Group, Institute for Social and Economic Studies (IESE), and Faculty of Economics, Eduardo Mondlane University, Maputo, Mozambique". *Review of African Political Economy,* *2014.* Vol. 41, No. S1, S26–S48, http://dx.doi.org/10.1080/03056244.2014.976363Routle dge, published online: 14 Jan 2015.

Coplan, D., and Thoahlane, T. (1995). "Motherless Households, Landless Farms: Employment Patterns among Lesotho Migrants" In Crush, J., and James, W. (eds) *Crossing Boundaries: Mine Migrancy in a Democratic South Africa.* Cape Town: Institute for Democracy in South Africa (IDASA) and the International Development Research Centre (Canada).

Crush, J. (1995). "Mine Migrancy in the contemporary era". *Crossing Boundaries: Mine Migrancy in a Democratic South Africa,* 14–32.

Crush, J. (1997). "Contract Migration to South Africa: Past, Present and Future". In Crush, J., and Veriava, F. (eds.), *Transforming South African Migration and Immigration Policy.* Papers Presented to the Green Paper Task Team on International Migration retoria: Department of Home Affairs.

Department of Labour (DoL). (2007). "Labour Migration and South Africa Parts 1 & 2". Annual Report. Labour Market Review. Retrieved May 5, 2017 from http://www.lab our.gov.za/DOL/.

Dodson, B. (1998). *Women on the move: Gender and cross-border migration to South Africa.* Idasa.

Fakier, K. (2012). "*Mobile Care*: Subverting Traditional Notions of Motherhood in a Precarious Society". University of Pretoria/SWOP.

Fine, J. (2014a). *Restriction and Solidarity in the New South Africa: COSATU's Complex Response to Migration and Migrant Workers in the Post-Apartheid Era.* Rutgers.

Fine, J. (2014b). "Movements Wrestling: Union Engagement with Migrant Worker Policy and Organizing in Comparative Perspective". Conference: XVIII ISA World Congress of Sociology, July 2014.

Forrest, K. 2013. "Marikana was not just about migrant labour". Mail & Guardian Online; 13 September 2013. mg.co.za/author/kally-forrest.

Gotz, G. and L.B. Landau (2004). Introduction in Landau, L.B. (ed.) "Forced Migrants in the New Johannesburg: Towards a Local Government Response". Forced Migration Studies Programme University of the Witwatersrand.

Gramsci, A. (1971). *Prison Notebooks.* New York: International Publishers.

Hayem, J. (2013). "From May 2008 to 2011: Xenophobic violence and national subjectivity in South Africa". *Journal of Southern African Studies, 39*(1), 77–97.

Hlatshwayo, M. (2013). "Immigrant Workers and COSATU: Solidarity versus National Chauvinism?" *Alternation Special Edition* 7 (2013) 267–293.

HSRC (2005). "A Review of the Economic Profile and Structure of the Hospitality Industry in South Africa: Investigations into Wages and Conditions of Employment in the Hospitality Sector. P5–42". Human Science Research council Annual Report 2005. www.hsrc.ac.za/uploads/pageContent/641/Full%20report.pdf.

Jinnah, Z. (2012). "We have to go into the bush": Understanding the responses of NGOs and government in addressing conditions faced by cross border migrant workers in Musina. Limpopo, South Africa. ACMS Research report 1–56.

Jinnah, Z., and R. Cazarin (2014) "Making guests feel comfortable: Migrancy and labour in the hospitality sector in South Africa". Migrating for Work Research Consortium (MiWORC) Report. www.miworc.org.zaFES-policybrief-6-migrancy-and-labour-in-hospitality-sector-in-sa.pdf.

LRS 2012 ANNUAL REPORT 2012, Woodstock South Africa

Ludwig, C., & Webster, E. (2017). Changing forms of power and municipal worker resistance in johannesburg. In *Southern Resistance in Critical Perspective,* Paret, Marcel, Carin Runciman, and Luke Sinwell, eds. (pp. 137–152). London: Routledge.

Milkman, R. (2006). *L.A. Story: Immigrant Workers and the Future of the U.S.* Labour Movement, New York: Russell Sage Foundation.

Misago, J.P. (2011). "Disorder in a Changing Society: Authority and the Micro-Politics of Violence". In Landau, L. (eds.) *Exorcising the Demons Within. Xenophobia, Violence and Statecraft in Contemporary South Africa.* Johannesburg: Wits University Press.

Mujere, J. (2015). "Platinum, poverty and protests: platinum mining and community protests around Rustenburg". Paper presented at a seminar hosted at Wits University's Society, Work and Development Institute (Swop).

Munakamwe, J. (2021). "'Selective Amnesia' and trade union exclusionary strategies in contemporary South Africa". *International Unions Rights, Vol 28, Issue 1.*

Munakamwe, J. (2020). "Looking at the facts, the law and the situation on the ground when it comes to migrants and the labour sector". *Paper presented at "Changing the Narrative on Migrants in South Africa and the region" Migration Workshops.* Internews and the African Centre for Migration Studies and Society. September – October, 2020.

Munakamwe, J. (2018). "Emerging political subjectivities in a post migrant labour regime: Mobilisation, participation and representation of foreign workers in South Africa (1980–2013)". Unpublished Thesis. Johannesburg: University of the Witwatersrand.

Munakamwe, J. (2008). *Challenges in Organising the gendered Home-based care workers in post-apartheid South Africa.* Unpublished thesis. Johannesburg: University of Witwatersrand.

Musabayana, J. (2014). *Support towards strengthening the labour migration governance in the SADC region. An update on process and issues.* Wits University 19 March 2014.

National Labour and Economic Development Institute (NALEDI) (2005). "Overview of South African Tourism and Hospitality Sector, South Africa". 1–101. Durban: University of Natal.

Nel, P.S., and R.H. Rooyen (1993). *South African Industrial Relations; Theory and Practice.* Second revised edition. National Book Printers, Pretoria.

Neocosmos, M. (2015). "The sickness of xenophobia, and the need for a politics of healing". *The Daily Maverick,* 2 February, 2015.Accessed April 8, 2019. https://www .dailymaverick.co.za/opinionista/2015-02-02-the-sickness-of-xenophobia-and-the -need-for-a-politics-of-healing/#.

Phanyeko, L. (2017). "OutsourcingLabourBrokingMustFall. R10, 000 Now!!" In Labasebenzi I. *Marxist paper of the Workers and Socialist Party.* February –July 2017. www.workers socialistparty.co.za.

Ryan, B. (ed.) (2005). *Labour Migration and Employment Rights.* London: The Institute of Employment Rights Johannesburg: Forced Migration Studies Programme. University of Witwatersrand.

Schierup, C.U. (2016). "Under the rainbow: Migration, precarity and people power in post-apartheid South Africa". In Schierup, C.U., and Jørgensen, M.B. (eds.) *Politics of Precarity: Migrant conditions, struggles and experiences,* Leiden: Brill: 276–316.

Segatti, A., and Munakamwe, J. (2014). "Mobilising Migrant Workers in the South African Post-Migrant Labour Regime: Precariousness, Invisibility and Xenophobia". *Paper presented at the International Sociological Association (ISA) Congress, XVIII ISA World Congress,* Yokohama, Japan. July 13–19, 2014.

Seidman, G. (1995). "Shafted: The Social Impact of Down-scaling in the OFS Goldfields" In Crush, J., and James, W. (eds.) *Crossing Boundaries: Mine Migrancy in a Democratic South Africa.* Cape Town: Institute for Democracy in South Africa (IDASA) and the International Development Research Centre (Canada).

Standing, G. (2011). *The Precariat: The new dangerous class.* London: Bloomsbury Academic.

Simelane, X., and Modisha, G. (2008). "From Formal to Informal Migrant Labour System: the impact of the changing nature of the migrant labour system on mining communities in Lesotho and Mozambique". *Paper presented at the XIV SASA Congress. 7th -10 July 2008.* Stellenbosch University.

Ueno, K. (2011). *Life Strategies of Women Working as Domestic Workers in Asia.* Kyoto: Sekaishisosha (in Japanese).

Ueno, K. (2014). *Facebook Activism by Foreign Domestic Workers in Singapore.* Conference Paper. XVIII ISA World Congress of Sociology. July 2014.

Underthun, A. (2015). "Stretching liminal spaces of work? Temporality, displacement and precariousness among transient hotel workers in Jordhus". In Lier, D., and

Underthun, A. (2015). *A Hospitable World? Organising work and workers in hotels and tourist resorts.* Oxon& New York: Routledge.

Valiani, S. (2012). *Rethinking Unequal Exchange: the global integration of nursing labour markets.* University of Toronto Press.

Valiani, S. (2013b.) "The Shifting Landscape of Contemporary Canadian Immigration Policy: The Rise of Temporary Migration and Employer-Driven Immigration". In Goldring, L., and Landolt, P. (eds.) *Producing and Negotiating Non-Citizenship: Precarious Legal Status in Canada,* pp. 55–70. Toronto: University of Toronto Press.

Von Holdt, K. (2002). "Social Movement Unionism: The Case of South Africa," *Work, Employment, and Society,* 16(2), 283–304.

Webster, E., R. Lambert, and A. Bezuidenhout (2008). *Grounding Globalisation: Labour in the Age of Insecurity.* Oxford: Blackwell.

Webster, E., and C. Bischoff (2011). "New Actors in Employment Relations in the Periphery: Closing the Representation Gap amongst Micro and Small Enterprises". *Relations Industrielles/ Industrial Relations* Vol. 66, No.1. 2011, p. 11–33. DOI: 10.2307/23078241.

Wilderman, J., R. Grawitzky, L. Lenka, C. Morris, J. Munakamwe, and A. Ryabuchuk (2016). "Worker Advice Offices in South Africa: Exploring Approaches to Organising and Empowering Vulnerable Workers". Johannesburg: Chris Hani Institute (CHI) and NALEDI.

Wolpe, H. (1972). "Capitalism and Cheap Labour-Power in South Africa: From Segregation to Apartheid". *Economy and Society* 1 (4): 425–5.

CHAPTER 6

Tactical Cosmopolitanism as Urban Negotiation

Diversity Management 'From Beside'

Loren B. Landau and Iriann Freemantle

The concepts of immigrant integration, transnationalism, and the nature of urban publics remain at the center of popular and political debate across much of the western world (Spencer and Charsley 2021; Schinkel 2018).[1] Although such concerns have been less evident in discussions of African cities and mobilities, increased interest in mobility within the global south is drawing additional attention to the urban spaces serving as destination and stations for migrants on the African continent (Cities Alliance 2021, OECD 2021). This raises fundamental questions about the actors, process, ethics and scales associated with urban becoming and community making (Landau 2021). The social heterogeneity and translocality of such spaces are fertile grounds for social experimentation drawing on variegated histories and moral systems (Simone 2001, 2004; Appadurai 1996).

Amidst these transforming and emergent urban spaces, this chapter identifies a form of 'tactical cosmopolitan' that outsiders develop through interactions with potentially inhospitable people and places. Unable – or uninterested – in addressing sources of structural exclusion, this discursive mechanism reflects a kind of usufruct ethics: a means of establishing rights to space aimed at achieving protection and benefit without communal membership or community cohesion. Rather than a coherent philosophy, this is a form of 'cosmopolitanism from below' (Portes 1997), an amalgam of rhetorical and organizational tools chosen magpie-like from more established discourses and value systems. It is a kind of 'thin' cosmopolitanism (Roudometof 2005: 113) that instrumentalizes rather than commits to its power and universalist duties.

As 'tactical' cosmopolitans, migrants avoid the kind of lengthy battles associated with 'insurgent citizenship' (Holsten 2008), 'peripheral urbanization' (Caldeira 2017) or 'waiting' (Oldfield and Greyling 2015), oriented toward state recognition and incorporation into a stable, often sedentary polis. Rather, our

---

1 This chapter draws explicitly on three of the authors' previously published works: Landau and Freemantle (2016; 2010) and Landau (2015)

work in the 'urban estuaries' (Landau 2014) of Nairobi, Kenya and Johannesburg, South Africa, suggests a form of politics that challenges presumptions about the desirability of robust social connection, representation and spatially bound membership. For many of the residents described here, tactical cosmopolitanism is rooted in utilitarian extraction, not a desire for shared identity or enduring bonds. In the exploration of this practice, this paper contributes to ongoing debates on cosmopolitanism 'from below', conceptualized not as a philosophy but as a practice shaped by contexts of exclusion and marginality. In doing so, we problematize teleological discussions of immigrant integration by recognizing the multiple spatial and temporal scales which migrants seek and negotiate membership.

While an ethics of instrumentality and disconnection shape socialities in both Nairobi and Johannesburg, the sites' specific geography and history gives rise to varied forms of urban, site-specific novelty (cf. Robinson 2013). In Kenya, 'being cosmo' allows residents to brace themselves against the virulent ethicized violence and exclusion seen elsewhere in the East African country while opening space for multi-ethnic newcomers to pursue varied economic and social ambitions. In South Africa, the language of cosmopolitanism is often more variable and fluid to match the multiple, parallel ethics of coexistence, some violently exclusive, others remarkably tolerant. Underlying each is a desire for distance: either to overtly exclude or to maintain almost slippery neighborliness that resonates with a reluctance to root.

The significance of these findings extends beyond documenting varied forms of membership and coexistence in the thrown together, often informally governed spaces that comprise Africa's rapidly expanding urban peripheries (Kihato and Muyemba 2015). Rather, our approach draws attention to the spatial scale at which we locate social integration, as well as the very ethics and desired outcomes scholars often presume ought to underlie conviviality and co-existence in diverse societies (Ye 2016).

1   Managing Difference in African Urban Spaces

In this chapter, we build on and integrate a dual set of themes. The first theme and our theoretical locus is diversity and the modalities of 'managing' difference. Whether driven by intellect or instinct, such modalities typically establish both dialogical and practical engagements among ontological (i.e., who is the Other), ethical (how ought I address Others) and practical (how do we do this) premises. For the most part, scholars as much as policymakers approach questions of successful coexistence among diverse population with a presumption that healthy and functional societies are consensus-based, united and syner-getic (Jenson 1998; Heuser 2005; Cheong, et al. 2007, 32). Many consider a lack of social cohesion to be harmful to development, economic progress, redistri-bution and stability (Hirschfield and Bowers 1997, 1292; Jeanotte 2003; Heuser 2005, 8–9; Chipkin and Ngqulunga 2008; Lægaard 2010, 454–455).

This cohesion and integration imperative within urban planning and poli-cies has important practical consequences. Many countries seek to limit new immigration while insisting that migrants already there 'integrate' into their host society (Syrett and Sepulveda 2012, 240; Grillo 2010) (Letki 2008; Holtug 2010). Such moves have critics arguing that a renewed emphasis on integra-tion and cohesion clouds attempts to effectively assimilate migrants into hege-monic groups (i.e., the native, majority population), and exclude or alienate those who do not or won't conform to the majority culture (Young, et al. 2006; Yuval-Davis 2006; Vasta 2010).

Underlying both integration activists and critics are presumptions that (a) an identifiable majority culture exists, (b) that such culture is rooted in national formations; (c) that migrants strive to belong since full membership aligns with people's immediate and long-term objectives. While scholars are slowly beginning to unsettle these assumptions, there is a fair degree of resis-tance, and even these critiques rarely consider the kind of fluidity and social simultaneity (see Levitt and Glick Schiller 2004) that inform the emerging socialities in Africa's most dynamics urban sites.

Africa's rapid urbanization – the second main theme of this chapter – has largely occurred in environments of limited state capacity or structured economic opportunities. This is a kind of 'DIY' urbanism contrasting with the historical growth of European and North American cities driven largely by industrialization and political consolidation (Weber 1976; Simmel 1975). African cities are growing in the absence of expanding formal employment or state services (Götz and Simone 2001, Simone 2004; Banks 2011; Robinson 2013; Mbembe and Nuttall 2004). The townships and peri-urban settlements in which migrants most often reside largely lack formal or informal mecha-nisms able to establish economic, coercive, or identitive hegemony. The peo-ple occupying highly transient peripheral urban gateways often see them as entry points to local economic opportunities or passage onward. Rather than a place to 'belong' to, cities remain places stations, not permanent destina-tions. While migrants' activities and presence there may further their social standing, the networks and registers of belonging that typically matter to them remain elsewhere. These subjective understandings of the city have import-ant implications for the enacted nature of urban life and governance while potentially reframing how we understand the objectives and ethics of social membership and integration. The absence of the disciplining force of formal markets and institutions means cities are unlikely to facilitate the kind of identitive, often national consolidation seen elsewhere. It also raises the specter of conflict. Yet for all of their fluidity, inequality, and informality, many African cities remain remarkably accommodating, facilitating a kind of ground-up diversity management.

Bringing together these two themes – the nature of African urbanization and dominant discourses on diversity and cohesion – we interrogate the modalities of coexistence in some of the most rapidly transforming sites within two ethnically heterogeneous African cities. In Kenya, our work largely concentrates on Ongata Rongai, an area to Nairobi's South. In South Africa the work considers both sites in the city center and in its peripheral townships (particularly Katlehong). Across the sites, we document negotiations over accommodation and tolerance that do not stem from a clearly articulated vision, let alone one aimed at cohesion and synergy. Rather, due to the precarity of employment and the urgency to maintain multiple local and translocal networks (Simone 2004; Kankonde 2010; Madhavan and Landau 2011), successful accommodation in many African cities – as understood from the perspective of those involved – is best measured by people's ability to 'get along': to co-exist and work towards one's own individual goals without being bound by the demands of full membership. In short, conviviality is achieved *without* an emphasis on "consensus over values and a sense of common belonging" (Syrett and Sepulveda 2012, 240). Tactical cosmopolitanism allows migrants to achieve exactly this: partial inclusion without becoming bounded.

What we observe here are the dynamics of poly-centric, 'horizontal' or social relationships that incorporate or exclude. In this way the socialities explored here differ from those described (or prescribed) in the 'north' which often analytically privilege the roles of centralized states and business-centered mechanism to uniformly discipline and shape the relationships between hosts and new arrivals. The kind of management 'from below' (or really, from beside) described here relies less on the coercive and normative power of state institutions, churches or regulated markets than on varying vernacular discourses and practices of inclusion and exclusion, tolerance and hospitality. This further rescales the discussion of urban transformation and integration through an explicit recognition that across Africa and in other rapidly urbanizing, multi-ethnic societies, presumptions of a dominant, host society and immigrant minorities often fall short. Especially when viewed at the level of the sub-urban estuaries (Landau 2014) emerging within and on the edge of cities, populations are typically too heterogeneous, too mobile, and too freshly arrived to sensibly speak in such dichotomous terms.

The remainder of this paper proceeds through four sections. After a definition of tactical cosmopolitanism and a brief review of our conceptual and
methodological foundations, we schematically review the forces that tactical
cosmopolitanism has emerged to resist: threats of both formal and informal
socio-political exclusion as well as generalized economic precarity. We then
outline the facets of tactical cosmopolitanism and review its empirical manifestations: the rhetoric of claims to space, the fragility and fragmentation of
migration associations; and efforts to elude 'capture' by national and local
socio-political institutions and other migrants. We end by raising a series of
empirical questions that, when answered, will add depth to our discussion by
speaking to the dimensions, prevalence, persistence and social importance of
tactical cosmopolitanism.

2   Tactical Cosmopolitanism Defined

Tactical cosmopolitanism is a reaction to exclusion: a way of claiming space
without adopting space-bound identities or values. In both Johannesburg
and Nairobi, new arrivals confront longer-term residents who are themselves
deeply and intersectionally divided by locally understood categories of race,
ethnicity, religion, and class. While these often map onto forms of spatial
segregation – based largely on class in Kenya and race and wealth in South
Africa – many areas are remarkably heterogeneous. Such diversity, coupled
with demographic dynamics, often leave the position of the 'other' as unclear
or emergent. Irregular alliances can identify and exclude individuals or groups
along any number of criteria, real or fictive. Coupled with the precarity of
uncertain economies, legal status, and political interventions, this generates
an unknowability about the urban environment that demands a mode of existence that is itself adaptable and thus difficult to define.

Before describing tactical cosmopolitanism's empirical manifestations, it
is worth reiterating that this is not a coherent set of tactics grounded in normative ideas of 'openness'. While migrants draw heavily from cosmopolitanism's philosophical foundations, they do this without necessarily adopting its
universalized concern for others. Drawing on various and multi-scalar, often
competing, systems of rights and rhetoric to insinuate themselves, however
shallowly, in the networks and spaces they require to achieve specific goals.
Unlike transnationalism, which is often about belonging to multiple communities, these are more 'decentered' tactics. This leaves them, in Friedman's words,
"betwixt and between without being liminal [...] participating in many worlds
without becoming part of them" (in Vertovec 2006: 3–10; cf. Simmel 1964). As

new arrivals encounter and attempt to overcome the risks associated with their presence in urban areas, they draw on a variegated language of belonging that makes claims to the city while positioning them in an ephemeral condition enabling them to escape localized social, political, or ethnic obligations. The remainder of this paper explores the content of this fragmented and heterogeneous discourse – what we term tactical cosmopolitanism – and how it draws on pan-Africanism, human rights rhetoric, religion, and language of the global elites. In doing so, it illustrates outsiders' agency in mitigating the effects of xenophobia by at once inserting themselves into city life and distancing themselves from it.

3   Conceptual and Methodological Foundations

Our inductive efforts to reveal migrants' 'tactical cosmopolitanism' help loosen the concept from the two pairs of capstans that have long pulled it in conflicting directions. Two of these pulleys are worked by philosophers who speak of what Beck and Sznaider (2006) term, 'the cosmopolitan condition' (see, for example, Beck 1998; Appiah 1998). This includes those celebrating the potential of transgressing nationalism and others who are distressed by cosmopolitanism's threat the communitarian bases of human society. Others fear cosmopolitanism as a nefarious, Trojan horse for elite, 'western', capitalist and consumerist values (see Walzer 1982; Carens 1987; Waldron 1992). The remaining pulleys are worked by prophets who, on one side, speculate about a new world of pastiches and hybridity. On the other, they explain and fret over the reassertion of localized identities emerging in response to pressures of globalization (see Geertz 1986: 121; Smith 1995: 20; Featherstone 1990; Sassen 2002; Geschiere 2006). In almost all cases, the philosophers ponder how we should react to these opportunities or threats: policy response, a new ethics, and new ways of being in the world.

   What these accounts too often miss are the forms of 'actually existing cosmopolitanism' (Robbins 1998; also Beck and Sznaider 2006: 6; Vertovec 2006) that emerge as ordinary people in relatively poor countries address quotidian challenges to meet their broader individual and collective objectives. Even among those focusing on existing cosmopolitanisms, attention is usually on economically privileged individuals and societies (cf. Furia 2005). Some go so far as to overtly deny the cosmopolitan potential of the poor and, more specifically, poor migrants. Hannerz (1990: 243), for example, claims a majority of migrants are not cosmopolitan, as their "involvement with another culture is not a fringe benefit but a necessary cost, to be kept as low as possible". Without claiming that all migrants are inherently cosmopolitan, we argue it is unfair to dismiss the poor's cosmopolitan potential even when it emerges from pragmatic concerns. In doing so, we share Beck's (2002: 21) view that "in the struggles over belonging, the actions of migrants and minorities are major examples of dialogic imaginative ways of life and everyday cosmopolitanism".

To begin revealing these innovations, this chapter draws on an ecumenical set of data in illustrating the emergence of tactical cosmopolitanism in Johannesburg and Nairobi. As their respective regions'primary cities and migrant destinations, they are palimpsests in which new patterns of investment, belonging, and mobility are being inscribed over legacies of apartheid and colonial planning, social fragmentation, and new patterns of migration. As there is a spatial concentration of wealth in urban areas (see Sassen 2002; Brenner and Schmidt 2012), people are moving to African cities as never before (OECD 2020). Many of those moving in are citizens, some are not. In Kenya, almost all have arrived to take refuge from the city center or are moving in from other small towns and rural areas. In Johannesburg, newly urbanized South Africans meet people from across Southern Africa, elsewhere on the continent, and parts of South Asia and the Middle East.

Kenya and South Africa represent two of the continent's most urbanized or urbanizing countries. Although their cities are smaller than West-Africa's sprawling monsters – Nigeria's greater Lagos has more than 20 million people compared to Johannesburg's 7.5 and Nairobi's 3.5[2] – they nonetheless attract significant and diverse migrant streams from within and beyond their national borders (see Kihato and Muyemba 2015). Through this mobility, the population has become increasingly diverse, representing not only the countries'varied ethnic groups (South Africa has 11 national languages; Kenya recognizes 42 tribes), but refugees and economic migrants from throughout the region and beyond (ECA UN 2010).[3] Although migration is but one component of rapid urban growth, the expanding social and physical footprint of cities has rapidly outstripped institutional capacities to provide or regulate service delivery (water, housing, schools, clinics) or infrastructure development (ECA UN 2011). Equally important, the most rapid growth – especially the most rapid growth due to human mobility – is not in the relatively established city centers, but rather on the less expensive and infrastructurally underendowed urban peripheries. The convergence and almost tidal movements of people through these ever evolving, informal urban spaces – what Landau (2014) terms 'urban

---

2   Data compiled by Thomas Brinkerhoff from official records. Downloaded from www.citypop ulation.de.

3   International Migration and Development in Africa: The Migration and Climate Nexus.

estuaries' – give cause to question the distinctions between hosts and outsider or the possibility of enduring, site specific forms of membership.

The data employed here stem from a series of projects considering the changing nature of African urbanism, governance and political identities. The Kenya work began in 2006 when the African Centre for Migration & Society co-organized a survey on migrant livelihoods and politics in Nairobi (results appear in Landau & Duponchel 2011; Madhavan and Landau 2011; and elsewhere). While Rongai was excluded for falling just beyond the municipal boundaries, it attracted attention as one of greater Nairobi's most rapidly transforming spaces due to domestic migrants from across the country. Returning later to Rongai, we conducted two studies explicitly exploring the people and institutions emerging in this peri-urban space. This included close to forty extended interviews with a broad swathe of residents and weeks in the area observing interactions and the sites social and physical geography, and participating in discussions – some orchestrated, some spontaneous – with residents in a variety of settings. Our South African material is drawn from multiple projects. This includes original survey research (2003, 2006[4]) complemented by formal and informal interviews with migrants, service providers, advocates, and local government representatives between 2002 and 2020. In all, we have included a range of sites within the city, all of which are linguistically and culturally diverse (Statistics South Africa 2020).

Given such eclectic data sources, this account should be seen as a kind of provocation rather than a conclusion. Even the most casual observer will note that the axes of difference discussed here differ remarkably between the two cases. In Kenya we largely consider the convergence of people from within the country's territorial boundaries; in South Africa the primary points of contention relate mostly to nationality although diversity tied to internal mobility and ethnicity also features. While there are obvious concerns with lumping these cases together, our position is effectively that studying African urban realities means, as Meyers (2011) suggests, moving beyond documenting the specificities of place. So, while the significant dimensions of difference between the two sites are highly contextual, they are not essential. Nationality need not be more or less significant than ethnicity, language or other potential markers of difference. Moreover, the resonance of our findings across the two cases suggests the value of such comparisons in ways that lets us raises broader more substantive – if still conceptual and methodological – points around the

---

4   The migration survey was a collaborative project among Wits University (Johannesburg), Tufts University (Boston), the French Institute of South Africa and partners in Maputo, Lubumbashi, and Nairobi.

meaning of hosts and guests, debates around immigration and integration and discussions of nationalism and the accommodation of domestic diversity. While our work is by no means comprehensive, it nevertheless provides critical illustrations of trends and the possibilities of new forms of socio-political organization and categories of belonging.

4   Manifestations of Tactical Cosmopolitanism

In a chapter of this scope, it is only possible to illustrate with signs of cosmopolitanism. There are four areas where we see signs of cosmopolitanism; three that demonstrate a form of tactical cosmopolitanism. The first example of migrant cosmopolitanism is linked to the composition of the population and their relations to people outside of the areas in which they reside, a *de facto* cosmopolitanism, although one that may be easily confused with an elaborate transnationalism or translocalism. The second is the rhetoric of self-exclusion and transient superiority that distances this group from a particular vision of nationalism and transformation. The third is in the rhetoric they use to claim membership, a varied mix of pan-Africanism and other liberation philosophies. The fourth, and most critical to the tactical component of our argument, is in how they organize to avoid the ethics of obligation to other migrant groups and their home communities. It is this mix of atomization and fluid association that is unique to this form of life: it is not an alternative way of belonging, but a use of cosmopolitan rhetoric and organizational forms to live outside of belonging while claiming the benefits of it.

4.1   *De-facto Cosmopolitanism and Orientation to Other Places*

As one of its core constituents, cosmopolitanism describes 'a practice or competence' (Vertovec 2002: 13) to familiarize oneself with a multiplicity of cultural systems (cf. Hannerz 1990: 293; Vertovec 2002: 14). In both Johannesburg and Nairobi, many migrants had lived elsewhere, often in multiple locations. Tactical cosmopolitans acknowledge the benefit they gain from these experiences and interactions. Their practices are not necessarily based on "respect and enjoyment of cultural difference" (Vertovec 2002: 13). Rather, they have developed the tools and the narratives that enable them to adeptly negotiate difference in ways that further their own objectives, as a Zimbabwean migrant explains: "I lived in Botswana, I was in Mozambique, Zambia, it's like when you are in a country which is not your home country, just try and get cash you see, you don't have much time to look for entertainment, all you do is part of life, whether you like it or not".

It is not only such instrumental familiarization that is at work here, but also persistent connections to 'multiple elsewheres'. Johannesburg's migrants are not only transnational – although many remain regularly in touch with people in their home communities – but they retain an extraordinary array of contacts with friends, relatives, and associates across the world. In Kenya, 'real' life is often thought of as elsewhere. Indeed, one's urban existence may be largely about establishing credibility and status in sites well beyond the city. Through these connections, migrants develop multi-sited families, economies, and categories of belonging that transcend borders and are, in some cases, so fluid that almost transcend territory all together. The frequency with which people are in contact with relatives and kin elsewhere suggests that these migrants are, in Benedikt's words, nomads "who are always in touch" (quoted in Bauman 2000: 78).

The tactical cosmopolitanism we describe also features a strong orientation to yet unknown and untraveled places outside of both host and home country. Critically, journeys home or onwards often remain practically elusive for reasons of money, safety, or social status. This leaves large sections of Johannesburg's non-national population effectively marooned in the city, but not necessarily planning to be here.

In Kenya, the site of residence was invented as a kind of de-ethnicized space that effectively belongs to no one in particular. An amalgam of different ethnicities, in the 1980s, the population of Rongai exploded (and again after the post-election violence in 2008), almost all property near the roads and rivers was sold to people from elsewhere with the 'indigenous' Maasai population decamping south towards Tanzania. In the minds of many residents, this is a space where everyone is welcome and no-one is from: a kind of terra incognita. Onyango (author interview, 7 January 2014) explained:

> This was their land but they have left to leave us all as visitors here. As a result of this, everyone can say we are brothers. None of us can say we are on someone else's place or that they're on ours … we are all visitors, we are all foreigners … Once you buy land here, you are a member of the community.

So while the Kikuyu – who most agree comprise the largest group of landowners – could not consider welcoming others to their ancestral lands on Mount Kenya's slopes, Rongai offers a different story. In Nderitu's words: "Kikuyus here can't be hostile: it's not their space. If you go up to Thika [in Central Province], people won't buy or live there unless they're a Kikuyu. But on this side here it is everyone's take. So, anyone can come here". Njoroge (author interview, 5

January 2014) concurs: "Here the natives are the Maasai, but the language that everyone speaks is Swahili. People have just come in and they can't fight". As the literature on Kenyan politics makes abundantly clear (Onguny and Gillies 2019), exclusive, indigenous claims to land are a hallmark of the country and a continual source of friction. They also serve as the foundation for an ethni- cized political system in which people's political legitimacy is typically about representing a space and the particular ethnicity that occupies it rather than a geographic space and the people who occupy it. Yet, in Rongai, the origin myth of a population that voluntarily ceded its territory to a welcomed and diverse 'other' does considerable work in helping new owners justify their claims.

4.2   Rhetoric of Self-exclusion

In response to the violence and discrimination they experience in Johannesburg, many migrants have developed a rhetoric of self-exclusion that fetishizes their position as permanent outsiders removed "from all connections and com- mitments" (Said 2001: 183; see also Malauene 2004; Simone 2001). Instead of striving to integrate, migrants' interactions with South Africans lead, as Barth (1969) predicts, to a reification of differences and a counter-idiom of transience and superiority. One migrant from Lesotho, who has lived in Johannesburg for four years, reveals many dimensions of this discourse of non-belonging: "I don't think any right-thinking person would want to be South African. It's a very unhealthy environment. South Africans are very aggressive, even the way they talk".

Ironically, foreigners often brand South Africans with the same flaws the latter levy against them: dishonesty, aggression, and pathology. Very few trust South Africans and the minority speaks of close relationships with them. All this is further complemented (and justified) by a sense that South Africans are uneducated or do not appreciate the opportunities they have for education (or other social services); are promiscuous or overly tolerant (especially regarding the acceptance of homosexuality); and unreligious.

Clinging to the status afforded those belonging to the 'mobile classes' (see Bauman 2000), migrants in Johannesburg hover above the national soil by retaining loyalties to their communities of origin and orienting themselves towards a future somewhat beyond the national project. This emerges from a combination of both original intent (i.e., why people came to a given city), and a counter response to the real and potential hostilities they face on arrival. For them, allochthon status is not a scarlet letter, but represents their own, alterna- tive form of deterritorialized inclusion. While many more foreigners would like their children to learn English or another South African language, they remain wary of them ever considering themselves South African.

The tactical cosmopolitans in Kenya may not distance themselves from Kenya, per se, but from the locals in Rongai and from a national politics they deem overly violence and tribal. Although members of the Kikuyu ethnic group represent a plurality of residents, they by no means dominate the space or make exclusive claims to it. Indeed, no one does. Proudly advertising this distinction, residents' sentiments are well reflected in a categorical proclamation made by a local land developer who self-identified as a product of Kikuyu and Maasai parentage: "There's no tribalism in this place; we're all mixed together" (Mungai, author interview, 5 January 2014). When describing the variegated and fluid community, people regularly speak of themselves as "a people of peace" (Kiriaki, author interview, 21 November 2013). Nderitu, a Kikuyu priest who at the time of the interview had recently moved to Rongai from an almost exclusively Maasai area near the Kenya – Tanzania border, concluded: "I've never been somewhere where I feel like I'm so at ease. There's nowhere here where you go and you feel like you're out of place" (author interview, 6 January 2014). Throughout formal discussions and casual conversations, leaders and citizens almost universally reiterated the refrain of welcome, peace and tolerance.

The cosmopolitanism residents describe is not merely a passive, laissez-faire state of being. It is instead a carefully considered and articulated set of aspirations that valorize resistance to forms of ethnic political mobilization or exclusion. Rongai residents not only condemn the violence witnessed elsewhere, but deny the possibility of such violence ever surfacing among them. As one resident noted: "If we have enemies, they would be just economic and not ethnic or political" (Mwangi, author interview, 3 January 2014). When asked if violence occurred after the 2007 elections, Kiriaki (author interview, 23 November 2012), an elder, quasi-official interviewed in his Rongai office, said: "Not even a little. Only a few were around wanting to fight, but even if they had tried they would have been put down, possibly killed". A few years later, Njoroge (author interview, 5 January 2014) described Rongai's anti-autochthonous ethos:

> There were people here who tried tribalism in the last election, but it was not successful. We're now used to living together and there are too many connections [...] of course, you can come with your money and try to mobilize and people won't refuse. They'll take your money and say they'll go attack this or that person, but they won't do it. This is because we are politically mature.

In this we see many critical characteristics of Rongai's cosmopolitanism: an assertion of residents' almost essential propensity to peacefulness and tolerance;

clear distinctions between Rongai residents and other Kenyans – including family members and co-ethnics – and a moral condemnation of violence and the character of those straying from the community's convivial values.

Rongai provides a direct contrast to this almost deterministic perspective of Kenyan politics: not by denying the political utility of land or its links political violence, but in demonstrating that the powerful ethnicization and associated debates over autochthony and ownership fail to represent the entirety of Kenyan political discourses and subjectivities. Rather, people in Rongai have developed a counter narrative to the exclusivist discourses that have so often led to overt, violence conflict. In this regard, our findings resonate with Klopp (2010), who, borrowing from Lonsdale (1994: 131), notes that ethnic identification can include moral, inclusivist tenets. In describing Nandi-a subgroup of the often-conflictual Kalenjin collective – she notes forms of subjectivities that are not classically liberal (i.e., where everyone has a right to settle anywhere) but nor are they ethnically exclusive. Even if tactical cosmopolitanism discursively resonates with Lockean liberalism, it remains significantly ethnicized: ethnicity often remains a critical component of a person's political cosmology, with people remaining committed to ideas of indigenized spaces beyond while proclaiming Rongai a kind of ethnic-free zone. It nonetheless takes overtly ethical or moral character, as Rongai residents contrast themselves and their convivial coexistence with the conflicts elsewhere in Kenya. Rongai's cosmopolitanism is founded on residents' recognition of the profound inter-dependence of Kenya's ethnicities. This alternative subjectivity – or performance thereof – offers, in Klopp et al's words, "one of the few protections the ravages of nature and the shared experience of political despotism" 2010: 286–7).

4.3   Rhetoric of Rights: Inclusion without Membership

In the account of a Malawian migrant in Johannesburg, "Africa is a family, just to uplift Africa as a whole, as a continent, I think if it is us Africans, we should uplift one another, for the benefit of us as a family. You can't just let your sister or your mother starve". In a similar vein, the founder of a South African migrant association states, "we want to shift our patriotism to the continent, not to a country. We Africans share a history together; we are bound together ... in our day to day living we are all confronted with problems of nationality, ethnicity and so on. But when you have this [broader African] perspective you do not see these problems anymore" (cited in Kihato 2007). There is more to this than a desire to build a community of all Africans as an end itself. Rather, various evocations of Pan-Africanism are designed to penetrate barriers of exclusion: by helping South Africans to realize connections to their continental kin they undermine the legitimacy of the reasons South Africans may draw on in excluding foreigners.

In a remarkable twist for an era (and country) in which indigeneity has so often been elevated to the primary, naturalized basis for membership and morality, many of the Rongai's residents remain deeply suspicious of those with even modest roots in the site. Although a number of respondents are children of early migrants, they have clung to their settler, outsider identity to distinguish themselves from those they deem to be too localized or too rooted to space. Although this kind of self-alienation is common amongst even long-settled migrant communities (see Simmel 1964; Malauene 2004; Simone 2001; Keith 2005), it is unusual in a country where ideas of home and rootedness are often exalted.

The demonization of locality became most evident in discussions around Rongai's security conditions. Even while dismissing the faint possibility of ethno-political violence, most residents identify parts of Rongai as 'black spots', zones unsafe to traverse alone or after dark. These spots were clustered around Kware, the neighborhood settled by those working in the eponymous quarry. Many spoke of a kind of laziness and moral corruption that comes from being settled too comfortably. Waweru (author interview, 9 January 2014), an aspiring Kikuyu business-owner running a small restaurant on his father's property across town, concurred: "those who grew up here don't want to work; they are just waiting for their parents to move on or to give them things [...] The newcomers are always prepared to work. They know they don't have any-one helping".

Whereas Kenyan politics – and indeed Kenyans – are often suspicious of those without strong local roots, Rongai residents regularly denigrate settling or claims that one can find happiness only within 'home squared', the space where one is really from. While they do not deny the importance of having a homeland – and many speak powerfully about their connections elsewhere – the demonizing discourse largely serves to legitimate the arrivals of outsiders and newcomers, morally elevating them by extolling their work ethic, respect for law and general respect for others regardless of their origin.

By allowing people to retain ethnic, religious or other forms of extra-local loyalties – both religion and ethnicity remain highly visible in Rongai – res-idents may also inadvertently be generating a kind of radical multicultural-ism, a "pluralization of possibilities of being on the same territory" (Campbell 1998: 162). Were he alive, Levinas (1999) would undoubtedly be pleased by Ongata Rongai: if all are sojourners, then on what basis might one justify exclu-sion? But as Bank (2011) notes in his work on urban South African identities, evocations of fluidity and ethno-territorial fixity often circulate simultaneously, potentially within the words of a single person.

In both the Kenyan and South African cases, this is not openness without boundaries: but rather one that draws on multiple identities simultaneously without ever accepting the overarching authority or power of one. Nowhere does this new language speak of maintaining ties to a specific location. Rather, it is a tactical effort to gain access to the city, but without a view of becoming exclusively or even partially bound to it or any other concrete locale.

One of the most powerful forms of membership without spatial belonging comes through forms of Pentecostalism operating in both Johannesburg and Nairobi. These often fashion an organizational form that at once bridges barriers among various groups while preparing people for a 'life beyond' the local altogether. Many of these offers up 'health and wealth' promises seen elsewhere in evangelical communities, promises that offer an alternative to the material deprivation many migrants experience. Although there is not space here to reflect the diversity of testimonies and preaching included in even one five-hour 'mass', almost all reflect the lived experiences of people in the city. In some instances, the preaching bares only the faint influence of biblical pronouncements, but is instead fabricated out of contemporary challenges and generalized evangelical Christian philosophy. The promises and guidance offered within such oration also bring in South Africans to the community, generating one of the rare common spaces between nationals and foreigners in the city. As one Zimbabwean migrant in South Africa states: "In the church, they help us in many ways, no matter where you come from, they just help you".

With their strong links to communities in Nigeria, Ghana, and the United States, the churches also open further connections out of Johannesburg. For many of the churches founding pastors see South Africa primarily as a place where they can enter global discourse and influence the lives of people across the continent and beyond. In the words of the Nigerian Pastor at the "Mountain of Fire and Miracles church", "Africa is shaped like a pistol and South Africa is the mouth from where you can shoot out the word of god". And, consequently, anyone doing the work of God has divine right to South African territory.

Unlike the rhetoric of the street, church ideology is potentially generative of community with social pressures and disciplines that may transform tactics into a counter hegemonic strategy. However, they presently remain far too fluid and many of their pronouncements too pragmatic and flexible to offer a coherent, stable alternative organizational form. Instead, the churches are often functional units, helping people to find jobs, transcend boundaries, or find ways (physically or spiritually) out of Johannesburg's hardships. If successful, these resources often physically help people out of the city (or at least the inner-city) and onto more prosperous grounds.

4.4   Organization and Atomization

Due to it philosophical heterodoxy, tactical cosmopolitanism is both enormously flexible and unable to discipline its practitioners. This is clearly illustrated in the dynamic social configurations evident among the Johannesburg's migrants. Mang'ana (2004) reports, for example, that even people from the same country are careful to avoid the mutual obligations and politics that come from close association with other 'exiles". Although there are instances in which migrant groups assert a collective (usually national) identity, these are often based on instrumental and short-lived associations. Amisi and Ballard's (2005) work on refugee associations throughout South Africa, for example, finds an almost universal tendency towards repeated reconfiguration and fragmentation. As Götz and Simone suggest, "these formations embody a broad range of tactical abilities aimed at maximizing economic opportunities through transversal engagements across territories and separate arrangements of powers" (2003: 125). They are not associations founded on preserving identity, but rather use transient combinations of national, ethnic, and political affiliations for tactical purposes. In many instances, people cling to multiple points of loyalty that allow them to shift within multiple networks. These act as resources and provide the weak links needed to gather information while allowing a shift of affiliations and tactics at a moment's notice (cf. Granovetter 1973). By doing so, migrants avoid capture by friends, relations, and the South African state while inadvertently reshaping the city's social and political dynamics.

In Rongai, such distanciation largely takes the form of disguise. While people's accents and names often reveal their ethnic affiliation, a conscious strategy of residential mixing helps mask what are potentially strong communal loyalties. Kikuyu landowners surround themselves with Luo shopkeepers and residents from multiple groups to avoid easy ethnic mobilization among the population. More importantly, the appearance of disconnection and the physical imbrication of multiple groups makes attacks by one group on the other all the less likely. The denial of ethnicity and the public distancing from strong ethnic politics further delegitimizes tropes and actions that might imperil person and property.

In both cases, the building of community by distancing limits networks ability to foster permanent inclusion and settlement, but also allows a flexibility of membership and opportunity, with people shifting alliances and allegiances to the degree that it is tenable given their documentation, language skills, and appearance. As Simmel notes, these strangers are not fully committed to the peculiar tendencies of the people amongst whom they live. They can, therefore, approach them with a kind of skepticism, 'objectivity', and self-imposed distance. But they are also cosmopolitan for, as Hannerz (1990: 239) suggests they should, many demonstrate a great, personal ability to "make their way into other cultures, through listening, looking, intuiting and reflecting" as well as through carefully developed skills for meandering through systems of meaning and obligation.

5   Conclusion: Potential Consequences of Tactical Cosmopolitanism

Tactical cosmopolitanism is a heterogeneous set of practices that has emerged from a form of constant, if not always conscious, struggle against the harshness of the city and hostile attitudes. As Beck (2004: 134) observes, this is in some ways a 'side effect', something developed as a tool to achieve other economic, social, and even political goals. As such, it is not a unified, counter-hegemonic or 'strategic' movement that seeks to articulate an alternative order. Rather, this is a motley collection of actions undertaken by groups that are often fragmented by language, religion, legal status, and mutual enmity. They rarely control significant economic resources or organizational capital. However, they are able to swiftly combine disparate segments of the population according to current necessity.

Although it is possible that this current fluidity will preserve extraordinary levels of combinatorial freedom, it is likely that the repeated iterations of hybrid and novel mobilization strategies and rhetoric will generate new categories of belonging that may eventually crystallize in ways that exert disciplinary powers of inclusion and exclusion. It is too early to tell what the nature of these will be, but it is unlikely that they will conform to existing modes of belonging – although they are likely to resonate with aspects of them. Like the marginalized populations that developed Christianity, Islam, and other transcendent, deterritorialized membership, migrants in African cities may pioneer forms of membership that reshape how we understand our relationship to each other, space, and institutions. This may take on the form of "common norms and mutual translatability" (Cheah and Robbins 1998: 12) that help overcome the legacy of Apartheid and national formation. However, it is unlikely that the outcome will conform so closely to the philosophers' vision. If Mbembe and Nuttall (2004: 356) correctly identify Johannesburg and Nairobi as sites of imagination – of collectively enacting shared or individual visions – then we are indeed witnessing novel forms of citizenship representing "both resistance to domination and new hegemonic categories that perpetuate domination" (Basch, et al. 2020 268. See also Mandaville 1999).

These cases also raise fundamental challenges to ethical and philosophical accounts of welcome and hospitality. If, for example, we follow Bulley's (2006 assertion that "hospitality requires some notion of an 'at home' for its possible performance", what is integration when there are multiple homes, or where everyone is both host and visitor? Without dominant states, hegemonic markets or powerful, centralized social institutions, diverse, newly urbanized populations have nonetheless found means of accommodating each other. Drawing on elements from liberal cosmopolitanism to violent and exclusive ethno-national chauvinism, the underlying ethics and mechanisms of inclusion nonetheless challenge fundamental elements of our thinking on both of these. Perhaps most importantly, the urban spaces in which people contest or co-occupy are fundamentally no-one's home in an ontological sense. Even the most vehement and exclusive claims to space are driven by an instrumental desire to *use* rather than *own* and be bound by it.

Our findings challenge the literature's emphasis on cohesion as the basis of conviviality; that the ultimate goal of policy makers and residents is to turn everyday interactions into 'positive' and transformative encounters that produce a society based on respect, common goals and mutual recognition. Our discussion challenges a number of key assumptions informing the existing literature on diversity and accommodation: assumptions about the integration, homogeneity and sedentary nature of both hosts and new arrivals (although others have begun addressing this in advocating a paradigmatic shift towards 'super diversity', (see Vertovec 2007; Olwig 2013)) about the distinctions between – and indeed the very existence of – hosts and guests; assumptions about the centrality of the state and its agents in 'managing' difference; and assumptions about the nature of place, mobility, identity and membership.

By allowing people to retain ethnic, religious, or forms of extra-local loyalties – both religion and ethnicity remain highly visible in Kenya and South Africa – residents may inadvertently generate a kind of radical multiculturalism, a "pluralization of possibilities of being on the same territory" (Campbell 1998, 162). We are not suggesting that what we document should, or could, serve as a normative model of integration. In many ways it remains brutally violent, unstable or so historically contingent as to deny the possibility of conscious reproduction. In the absence of centralized, disciplining institutions, even the most inclusive practices of tolerance and hospitality can be rapidly undone by shifting alliances or incentives (Wrobleski 2012, 29). Derrida thus writes that there is "residual violence of the hospitable gesture, which always take place in a scene of power" (Leung and Stone 2009, 193).

Even if unsettling, the observations summarized in the previous pages provide valuable insights into the experiences of diverse populations and the ways
they find to 'get along', however precarious these may be. In doing so, they raise
fundamental questions about the naturalness with which we commonly, intu-
itively, imbue the link between integration and shared values, place-based
belonging and consensus. The important role of utilitarian and pragmatic elements in the engagement with Others resonates beyond well the continent's
cities, as for example Skrbis and Woodward's work on "limits of cosmopolitan
openness" (2007, 744–745) suggests. While such concepts of instrumentality
sit uneasily with dominant normative and moral concepts of society, they
are a reality in African cities as much as elsewhere that anyone – scholar, policy maker, ordinary citizen – will have to negotiate and acknowledge in their
attempts to understand and 'manage' diversity.

Beyond these normative and theoretical conclusions, this paper also draws
our attention to the specificity of space and place. Peri-urban Africa may not
be globally unique, but the rapid sprawl of urban spaces with little state regulation or public infrastructure creates distinct and potentially novel ways of
living together. There is a thrown-togetherness here, but one unlikely to result
in forms of membership others describe. Secondly, we must be more conscious
in our treatment of the putative host population's composition and intentions.
In the cases discussed here, it makes little sense to speak of a settled host with
a conscious conception of community or even a desire to build stable, place-
bound membership. Even where such populations are citizens, they remain so
internally fragmented and fluid as to belie sensible analytical aggregation and
may also wish to remain fluid and fundamentally fragmented as they navigate
the precarity of tenure, employment, and family demands. Given the history of
recent urbanization and ongoing mobility, people's most significant moral and
political communities may be elsewhere.

Although there will be those who may read this paper as an appeal for African
exceptionalism, the challenges we raise are anything but. Our attention to the
historical specificity of place is not intended to suggest that Africa is inherently
distinct. It rather surfaces the specificity of the Euro-American experience by
illustrating how its history of nationalism and urbanization during an era of
industrialization has shaped both practices and analytical presumptions about
membership, belonging and the trajectories of diverse societies. Such institutional and structural foundations present seldom in the cities and countries of
the 'global south', the sites of the most rapid forms of immigration and urbanization. We can no longer see these sites as deviations from a Euro-American
norm, either analytical or philosophical. Rather, the kinds of pragmatic, instrumental and horizontal patterns described here, however briefly, are likely to

become the new normal, and require us (Tonkiss 2003; van Leeuwen 2010) to conceptualize more manageable, pragmatic 'side by side' modes of urban co-existence that align with the diverse nature, needs and aspirations of city populations. Although Europe and North America may never face the kind of institutional frailty described here, there are clear parallels in the ghettos of the United States and the denigrated post-industrial spaces of Europe where host populations are themselves fluid and fragmented and state and cultural institutions remain only shallowly embedded. Although future urban sociality and modes of accommodating difference in the global North may look little like Johannesburg or Nairobi, unless we expand our range of analytical tools and normative standards along the lines described here, we may overlook the novel and important socio-political formations that ultimately emerge.

References

Amisi, B., and R. Ballard (2005). "In the absence of citizenship: Congolese Refugee Struggle and Organisation in South Africa". Forced Migration Working Paper #16. Accessed April 2005 at http://migration.wits.ac.za/AmisiBallardwp.pdf.

Appadurai, A. (1996), *Modernity at Large: Cultural Dimensions of Globalization*, University of Minnesota Press, Minneapolis.

Appiah, K.A. (1998). "Cosmopolitan Patriots", In Cheah, P., and Robbins, B. (eds.) *Cosmopolitics: Thinking and Feeling Beyond the Nation*. Minneapolis: University of Minnesota Press, 91–114.

Bank, L.J. (2011). *Home Spaces, Street Styles: Contesting Power and Identity in a South African City*. London: Pluto Press.

Barth, F. (1969). *Ethnic Groups and Boundaries. The Social Organization of Culture Difference*. Oslo: Universitetsforlaget.

Basch, L., Schiller, N. G., & Blanc, C. S. (2020). *Nations unbound: Transnational projects, postcolonial predicaments, and deterritorialized nation-states*. Routledge.

Bauman, Z. (2000). *Globalization: Its Human Consequences*. New York: Columbia University Press.

Beck, U. (1998). "The cosmopolitan manifesto", *New Statesman*, March 20: 28–30.

Beck, U. (2002). The cosmopolitan society and its enemies. *Theory, culture & society*, *19*(1-2), 17–44.

Beck, U. (2004). "Cosmopolitan realism". *Global Networks*, 4.2: 131–156.

Beck, U.and N. Sznaider (2006). "Unpacking cosmopolitanism for the social sciences: a research agenda". *The British Journal of Sociology*, 57.1: 1–23.

Brenner, N., and C. Schmid (2012). "Planetary Urbanization," In Gandy, M. (Ed.) *Urban Constellations*. Berlin: Jovis: 10–13.

Bulley, D. (2006). Negotiating ethics: Campbell, ontopology and hospitality. *Review of International Studies*, 32(4), 645–663.

Caldeira, T.P. (2017). "Peripheral urbanization: Autoconstruction, transversal logics, and politics in cities of the global south". *Environment and Planning D: Society and Space.* 35.1:3–20.

Campbell, D. (1998). *National Deconstruction: Violence, Identity and Justice in Bosnia.* Minneapolis: University of Minnesota Press.

Carens, J. (1987). "Aliens and citizens: the case for open borders". *The Review of Politics*, 49: 251–273.

Cheah, P., and B. Robbins, eds. (1998). *Cosmopolitics: Thinking and Feeling Beyond the Nation.* Minneapolis: University of Minnesota Press.

Cheong, P. H., R. Edwards, H. Gouldbourne, and J. Solomos. (2007). "Immigration, Social Cohesion and Social Capital: A Critical Review". *Critical Social Policy* 27.12: 24–49.

Chipkin, I., and B. Ngqulunga. (2008). "Friends and Family: Social Cohesion in South Africa". *Journal of Southern African Studies* 34.1: 61–76. https://doi.org/10.1080/03057070701832882.

Cities Alliance. (2021). *Annual Report 2020: Cities Alliance Joint Work Programme on Cities and Migration.* Brussels: Cities Alliance.

ECA, U. (2011). International migration and development in Africa: the migration and climate nexus.

Featherstone, M. (ed.) (1990). *Global Culture: Nationalism, Globalization andModernity.* London: Sage.

Furia, P. (2005). "Global citizenship, anyone? Cosmopolitanism, privilege and public opinion". *Global Society*, 19.4: 331–359.

Geertz, C. (1986). "The Uses of Diversity". *Michigan Quarterly Review*, 25:105–123.

Geschiere, P. (2006). "Autochthony and the crisis of citizenship: democratization, decentralization, and the politics of belonging". *African Studies Review*, 49.2: 1–7.

Götz, G., and A. Simone (2003). "On belonging and becoming in African cities", In Tomlinson, R., et al. (eds.) *Emerging Johannesburg: Perspectives on the Postapartheid City.* London: Routledge, 123–47.

Granovetter, M. (1973) "The strength of weak ties". *American Journal of Sociology*, 78.6: 1360–1380.

Grillo, R. (2010). "Contesting diversity in Europe: alternative regimes and moral orders". Max Planck Institute of Cultural and Religious Diversity, Working Papers WP 10-02 ISSN 2192-2357.

Hannerz, U. (1990) "Cosmopolitans and locals in world culture". In Featherstone, M. (ed.) *Global Culture: Nationalism, Globalization and Modernity.* London: Sage, 237–251.

Heuser, B. L. (2005). "The Ethics of Social Cohesion". Peabody Journal of Education 80.4: 8–15. https://doi.org/10.2307/3497049.

Hirschfield, A., and K. Bowers. (1997). "The Effect of Social Cohesion on Levels of Recorded Crime in Disadvantaged Areas". Urban Studies 34.8: 1275–95. https://doi.org/10.1080/004(2098975637.

Holsten, J. (2008). *Insurgent Citizenship*. Princeton: Princeton University Press.

Holtug, N. (2010). "Immigration and the Politics of Social Cohesion". *Ethnicities* 10.4: 435–51.

Jeanotte, S. (2003). "Social Cohesion: Insights from Canadian Research". In . Hong Kong. http://www.socsc.hku.hk/cosc/Full%(20paper/Jeannotte%(20Sharon_Full788.pdf.

Jenson, J. (1998). "Mapping Social Cohesion. The State of Canadian Research". CPRN Study No. F/03. Ottawa: Renouf Publishing Co. Ltd.

Kankonde, P.B. (2010). "Transnational Family Ties, Remittance Motives, and Social Death among Congolese Migrants: A Socio-Anthropological Analysis". *Journal of Comparative Family Studies* 41.2: 225–243.

Keith, M. (2005). *After the Cosmopolitan? Multicultural Cities and the Future of Racism*. London: Routledge.

Kihato, C.W. (2007). "Reconfiguring citizenship in African cities". paper presented to the Inclusive Cities Workshop, Wits University, Johannesburg (12 March 2007).

Kihato, C.W., and S. Muyemba. (2015). "The Challenges and Prospects of African Urbanisation: Forging Africa"s Economic Growth Through Sustainable Urban Policies," *Working Paper for the African Centre for Cities, University of Cape Town*.

Klopp, J. M., Githinji, P., & Karuoya, K. (2010). *Internal displacement and local peace-building in Kenya*. US Institute of Peace.

Lægaard, S. (2010). "Immigration, Social Cohesion, and Naturalization". Ethnicities 10.4: 452–69. https://doi.org/10.1177/1468796810378324.

Landau, L.B. (2006). "Transplants and transients: idioms of belonging and dislocation in inner-city Johannesburg". *African Studies Review*, 49.2: 125–145.

Landau, L.B., and M. Duponchel (2011). "Laws, Policies, or Social Position? Capabilities and the Determinants of Effective Protection in Four African Cities," *Journal of Refugee Studies* 24.1:1–22.

Landau, L. (2014). "Conviviality, Rights, and Conflict in Africa's Urban Estuaries," *Politics & Society* 42.3: 359–80.

Landau, L.B. (2015). "Being Cosmo: Displacement, Development and Disguise in Ongata Rongai," *Africa* 85.1:59–77.

Landau, L.B. (2021) (Forthcoming). "Asynchronous Mobilities: Hostility, Hospitality, and Possibilities of Justice," *Mobilities*.

Landau, L.B., and I. Freemantle, (2010). "Tactical Cosmopolitanism and Idioms of Belonging: Insertion and Self-Exclusion in Johannesburg". *Journal of Ethnic and Migration Studies* 36.3:375–390.

Landau, L.B., and I. Freemantle. (2016). "Beggaring Belonging in Africa's No-Man's Lands: Diversity, Usufruct and the Ethics of Accommodation," 2016, *Journal for Ethnic and Migration Studies* 42.6:933–951.

Van Leeuwen, B. (2010). "Dealing with Urban Diversity: Promises and Challenges of City Life for Intercultural Citizenship". *Political Theory*, June. https://doi.org/10.1177/0090591710372869.

Letki, N. (2008). "Does Diversity Erode Social Cohesion? Social Capital and Race in British Neighbourhoods". *Political Studies* 56: 99–126.

Leung, G., and M. Stone. (2009). "Otherwise than Hospitality: A Disputation on the Relation of Ethics to Law and Politics". *Law and Critique* 20.2: 193–206. https://doi.org/10.1007/s10978-009-9046-1.

Levinas, E. (1999). *Alterity and Transcendence*, Michael B. Smith (trans.), New York: Columbia University Press.

Levitt, P. and N. Glick Schiller (2004). "Conceptualizing Simultaneity: A Transnational Social Field Perspective on Society". *International Migration Review*. 38.3:1002–1039.

Lonsdale, J. (1994). Moral ethnicity and political tribalism. *Inventions and boundaries: Historical and anthropological approaches to the study of ethnicity and nationalism*, 11, 131–50.

Madhavan, S., and L.B. Landau (2011). "Bridges to Nowhere: Hosts, Migrants and the Chimera of Social Capital in Three African Cities," *Population and Development Review* 37.3:473–497.

Mandaville, P. G. (1999). Territory and translocality: discrepant idioms of political identity. *Millennium*, *28*(3), 653–673.

Malauene, D. (2004). "The impact of the Congolese forced migrants' "permanent transit" condition on their relations with Mozambique and its people". unpublished thesis, Masters of Arts in Forced Migration, University of the Witwatersrand.

Mang'ana, J.M. (2004). "The effects of migration on human rights consciousness among Congolese refugees in Johannesburg". Unpublished thesis, Masters of Arts in Forced Migration, University of the Witwatersrand.

Mbembe, A., and Nuttall, S. (2004). "Writing the world from an African metropolis". *Public Culture*, 16.3: 347–372.

Meyers, G. (2011). *African Cities: Alternative Visions of Urban Theory and Practice*. London: Zed Books.

OECD (2020). *Africa's Urbanisation Dynamics 2020*. Paris: OECD.

OECD (2021). *Local Inclusion of Migrants and Refugees*. Paris:OECD (https://www.oecd.org/regional/Local-inclusion-Migrants-and-Refugees.pdf).

Oldfield S., and S. Greyling (2015). "Waiting for the state: a politics of housing in South Africa". *Environment and Planning A: Economy and Space*. 47.5:1100–1112.

Fog Olwig, K. (2013). "Notions and Practices of Difference: An Epilogue on the Ethnography of Diversity". *Identities* 20.4: 471–79. https://doi.org/10.1080/1070289X.2013.822378.

Onguny, P., and T. Gillies. (2019). "Land Conflict in Kenya: A Comprehensive Overview of Literature". *East African Review* 53. https://journals.openedition.org/eastafrica/879.

Portes, A. (1997). "Globalization from below: the rise of transnational communities". UK Economic and Social Research Council, Transnational Communities Programme Working Paper Series, WPTC-98-01. (www.transcomm.ox.ac.uk).

Robbins, B. (1998). "Introduction part I: Actually existing cosmopolitanism". In Cheah, P., and Robbins, B. (eds) *Cosmopolitics: Thinking and Feeling Beyond the Nation*. Minneapolis: University of Minnesota Press: 1–19.

Robinson J. (2013). "The Urban Now: Theorising cities beyond the new". *European Journal of Cultural Studies*. 16.6:659–677.

Roudometof, V. (2005). "Transnationalism, cosmopolitanism and glocalization". *Current Sociology*, 53.1: 113–135.

Said, E. (2001). *Reflections on Exile and Other Essays*. Cambridge: Harvard University Press.

Sassen, S. (ed.) (2002). *Global Networks, Linked Cities*. London: Routledge.

Schinkel, W. (2018). "Against "Immigration Integration": For an End to Neocolonial Knowledge Production". *Comparative Migration Studies* 6.31. https://doi.org/10.1186/s40878-018-0095-1.

Simmel, G. (1964). *The Sociology of George Simmel*. Translated by Wolff, K. New York: Free Press.

Simmel, G. (1975). *The Metropolis and Mental Life*, New York: Free Press.

Simone, A. (2001). "On the Worlding of African cities". *African Studies Review*, 44.2:15–41.

Simone, A. (2004). *For the City Yet to Come: Changing African Life in Four Cities*. Durham: Duke University Press.

Skrbis, Z., & Woodward, I. (2007). "The ambivalence of ordinary cosmopolitanism: Investigating the limits of cosmopolitan openness". *The sociological review*, 55(4), 730–747.

Smith, A.D. (1995). *Nations and Nationalism in a Global Era*. Cambridge: Polity.

Spencer, S., and K. Charsley (2021). "Reframing "Integration": Acknowledging and Addressing Five Core Critiques". *Comparative Migration Studies* 9.18 https://doi.org/10.1186/s40878-021-00226-4.

Statistics South Africa. (2020). *Mid-Year Population Estimates*. Statistical Release P0302. Pretoria: Statistics South Africa (31 July 2021).

Syrett, S., and L. Sepulveda. (2012). "Urban Governance and Economic Development in the Diverse City". *European Urban and Regional Studies* 19.3: 238–53. https://doi.org/10.1177/0969776411430287.

Tonkiss, F. (2003). "The Ethics of Indifference: Community and Solitude in the City". *International Journal of Cultural Studies* 6.3: 297–311. https://doi.org/10.1177/13678779030063004.

Vasta, E. (2010). "The Controllability of Difference: Social Cohesion and the New Politics of Solidarity". *Ethnicities* 10.4: 503–21.

Vertovec, S. (2006) "Fostering cosmopolitanisms: A conceptual survey and a media experiment in Berlin". In Lenz, G.H., Ulfers, F., and Dallmann, A. (eds.) *Towards a New Metropolitanism: Reconstituting Public Culture, Urban Citizenship, and the Multicultural Imaginary in New York and Berlin.* Heidelberg: Universitätsverlag, 277–98.

Vertovec, S., and R. Cohen (2002). "Introduction: conceiving cosmopolitanism". In Vertovec, S., and Cohen, R. (eds.) *Conceiving Cosmopolitanism. Theory, Context, and Practice.* Oxford: Oxford University Press.

Vertovec, S. (2007). "Super-Diversity and Its Implications". *Ethnic and Racial Studies* 30.6: 1024–54.

Waldron, J. (1992). Minority Cultures and the Cosmopolitan Alternative. *University of Michigan Journal of Law Reform*, 25: 751–793.

Walzer, M. (1982). *Spheres of Justice: A Defense of Pluralism and Equality.* New York: Basic Books.

Weber, E. (1976). *Peasants into Frenchmen: The Modernization of Rural France, 1870 – 1914.* Stanford: Stanford University Press.

Wrobleski, J. (2012). *The Limits of Hospitality.* Liturgical Pres.

Ye, J. (2016). "Spatialising the politics of coexistence: *gui ju* (规矩) in Singapore". *Transactions*, 41: 91–103.

Young, C, M. Diep, and S. Drabble (2006). "Living with Difference? The "Cosmopolitan City" and Urban Reimaging in Manchester, UK". *Urban Studies* 43. 10: 1687–1714.

Yuval-Davis, N. (2006). "Belonging and the Politics of Belonging". *Patterns of Prejudice* 40.3: 197–214.

CHAPTER 7

Yellow Vests in Metropolis

A Chance for Transversal Solidarity

Christophe Foultier

The *Yellow Vests* is an urban protest movement that took off in France in November 2018. It initially contested the increase of petrol tax proposed by Macron's center-right government. Subsequently however, it developed into a multifaceted anti-austerity movement. Due to the multifaceted nature of the protests, the Yellow Vests' movement has fueled a series of speculations in the media, reinforced by local expressions of anti-semitic allegations, and isolated sexist and racist acts during demonstrations and protests (Guérin 2018; Bornstein 2019). In particular, the Yellow Vests have been reduced to being a mouthpiece for populist claims on the part of the 'left-behinds' that emerged from the peri-urban areas of the French regional centers.

Through the notion of transversal solidarity, this chapter explores possible mediations if not alliances between a heterogeneous 'white' French precariat in suburban areas and that of *'les exclus'*, alternately designated as 'immigrant', 'Muslim' or 'black' in the racialized urban spaces of the French republic. The first part of the text presents key theoretical aspects on transversal solidarity, in order to position the Yellow Vests' movement in terms of a research perspective. The second part focuses on the depiction of the Yellow Vests as a populist movement. As the debates in the media evolved, social justice issues were eclipsed by discussions of the movement's political ideology. Through metaphors and historical analogies, several commentators and editorialists contributed to entrenching the movement in French national mythology as encapsulating a protest of the shapeless masses of the conurbations, often associated with the pejorative word *populace* in French.

In the third part, I argue that the media's reduction of the movement to populism has contributed to forming a racialized cartography of metropolitan areas: in this, the political rhetoric defines social justice movements as imagined community spaces, where residents and activists are categorized through racialized identities (Geisser 2019, 6). Further, I examine how ideological representations map the 'white trash' movement *à la Française* in metropolitan spaces. In media debates, commentators in the national media mention that the invisibility of non-white residents during the Yellow Vests' protests constituted a lack of solidarity from the residents and social justice movement in *les banlieues*; an argument that served to establish a dichotomy between the racial and the social in social justice matters. This argumentation reinforced racial identities in metropolitan spaces, between *les banlieues* and the peri-urban areas. From the fragmentation of metropolitan spaces to ethnic separatism, this recurrent discourse in the media turned the notion of solidarity into a non-sense: the populist ideology would exclusively generate irreconcilable positions with other justice movements in *les banlieues*.

In the fourth part, I consider transversal aspects that highlight to what extent a mobilization locally encompasses multiple political positions: heterogeneous, changing, uncertain, controversial and ambiguous. Such an analysis questions our traditional ways of understanding 'protest movements' in metropolitan spaces. Indeed, the spatial strategy of the Yellow Vests testifies to a capacity for mobilization in unconventional spaces such as roundabouts, parking facilities as well as in public infrastructure. In this perspective, the notion of transversal solidarity is valuable for researchers because it provides a theoretical line of analysis that allows for extending the comprehension of conflictual relations and also mediations on identity issues and membership.

In the fifth section, I examine to what extent the consensual arguments and irreconcilable positions presented by activists and representatives of suburban youth, renew the debates on solidarity issues. The Yellow Vests are primarily a political movement that promotes direct participation in public decision-making and proposes a series of reforms in matters of public policy and social justice. This political positioning reveals heterogeneous attitudes both within and outside of the movement.

In the concluding section, I argue that the Yellow Vests extend the content and form of democratic processes in metropolitan areas. Through public spaces, which are composed of a variety of places, local networks and grassroots organizations, the Yellow Vests' movement initiates debates and confrontations on race and social issues. In doing so, conflictual sociopolitical positionings do not contradict the potential of transversal alliances. Rather, the Yellow Vests generate ambivalent positions, as well as sometimes-irreconcilable views. However, they also generate points of convergence between groups and places that can contribute to recast citizenship issues in metropolitan areas.

The methodology of the analysis is a literature review. Its purpose, though, is not simply to provide an overview of the writings on the movement, but to use the perspective of transversal solidarity – seen in this paper as "a new line of theory" (Hart 2018, 38) on urban justice movements – to understand the specifics of the Yellow Vests' movement. The literature review draws on several sources of documents. Firstly, a series of elements has been collected from newspapers, social media and websites in order to trace the gatherings and the cartography of the movement in cities. Secondly, I have chosen the two biggest French newspapers, *Le Monde* and *Le Figaro*, to understand the way the Yellow Vests' mobilization was perceived and problematized during the initial formation of the movement. I have also collected information from international newspapers, *The New York Times* and *Aljazeera*, in order to highlight the way the movement was perceived outside Europe, in several parts of the world.

The movement has generated widespread confusion, suspicion and controversies in terms of political positioning. However, as this chapter makes clear, the Yellow movement is more than a series of populist claims made by a white trash movement in peri-urban areas– or what President Macron depicted as a 'hateful mob' in a televised speech (Nossiter 2018). Seen as an expression of populism, the Yellow Vests were even depicted as contrasting with previous movements such as *Nuit Debout* – which occupied several cities in order to protest against French labor reforms in 2016 – and the urban justice movement that took place in 2005, rooted in French suburban areas, the so-called *banlieues*. Against the attempt to understand the Yellow Vests' movement according to an extreme right-wing populist ideology, this text interprets their mobilization as an occasion to develop transversal dialogues based on issues of race and class as well as mediations in matters of social justice.

In broad terms, the Yellow Vests can be seen as a movement that initiates new forms of protest in unconventional metropolitan spaces. From 2018 to 2019, the development of the movement indicates a both massive and multifarious potential for popular mobilization, along with a latent capacity to reformulate basic rights in terms of civic participation, mobility or even access to welfare services in metropolitan areas. Thus, besides the media's focus on violent incidents involving the police forces and the resulting serious injuries among the protagonists, the mass mobilization reveals a wish by the movement to position itself in public spaces in opposition to the deficient national political representation.

Moving on from there, I will proceed to discuss the extent to which this grassroots movement initiates a new form of protest in metropolitan areas. I demonstrate how the Yellow Vests promote a capacity for civil society – citizens, precarious workers, activists, migrants and racialized groups – to take part in summits and dialogues in unconventional urban spaces, such as roundabouts, tollgates and public transport infrastructure. Gatherings in such places have a symbolic role to play in the development of mobilization, in that these spaces radically contrast with the conventional spaces that the French institutions propose – public consultations and participatory strategies in public projects – and the routes that trade union movements use during traditional demonstrations – in streets, boulevards and public places in city centers.

1   On Transversal Solidarity: A Theoretical Perspective

In the social sciences, the notion of transversal solidarity provides an analytical grid for understanding social transformations in metropolitan areas in a new way. While multiple local movements take place in heterogeneous spaces, the notion of transversal solidarity emphasizes the viewpoints of the governed. This point is particularly relevant when it comes to analyzing several types of discourse and practices in a 'regime of citizenship'. (Jobert 2008, 407).

Through the dynamics of urbanization and globalization, social justice movements such as the Yellow Vests' mobilization testifies to a growing will for mediation and social adjustments within civil society. In particular, the Yellow Vests show an astonishing capacity to propose radical changes outside of the traditional policymaking process. The idea of transversal solidarity can help understanding the extent to which diverse social groups, that radically reject traditional political organizations and institutions, propose new forms of mobilization and develop innovative spatial strategies and modes of affiliation in metropolitan spaces.

Following Martin Bak Jørgensen and Carl-Ulrik Schierup's argumentation (2020) on transversal solidarity, I will focus on the understanding of the public realm when the Yellow Vests mobilized in French metropolitan spaces. The aim is to identify new practices of mobilization that take place on the fringes of the cities. Understood as heterotopias, these unconventional spaces can be described as follows:

(1)   heterogeneous places, which are targeted in order to define new social functions: the gatherings of the Yellow Vests in transport infrastructure and roundabouts, transform these spaces into assemblies.

(2)   spatial practices of mobilization that give the Yellow Vests the opportunity to expose social cleavages, spatial thresholds, and cultural borders in line with social justice issues.

(3)   new 'spatio-temporal units' in metropolitan areas: taking the temporal dimension in a massive mobilization into account, practices of transversal solidarity vary and change with both time and space according to the evolution of the mobilization.

In this chapter, I argue that the notion of public realms in metropolitan centers incorporates new forms of political commitment. Members of civil society gather in unconventional spaces to discuss interrelated issues of racism, gender inequality and social injustice. These forms of mobilization are not seen through an essentialized lens of political membership, in particular in matters of gender and ethnicity; the transversal dimension of solidarity movements is not defined according to identity interests. On the contrary, issues of identity, social justice and political membership are transversal stakes that must be examined with a sense of equality (Jørgensen and Schierup 2020). In the case of the Yellow Vests, I argue that the rise of heterogeneous movements in metropolitan spaces led politicians and commentators to essentialize the claims of the protesters according to simplistic spatial affiliations. This means that traditional borders in term of cultural affiliation, ethnicity and gender identity are reaffirmed.

I also draw on the analysis of Óscar García Agustín and Martin Bak Jørgensen (2020), who argue that transversal solidarity encompasses three fundamental dimensions: *space, organizations* and *identity*. This analytical grid allows me to establish relevant factors for the case of the Yellow Vests.

Firstly, it gives me the opportunity to clarify the spatial vocabulary that will be used in this chapter. In France, the spatial understanding of the metropolitan dynamic is strongly influenced by a bureaucratic view, mostly rooted in earlier official documents such as *Le Schéma directeur d'Aménagement Urbain* (SDAU): the metropolitan spaces are defined through the prism of radioconcentric vision. Let me explain in greater detail the consequences of this institutional vision. In the French institutional documents, the first spatial belt of the metropolitan spaces, such as Paris, Lyon or Marseilles, often corresponds to the city-center. This first spatial belt has generally undergone a gentrification process. The second belt of the metropolitan organization is historically structured by industrialized zones and the massive social housing developments initiated by the French state after the Second World War. It is commonly called *la proche banlieue* (the inner suburb), a stigmatized space comprising most of the vulnerable areas that are targeted through official documents. They are described as *quartiers populaires* (working-class neighborhoods), *les quartiers sensibles* (vulnerable districts) and this is also where multi-ethnic groups live. The third belt, which is a collage of cities and semi-rural spaces, massive transport infrastructure dedicated to road traffic, collective houses and villas, is located at the outskirts of the regions. It is this third belt, called 'peri-urban spaces', that has been associated with the Yellow Vests.

I use the notion of 'metropolitan spaces' in order to introduce three distinctive metropolitan dynamics: gentrification, segregation and peri-urban development. In the French field of urban studies, the production of metropolitan spaces is analyzed in relation to these socio-spatial dynamics. In this text, however, I argue that this institutional classification of metropolitan spaces is too simplistic to establish a clear understanding of social and political belonging in space. It seems to me that the Yellow Vests is not a 'peri-urban movement' that can be easily dissociated from previous social justice movements such as *Nuit Debout* or the 2005 riots in France.

Secondly, and consequently, I postulate that organizations and institutions such as the state and the French media have substantial difficulties in understanding and interpreting these emerging movements, decentralized and powerfully organized through local networks. Alexander C. Diener (2017, 36) rightly points to this phenomenon when he argues: "increasing mobilities and communication technology, supra and sub-state political communities, as well as cross-border relationships and the daily practices of integration [...] pervade contemporary human existence".

In other words, institutions such as the national police forces cannot cover a mobilization of such magnitude, and the media debates do not easily take into account the complexities of these metropolitan dynamics. In this chapter, controversies between organizations and movements provide an opportunity to grasp the effects of misunderstandings and contentious relations – if not rejections of these – between various organizations in a political space exclusively based on political representativeness.

The third and last dimension of transversal solidarity, identity and membership in space, is problematized through categories of political belonging. In that perspective, Rainer Bauböck remarks that citizenship membership understood as political community requires critical discussion of the "democratic boundary problem". He further argues that "principles of democratic inclusion need to be differentiated for various stages of the democratic process and different types of polities" (Bauböck 2017, 60). For him, this implies complex forms of citizenship or categories of membership that are not "necessarily impermeable, stable or bright boundaries" (ibid.). As Yuval-Davis (1999, 96) remarks, all participants in a transversal dialogue "bring with them the reflexive knowledge of their own positioning and identity".

The case of the Yellow Vests demonstrates that the dominant discourse reproduces a republican vision of citizenship, which is embedded in patterns of loyalty to republican principles. Contemporary issues of citizenship can broadly refer to discourse on the nation but also discourses rooted in neo-conservatism, in a transatlantic third way or in more inclusive ways of living (Jobert 2008, 407). For this reason, the movement that promoted decentralized actions, and hybrid forums based on innovative ways of communication, as well as gatherings, controversial discussions and protests between diverse social groups including minority groups, is rejected. The problem that I would like to highlight concerns the political discourse on the racialization of spaces in the republic and its consequences for solidarity issues during the Yellow Vests' movement. This nationalist view of citizenship leads to the subjection of civil society to regime of divide and rule.

2   The Yellow Vests: A Movement Examined through the Populist Spectrum

Experts and editorialists who first commented on the emerging movement of the Yellow Vests saw it as an unexpected event. In particular, there was no clear mobilization strategy behind it nor support from the French trade unions. As Didier Fassin and Anne-Claire Defossez (AOC 15 March 2019) put it, the movement arrived "an unidentified political object" in the media landscape. The massive protests erupted spontaneously in the outskirts of the French metropolitan areas. They signaled *un ras-le-bol general* – a sort of frustration mixed up with a general feeling of dissatisfaction among the working class and the lower middle-class representatives.

The first protests emerged after the proposed increase of the tax on petrol, but the feeling of frustration had appeared previously in the wake of a set of reforms in relation to road code dispositions: these reforms concerned speed limits on country roads, new settings of speed radars, and the delegation of authority to private societies for speed control. Since the residents of the peri-urban sectors depend on road infrastructure, the increase of fuel taxes was experienced as an unfair reform. In the peri-urban areas, these vast conurbations which are located at the outskirts of the metropolitan centers, mobility issues were also associated with various forms of deterioration in the immediate environment. This deterioration in the environment of the residents of peri-urban areas had several features: the decline of traditional commerce in favor of the profit of peripheral mall centers; the devitalization of city centers; the increasing precariousness of local labor markets; and the growing commuting distances that turn peri-urban residents into long-distance travelers. In sum, the Yellow Vests present new perspectives on social issues that emphasize the neoliberal drifts of successive French governments. On the initiative of a local member of the Department of Sarthe, in northwestern France, an inventory of 42 claims was published by the Yellow Vests on social media on 29 November 2018 which called for radical reforms on matters of fuel taxes, the minimum wage, public policy and direct democracy.

Out of these 42 demands, 20 propositions concerned the reduction of social inequalities: zero homelessness; the minimum wage to be set at 1,300 euros net; a fixed threshold for pensions at 1,200 euros; the creation of jobs for the unemployed; and the same social security system for all, etc. Ten propositions related to neoliberal policies and privatization: the use of money from motorway tolls for the maintenance of motorways and roads, as well as for road safety; and a stop to the selling off public property such as dams and airports, etc. Five orientations were to promote the development of public services: substantial means were to be granted to the justice system, the police and army; and there should be a stop to the closure of small post offices, schools and maternity wards, etc. Eight propositions concerned the implementation of ecological transition. Eight propositions were dedicated to a fair tax reform (e.g. a more progressive income tax, and a tax on maritime fuel and kerosene). Four dealt with the dignity of migration and the tackling of the causes of forced migration: asylum seekers should be well treated; integration policy should be strengthened in matters of education and culture; and there should be deportation for asylum seekers in irregular circumstances, etc. There were also calls for reform of the political system to facilitate democratic renewal (e.g. popular referendums in the constitution, and a seven-year term for the election of the president of the republic) (Joumard 2018).

Without a clear political affiliation, the Yellow Vests became subject to multiple interpretations. On the one hand, this movement could not be easily compared to traditional social movements. On the other hand, the demonstrations were not led by a charismatic leader. Without representativeness and civil support, the historian and editorialist Jacques Julliard referred to the political positioning of the movement as a "dangerous ideology of the common man" (Higgins 2018).

For the historian Gerard Noiriel, this mobilization was a challenge for commentators – politicians, editorialists and experts – and they tended to 'historicize' the movement. On 17 November 2018, the presence of 300,000 Yellow Vests on the streets, and on motorway tolls and roundabouts was mostly spelled out as a popular revolt, *à la manière des Jacqueries* (Brochet 2018). Jacquerie – a sobriquet for French peasants – refers to a popular revolt against taxes in the north of France in the Middle Ages. The term *Jacquerie* is a degrading comment which accompanied the depiction in the national newspaper *Le Figaro* of the Yellow Vests as "spontaneous, unstructured, both targeted and broad" (Brochet 2018). The movement was also associated with the French revolutionary period in which *les Sans-culottes* (without knee breeches) were used by the lower social groups who were opposed to aristocrats. They were further compared with the right-wing populism called *poujadisme* – an antiparliamentary movement that protested against taxes in the 60s – in order to signal their anti-establishment positioning. I would like us to get out of a form of contemporary *poujadism* Emmanuel Macron stated during an interview on television in November 2018 (Perrault *Le Figaro* 15 Nov 2018).

For Noiriel (2019), this burdensome heritage allows commentators to present a pejorative vision of the Yellow Vests as one of the *populaces*. With the symbols *Jacquerie, League or Sans culottes*, politicians and commentators contributed to making the Yellow Vests' movement into being a national identity issue. As E. Tunbridge and G. J. Ashworth put it (1996, 6), the 'selective use of the past' is deliberately open to interpretation and controversy. The multiplication of symbols rooted in French national mythology reflects multiple approaches within the Yellow Vests' movement: criticism of neoliberal policies on the one hand and demands for deportation of asylum seekers on the other. Both the radical left and far-right extremists have considered taking the opportunity to support the movement (Higgins 2018). While Steeve Briois, mayor of Hénin-Beaumont and leader of the National Rally party (previously the National Front), allowed the Yellow Vests to protest in the public places of the municipality in November 2018, François Ruffin, member of the deputy assembly and the founder of extreme-left magazine Fakir, organized a mobilizing meeting with various French left-wing movements. Thus, these local manifestations were highly confusing. Nira Yuval-Davis (1999, 95) perfectly sums up the trap commentators fell into when they attempted to analyze the positioning of the movement during its initial phase: "While the first (interpretation) has proved to be ethnocentric and exclusionary, the second has proved to be essentialist, reifying boundaries between groups and, by homogenizing and collapsing individual into collective identities [...]".

This analysis helps in understanding the terms of the national debate on the Yellow Vests. While the ethnocentric vision of the commentators tends in the media to depict the peri-urban movement as an exclusive *rendez-vous* for white people, the essentialist perspective presents the Yellow Vests as a populist collective walking in the steps of the *poujadistes* of the 60s.

3   From Fragmentation to Separatism: A Racial Cartography of
       Metropolitan Spaces

Drawing on Yuval-Davis, I argue that the discourses on the Yellow Vests have fueled ethno-racial stereotypes through a series of spatial metaphors. The spatial dimension is central for understanding the way in which the Yellow Vests movement served to establish a dichotomy between the racial and the social in social justice matters. While the *populace* of Yellow Vests, rooted in peri-urban spaces, would, according to a prevalent discursive stereotyping, follow a populist ideology, the ethnic minorities and grass roots' organizations in *les banlieues* would choose to disengage and favor ethnic insularities in metropolitan spaces.

As Mustafa Dikec remarks (2007, 21), the close relationship between spatial and political issues often "involves spatial ordering through descriptive names, categorizations, definition, designation and mapping". Based on this theoretical view, the notion of racial cartography explains to what extent the Yellow Vests' movement's political identity is associated in the media with racial stereotypes in metropolitan areas. In other words, the Yellow Vests have become a 'white' movement that emerges from the peri-urban spaces. Political scientist Nedjib Sidi Moussa critically analyzed the emerging racial views on urban spaces in newspaper articles on the Yellow Vests at the beginning of the protests. A quote from a far-right magazine sets the tone:

> We are facing, with the yellow vests, native-born French people: no Malika, Akim, Shlomo, N'Golo or Abdel in their ranks, but local ordinary people, (who live) far from the hordes of scum who come from the (Department) 93 to do their Christmas shopping in Paris, at the end of the day, during the first four Saturdays of December.
>
>   quoted in MOUSSA 2019, my translation

These ethno-racial stereotypes are not an exclusive construction of the far right and of extremists. During the demonstrations by the Yellow Vests in November and December 2018, even television journalists and commentators maintained that *les quartiers sensibles* – the French term for vulnerable areas, similar to *banlieue* – were 'underrepresented' and that the suburban grass-root organizations remained silent. A quote from Claire Rodineau, a journalist from BFM television, exemplifies the spatial metaphors, such as 'Les quartiers', used by journalists to describe a presupposed lack of political support among migrants and 'non-white' residents:

> Apart from a few calls to protest, [...] *les quartiers sensibles* were not much represented in the first two acts of the revolt. [...] Another factor that could explain the silence of *les quartiers* is that the associations of *les banlieues* seem to have had the same fear of being associated with the violence [...].
>
>   RODINEAU BFMTV 2018, my translation

Another journalist, Richard Bonnet from the Arte TV channel, emphasizes the lack of visibility of minorities and migrants during gatherings and protests. As an introduction to a television report on the absence of Yellow Vests' mobilization in suburban areas he wrote the following text:

> They (the inhabitants of the French suburban areas) do not belong to the same sociological and cultural group, as the yellow vests, the inhabitants of *les quartiers*, mostly with an immigration background, have not joined this movement. However, they have the same difficulties at the end of the month.
>
> BONNET *Arte* 18/02/2019, my translation

Thus, according to several journalists and commentators, the minority groups remained silent during the protests because the solidarity issues supported by the Yellow Vests are not central to suburban youth and ethnic minorities. In the quotes, the spatial metaphor – *les quartiers sensibles* – serves to amalgamate issues of political membership and identity in metropolitan spaces. The lack of solidarity expressed by *les quartiers sensibles* towards the Yellow Vests is an argument that also went viral in international newspapers: "It's a white movement. The question of minorities and their specific concerns are not central to the Yellow Vests", argues for instance a legal expert (Kantor 2019). One major argument is that the Yellow Vests' movement generates racist acts and homophobic comments, such as in Cognac or in Châteaufarine (Guérin 2018).

Through this cartography, the Yellow Vests that come from peri-urban areas are explicitly defined in contrast with *les quartiers de banlieue*, those districts in which suburban cultures are conceived of as composed of 'non-white' residents: Africans, Muslims and migrants. The multiplication of dual references – the use of cars in peri-urban spaces versus public transport in suburbs; semi-rural spaces versus dense urban fabric; houses with gardens versus high-rise estates – strengthens differences between the life style of 'white trash' representatives in peri-urban areas and the non-white residents in *les quartiers sensibles*.

The analyses by geographer Christophe Guilluy (2014), who argues in his book *La France périphérique* that the French elite has lost contact with the residents of the peri-urban and semi-rural spaces, were used as a key argument by commentators. The peri-urban areas become the 'forgotten spaces' of the republic, which are distinguished from *les banlieues* or *quartiers sensibles* where the migrants and the members of ethnic minorities are presented as threats to the cohesion of republican territory.

This variable racial cartography of metropolitan spaces, which categorized the Yellow Vests as a homogeneous ethnic group that lives far away from the wealthy regional centers and *les banlieues* – these "badlands of the republic" – to borrow an expression from Dikec (2007), provides a dystopic vision of the metropolitan spaces, increasingly specialized and segregated, and where insularities or all other forms of urban separatism were presented in the media as a threat.

4   The Rise of Transversal Solidarity in Unconventional Spaces

Against this dual representation of spaces, it seems urgent to explain to what extent issues of social justice can be interpreted as providing a chance for transversal solidarity in multiple metropolitan areas. In the case of the Yellow Vests, the mobilization was made possible through interrelated networks: social network-based and cross-class alliances; grassroots organizations connected to marginalized groups; as well as social media and places. This mobilization appears as a sort of 'rhizome', to speak with Gilles Deleuze, a sort of network that has no established origin, no hierarchy or precise purpose. Rather the mobilization can generate connections between social groups, and simultaneous meeting points in places. The notion of unconventional spaces can be associated to the concept of 'heterotopias', to borrow the word of the philosopher Michel Foucault. Through this notion, heterogeneous spaces form new spatio-temporal units in which social hierarchies, thresholds and conventions in society are called into question (Defert 2009, 41–42). Let us present some aspects of these new bounds of solidarity through the Yellow Vests' movement.

Firstly, the spatial dynamics of mobilization in unconventional spaces – the occupation of roundabouts, blockages of public infrastructure and demonstrations – reveals a new spatial strategy. At the very local level, the gatherings in roundabouts and infrastructure are "points of contact between the Yellow Vests and other social forces, for instance unionized workers" (Kipfer *IJURR* 2019). This contributes to changing the function of these unconventional places, which become spaces for discussions and mediations for social issues and police brutality.

Secondly, the meeting points – roundabouts, transport infrastructure and tollgates – are correlated with online mobilization. The gatherings were initially planned by hundreds of social groups on social media such as Facebook, Twitter and WhatsApp (Boyer, et al. 2019, 10). A series of calls communicated by collectives of Yellow Vests on the web is highly significant in the way they targeted local networks:

> Based on the success of our first call, we propose to organize it (the second call) democratically, in January, here in Commercy, with delegates

from all over France, in order to gather our demands in books [...]. We also propose to discuss the consequences of our movement together. Finally, we propose to decide on a collective way of organizing yellow vests, authentically democratically [...]. Together, let us create the assembly of assemblies, the Commune of Communes. It is the sense of history; this is our proposal.

> COLLECTIF 2018; my translation

This communication strategy shows to what extent social networks can mobilize online and simultaneously coordinate decentralized actions all over the country (Piquet 2018). In the initial phase of the development, on 17 November 2018, the movement was composed of 1,500 groups on Facebook. By 13 December 2018, they included in total 4,263,693 members (Boyer, et al. 2019, 7). Through social networks, the movement was able to plan 700 points of contact in the whole country. The Yellow Vests' movement has shown a broader spatial diffusion compared to the 2016 social justice movement *Nuit Debout* that generated 1,300 assemblies in 215 locations in total (Baciocchi, et al. 2019).

Thirdly, the longevity of the movement demonstrates that the protest registers of the movement can change significantly over time and space. In the initial phase of the movement, the Yellow Vests pointed out social justice issues related to tax reforms, while in February 2019 the protesters denounced the injuries caused by police violence during previous demonstrations. The multiplication of registers – that are changing and heterogeneous – indicates to what extent local groups of protesters are confronted with transversal discussions. On race and social issues, police brutality and precariousness, which are two major critical arguments of the Yellow Vests movement, these can both lead to shared convictions *and* controversies relating to representatives of grass-root organizations in *les banlieues*.

Fourthly, the construction of racialized categories in metropolitan spaces through suburban areas – *the badlands of the republic* – or the peri-urban spaces – the 'forgotten spaces' of the republic – does not explain the reasons for the mobilization. Rather it conceals potential transversal discussions on solidarity at the metropolitan level. The fact that minority representatives in *les banlieues* experience ethnic and racial discrimination on a regular basis does not occult the fact that they experience precariousness and constraining long-distance travelling patterns. For instance, regional studies and sociological surveys conducted by the Department of Seine-Saint-Denis testify to the dramatic rise of precarious employment in *les banlieues,* a phenomenon that is comparable to unemployment (Observatoire Départemental des Données Sociales de la Seine-Saint-Denis 2018). Signs of structural poverty are also identified on the edge of the Paris municipality – squats, homelessness and other indecent conditions of living – in parallel to the gentrification of Paris' central districts.

These four transversal aspects explain to what extent a mobilization locally encompasses multiple political positions: heterogeneous, changing, controversial and ambiguous. These dimensions also highlight how complex the dynamic of mobilization in urban spaces can be, and how the role of social media and local networks provides a basis for a 'communality' project. The notion of communality can be related to the assertion of Marc Purcell (2009, 312) that describes the development of a "horizontal network of interconnected underground roots". The capacity for mobilizing local networks becomes a sort of pre-condition for an active solidarity (Rosanvallon 2011, 381).

5   From Mobilization to a Participatory Democracy: Consensual
       Arguments and Irreconcilable Positions

During the period of protests, the Yellow Vests' movement did not explicitly converge with other social movements. However, this protest movement presents striking similarities and clear differences with past civic rights movements such the suburban uprising in 2005. Let us present the way theses similarities and differences can be understood through transversal dialogues. In the case of the Yellow Vests, the movement emerged outside of traditional political frameworks, without any established leaders or representative committees. On this matter, Robert Castel (2007, 15; my translation) wrote apropos the 2005 uprising in *les Banlieues*: "What is striking at first glance is the absence of recognized leaders, structured organizations, stated objectives or specific claims that are likely to lead to results".

As with the previous suburban uprising in 2005, the Yellow Vests experienced major difficulties in accessing public spaces. The motives of those involved in the Yellow Vests' movement is often correlated to the movement's abstention during the presidential election of 2017, which indicates that a substantial part of the Yellow Vests tend to reject the national electoral process (Boyer, et al. 2019, 15). The Yellow Vest symbolized the absence of political representativeness since the gatherings were planned without a formal 'hierarchy' in the movement nor a clear leading function in political activity. Among other things, the political behavior of the Yellow Vest supporters varied from one city to another, and the positive opinions expressed about the movement can be interpreted as related to the rise of far-right extremism, as well as that of radical left parties or also of abstention, depending on what city is considered (Procher 2019).

In response to racial stereotypes on suburbs – *les banlieues*, experts such as Eric Marlière have highlighted the viewpoints of suburban youth on the Yellow Vests movement. Marlière's empirical studies demonstrate that many suburban activists support the Yellow Vests on social issues. However, the young residents of *les banlieues* do not adhere to the conservative elements of the mobilization. As Marlière (2019) puts it, the suburban activities and residents legitimate the claims of the Yellow Vests but also distance themselves from the movement. Let us illustrate this point.

While the Yellow Vests protests were mostly focused on the 'inability to pay the bill'", social vulnerability has become an experience common to heterogeneous sociocultural groups in metropolitan areas. A round table organized by the research project Pop-Part, with young activists involved in social justice movements, brings to light a commonality of their views with the Yellow Vests:

> The *banlieues* have always been *Gilets Jaunes* [at heart], and yet in 2005 they were harshly criticized and received very little support. So today I understand why they don't want to be in the spotlight anymore, even though the demands made, in social terms, are exactly the same. Argues Karima during the round table.
>
> AHMED, et al. 2019

Thibaud, another young activist, adds:

> We are reaching such a point of economic and social asphyxiation that people are coming together in the same movement, but that does not mean that they all agree. On immigration, for example, if you take 10 *Gilets Jaunes*, there will always be differences. That's where you have to be very careful. Identifying as a *Gilet Jaune* does not mean agreeing on ideas, it means being in a state of mind to challenge them.
>
> AHMED, et al. 2019

Social justice issues have even generated support among a few suburban residents – mostly those who already have a working experience through trade unions for instance (Marlière 2019). This support demonstrates that transversal discussions exist in the Yellow Vests' movement. Thibaud, the activist quoted above, points out that local connections between Yellow Vests and other social justice movements have resulted in discussion forums in various regions.

> We work with the Adama Committee, set up by Adama Traoré's sister,
> which from the outset has led to meetings with the *Gilets Jaunes* of
> Rungis [a town in the southern Paris suburbs, home to France's largest
> wholesale market] and Saint-Nazaire [a port town on the Atlantic coast,
> near Nantes in western France], and with anti-racist activists. This cre-
> ates connections, but it's still very fragmented.
>
> AHMED, et al. 2019

The young generation of *banlieue* activists, who retrospectively experienced a
strong feeling of distrust towards several institutions such as the police and the
justice system, perfectly understand the critical position of the Yellow Vests on
police violence. However, as one activist expresses it, having observed racism
and xenophobia in the movement, his support of the Yellow Vests' movement
remains uncertain.

Ahmed's argument succinctly illustrates this viewpoint:

> I don't feel concerned in the sense that the *Gilets Jaunes'* problems are
> problems that our grandparents and our big brothers and sisters have
> always experienced. Everything they're protesting about – unemploy-
> ment, insecure and low-skilled jobs, police violence – we've always borne
> the brunt of that. But when immigrants tried to demonstrate, they were
> told: "You're not in your country, you can't do this, you can't complain.
> You should be happy to be here". My father was born in Algeria, he came
> here when he was 18. He was always told: "You're not French, you don't
> get to speak". There was this state of mind, we're not at home, so we keep
> our mouths shut.
>
> AHMED, et al. 2019

Suspicion and distrust towards institutions and the mass media are also common ground for activists who are involved in today's urban justice movements.
The case of the Yellow Vests testifies to the growing disconnection between
the experience of city dwellers, in terms of living conditions, and the analyses of the movement presented in the media. With the unprecedented media
coverage – 20 percent of the topics on television concerned the mobilization
between November 2018 and March 2019 – the movement has been associated with a dystopic vision, focusing on violent events perpetrated by protesters. According to Geraldine Poels and Véronique Lefort (2019), as early as in
December 2018 the media focused on multiple forms of violence, including
the violent treatment of the police forces and vandalism, with businesses damaged and pillaged.

Finally, the racial acts that occurred in the Yellow Vests' movement have been interpreted differently by activists. The first informant tends to marginalize racial acts within the Yellow Vests' movement, whereas the second one sees a clear racial issue throughout the Yellow Vests' movement. The media controversies and the multiple networks across cities do not facilitate debates on class and racial issues:

> One activist argues: For a long time, we were told that the rural classes that had mobilized were people concerned about cultural insecurity, [with] a fear of the other, a fear of immigrants, whereas we've seen that such concerns are in fact very much on the margins. There were two or three demands made by certain GMS regarding migrants, but we talk much more about social problems.
>
> AHMED, et al. 2019

A second activist asks: "Why are they (the Yellow Vests) going against us instead of rallying us against a system that makes us all in the same galley? Whether you are Arab, black or white, you have the same difficulties" (Ahmed, et al. 2019).

This critical debate on transversal solidarity is not limited to the viewpoints of young activists. The American critical theorist Bernard Harcourt, for instance, recalls that his "reluctance to wear a yellow vest comes from the identity orientations that are present in the movement and the use of patriotic and nationalist symbols" (Maximin *Le Grand Continent* 14 Feb 2019); whereas the historian Ludivine Bantigny remarks that "the act of brandishing a tricolor flag (during the demonstrations) can have very different meanings, which cannot be summed up in an identity logic, quite the contrary. It is also a reference to the French Revolution, as there are many others in the movement, including grievance books" (Maximin *Le Grand Continent* 14 Feb 2019).

Thus, while consensual viewpoints emerge on social issues among suburban activists and potential supporters, this does not systematically lead to cohesion or political support. According to Marlière (2019), these hybrid forms of involvement are complex to analyze in situ, during the formation of the movement, since the degree of involvement depends upon familial patterns, semi-professional categories, age-bracket, geographic distribution, religious belonging and gender identities.

The fact that the Yellow Vests were able to define common views through a list of propositions cannot alter the fact that the Yellow Vests' movement recovers different social views and political values. Through a radical democratic vision, their aspiration combines with powerful political disaffiliation regarding political parties and a distrust of institutions such the police and the justice system (Forray 2019). A few anti-racist movements officially announced their support of the Yellow Vests in 2018, but suburban youth and activists remained distant.

6   Recasting Solidarity in Metropolitan Spaces through Transversal Practices

This concluding section aims to clarify the role that transversal solidarity plays for the social justice movement of the Yellow Vests. I will focus on two theoretical dimensions in order to determine to what extent the transversal solidarity represent a chance for social justice movements: the first dimension focuses on transversal solidarity as a new way of defining complex political affiliations in metropolitan areas, whilst the second one highlights transversal dialogues as a practice of solidarity.

Firstly, I argue that the political values of the Yellow Vests must be problematized at the local level and not at the national level if one is to understand how transversal dialogues can emerge through local networks. Indeed, the Yellow Vests' movement shows that emergent socio-political forces in metropolitan spaces forged transversal dialogues through social networks in embracing political support both to the left and to the far right of the national political scene. Such positions can generate conflictual viewpoints, political paradoxes and contrary social dynamics, but also make transversal dialogues possible. This is mainly because the Yellow Vests' movement is composed of diverse groups on social media that create points of contact all over France. "People are coming together in the same movement, but that does not mean that they all agree", a young suburban activist of the Yellow Vests points out (Ahmed, et al. 2019). A discourse on anti-discrimination, which was carried out by local representatives in the city of Rungis, does not make racial acts perpetrated in Cognac disappear, for instance. Thus, the existence of or opportunity for transversal dialogues depends on the local network and the social media where gatherings emerge.

The Yellow Vests' movement has to be considered in a decentralized perspective in order to understand potential alliances. Since the 90s, successive French governments initiated neoliberal policies that promoted a withdrawal of the state in metropolitan areas and the multiplication of public debates in decentralized contexts (Gaudin 2008, 263–265). From this local perspective, the movement questions the neoliberal tendencies of the government – how compatible the reduction of social inequalities are with neoliberal policies and privatization, for instance – as well as the authoritarian reflexes of *La République Française*. In particular, the Yellow Vests have initiated acts of solidarity and forms of communality that go against the neoliberal principle of individual accountability, rather than simply resisting the call to political action.

The growing disconnection between the conception of national policy orientations and the implementation of solidarity strategies in cities has also contributed to a depoliticization of the masses in metropolitan spaces. As mentioned previously, it is not surprising to observe that the Yellow Vests were substantially abstentionists during the 2017 presidential election. (Boyer, et al. 2019, 15) This sign of depoliticization suggests that the mass mobilization and gatherings in unconventional spaces testify to a will to redefine the role of citizens in urban regimes.

Secondly, the Yellow Vests give rise to interesting standpoints on transversal solidarity, since the political viewpoints are heterogeneous and changing both within the movement and outside – among local supporters and suburban activists, for example. Unified by a yellow uniform, the local networks tend to eclipse the function of representativeness in political dialogues and promote the function of *expressiveness in public spaces*.

I have previously described how the rise of transversal alliances in metropolitan areas have emerged in contrast to the national identity discourse. Through a series of dual references, the national discourse that is diffused in the media provides a racialized cartography in metropolitan spaces: suburbs versus peri-urban spaces, racial segregation versus social insecurity, civic rights versus social rights, as well as black and Muslims versus 'white trash' groups. This phantasmagoric vision of metropolitan spaces reinforces the idea that the republican state would remain the keystone of the social cohesion in French metropolitan areas. The 'dangerous' masses in metropolitan spaces, which the republican elite traditionally fear (Sintomer 2011, 246–247), provide an easy target for racial comments in the media.

Through local networks, however, expressions of transversal solidarity can emerge. These networks work without offices, localities, hotlines or addresses. Rather, the Yellow Vests who are affiliated to the movement through social networks, communicated through messages and hashtags. In particular, the existence of 1,500 groups over the country explains why Yellow Vests' fractions were opened to alternative movements, new narratives and experiences such as was the case with *Le Comité Vérité* and *Justice pour Adama Traoré*. Local networks created democratic channels that account for both social and racial justice in multifaceted metropolitan areas.

The notion of public space is useful for the understanding of these new ways of mediation. As Thierry Paco (2009) reminds us, the notion of 'public space', the so-called *espace public* in the French language, is a polysemic term that can designate at least (1) the expression of opinions in the political sphere, (2) the development of public opinions in the traditional media and social media and (3) the urbanity spaces made up of streets, public places and parks. In the light of the Yellow Vests' experience, the notion of public space can be seen as an arena that simultaneously is composed of a *space of circulation* and a *space of communication,* as Isaac Joseph puts it (1995, 13). The Yellow Vests and the roundabouts have a political sense in these public spaces since these meaningful objects help people to gather in the city.

Through local networks, the new public arenas are deeply connected to new practices of engagement. While the national perspective gives a profoundly racialized representation of the suburban and peri-urban spaces of metropolitan centers, the Yellow Vests movement allows for the bridging of local networks without representation or hierarchy. In unconventional spaces, practices of solidarity involve intense mediations in which irreducible positions alternate with consensual viewpoints. Interviewed by France Culture in the city of Limay, Saïd illustrates the possible mediations that occur in unconventional spaces during the gatherings: "I have talked to the 'yellow vests' who vote for the National Front. We realize that this is a dissatisfaction vote, not an ideology" (Chaudet *France Culture* 21 Feb 2019, my translation).

The reflexivity on position and identity constitutes a prerequisite position for establishing a common view on precariousness in metropolitan spaces. While the dialogue on identities allows one to define a position, issues of alterity can emerge and be discussed across boundaries: tax, transport, migration, housing, health, pensions, work conditions and participatory strategy. Based on flexible and adaptable networks, the transversal movement provides a capacity to discuss political events and reject media speculations in a timely manner. For instance, an isolated sexist and racist act during a gathering in Cognac was followed by its denunciation through social media by a representative of the local grassroots movement (Guérin 2018).

The Yellow Vests reject traditional political affiliations and media channels in order to make possible the exploration of new mediations in the public realm. The notion of transversal alliances is not an ode to the convergence of struggles. (Yuval-Davis 1999; Tazzioli 2020). Rather it implies confrontations, conflictual debates, ambivalent positions, reflexivity and partial cohesion. Tensions that rise between movements and individuals can generate sexism, racial stigma or social labelling in metropolitan areas. However, those attitudes are not one exclusive position in the collective. Rather the Yellow Vests' movement contributed to explore hybrid approaches in matters of identity, place and solidarity. This new political expression appears to imply a new era for urban justice movements, in which citizenship aspirations become much more interrelated with the development of transversal dialogues and mediations in matters of social justice.

The amplitude of mass mobilization during 2018 and the achievements of the Yellow Vests in 2019 were sufficiently unexpected and astonishing to reverse the famous quote of Karl Marx (1926) in his book *The Eighteenth Brumaire of Louis Bonaparte*: when *you play* the *fiddle* down below, what *else* is to be expected but that those at the *top* of the *state* dance? The event of the Yellow Vests reveals retrospectively to what extent the French state and its institutions have been deeply shaken by actions at ground level. Indeed, a series of national reforms focuses on the aspirations of the Yellow Vests. From December 2018 to April 2019, the massive mobilization forced Macron's government to suspend the fuel tax increase and initiate a national consultation, the so-called *Grand Débat* (the great debate), which focused on four key social justice issues: taxation, the organization of public services, ecological transition, as well as democracy and citizenship. Recently, in April 2021, President Macron also announced the closure of l'*Ecole National d'Administration* (ENA), the school that forms France's elite civil servants, as a consequence of the Yellow Vests' protests. In early 2021, calls for mobilization and demonstrations sporadically emerged in Lyon, Paris and Bordeaux. Far from disappearing, the movement is looking for a new impetus out of the traditional political scene. More than 200 local delegations of the Yellow Vests exist today in France and constitute an assembly of assemblies, the so-called *Assemblée des assembles*, a decentralized body in which local delegates of the Yellow Vests discuss the way to prioritize objectives for the years to come. Will these facts contribute to recasting citizenship issues in metropolitan areas? The massive mobilization in unconventional spaces clearly shows that the convergence of views on social issues and the debates on political membership and identity can raise new transversal discussions in the public realm.

References

Agustín, Ó. G., and M.B. Jørgensen (2020). "On Transversal Solidarity: An Approach to Migration and Multi-Scalar Solidarities". *Critical Sociology*: 1–17.

Ahmed, Baptiste, Hachimia, Jeremy, Karima, Lisa-Marie, Louiza, and Thibaut (23 May 2019). "How the Youth of the Banlieues See the Gilets jaunes". *Métropolitiques*.

Retrieved August 17, 2020, from https://www.metropolitiques.eu/Gilets-jaunes-rega rds-de-jeunes-de-banlieue.html.

Baciocchi, S., L. Beauguitte, P. Blavier, and N. Lambert (2019). "Documenting the Diffusion of the 2016 French Nuit Debout". *Research Data Journal for the Humanities and Social Sciences*. Brill: 1–10.

Bonnet, R. (18/02/2019). "La banlieue, absente des gilets jaunes". *Arte journal*. Retrieved August 17, 2020, from https://www.arte.tv/fr/videos/087985-000-A/la-banlieue -absente-des-gilets-jaunes/.

Bauböck, R. (2017). "Political Membership and Democratic Boundaries". In *Oxford Handbook of Citizenship*, edited by Bauböck, R., Bloemraad, I., and Vink M., (eds.). Oxford: Oxford University Press: 60–78.

Bornstein, R. (2019). "En immersion numérique aves les «gilets Jaunes»". *Penser pour agir*, Paris: Fondation Jean Jaurès. Retrieved August 17, 2020, from https://jean-jau res.org/nos-productions/en-immersion-numerique-avec-les-gilets-jaunes.

Boyer, P. C., T. Delemotte, G. Gauthier, V. Rollet, and B. Schmutz (2019). *"Les détermi-nants de la mobilisation des gilets jaunes"*. Center for Research in Economics and Statistics.

Brochet, F. (09/11/2018). "Les gilets jaunes, une jacquerie numérique", *Le Figaro*. Retrieved August 17, 2020, from https://www.lefigaro.fr/vox/politique/2018/11/09/ 31001-20181109ARTFIG00317-les-gilets-jaunes-une-jacquerie-numerique.php.

Castel, R. (2007). *La Discrimination négative. Citoyens ou indigènes*. Paris: Seuil.

Chaudet, E., and Y. Mandelbaum (21/02/2019). "«Gilets jaunes» et banlieue: y aller ou pas". *France Culture*. Retrieved August 17, 2020, from https://www.franceculture.fr/ emissions/les-pieds-sur-terre/gilets-jaunes-et-banlieue.

Collectif (2018). "Deuxième appel de Commercy: l'assemblée des assemblées!" Retrieved August 17, 2020, from https://tendanceclaire.org/contenu/articles-pdf/ artpdf-1504.pdf.

Defert, D. (2009). *Foucault, Les corps utopiques, Les Hétérotopies*, Lignes: Paris.

Dikeç, M. (2007). *Badlands of the Republic: Space, Politics and Urban Policy*. Oxford: Blackwell Publishing.

Diener, A. C. (2017), "Re-Scaling Citizenship: From Polis to Empire to State Formation and Beyond". In *Oxford Handbook of Citizenship*, Bauböck, R., Bloemraad, I., and Vink M. (eds). Oxford: Oxford University Press: 36–59.

Fassin, D. and Defossez A. C. (15/03/2019). "Les gilets jaunes, objet politique non iden-tifié". *Analyse Opinion Critique*. Retrieved August 17, 2020, from https://aoc.media/ analyse/2019/03/15/gilets-jaunes-objet-politique-non-identifie/.

Forray, J. B. (01/02/2019). "Jacques Lévy: L'abandon des territoires périurbains est une légende". *La gazette des communes*. Retrieved August 17, 2020, from https://www .lagazettedescommunes.com/603895/jacques-levy-labandon-des-territoires-peri urbains-est-une-legende/.

Gaudin, J. P. (2008). "Politiques publiques : dispositifs participatifs et démocratie". In Giraud, O., and Warin, P. (eds) *Politique publique et démocratie*. Paris: La Découverte.

Geisser, V. (2019). "Les gilets jaunes et le triptyque " islam, banlieues, immigration ": une machine à produire des fantasmes identitaires". *Migrations Société* 19.1:175.

Guérin, J. (19/11/2018). "Cognac: des insultes racistes proférées sur un barrage des Gilets Jaunes". *Sud-Ouest*. Retrieved August 17, 2020, www.sudouest.fr/2018/11/19/cognac-des-insultes-racistes-proferees-sur-un-barrage-des-gilets-jaunes-5579190-882.php?nic.

Guilluy, C. (2014). *La France périphérique: Comment on a sacrifié les classes populaires*. Paris: Flammarion.

Hart, C. (2018). *Doing a literature Review: Releasing the Research Imagination*. 2nd ed. Sage Study Skills. London: Sage Publications Ltd.

Higgins, A. (16/12/2018). "France's Far Right Sees Gold in Yellow Vest Movement". *The New York Times*. Retrieved August 17, 2020, from https://www.nytimes.com/2018/12/16/world/europe/france-national-front-yellow-vests.html.

Jobert, B. (2008). "Des référentiels civils". In Giraud, O., and Warin, P. (eds) *Politique publique et démocratie*. Paris: La Découverte.

Joumard, R. (5/12/2018). "Analyse des revendications des Gilets jaunes". *Mediapart*. Retrieved August 17, 2020, from https://blogs.mediapart.fr/robert-joumard/blog/051218/analyse-des-revendications-des-gilets-jaunes/commentaires.

Joseph, I. (1995). "Reprendre la rue". in *Prendre place. Espace public et culture dramatique*. Colloque de Cerisy, Paris: Plan Urbain: 11–35.

Jørgensen, M. B., and C. U. Schierup (2020). "Transversal Solidarities and the City: An Introduction to the Special Issue". *Critical Sociology*: 1–11.

Kantor, A. (28/01/2019). "Why are France's yellow vest protests so white?" *Al Jazeera*. Retrieved August 17, 2020, from https://www.aljazeera.com/indepth/features/france-yellow-vest-protests-white-190127223757928.html.

Kipfer, S. (2019). "The Yellow Vest in France: A Few Snapshots". *International journal of Urban and Regional Research*. https://www.ijurr.org/the-urban-now/the-yellow-vests-in-france-a-few-snapshots/.

Marlière, É. (9/01/2019). "Les 'gilets jaunes' vus par les habitants des quartiers populaires". *La Tribune*. Retrieved August 17, 2020, from https://www.latribune.fr/opinions/tribunes/les-gilets-jaunes-vus-par-les-habitants-des-quartiers-populaires-803226.html.

Marx, K. (1926). *The eighteenth brumaire of Louis Bonaparte*. International Publishers.

Maximin, E. (14/02/2019). "Le Savant et le mouvement, quatre perspectives sur les Gilets jaunes", *Le Grand Continent*. Retrieved August 17, 2020, from https://legrandcontinent.eu/fr/2019/02/14/le-savant-et-le-mouvement/.

Moussa, S. N. (19/01/2019). "Gilets jaunes et banlieues françaises : une convergence impossible?" *Middle East Eye*. Retrieved August 14, 2020, from https://www.middle easteye.net/fr/opinion-fr/gilets-jaunes-et-banlieues-francaises-une-convergence -impossible.

Noiriel, G. (2019). "Gillets jaunes, la nouvelle Jacquerie?" *France Culture*, Retrieved August 14, 2020, from https://www.franceculture.fr/emissions/la-grande-table -2eme-partie/gilets-jaunes-la-nouvelle-jacquerie.

Nossiter, A. (31/12/2018). "Macron Vows Order 'Without Compromise' in Rebuke to Yellow Vest Protests". *The New York Times*. Retrieved August 14, 2020, from https:// www.nytimes.com/2018/12/31/world/europe/france-macron-yellow-vests.html?

Observatoire Départemental des Données Sociales de la Seine-Saint-Denis (2018). *"Portrait de territoire Plaine commune".* Retrieved August 14, 2020, from https://res sources.seinesaintdenis.fr/IMG/pdf/2018_portrait_territoire_ept_plaine_comm une.pdf.

Paco, T. (2009). *L'espace public*. Paris: La Découverte.

Perrault, G. (15/11/2018). "Qualifier les gilets jaunes de poujadistes, est-ce vraiment leur nuire?" *Le Figaro*. Retrieved August 14, from https://www.lefigaro.fr/vox/politique/ 2018/11/15/31001-20181115ARTFIG00341-guillaume-perrault-qualifier-les-822ogilets -jaunes8221-de-822opoujadistes8221-est-ce-leur-nuire.php.

Piquet, C. (2018). "Gilets jaunes: la carte des 700 rassemblements prévus le 17 novem-bre". *Le Parisien*. Retrieved August 14, from https://www.leparisien.fr/economie/gil ets-jaunes-la-carte-des-rassemblements-prevus-le-17-novembre-06-11-2018-7936 479.phpn.

Poels, G., and V. Lefort (13/11/2019). "Gilets jaunes: une médiatisation d'une ampleur inédite", *La revue des medias*. Retrieved August 14, from https://larevuedesmedias .ina.fr/gilets-jaunes-mediatisation-chaines-info-twitter.

Porcher, S. (2019). "Qui sont les Gilets Jaunes, Une étude sur les 10 plus grandes villes françaises". *HAL Archives ouvertes*. halshs-02357802. Retrieved August 14 2020, from https://halshs.archives-ouvertes.fr/halshs-02357802.

Purcell, M. (2009). "Hegemony and Difference in Political Movements: Articulating Networks of Equivalence". *New political Science, A journal of Politics and Culture*. London: Routledge.

Rodineau, C. (30/11/2018). "Gilets Jaunes: les banlieues, grandes absentes du mouve-ment?" *BFMTV*. Retrieved August 14, from https://www.bfmtv.com/societe/gilets -jaunes-les-banlieues-grandes-absentes-du-mouvement_AN-201811300078.html.

Rosanvallon, P. (2011). *La Société des égaux*. Paris: Éditions du Seuil.

Sintomer, Y. (2011). "Délibération et participation: affinités électives ou concepts en tension?" *Participations*. 1:239–275.

Tunbridge, J. E., and G. J. Ashworth (1996). *Dissonant heritage: The management of the past as a resource in conflict*. Chichester, UK and New York, NY: John Wiley & Sons.

Tazzioli, M. (2020). "What is Left of Migrants' Spaces? Transversal Alliances and the Temporality of Solidarity" *Political Anthropological Research on International Social Sciences* 1.1: 137–161.

Yuval-Davis, N. (1999). "What is 'transveral politics'", Sounding special issue 12, *Transversal politics*. Retrieved August 14, 2019 from https://autonomorganisering .noblogs.org/files/2015/12/davis_transversal-politics.pdf.

CHAPTER 8

Forward through the Past? Reinventing the 'People's House' in Subaltern Stockholm

Carl-Ulrik Schierup, Aleksandra Ålund and Ilhan Kellecioglu

The People's House shall be its castle, from where they shall defend what they have already won, but above all with the arms of spirit and power undertake new achievements.

HJALMAR BRANTING 1898[1]

• • •

[T]he present is never at one with itself. It is riddled with time-holes torn open by the past's unfulfilled promises for the future.

JAN VERWOERT 2009[2]

•.•
:

1   Vistas of Another Rebirth

The Hunger[3] is the title of a book on the birth pains of an epochal social transformation that was with the winds of time to transpire as the 'exceptional' Swedish welfare state.[4] It confronts us, in the trails of a great famine, 1867–69, with historical memories of poverty, usurpation of the commons, arrogant ruling class neglect, and a massive overseas emigration as the 19th century drew to a close. Sweden was then one of the poorest countries in Europe, and only six percent of the population had voting rights. Industrialization was still at an

---

1   As quoted by Ståhl (2005: 11). Our translation from Swedish. Branting was a leading Social democrat.
2   Quoted from Verwoert (2009).
3   *Svälten* by Västerbro (2018).
4   An earlier version of the present text was published in the journal *Critical Sociology*, in 2020, September 16. Available through: https://doi.org/10.1177/0896920520957066.

early stage, with an incipient working class exposed to precarious livelihoods and working conditions, child labor and abject housing. It was a state of precarity that triggered critical thinking and politics of contestation. A broadening political subjectivity and unionization was supported by a solidarity network of self-governing commons, *The People's Houses*, (Swedish: *Folkets Hus*); cradles of democratic socialism across a changing nation (Ståhl 2005). The first People's House in Sweden was founded in the City of Malmö in 1893, and soon workers' assemblies were established throughout the country. The People's House drew its label from *Maisons du Peuple*, working class meeting places for unions and political associations, initiated by the socialist cooperative movement in Belgium. It was a time when 'the free word' was still a vision (Ståhl 2005: 13) and autonomous workers-driven meeting places seen as an essential ground for the struggle for freedom of speech and assembly.

The Swedish labor movement was to become pillar of one of the most successful models of democratization, economic development, and social welfare of the 20th century. At its zenith by the mid-1970s it promised, under the insignia of international solidarity, the inclusion on equal terms of fellow humans fleeing wars and persecution, into a ramifying edifice of social, political, labor, and cultural rights (Ålund and Schierup 1991). This historical rebirth of the nation carries a critical message to our present when Sweden can no longer legitimately claim 'exceptionalism' in terms of inclusionary solidarity and social justice (Schierup and Ålund 2011). Indeed, Sweden figured in one of the world's most prominent economic magazines (Financial Times 2013) as a "hazardous neoliberal experiment", in an editorial comment on a youth uprising in Stockholm's racially stigmatized suburbs, 2013 (see Schierup, Ålund and Kings 2014). These 'riots', stated the Financial Times, could hardly be seen as related to matters of migration or ethnicity, but to an obsessive dismantlement of the welfare state. Disregarding this, the so-called 'Swedish Model' continues to figure internationally in visions for an inclusive democratic socialism as "the most livable society in history" which "got the furthest along in undermining capital's power" (Sunkara 2019: 105–6).

At home, however, in contemporary Sweden's precarious urban communities, ridden by poverty, discrimination and racializing stigma, we could recognize a more convincing reception of this mythological past in the agenda for social justice of an anti-racist movement by young post-migrants; a "renaissance from the margins", building transversal solidarity across ethno-cultural identities, confessional affiliations, and institutional confines (León Rosales and Ålund 2017; Sernhede, León Rosales and Söderman 2019). In the following we address the trajectory of their activism as it transpired as a new political subject, encompassing the 'reinvention' of the old working class common of the 'People's House'. In focus stands the case of the community center, *Folkets Husby* (Husby of the People), founded in 2016 in the Stockholm neighborhood of Husby from where the 2013 uprising took off. The new community center was envisioned as an "oasis for organization" (Al-Khamisi, et al. 2019); a mouthpiece for social justice in a capital torn apart by socio-spatial polarization. This vision is reminiscent of Bollier's (2015) conception of the common as a "paradigm for social transformation".

On this background we ask whether a new beginning is posited in which an "unlost heritage takes possession of itself"? (paraphrasing Bloch 2000 [1917], 3). It is a question that needs to address the enigma of commoning in precarious times (Schierup and Ålund 2020). It calls for a discussion on how a postpolitical hegemony could be challenged, and what could, under the burden of a neoliberal urban governance regime, be the comportment of 'civil society'. On these premises we scrutiny a growing engagement of professionalized NGOs in politics for redemption of the most disadvantaged and its impact on the space, position, and agency of a contestative urban activism. The central issue is an assessment of openings for what Yuval-Davies (1999) has referred to by the concept of 'transversal politics', implicating dialogue between disparate actors on equitable terms and gaining a voice for subordinated people on their own terms. In connection with this the notion of the 'subaltern', coined by Antonio Gramsci (1971), is central. Through it we focus on identities subject to a cultural hegemony, excluding agency and voices of subordinated social groups from democratic participation.

We build the following analysis and argument on, still ongoing, research, 2012–21. It is grounded on a continuous interchange with movement activists in Stockholm's disadvantaged neighborhoods, on sustained participant observation (on site and through netnography on social media), on interviews with representatives of CSOs/NGOs and the Stockholm city administration, and on critical reading of official documents and secondary sources (investigative reports, journal articles, and academic books). Our approach is informed by a 'third option' for engaging with contentious social movements, aiming to bridge the divide between a detached 'invocating' academic objectivism and a solidaristic 'advocating' engagement with movements (Haiven and Khasnabish 2014).[5] This rationale aims at consolidating what Haraway (1988) refers to as

---

5   Ilhan Kellecioglu, co-author of this chapter and research fellow at Uppsala University, has
     himself a background as an activist in the community of Husby, including *Megafonen*. At
     present he interconnects his position as scholar and engaged activist within the organization
     Ort till Ort, a section of the *Social Centre*, locating its counselling activities at Folkets Husby
     (see later in this chapter). Ålund and Schierup, researchers at Linköping University, are both

'situated knowledge' related to a positional perspective, framed by a double engagement in social movements and critical academic research.

2 A Post-political Time Hole

Under the banner of 'flexibility' the great neoliberal ideological and political-economic transformation has posited contingent employment, a truncated citizenship, and fragmented livelihoods as a new global norm. A multifarious precariat in search of identity has entered world history (Schierup and Jørgensen 2016). Its predicaments are forged by deep changes in the relations between market, state, and civil society; It bespeaks a crisis of liberal democracy, but also the genesis of new contestative movements, emerging out of a gaping post-political time hole, torn open by the past's unfulfilled promises for the future.[6]

2.1 Anatomy of a 'Stealth Revolution'

Precarious conditions of work and citizenship arrive in tandem with a transformation of a redistributive welfare state into a neoliberal 'regulatory state' (Majone 1997). Seen from this perspective, the state is "not anymore ... the mediator or 'the shield' protecting society from the tensions between capital and labor through ... redistributive policies" (Sommer-Houdeville 2017, 162). It is a transformation of the state in which innumerable new regulations are tailored to undermine citizenship, the capacity to mobilize contentious resistance and to form political constituencies, giving way to a hypertrophy of technocracy and the executive (cf. Sassen 2006). Trapped in consensual 'post-politics' (Mouffe 2005), old political parties have deserted visions of solidarity, equality, and social justice, and are losing popular legitimacy. Democracy has taken the form, asserts Ali (2018, 147) in speaking of Tony Blair's 'Third Way' Britain, of an 'extreme center, in which center-left and center-right collude to preserve the status quo'. It has been depicted in terms of a "stealth revolution" (Brown 2015) which spells the end of liberal democracy by casting its very moral reason and institutional foundations in the mold of market rationality; an 'undoing the demos' that holds implications for the role of civil society. In the global North as well as the South, renegotiated social contracts, signified by state marketization and the expansion of a technocratic 'participatory

---

participating in international movements for social justice, concerned with precarity, civic and migrant rights.

6   Alluding to the introductory quotation by Verwoert (2009).

governance', are matched by growing prominence of a reconfigured, professionalized and NGOized civil society, with a role as service providers rather than as a mobilizing force in politics (O'Brien and Penna 1998; Kaldor 2003).

Even in Sweden center-right and center-left have come to converge towards a new hegemonic normal defined by a dogmatism of neoliberal austerity. "[Bourgeois and Social Democratic] led coalitions", muses Therborn (2018, 3), "that have alternated in power since 1991 have operated as relay runners in the promotion of inequality and profiteering. Together they have lowered taxes on inheritance, wealth, and residential property to zero, made capital income less taxable than labor income, and tightened the scale of social benefits, while making them harder to access". It is a politics that, in the 2000s has kept company with a fear-mongering racist discourse on the 'non-belonging' Other as a floating post-political signifier. This is, evidently, the significate trademark of the so-called *Swedish Democrats* (Mulinari and Neergaard 2017), with roots in the pre- World War II Swedish Nazi party, step by step spinning itself into the position of today's third largest political party in the polls (as of June 2021). Yet, it is a racializing political agenda that center-left as well as center-right have bought into, in vying for the votes of a disorientated electorate to whom appeals to welfarist solidarity do not sound convincing any more (Schierup and Scarpa 2017).

A xenophobic and racializing discourse has, in consequence, been instrumentalized by a Swedish corollary of the 'extreme center' with the effect of suppressing democratic deliberation on ground causes of a welfare institutional, so-called 'system collapse'.[7] It has been exploited to paint over structural disjunctions of a financialized political economy, precarisation of labor, and a fragmenting commodification of the entire welfare institutional system (Schierup and Scarpa 2017; Allelin, et al. 2018); a state of the nation, coupled with a polarizing urban segregation in terms of class and race. It is a state of apparent apoliticality that disguises or represses political antagonisms (cf. Mouffe 2005), rendered void of democratic deliberation in favor of expert rule driven by New Public Management. From a state in the 1980s, still with a reputation for being one of the world's most egalitarian societies, Sweden has become one of the most unequal societies in the world in terms of the distribution of wealth, and the OECD member with the fastest growth of inequality of income, which has, alleges Therborn (2018, 4), been taken back close to the state of the late 1930s.

---

7   Idiom coined by the Swedish minister of foreign affairs, Margot Wallström, in 2015.

2.2   'Spaces of Outsidership'

A former Swedish 'exceptionalism' has been transmuted into a 'state of exception' (Schierup, et al. 2014);[8] an immanent condition by which civil, political, and social rights pertaining to citizenship are truncated. A systemic precarisation of citizenship, labor and livelihoods is most obvious in extended rental housing complexes on the periphery of the major cities, predominantly populated by immigrants and post-immigrants with their backgrounds in Asia, Africa, and Latin America. These marginalized urban spaces are parts of the Swedish post-political polis from which vital social institutions have been evacuated or depreciated. Youth in these areas suffer, in particular, from the consequences of an extreme commodification of primary and secondary education, producing a cumulative, spatially articulated, race and class inequality (Kornhall and Bender 2018).

Yet, the precariousness of these so-called 'spaces of outsidership' (*utanförskapsområden*) (e.g. Folkpartiet 2004) is functional from the perspective of a prevailing 'accumulation by dispossession' (Harvey 2004). They offer 'occupational ghettoes' (Feuchtwang 1982) in which devalued welfare provisions and disciplinary workfare generate cheap, hands down exploitable labor reserves for the service economy of the post-political metropolis (Schierup, et al. 2006, 195–230). They are, moreover, the lucrative prey of transnational housing companies, reaping hyper-profits through bogus takeovers, exclusivist gentrification, sham renovation, and the illicit raise of rents. The resulting stress on the budgets of families subsisting on precarious livelihoods has forged housing congestion and eviction of impoverished tenants (Polanska, et al. 2019); a condition contingent on a 'monstrous hybrid', creating and reproducing socio-economic inequality (Christophers 2013).

These deprived metropolitan areas have in the course of the 2010s become hotspots for politics of securitization, involving militant policing and racial profiling (Schclarek Mulinari 2020). Still a militant securitization continues to keep company with a soft biopolitical twin, involving interventions through a broad repertoire of technologies by police and social workers (Dahlstedt and Lozić 2017; Gressgård 2017), focused on therapeutic fostering of potentially 'delinquent youth', on responsibilization of 'dysfunctional parenting', and on redemption of 'traditionalist migrant women' (Mulinari and Lundqvist 2017).

The idea of 'spaces of outsidership' – later renamed 'particularly exposed areas' (*särskilt utsatta områden*) – which continues to guide government intervention, social work and prescribed activities of NGOs in precarious urban

---

8   Referring to Agamben (2005).

neighborhoods – was first masterminded by the center-right People's Party[9] in 2004 (Folkpartiet 2004). It speaks, in terms of the 'culture of poverty' thesis,[10] about areas of a 'particularly deep outsidership', suffering abject exclusion; a state reproduced by deviant cultures, transmitted from generation to generation. Here, perceived 'cultural differences' vis a vis an autochthonous so-called 'majority' are supposed to condition "situations in which groups living in outsidership do not ... understand how ... central social arenas function and neither the set of values and cultural points of reference that lend these arenas their cohesive cultural glue" (Folkpartiet 2004, 8). The cure is prescribed as 'empowerment against outsidership'. It is a formula operationalized in terms of training for 'entrepreneurship', embedded in politics for social cohesion, fostering the deviant Other into values of liberal democracy in the encounter with "situations of conflict when mutually irreconcilable individual and group-related value systems, goals and ambitions meet"(Regeringen 2008, 59).

3 A Predicament of Counter-Hegemony: Invited versus Invented Spaces

Yet, the perceived victims of 'outsidership' were to strike back. Reclaiming the city from commodifying politics of enclosure under the banner of 'place struggle' a new urban justice movement was, as we discuss further ahead, spearheaded by young post-migrant 'organic intellectuals'[11] (León Rosales and Ålund 2017). They proved to possess a critical understanding of how the 'central arenas' of society work and of the conditionality of civic activism, exposed to an ever-present risk of being deemed 'uncivil', beyond the pale of 'liberal democracy'.

Scrutinizing this predicament, we use two interconnected notions on the performance of citizenship: *invented and invited spaces of citizenship* versus *active and activist citizenship*.

The concept of 'invited spaces' originates from the work of Karen Brock, Andrea Cornwall and John Gaventa (2001). It was further developed in

---

9   Renamed 'The Liberals' (*Liberalerna*) in 2015.
10 The term "culture of poverty" was coined by Oscar Lewis (1968), arguing that the values of people in poverty play a significant role in sustaining their impoverished condition, thus reproducing a 'cycle of poverty' across generations.
11 "Organic intellectuals" is a term devised by Gramsci (1971) to signify socially engaged practical intellectuals emanating from and articulating imaginaries and strategies of civil society.

different contexts by, for example, Cornwall (e.g. 2002), Gaventa (e.g. 2006) and Miraftab (2009, 2004). Invited spaces are, as argued by Gaventa (2006, 26–27), related to 'participatory governance', formalized at different levels from local government to national policy and even in global policy forums (e.g. Ålund and Schierup 2018). Aiming at the creation of more open arenas for citizen participation, citizens are 'invited' to participate by various kinds of authorities and organizations, be they governmental, supranational agencies or non-governmental organizations. These spaces are "either institutionalized ongoing, or more transient, through one-off forms of consultation" (Gaventa 2006, 26–27).

Any movement of civil society, operating within the framework of dominant institutions – be they local, national, or transnational – face risks of NGO-ization, that is dependence on donors, and involving de-politization (Ålund and Schierup 2018), connected with limitations of invited spaces for civil society participation in contemporary forms of participatory governance. This is connected to transformation of civil society from an 'activist' into a neoliberal model (Kaldor 2003) with civil society becoming institutionalized, as service providers replacing a retiring welfare state.

In Sweden, a comparable conditionality of contentious movements has been brought about by an exceptional decentralization of urban governance. The Social Democratic party, governing uninterruptedly for 44 years (1932–76), was originally an integrated part and the political vanguard of self-directed popular movements surging during the early phase of industrialization. In the period of coordinated capitalism after World War II these movements were incorporated into a centralized welfare state through institutionalized strategies of consensus making, including state funding (Peterson, et al. 2017). This political culture was increasingly challenged by the new social movements from the late 1960s onwards, including in the 2000s the post-migrant led urban justice movement. It gave rise to a multiplicity of disciplinary measures in terms of soft repression as well as militant policing of protests. As the neoliberal transformation grew in depth from the early 1990 strategies for reforming a consensual political culture have become framed by decentralized, business-friendly public-civil society 'partnerships' (Peterson, et al. 2017, 383). Seen from this perspective, 'partnership' is ideopolitical newspeak for the co-optation of an NGO'ized 'civil society', with a role as vicarious welfare producer rather than as a mobilizing force for political influence (Wikström and Lundström 2002). It is a version of civil society vying for conditioned public funding to execute welfare services, crisis driven projects or special purpose experiments in social engineering that a downsized public sector is no longer capable to cope with or wishes to expose to competition (Papakostas and Kings 2021). This transformed neoliberal management regime forges, maintain Kings, Ålund and Tahvilzadeh (2016), a dependency or conditionality that tends to undermine "local civil-society associations as well as their cooperation around more radical visions concerning issues of democratic participation".

These limitations have been challenged by inventive forms of activism that, as in the following example from Stockholm, have come to expression within urban justice movements driven by youth from a socially disadvantaged and institutionally segregated multi-ethnic suburbia. We speak of an activism that contests a deficit of democratic participation in local decision making and the lack of, or shortcomings, of invited spaces for formal democratic deliber-ation. It designates a politics taking off from the informal sphere of civil soci-ety, contingent on lack of recognition, legitimacy of claims and with marginal influence of youth within formal spaces for democratic participation. In this context we locate the notion of *invented spaces*.

Miraftab (2004), in her writings on participatory governance in Cape Town, develops the notion of *invited spaces* and relates it to that of *invented spaces*. She defines invited spaces "as the ones occupied by those grassroots and their allied non-governmental organizations that are legitimized by donors and government interventions" (Miraftab 2004, 1). Invented spaces are in contrast those also occupied by the grassroots and claimed by their collective action, but directly confronting the authorities and the status quo. The prevailing urban governance regime and mainstream media promote, Miraftab argues, the imaginary of an 'authentic' civil society operating within invited spaces, opposed to an image of an 'outcast' civil society referring to contestative civic action positioned in invented spaces. However, grassroot strategies are flexi-ble and their collective actions move between these spaces to advance their cause. Miraftab (2009) relates further this flexibility to the Gramscian notion of 'hegemony',[12] defined as a consensual ideopolitical rule, and uses the notion of "counter-hegemony" to describe flexible practices that destabilize relations of power in urban governance. She illustrates how grassroots movements use the hegemonic system's political openings to determine their own terms of engage-ment and participation in order to "expose and upset the normalized relations of dominance" (Miraftab 2009, 34). Or spoken through a Gramscian terminol-ogy: They launch a counterhegemonic 'war of position' acting within, being subordinated to, but also challenging the institutions of urban governance.

The notion of invented spaces of citizenship participation calls for a per-spective on urban activism among subaltern youth that moves beyond a

---

12   In Gramsci (1971).

conventional understanding of the 'political'. It represents a praxis that culti-
vates spaces of action beyond formalized political participation – such as voting, party politics, and sanctioned activities of mainstream CSOs, bounded by
frameworks of conditioned 'participatory governance'.

Isin (2009) contrasts this conventional normality contained in the established discourse of 'the active citizen', bounded by formalized political domains,
to that of 'activism' as critical and contestative 'rights claiming', which he sees
as a fundamental property of a substantive citizenship. These 'enacted processes' are an expression of how subjects act to become citizens. It is, he states
(Isin 2009, 371–2) through enacted "claims to citizenship as justice that citizenship becomes a site of rights (and obligations)". Thus, Isin merges the notion of
citizen and acts, concluding that "to be a citizen is to make claims to justice: to
break habitus and act in a way that disrupts already defined orders, practices
and statuses". (Isin 2009, 384). So, the birth of new 'acts of citizenship', enacted
through struggles for rights and justice, illuminates how acts produce new
subjects as *activist citizens* and "new sites of contestation, belonging, identification and struggle ... different from traditional sites of citizenship, such as
voting" (Isin 2009, 371).

Pairing this distinction between *active/activist* with the meaning of *invited/
invented* spaces of citizenship, we discuss in the following activism of subaltern urban youth as a critical response contending interconnected processes
of contemporary participatory governance, neo-liberal transformation, and
racialized segregation in metropolitan Stockholm.

4   'Place Struggle'

Youth uprisings, coming to expression through fervent riots in the cities of
Malmö, Gothenburg and Uppsala in 2009, and in Stockholm in 2013 (Schierup
and Ålund 2011; Schierup, et al. 2014), brought into focus disadvantaged citizens' claims for social justice. These claims became intellectually and organ-
isationally substantiated through an articulate social movement emerging
from Sweden's stigmatised suburbia (*förorten*); home to disadvantaged population groups with a preponderance of immigrants and their descendants
(Dikeç 2017, 130–55). Precarious living conditions in segregated neighborhoods exposed to racializing stigmatization, welfare cuts, lack of spaces for
democratic participation in urban planning and decision making have during
the 2000s contributed to growing and widely expressed feelings of frustration among post-migrant youth. Through a multiplicity of activism these feelings have been converted into collective learning processes, creating critical

awareness both within the movement and in addressing the wider society (Sernhede, et al. 2019). By re-inscribing their communities into the city and the wider space of the Swedish state and society they have produced a 'differential space' (Lefebvre 1991), or what among Swedish suburban activists came to be referred to as *place struggle* (León Rosales and Ålund 2017), reading predicaments of the political on their own terms. They badged themselves *the suburban movement (förortrörelsen)*, with connotations of *förorten* (the Swedish word for 'suburb') matching the social, cultural, and racial inferences of the French idiom of the *banlieu*. An important activist group was the Stockholm based *Megafonen* (Swedish for 'The Megaphone'), striking a note of glocal solidarity through its slogan, "A united suburb will never be defeated!"

Megafonen emerged originally as an activist group in Husby, a precarious neighbourhood of 12.000 inhabitants in the area of *Järvafältet* in metropolitan Stockholm (e.g. León Rosales and Ålund 2017). Järvafältet is an area with a population close to 100.000 marked by a disorganic social geography. It harbours Kista Science City, one of the world's most important ICT clusters, side by side with poor communities, like Husby, with a majority of low income households with vulnerable livelihoods, dependent on precarious labor and a fluctuating gig-economy. Livelihoods in this originally well planned and built municipal rental housing area have deteriorated due to consecutive privatisations and corporate take overs, coupled with lack of maintainance, sham renovations, illicit increase of rents, and congested living.[13] The deterioration of livelihoods in the area is further exacerbated by a dwindling presence of public institutions on health and education.

Still, concludes a detailed survey, published in 2016, the inhabitants of Husby conveyed a view of their community as beautiful, safe, orderly and convivial, in contrast to a prevailing image of Husby among outsiders in greater Stockholm of a 'dangerous', 'chaotic' and 'ugly' no go area; a stigma, "which deeply affects their lives and their access to labour" (Fischer, et al. 2016, 67).

4.1   An Invented Space in Making: Becoming Activist Citizens

On the other side of the coin, Husby is a neighbourhood with a strong sence of community and a deep rooted trajectory for popular mobilisation (Sernhede, et al. 2019; Dikeç 2017). The activist group of Megafonen was formed (2008) at a critical juncture when segregation in Järvafältet was developing in an

---

13   At present (2021) a major corporate player in the context is the housing company Hembla, owned by the transnationals Blackstone and Vonovia, ill-famed among locals due to illicit rent increases and severely neglected maintenance of their housing stock (Johansson and Kellecioglu 2021).

increasingly precarious direction, with growing unemployment among youth in communities like Husby, and closure of public welfare institutions such as youth centres and schools, health centers, the post office, the municipal office, the social insurance office, etc. Megafonen emerged invigorated out of the time-hole blasted by the 2013 Stockholm uprising. At the time, Megafonen was treated in mainstream media as an example of an untrustworthy insurgent activism, involving direct action against gentrification and demonstrations against the selling out of public housing in Stockholm to speculative venture capitalists. Yet, with its efforts to publicly *explain* the wider structural-institutional *causes* and predicament of the 2013 uprising it became a public voice of Sweden's precarious urban communities, nationally and internationally (Schierup, et al. 2014).

Megafonen's engagement had roots in contestation of racializing stigmatization and criminalization of youth in Sweden's disadvantaged urban communities, but also in struggles against broken promises from the local city administration (León Rosales and Ålund 2017). Related to this, their first major intervention in a public debate took place in 2012, after young people in Husby had been invited by the district administration to present their view and ideas on the urban development program, *Järvalyftet*. This was an import experience of participation within an *invited space* for so-called 'citizens dialogue' (*medborgardialog*). Järvalyftet was launched in 2007 by the conservative majority in the Stockholm City Hall with the purpose of stimulating economic growth by integrating the area into the development of greater Stockholm as a whole. This developmental program invited citizens' participation in the planning process and promised space for the influence of local inhabitants. However, an actual boundedness of this invited space became a source of disappointment and frustration for local activists, including Megafonen, as formulated by Al-Khamisi (2015) in a retrospective view under the heading of "A dialogue that ended up as a monologue".

This experience was followed up by Megafonen through interventions in national media, and became a springboard for further development of alternative invented spaces for civic activism (León Rosales and Ålund 2017). This was, not least, achieved through a series of public lectures engaging researchers, politicians and administrators, and by becoming a voice in public debates with capacity to articulate a critical perspective on conditions of precarious neighborhoods and urban governance in general. Petitions were made to local authorities, actions set up to confront sham renovations and evictions, and a wider protest movement and demonstrations organized against privatization and corporate take-over of municipal housing (León Rosales and Ålund 2017).

Megafonen's political program, published on their home-page,[14] aimed at making "a society for all free from racism, sexism and class oppression" by "mobilizing the power that repression in suburbia gives birth to" (quoted in Schierup, et al. 2014, 14). The program conveys what Isin (2009) defines as attributes of 'activist citizens' making contestative claims. In it Megafonen claimed opportunities for people in socially disadvantaged and racially stigmatized urban neighborhoods to influence politics. This pertains to investment in public services and for facilitating social activities in disadvantaged suburbs, the establishment of a fair educational system guaranteeing the achievement of high quality results in all schools, decent work for all independent of background, development of proactive social programs, and a housing policy recognising the right to decent livelihoods.

By time organic intellectuals originally organized in Megafonen have become engaged with different networks and organizations of civil society, human rights movements and critical thinktanks. One instance was the first public presentation, at an internatinoal UNESCO-sponsored workshop in 2015, of a report on Social movement lawyering (Al-Khamisi 2017); a report commissioned by the leading Swedish leftist think tank, Arena Idé.[15] The workshop brought together activists from Sweden, the United States, South Africa and France. The report discusses potentials of movement lawyering with reference to discriminated inhabitants in Sweden's disadvantaged urban communities. It was followed up by the foundation of an Academy for Movement Lawyers; an autonomous educational common that draws on the experience of Black Lives Matter as well as lawyers and movements linked to Brazil's *favelas* and South Africa's precarious *townships* (Al-Khamiisi and Kakaee 2019).

In contrast to earlier organizations with their background in post-World War II migration to Sweden, depoliticized through ethicizing funding strategies by the state (Schierup 1991), Megafonen built its impact on self-directed politics of solidarity traversing ethno-cultural and confessional divides. This evokes memories of the legendary Rainbow Coalition in Chicago of the late 1960s, which continues to stand out as exemplary today (Williams 2013). It entails a transversal solidarity, embodying the intersectionality of race, gender, and generation, respecting variable identities while focusing on shared burdens of social dispossession and racism as collective unifiers. The strategy of Megafonen included, what is more, dialogue and collaboration with established CSOs, sympathetic to their cause, as for example, in the case of

---

14   Latest accessed, January 2014. No longer available.
15   Arena Idé is sponsored financially by the Swedish blue collar trade union federation, the LO.

Movement Lawyering, mentioned above. Other examples are civic dialogue and collaboration with the PRO (The National Organization of Pensioners), the National Tenants Organization, Save the Children, and the Red Cross.

5   Soliciting a Renaissance of 'The People's House'

The liaison of Megafonen with a wider civil society was accentuated in connection with local struggles for a citizen-driven community center, which was eventually to converge on the 'reinvention' of the old working class common of the 'People's House'.

The chief meeting place for Megafonen was originally *Husby Träff*, harboring an assembly hall located in a property owned by the housing company *Svenska Bostäder*. It was managed by the Red Cross until 2012, when citizens were informed by the local administration that this popular meeting place should be replaced by smaller premises of a former pub. This led to protests in the area and the occupation of Husby Träff; a campaign that could rely on a remarkable community solidarity. Megafonen, a driving force in the occupation, could for instance count on support from the local branch of the PRO, the Swedish pensioners' association; however, without lasting result. Following a process of continued community mobilization for the constitution of a new meeting place, in which Megafonen played a major part, a new People's House, named *Folkets Husby* (Husby of the People), could finally open its doors in 2016.

5.1   Post-riot Fireproofing
The wider context of this battle for a new meeting place is that of a conspicuous engagement of several large established NGOs in the community of Husby after the 2013 uprising. They were welcomed by local and national political bodies, with unrest in the community as a spur for setting up projects for 'integration' and community development. This process of systemic fireproofing represented, argues Kellecioglu (2017), a potential window of opportunity, which could, arguably, turn into a stranglehold on local activism.

The most influential NGO in Husby became *Fryshuset*, an organization with a focus on youth, education and entrepreneurship, and the rehabilitation of delinquent youth. It is an expansive non-profit organization, proudly announcing itself on its homepage as "Sweden's largest organization for young people" (Fryshuset 2021). This influential NGO benefits from significant public-political and economic support and enjoys celebrious publicity. Its board includes directors and influential entrepreneurs deriving from several business corporations, including media and communications companies, as well as trendsetting NGOs engaged in business management, sustainable development, and human rights.[16]

Another main post-riot actor in Husby, with a different background and setup, is *Folkets Hus och Parker* (The People's Houses and Parks. Henceforth 'PHP'). It is an umbrella organization founded in 2000 as a nonpartisan central organization, designating itself as a popular movement. It has more than 500 local member associations – that is People's Houses and Parks– across Sweden, receiving a substantial public funding for their activities.

In their post-riot engagement in the local community Fryshuset and PHP built separate *coalitions.* Fryshuset gathered forces together with Initiative of Change, a UNESCO-funded organization, and with Rotary (Kellecioglu 2017). It was licensed by the municipality, to open a school, which provides classes from preschool to high school in competition with public schools in the area. With support from the local district committee, it was licensed to open premises for youth activities, oriented towards entrepreneurship training. The PHP developed alliances with Save the Children, and with the Workers Educational Association (ABF) and the Swedish Tenants Association– two large national NGOs with their heritage in the popular movements that build the Swedish welfare state. This latter coalition backed the constitution of a new People's House in Husby in 2015, following up a common declaration of intent (2014) signed by PHP, the local district committee (Rinkeby-Kista Stadsdelsförvaltning) and the municipal housing company, Svenska Bostäder. The new people's house was named *Folkets Husby* (Husby of the People), and formally opened in 2016. In setting off the new people's house benefitted from banking on the PHP, its historical trajectory, its experience, organizational resources, and alliances.

5.2   *Husby of the People*

Folkets Husby has presently (2021) become a celebrated social experiment (Kings, et al. 2021). It has currently more than fifty member associations, local ones, as well as organizations based in greater Stockholm, and some of national extent. It has close to 85.000 visitors yearly.[17] Its board and staff are residents of, or persons with established connections to the community, which

---

16   The chairman of Fryshuset (state 2017), Christer Thordson, has a professional background in international corporate law and governance, and a record counting positions in management boards in business and academia. Fryshuset's project leader in Husby (board member until 2017), Christian Jochnick, is heading a technology company, and has a past record as Investment Banking Analyst on Goldman Sachs, according to information on the organisation's homepage: https://fryshuset.se/om-fryshuset/styrelse-och-lednin gsgrupp.

17   Before the Covid-19 Pandemia.

motivates the house's self-presentation as a citizens-driven community center. The house serves as a lively center for socializing and the exchange of experience across ethno-cultural and confessional divides, due to engaged social support and counselling, and based on an array of cultural and educational activities. It invites meetings of organizations, cultural events and educational pursuits, and collaboration with the wider civil society, the municipality, business, and academia.

A principal vision, laid down in the house's statutes (Scribd 2016), is to be a vital node in development of the community "with an ear to the ground and gazing ahead".[18] This is understood as a professed commitment to the needs and participation of inhabitants of all ages in public and political life. Adjoining this vision comes the principled direction by PHP that the founding of new and permanent meeting places, where such are lacking, needs to depart from local initiatives, yet that partners such as established CSOs, educational associations, housing companies and municipalities should participate and collaborate in their founding and operation. The house has during its short life developed a rich diversity of activities related to social wellbeing and popular education, including a reading library set up in 2021 as service to locals.[19] A sizeable rent demanded by the owner of the location, the public housing company, Svenska Bostäder, obliges the house to charge its member organizations considerable fees for use of the premises, which may discourage the organization of meetings and activities on burning political issues by impecunious member organizations. The staff emphasizes, however, that exceptions are made for users without access to adequate means, and that there is always an 'open door' for use of the house's premises for young people.[20]

As it were, the house appears to have asserted itself with comparative success in a local environment subject to competition for public funding and financing of educational and social policy programs, operating under conditions stipulated in funding agreements with the city administration, regional government, and state agencies, which finance a major part of the house's budget. A longer-term grant to Folkets Husby from the local district administration was obtained in 2018 through an *IOP* agreement (Rinkeby-Kista Stadsdelsförvaltning 2018) for the establishment of a so-called 'Idea Driven Public Partnership'[21] (see further, the discussion below). Other financing

---

18 Swedish: "Vi har örat mot marken och blickar framåt!" The watchword of the PHP, repeatedly referred to our discussion with members of staff in Folkets Husby.
19 https://www.nyhetsbyranjarva.se/folkets-husby-har-blivit-med-lasebibliotek/.
20 Zoom meeting with members of staff.
21 Swedish: *Idéburit offentligt partnerskap.*

has been granted by the National Board of Housing, Building and Planning (*Boverket*), supporting premises for youth activities, and from the Swedish Agency for Youth and Civil Society (*MUCF*), in support of projects for enhancing voting and democratic participation and building links between youth and established civil society. Other pursuits oriented towards youth involve a media-study, in which film, music and pod-programs are produced through collaboration with ABF (the Workers Educational Association), Sweden's largest NGO for popular education. A major project on mental health conditions among youth is supported directly from the administrative board of the greater Stockholm region (myNewsdesk 2019). Yet, as we discuss further on, this apparent success in competition for funding may come with stealthy conditions blocking criticism on these very funders; that is obstructing the emplacement of a critical positionality professed to be an essential *raison d'être* for the reinvention of the people's house in the first place.

We shall return to a discussion of this quandary further on.

5.3   *'Oases for Organization': A Vision for Activist Citizenship*

The institution of Folkets Hus och Parker (PHP) as a national umbrella organization for People's Houses across Sweden followed upon a long period of depoliticization of the People's House, as an institution (Ståhl 2005). However, the involvement of PHP in initiating Folkets Husby did indeed look like part of a new beginning. It came to be as an integrated part of a wider project targeted at revitalizing the social engagement of PHP through the establishment of People's Houses as new genuine 'citizens-driven meeting places' in twelve of Sweden's most precarious urban areas. The head of the PHP, Calle Nathanson (in Léon Rosales 2019, 2), branded the purpose of this ambitious reinvention of the People's House as an inclusive and socially engaging institution, building "platforms for the people in disadvantaged urban areas so that they can raise their voice in the democratic society"; spaces out of which they can "create greater opportunities to influence their own lives and the development of the wider society". It is "basically about empowerment" (Swedish:*egenmakt*), Nathanson sums up.

In his commissioned report to PHP Léon Rosales (2019), emphasizes that, alongside the necessity of securing stable financing of these reinvigorated People's Houses, it is essential to develop *shared visions* that facilitate transversal collaboration across age, confessional and ethnic divisions. These would be intercultural spaces for communal creativity, facilitating inclusive meetings and activities in diverse local communities. Individuals anchored in the community and enjoying trust among a heterogeneous array of sociocultural groups would ideally be key-bridge builders between local and national CSOs.

In conformance with this, experienced local community organizers, with a background in Megafonen and as activists in the area, were engaged in 2018. They were entrusted by the boards of the People's Houses in Husby, and in the nearby community of Rinkeby, with the task of investigating needs and conditions and to elaborate a vision for developing innovative and sustainable citizens-driven meeting places. In the resulting report Al-Khamisi, et. al. (2019)[22] assess in detail how People's Houses in the two local communities could be developed into vital *Oases for Organization*. This is projected to include, among other, independent media-production to challenge a stigmatizing public-political discourse and to involve a broad engagement in critical education and research in collaboration with universities and other centers of learning. It is envisaged to involve the consolidation of platforms for citizens' influence on education and the labor market. Moreover, networking between People's Houses across urban local communities would boost community power to influence strategic decision makers. Consolidating a local space for meetings, traversing gender, age and confession, would follow in the footsteps of the community's past record for solidarity and commonality, the authors argue: that is the development of "collective power uniting people in demonstrations, manifestations, and protests", contending welfare cuts, the selling out of public housing, the closure of institutions, and a stigmatizing media discourse (Al-Khamisi, et al. 2019, 26).

6   Ambiguous Emplacement

In the case of Folkets Husby a range of activities, discussed in the report, are indeed taking place. Nevertheless, the vision of 'oases for organization', echoing the community of Husby's record for contending activism, is exposed to a process of ambiguous emplacement of this new dynamic meeting place. It poses the problem of striking a balance between being positioned as a conditioned service providing NGO, entangled in bounded public-civil society 'partnerships', and the upholding of the contestative activism rooted in the local community and in wider alliances for social transformation.

In line with the theoretical and analytical propositions discussed in the preceding we use the idea of *ambiguous emplacement*[23] to capture the enigma

---

22   Reference to the first draft of the report, kindly made available by courtesy of the authors autumn 2019. A final version of should be forthcoming according to. Information available at the home page of Folkets Husby: https://folketshusby.se/kunskap-rapporter/.

23   For a detailed discussion of the concept and idea of 'emplacement' related to the building of contending urban spaces, see, e.g., Hansen (2019).

experienced by contestative activism in putting spaces of solidarity in place, under conditionality of participatory governance. It is a perspective related to the Gramscian (Gramsci 1971) perception of 'civil society' placed in an ambiguous position between hegemonic consensus building and 'war of position'; that is the predicament of contestative civic struggles, which are at the same time subordinated to and challenging the post-political hegemony. It is, as discussed in the preceding, an enigma with historical antecedents, albeit in an altered configuration, in connection with the ascent of public-civil society partnerships as a prevalent ideopolitical technology for transforming a contestative civil society into NGOized service providers.

As we shall discuss in the following, the development of Folkets Husby brings to light this double bind of civil society: *on the one hand* the commitment to function as a vital node of community development with ambitions to realize visions for becoming a crucial 'oasis for organization' as sketched out in the principled report referred to in the preceding; *on the other hand*, being dependent on financing through an array of public-civil society 'partnerships'. However, the dependence on such 'partnerships', as well as the degree and type of conditionality they imply, vary from activity to activity emplaced in the house. Not all eggs are alike. Nor are they placed in the same basket.

6.1   *The Social Centre: Emplacement of a Transversal Movement Alliance*

At one end of a scale of activities, along an axis of invited and invented spaces, is *The Social Centre*, member of Folkets Husby, and with counselling activities once a week for inhabitants of the Järva district located in the house. The center is a movement-based coalition of activist organizations combining unsalaried social work with local, national, and international popular mobilization for social transformation. Their local activism in Husby, Järvafältet and Stockholm is equivalent to the trajectory of Megafonen, described in the preceding, in capacity of a selective and flexible approach to collaboration and alliance-building with activist groups, NGOs, institutions, organizations, and political parties, sympathetic with their cause, but also in keeping aloof from dependency on governmental funding and conditioning 'partnerships'.

The Social Centre has its origin in actual social problems and perceived feelings of insecurity and powerlessness in the area. These are linked to discrimination, to poverty, closures of public welfare service, suffering from insolent monitoring, surveillance, and police harassment, and lack of information and influence that produces a crippling feeling of rightlessness (e.g. Al-Khamisi 2017; Al-Khamiisi and Kakaee 2019; Al-Khamisi, et al. 2019). An important background concerns increases of rents connected with the privatization of apartment housing, fraudulent renovations, and a foreboded introduction of profit driven rent setting, potentially devastating for precarious households (Johansson and Kellecioglu 2021).

The Social Centre has been developed as a platform for managing these uncertainties through professional counselling and process support by lawyers, trade unionists and housing activists. The center engages activists, professionals, and a range of critical CSOs, anchored locally and active nationally and internationally. It operates a ramifying transversal solidarity network, based on a coalition of three organizations that, within the frame of Folkets Husby, offer free of charge legal advocacy and organize workshops on housing, judicial, labor and welfare issues. *Folkrörelsejuristerna* (The People's Movement Lawyers) offers counselling on migration law, labor law, and family law, and can draw support from a wider network of lawyers engaged with social movements. SAC *Syndikalisterna*, an old leftist labor union that has engaged in many labor disputes, offers support on issues of work under substandard conditions. It can draw on experienced activists, seasoned through the organization of demonstrations and campaigns. *Ort till Ort* ('Place to Place'), member of the European Action Coalition of housing activists, aids households exposed by evictions and inflated rents connected with sham renovations. The organization links activists in solidarity networks across precarious communities.

An example of the critical involvement and popular mobilization of members of the tripartite coalition, constituting the Social Centre, is the engagement of Ort till Ort in raising a national protest movement against a pending legislation (2020–2021), stipulating extended market-driven rent setting in the housing sector: thus, slashing one of the traditional Swedish model's crucial welfare regulations in favor of a further aggravation of an already rampant commodification of housing driven by corporate take overs. If the law is passed, despite widespread popular resistance, it will exacerbate the precarious situation for tenants in poor urban communities. In collaboration with Hyresgästföreningen (the national tenants association), the *Norra Järva* Stadsdelsråd[24] and *Välfärdslliansen* (the Welfare Alliance),[25] Ort till Ort organized a start-up meeting for Stockholm in Folkets Husby in February 2020, as part in the mobilization for an all-out national protest rally against a pending law proposal on profit-driven rent setting (Swedish: *marknadshyror*). Restrictions in the footsteps of the Covid-19 crisis temporarily thwarted these plans. However, in the beginning of January 2021 meetings continued in

24   A citizens' district council for 'voice and power' to inhabitants and activists in Husby and the neighbouring communities of Akalla and Kista. Link: https://www.facebook.com/norrajarvastadsdelsradet/.

25   A collaborative network for tenants' organisations and several labour unions.

a digital format, targeted at organizing ('Covid-19 safe') demonstrations, which on 18 April 2021 took place on 150 localities across Sweden. Their staging by more than seventy organizations, networks and local associations manifested a place based popular mobilization traversing generations and bringing together a plethora of local communities, civic rights organizations, established CSOs and trade unions.

This popular mobilization reflects potentials of what Castells has called a 'counterpower of places' (Castells 1996, 498), as a critical response to the dismantlement of the welfare state and polarization of the city in terms of class, race and place. When such mobilization involves a heterogeneity of participants moving at the same direction, we can speak of a counterhegemonic 'network of equivalence'[26] (Purcell 2009), which epitomizes the idea of transversal solidarity. Seen in this perspective Folkets Husby harbors, through the Social Centre, an activism of relevance beyond the local community.

Also, the following case illustrates a trans local momentum of agency emplaced within Folkets Husby.

6.2   'Mental Disorder' or Systemic Oppression? Cultivating a Sub-altern Subjectivity

The case concerned pertains to activities driven by the non-profit association Unity & Cultivation (Unity & Cultivation 2021) located at Folkets Husby. Unity & Cultivation vas grounded in 2017 by young people with roots in Husby. It is at present (2021) headed by one of the original initiating members, employed at Folkets Husby as 'process leader'. The activity is focused on youth and mental health and ways of confronting taboo, and stigma related to psychological disorder. The project, which was first driven by unsalaried voluntary labor, is presently (2021) financed by a three years grant from Region Stockholm, professing a readiness "to learn from Folkets Husby".[27] It is centered around young people's active participation, knowledge promotion and empowerment in an individual and collective perspective. This includes social gatherings; presentation of life stories (Unity Talks) with related discussion, cultural creativity, development of podcasts, lectures by locally based activists, and artists. Participation in social media and related dissemination of experiences within the Järva area (where Husby geographically belongs), has been appreciated in various marginalized areas in Stockholm and in other Swedish cities.

---

26   On the notion of 'networks of equivalence', see further the introduction to this volume.
27   As reported by Wettergård (2019).

The work of Unity & Cultivation echoes the critical pedagogy of Paulo Freire (Freire 1970) in developing emancipatory education. The project relates mental health to structural problems, social and class divisions and to racialization of stigmatized urban communities. It contests accordingly a hegemonic discourse that considers mental health an individual problem, separate from inequality of life conditions, social polarization, segregation and the wider normative, political and economic order. This recalls the assertion by Stuart Hall (1990) that the living memory and practices of being affect conditions of becoming. Interconnecting experiences of racialization with relations of power may ground bottom-up knowledge production and the becoming of a critical political subject (Choudry and Kapoor 2010). In this process, different and changing conditions of *being* interconnect experiences of youth and their parents (Ålund and León Rosales 2017).

Composite strategies employed in the project can be summarized in terms of searching ways to develop knowledge on collectively shared experiences of territorialized subordination through emancipatory subjectivation confronting dominant normative discourses. Following Manojan (2019), what transpires through this process is a collectively developed praxis to unravel "potentialities within subalterns through their wisdom, practical knowledge and everyday common sense and thereby transforming educational regimes as spaces of social justice and human liberation" (Manojan 2019, 123). It is a process targeted at breaking taboos and stigma linked to mental illness through creation of a platform that offers safe spaces for conversations and dialogues among youth. Here, Folkets Husby, with its premises and cultural activities engaging young people, has become a meeting place which has resulted in a broad participation of youth, female as well male.

A key element in initiating Unity & Cultivation was originally personal experiences of the initiators about growing up in families exposed to economic vulnerability and race and cultural stigmatization of the area and its inhabitants. Growing up was infused by experiences of discrimination, surveillance, and police harassment. These experiences have contributed to health problems and related feelings of insecurity. Group identification through sharing experiences and staging the project as a joint venture, has been central. In this endeavor Folkets Husby has come to be experienced as a 'safe place' offering a range of opportunities; a meeting place, for building support, participation, and awareness among youth, confronting challenges of the future:

The activities undertaken by Unity & Cultivation demonstrate how a safe space of communication can be read as a counterspace to 'unsafeness' and problems of health connected with an 'aesthetics of order' (Smith, et al. 2021) staged by camera surveillance, race-profiling stop and search, and

other measures of a stigmatizing securitization. On the road ahead activities of Unity & Cultivation have been supported by exchanging experiences
with activists in the area and by established CSOs. This counts representatives
of, among others, ABF (the Workers Educational Association) and Save the
Children. But a supporting network includes also apparently open-minded
public servants of Region Stockholm, inviting an "equal partnership" of "critical friends" (Wettergård 2019). It represents an example of a potentially
successful avoidance of barriers between invented and invited spaces as civil
society moves between these spaces to advance their cause (cf. Miraftab 2004,
4). This, in effect, demonstrates that state-power in liberal-democratic systems is not monolithic. It is, embedded in a complex cultural hegemony, criss-
crossed by bounded but latently conflicting political perspectives (Gramsci
1971; Poulantzas 1978). However, it is thereby also subjected to capricious con-
ditionalities depending on shifting coalitions of political forces and administrative vicissitudes.

6.3   'Partnership for Trust': A Contradiction in Terms?

All the same, the partnership described above harbors far from a universal
experience with participatory governance in Sweden's disadvantaged urban
areas. Public-civil society 'partnerships' have often been mired with problems
and obstacles, especially when city administrations are confronted with criticism by involved CSOs (Kings, et al. 2021; León Rosales and Ålund 2017). One
example of perceived arrogance discussed above, leading to broken relationships, was (2012) when the founders of Megafonen, as noted by Al-Khamisi
(2015), experienced a supposed 'dialogue' with the city administration bespeak-
ing a 'monologue', silencing the voices of concerned citizens. This is the kind
of stalemate that the building of Folkets Husby as an 'oasis for organization'
has been projected to break. Yet, as we discuss below, through the mirror of
the past the experience of Folkets Husby with a supposed 'dialogue' with the
district administration, one decade later, comes as proof of the wisdom that
history tends to repeat itself, albeit dressed in different robes.[28]

  The context is that of a continued and increasing lack of trust in the local
administration; a predicament spelled out in the report by Al-Khamisi, et. al.
(2019) that we have referred to in the preceding. In it they voice a bitter critique
of the politics and measures of the city administration. Precarisation in Husby
and neighboring communities have, they claim, been impaired by escalating

---

28   That historical events tend to unwittingly repeat themselves, is a famous dictum from *The
      18th Brumaire* by Karl Marx' (1943[1852]).

closures of public services, such as schools, health centers and local meeting places and by the unbridled and fickle commodification of rental housing. They see it as the product of a stealthy decision making that has seldom
involved locals or considered basic needs of the inhabitants. Despite a broad
local organization, the inhabitants have routinely been run over, they argue,
exposing a glaring lack of opportunities for influence. The district administration's nonchalant handling of citizens' proposals has caused a widespread
feeling of powerlessness and lack of trust in the local administration. On this
background, the authors of the report imagine Folkets Husby as a concerted
actor that could boost the capacity of citizens to launch formal proposals and
follow up the district administration's processing of them. This would, they
suggest, supposedly also stimulate an increase of mutual trust between citizens and the administration.

An investigation by the Commission for a Sustainable Stockholm (Löfvenius
2016) published in 2016 reports a lower degree of trust in the city administration in Stockholm's most disadvantaged districts than in other parts of the
city. On this background it is hardly by change that the issue of enhancing
mutual trust (Swedish: *tillit, förtroende*) was made focal in a new major so-
called 'Idea Driven Public Partnership' (IOP) signed between Folkets Husby
and the local city administration in 2018 (Rinkeby-Kista Stadsdelsförvaltning
2018). This IOP, one among several entered between the administration and
different CSOs in the district that year, entailed a substantial three-year budget
with prospects for prolongation. It was to be monitored by a common steer-
ing group and bipartisan working groups including representatives of Folkets
Husby and the local city administration. The stated purpose was that of "building a strong city district with a meeting place open for all, and to increase trust
between public administration, the idea-driven voluntary sector and the citizens". The budget granted was conditioned by the obligation to develop the following long term projects, 1) A Parental Group (*Föräldrargrup Folkets Husby*),
including a range of activities aiming at "strengthening parents in their parental role"; 2) A Women Centre (*Kvinnocenter Folkets Husby*) aiming at empowering women in a community marked by perceived male dominated meeting
places; 3) A project for the development of Local Democracy and Participation
(*Lokal Demokratiutveckling och Delaktighet*) aiming at "taking advantage of the
engagement of the inhabitants and to increase trust in the public sector".

The mutual engagement of Folkets Husby and the district administration
in the context of the IOP was perceived by the staff and responsible process
leaders of Folkets Husby as an opportunity to embark on a constructive dialogue with the district authorities. However, the IOP was soon to turn into a
field of conflict between different perspectives. It appears credible to conclude

that this reflects two mutually opposed readings of the IOP. On the one hand, the very phrasing of the document appears to reflect a dominant ideopolitical discourse focusing attention on certain 'non-integrated' target groups, seen as 'problems' in political and media discourse, in need of education for democratic responsibility, gender equality and norm-conforming family relations. Staff and process leaders of Folkets Husby have obviously applied a different reading. They speak of processes of the IOP as common spaces within which participants could deepen a sense of community, voice collective grievances, and develop critical deliberation, organization, and proposals for action contending politics of precarisation in a divided city.

In any event this, apparently troubled, 'partnership' was brought to an unexpected end.

According to the district committee's program of operations presented in February 2021 the district's IOPs would be prolonged after 2021, except for the one with Folkets Husby. No explicit explanation was given by the administration for this exception, apart from that this particular partnership had "played out its role" and "reached the end of the road".[29] However, in the opinion of the seasoned community organizer, Anders Cardell (Cardell 2021b, 2021a), this stands for a calculated decision to break down opportunities for local social mobilization and the struggle for equality and community involvement by one of the few organizations, developed by and for citizens, in one of the capital's most precarious areas, most severely hit by consequences of the Covid-19 crisis. It took place, moreover, in a period when several popular activities in the area, functioning as free spaces for youth, were closed. With plans to start a new 'House of the Future' (*Framtidens Hus*) in the area, the district council appears to have taken action for strengthening its control on the organization of activities for youth. It is a local venture in which the above-mentioned NGO, Fryshuset, focused on the rehabilitation of delinquent youth and entrepreneurship training, is supposed to take a leading role, boosted by additional funding by the district administration (Löf Hagström 2021).

One reason for a tensed-up relation between Folkets Husby and the district administration, brought up by staff and process leaders, is that the house provided free action space for youth protesting the closing down of the popular youth facility, Reactor (Husbys unga 2020). Another bone of contention pointed at, supposedly upsetting the local administration, is that of a critical *Investigation on Safety, Exposure and Community* (Schlarek Mulinari and

---

29   The chairman of the district committee, Ole-Jörgen Persson, as quoted in report on the
      program of operations of the city district for 2021 (Löf Hagström 2021).

Wolgast 2020) in the Järva district by researchers at Stockholm University, initiated and published by Folkets Husby. In it the authors, Schlarek Mulinari and Wolgast, take issue with a dominant securitization focused discourse and prevalent politics on 'safety' in Sweden's 'particularly exposed' urban areas. The investigation offers an area related perspective on the general argument of a recent doctoral thesis on race, social structure, and the neoliberal social order (Schclarek Mulinari 2020). It conveys an inherent critique on racial profiling and how politics and policies targeted at Stockholm's and Sweden's most disadvantaged communities are operated. The investigation builds on deep interviews with parents and young adults and on a survey with 715 inhabitants in the Järva area, predominantly young adults. It conveys that the great majority of the surveyed are devoted to and have trust in fellow citizens in their community. In contrast, most of the interviewed state that they have no or a low degree of trust in the authorities in general, and for police and security guards in particular. However, the most glaring lack of trust stated pertains to journalists and to the ways in which media report on the residential areas of the respondents. The experience of racism is widespread as well as that of discrimination in terms of a lack of acknowledgement of formal education or of actual work-related competence. Although violence in the area, related to criminal networks, is experienced as a serious problem, trust in securitization for 'safety' through the prevalent methods and means of police and guards is exceedingly low. An excessive stop and search pursuit is experienced as abrasive, unwarranted, and inefficacious, and often coupled with offensive treatment and unjustified brutality (cf. Al-Khamiisi and Kakaee 2019).

Altogether, circumstances of the broken 'partnership' discussed above demonstrate how 'participatory governance' may obscure inequalities of resources and power, and blur distinctions in positionality between policymakers and popular movements.[30] Civic engagement in participatory governance may not by itself be counterproductive. However, once they voice inopportune concerns CSOS may encounter an incapacitating conditionality, enforced by the same hegemonic order that represents the object of contestation.

7   Will an Unlost Heritage Take Possession of Itself?

Visions for energizing the 21st century's reinvention of the People's House as a critical community driven meeting place of and for Sweden's most

---

30   Cf. Gaventa (2006).

disadvantaged appear to echo the initially quoted memo addressed to the nation's workers by the social democratic leader, Hjalmar Branting, in the twilight of the 19th century: 'The People's House' represented as their castle from where they should "with the arms of spirit and power undertake new achievements". We have in the introduction posed the question of whether the reinvention of the People's House, loaded with hopes of building citizens driven 'oases for organization', could indeed take possession of the legendary heritage of Sweden's incipient labor movement? Yet, considering our examination of the experience exemplified by Folkets Husby we need to pose the counter-question of whether a convoluted history of the People's House movement in the 20th century may not come to repeat itself in the 21st?

The first People's Houses were built, crowdfunded and managed co-operatively by the workers themselves (Ståhl 2005, 21). Developing their assemblies, independent of external funding, was seen to precondition democratization. The political radicalism associated with this worker driven common was, however, understood as a threat by the political right, which attempted to block the availability of meeting places outside the dominion of state and market. After World War II funding of The People's Houses was eventually transferred to state and municipalities, with their activities supposed to be politically neutral. This was a development adjacent to the consensualist disciplining of social movements in the post-World War II period (Peterson, et al. 2017). It dovetailed the building of Sweden's ramifying welfare edifice with Social Democracy as vanguard, yet dependent on a compact between capital and labor as well as a political 'cow deal' with the center-right (Schierup and Scarpa 2017).

Will then, by analogy, Folkets Husby, with its many activities answerable to funding by state, municipalities and regions, come to fare similarly in terms of de-politicization? This question needs to be posed in a fundamentally different historical context. Before, processes of depoliticization were subjected to the disciplinary logics of an ascending social democratic welfare state. Today the question needs to be posed at a pointed conjuncture of political crisis and exacerbated precarity of labor, livelihoods, and citizenship. It is an ominous historical moment with the mainstream of the political spectrum increasingly dancing to the pipe of the extreme xenophobic right (Schierup, et al. 2017). It depicts the country's disadvantaged urban neighborhoods as an 'unintegrated' security threat to the 'nation' with its inhabitants represented as a costly, culturally alien social burden to public welfare (Schierup and Scarpa 2017).

Branting's memo to the incipient labor movement was formulated as the 19th century drew to its close, in the cruel aftermath of the great famine striking Sweden's poor, 1867–69. We have written this essay at the time (2020–21) of another deep social crisis: that triggered by Covid-19. It has been prospected by the World Food Program (WFP 2020) to lead to "hunger of biblical dimensions"; a threat, in particular, to precarious populations in the Global South, but over-throwing livelihoods of the most disadvantaged in the North as well. Even in Sweden many children in disadvantaged urban communities have been forced to go hungry under the impact of Covid-19, and charity programs for distribution of food to poor families have mushroomed (Perkins 2020).[31] It is about an exacerbated precarity directly related to the widespread vulnerability of livelihoods of many in these communities and the burden of a vastly unequal share of rising unemployment, triggered by Covid-19. In this context, moreover, illicit apartment rents related to predatory take overs by transnational venture capital have become extraordinarily taxing for poor families. It appears symptomatic for the gravity of this quandary that evictions in Sweden reached an all-time high during the pandemia, without no serious countermeasures taken by the government (Annebäck and Pogorzelska 2021; Kierkegaard 2021), and despite warnings and appeals for restraint by the United Nations' Special Rapporteur on the right to adequate housing (Rajagopal 2020).

Consequently, Covid-19 has exacerbated the impact of already existing structural disjunctions. These can be projected to persist or to be further sharpened after the pandemic; at least if no critical transformation of the post-political hegemony and the contingent urban governance regime is accomplished. The pending (2021) law on free commercial setting of rents in housing threatening the livelihoods of poor households, referred to about, comes together with discriminatory provisions, targeted at loosening regulations on employment security, from which precaritized populations in disadvantaged neighborhoods are likely to bear the brunt. So, these and other concerns of livelihoods and labor that originally mobilized Sweden's urban justice movement remain as topical as ever. They are, truly, inciting a new surge of contestation.

The question remains, how far a reinvented People's House, to the degree that it may be conditioned by the very hegemony that stands behind the current austerity politics, could be a catalyst in this pursuit?

We have argued that a changing environment after the 2013 riots, marked by the entry of influential NGOs into the community of Husby, and a related competitive drive for project related funding, plaid in the hand of a trajectory resting on conditioned financial support through 'partnerships' with the city administration and other public funders. The activities and premises of Folkets Husby have become in need of catering to specific topics. Expectations

---

31   An act of solidarity in which also Folkets Husby has taken an active part.

from donors appear to be predominantly focused on individual empowerment through therapeutic responsibilization and training for democratic participation subject to prescribed norms. The interrupted collaboration between Folkets Husby and the district administration, discussed above, appears concomitantly to flag a sign of warning against critical mobilization for democratic influence.

Yet, activities in Folkets Husby give witness to a 'war of position' beyond or within conditioned frames. We have highlighted this point through the example of the contestative transversal solidarity movement driven by The Social Centre, emplacing an important invented space in Folkets Husby. Another is the critical investigative report on safety, vulnerability and community in the Järva district (Schlarek Mulinari and Wolgast 2020) published by Folkets Husby. A third example is project Unity & Cultivation focused on youth and mental health, discussed in the preceding. Traversing invented and invited spaces it takes issue with systemic discrimination and internalized oppression through collective learning processes. Taken together, critical organic intellectuals are, in different positions, active in Folkets Husby, as process leaders for ongoing projects or as board members, and some have gained positions of influence across an array of established CSOs and governmental agencies. They share an understanding of the institutional and structural conditions generating the individual and social problems of subaltern groups and stigmatized local communities. It implicates a crucial potential of situated knowledge for critical thinking and training.

But the predicament remains that Folkets Husby encounters challenges in terms of a disciplinary conditionality, like those the working class common of the People's House confronted in the past yet dressed in different robes. The reinvigorated People's House, Folkets Husby, rooted in the activism of the urban justice movement of the 2000s, makes visible the enigma of commoning encountering austere conditionality of civic participation in urban governance. Moving forward, recalling lessons of the past, implicates the necessity of a continuous revival of urban commons as invented spaces for social transformation.

Acknowledgements

We wish to express our gratitude to René Léon Rosales, Anders Neergaard, Charles Woolfson, Rami Al-Khamisi, Hedvig Wiezell, Atusa Rezai, Basar Gerecci, and Faisal Muse for commenting on drafts of this text in process.

References

Agamben, G. (2005). *State of Exception*. Chicago (IL) & London: The University of Chicago Press.

Al-Khamisi, R. (2015). "Dialogen som blev en monolog". In Lindholm, T., Oliveira, S.C., Wiberg S. (eds.). *Medborgardialog – demokrati eller dekoration?*. Arkus 72. Klippan: Ljungbergs tryckeri, 159–69.

Al-Khamisi, R. (2017). *Movement Lawyers: The path toward social change through law – on power, civil society and the need for a new breed of lawyers*. Stockholm: Arena Idé.

Al-Khamisi, R., A. Rezai and Anonymous (2019). *Organiseringens oaser – en rapport om lokalt inflytande i Järva utifrån Folkets Husby och Rinkeby Folkets Hus*. Unpublished manuscript made available by courtesy of the authors. Forthcoming as report to be published by Folkets Husby. Information at: https://folketshusby.se/kunskap -rapporter/.

Al-Khamiisi, R., and M. Kakaee (2019). *Rörelsejuridiken som motstånd*. Stockholm: Arena Idé.

Ali, T. (2018). *The Extreme Centre. A Second Warning*. Brooklyn (NY) and London: Verso.

Allelin, M., M. Kallifatides, S. Sjöberg, and V. Skyrman (2018). *Välfärdsmodellens omvandling. Det privata kapitalets utvidgning i den offentliga sektorn*. Katalys publikationer. Stockholm: Katalys.

Annebäck, K., and A. Pogorzelska (2021). "Fler vräks från sina hem – trots pandemin". *Dagens ETC*. Stockholm 8 April.

Bloch, E. (2000 [1917]). *The Spirit of Utopia*. Redwood City (CA): Stanford University Press.

Bollier, David. (2015). "Commoning as a Transformative Social Paradigm". The Next System Project. Available at: http://www.thenextsystem.org/commoning-as-a-tra nsformative-social-paradigm/.

Brock, K., J. Gaventa, and A. Cornwall (2001). *Power, knowledge and political spaces in the framing of poverty policy*. Brighton: IDS.

Brown, W. (2015). *Undoing the Demos: Neoliberalism's Stealth Revolution*. New York (NY): Zone Books.

Cardell, A. (2021a). "Kan vi tala om den politiska majoritetens haveri på Järva?". *Nyhetsbyrån Järva*. Available at: https://www.nyhetsbyranjarva.se/kan-vi-tala-om -den-politiska-majoritetens-haveri-pa-jarva/.

Cardell, A. (2021b). "Ett medvetet beslut för att slå sönder Folkets Husby". https://www .nyhetsbyranjarva.se/ett-medvetet-beslut-for-att-sla-sonder-folkets-husby/.

Castells, M. (1996). *The Rise of the Network Society*. Oxford: Blackwell.

Choudry, A., and D. Kapoor (eds. 2010). *Learning from the ground up, Global perspective on social movements and knowledge production*. New York (NY): Palgrave Macmillan.

Christophers, B. (2013). "A monstrous hybrid: The political economy of housing in early twenty-first century Sweden". *New Political Economy* 18 (6), 885–911.

Cornwall, A. (2002). "Locating Citizen Participation". *IDS Bulletin* 33 (2), 49–58.

Dahlstedt, M., and V. Lozić (2017). "Problematizing parents: Representations of Multi-Ethnic Areas, Youth and Urban Unrest". In Ålund, A., Schierup C.U., and Neergaard, A. (eds.). *Reimagineering the Nation. Essays on Twenty First Century Sweden.* Frankfurt am Main and New York (NY): Peter Lang.

Dikeç, M. (2017). *Urban Rage. The Revolt of the Excluded.* New Haven (CT) and London: Yale University Press.

Feuchtwang, S. (1982). "Occupational Ghettos". *Economy and Society* 11 (3), 251–91.

Financial Times (2013). "The challenges of the Swedish model". *Financial Times* http://www.ft.com/intl/cms/s/0/ba2fb9ee-c47e-11e2-9ac0-00144feab7de.html.

Fischer, S., M. Pochadt, and S. Schrader (2016). *Segregated but Equal? The Perception of the Access to the Labour Market of Young Adults from Stockholm-Husby.* Osnabrück: Institute of Geography.

Folkpartiet (2004). *Utanförskapets Karta. En kartläggning över utanförskapet i Sverige.* Stockholm: Folkpartiet.

Freire, P. (1970). *Pedagogy of the Oppressed.* New York: Seabury Press.

Fryshuset (2021). https://fryshuset.se/.

Gaventa, J. (2006). "Finding the Spaces for Change: A Power Analysis". *IDS Bulletin* 37 (6), 23–33.

Gramsci, A. (1971). *Selections from the prison notebooks of Antonio Gramsci.* New York: International publishers.

Gressgård, R. E. (2017). "Welfare Policing and the Safety–Security Nexus in Urban Governance: The Expanded Cohesion Agenda in Malmö". In Ålund, A., Schierup C.U., and Neergaard A. (eds.) *Reimagineering the Nation: Essays on 21st Century Sweden.* Frankfurt and New York (NY): Peter Lang, 235–56.

Haiven, M., and A. Khasnabish (2014). *The Radical Imagination. Social Movement Research in the Age of Austerity.* Halifax & London: Halifax & Winnipeg/Zed Books.

Hall, S. (1990). "Gramsci och vi", *Zenit* 109/110 (3–4), 61–69.

Hansen, C. (2019). *Solidarity in Diversity: Activism as a Pathway of Migrant Emplacement in Malmö.* Malmö: Holmbergs.

Haraway, D. J. (1988). "Situated Knowledges: The Science Question in Feminism and the Privilege of Partial Perspectives". *Feminist Studies* 14 (3), 575–99.

Harvey, D. (2004). "The new 'imperialism': Accumulation by dispossession"., *Socialist Register,* 40, 63–87.

Husbys_unga (2020). "Vi vill vara med och bestämma om vår framtid". Nyhetsbyrån Järva, https://www.nyhetsbyranjarva.se/vi-vill-vara-med-och-bestamma-om-var-framtid/.

Isin, E. (2009). "Citizenship in Flux: The Figure of the Activist Citizen". *Subjectivity* 29 (367–88).

Johansson, A., and I. Kellecioglu (2021). "Sveriges Allmännytta måste säga nej till ful-värdarna". https://www.dagensarena.se/opinion/sveriges-allmannytta-maste-saga-nej-till-fulvardarna/.

Kaldor, M. (2003). *Global Civil Society. An Answer to War*. Cambridge: Polity Press.

Kellecioglu, I. (2017). *NGO Participation in Local Politics: A case study of Husby*. School of Social Sciences. Stockholm: Södertörn University.

Kierkegaard, S. (2021). "Enkelt att stoppa vräkningarna". *Dagens Arena*. Available at: https://www.dagensarena.se/opinion/enkelt-att-stoppa-vrakningarna/.

Kings, L., A. Ålund, and N. Tahvilzadeh (2016). "Contesting urban management regimes: The rise of urban justice movements in Sweden". In Agustín, Ó.G. (ed.). *Solidarity without Borders*. London: Pluto Press, 186–202.

Kings, L., I. Kellecioglu, A. Rezai, and Z. Kravchenko (2021). "Civilsamhället och marginaliserade områden. Att vara på plats och att göra plats". In Gawell, M., and Papakostas, A. (eds.). *Att göra stad i Stockholms urbana periferi*. Stockholm: Stockholmia, 189–2009.

Kornhall, P., and G. Bender (2018). *Ett söndrat land. Skolval och segregation i Sverige*. Stockholm.

Lefebvre, H. (1991). *The Production of Space*. London: Verso.

León Rosales, R., and A. Ålund (2017). "Renaissance from the Margins: Urban Youth Activism in Sweden". In Ålund, A., Schierup C.U., and Neergaard A. (eds.) *Reimagineering the Nation. Essays on Twenty First Century Sweden*, Political and Social Change. Frankfurt am Main and New York (NY): Peter Lang, 351–74.

Léon Rosales, R. (2019). *Medborgardrivna mötesplatser i socioekonomiskt utsatta områden. En rapport framtagen av Mångkulturellt Centrum på uppdrag av Folkets Hus och Parker*. Stockholm: Folkets hus och parker.

Lewis, O. (1968). "Culture of Poverty". In Moynihan, D.P. (ed.) *On Understanding Poverty: Perspectives from the Social Sciences*. New York: Basic Books.

Löf Hagström, E. (2021). "Folkets husby får inte förlängt avtal". *Mitt i Kista/Rinkeby/Tensta*. Available at: https://www.mitti.se/nyheter/folkets-husby-far-inte-forlangt-avtal/repuay!v3FOfiOJBfEnVSUDGvZjfg/.

Löfvenius, J. (2016). *Stad i samverkan. Stockholms stad och civilsamhället. Delrapport från Kommissionen för ett socialt hållbart Stockholm*. Stockholm: Kommissionen för ett socialt hållbart Stockholm.

Majone, G. (1997). "From the Positive to the Regulatory State: Causes and Consequences of Changes in the Mode of Governance". *Journal of Public Policy* 17 (2), 139–67.

Manojan, K. P. (2019). "Capturing the Gramscian Project in Critical Pedagogy: Towards a Philosophy of Praxis in Education". *Review of Development and Change* 24 (1), 123–45.

Marx, K. (1943[1852]). "The Eighteenth Brumaire of Louis Bonaparte". London: Bradford & Dickens.

Miraftab, F. (2004). "Invited and Invented Spaces of Participation: Neoliberal Citizenship and Feminists. Expanded Notion of Politics". *Wagadu* 1 (Spring 2004), 1–7.

Miraftab, F. (2009). "Insurgent planning: Situating radical planning in the global south". *Planning Theory* 32 (8), 32–50.

Mouffe, C. (2005). *On the Political.* London: Routledge.

Mulinari, D., and Å. Lundqvist (2017). "Invisible, Burdensome and Threatening: The Location of Migrant Women in the Swedish Welfare State". In Ålund, A., Schierup C.U., and Neergaard A. (eds.) *Reimagineering the Nation. Essays on Twenty First Century Sweden.* Frankfurt am Main and New York (NY): Peter Lang, 119–38.

Mulinari, D., and A. Neergaard (2017). "From Racial to Racist State? The Sweden Democrats Reimagining the Nation". In Ålund, A., Schierup C.U., and Neergaard A. (eds.) *Reimagineering the Nation. Essays on Twenty First Century Sweden*, Political and Social Change. Frankfurt am Main and New York (NY): Peter Lang.

myNewsdesk (2019). "Samverkan som främjar psykisk hälsa". *MyNewsdesk.* Available at: https://www.mynewsdesk.com/se/mp-sll/pressreleases/samverkan-som-fraem jar-psykisk-haelsa-2929403.

O'Brien, M., and S. Penna (1998). *Theorising Welfare. Enlightenment and Modern Society.* London: Sage.

Papakostas, A., and L. Kings (2021). *Coronapandemin och det ömsesidiga beroendet – Reflektioner över civilsamhällets roll i den segregerade staden.* Diarienummer: 2020-4.1.1-351/83. Stockholm: DELMOS.

Perkins, Y. (2020). "De kraftsamlar för att ge familjer mat på borden". *Dagens ETC.* Stockholm 23 June.

Peterson, A., H. Thörn, and M. Wahlström (2017). "Sweden 1950–2015: Contentious Politics and Social Movements between Confrontation and Conditioned Cooperation". In Mikkelsen, F., Kjeldstadli K., and Nyzell S. (eds.). *Popular Struggle and Democracy in Scandinavia.* Palgrave Studies in European Political Sociology. London: Palgrave Macmillan, 377–432.

Polanska, D., S. Degerhammar, and Å. Richard (2019). *Renovräkt!: Hyresvärdars makt(spel) och hur du tar striden.* Stockholm: Verbal.

Poulantzas, N. (1978). *State, Power, Socialism.* New Left Review Editions. London: NLB.

Purcell, M. (2009). "Hegemony and difference in political movements: Articulating networks of equivalence". *New Political Science* 31 (3), 291–317.

Rajagopal, B. (2020). *COVID-19 and the right to adequate housing: impacts and the way forward. Report to 75th UN General Assembly by the Special Rapporteur on the right to adequate housing.* New York: OHCHR.

Regeringen (2008). *Egenmakt mot utanförskap – regeringens strategi för integration.* Stockholm: Regeringen.

Rinkeby-Kista Stadsdelsförvaltning (2018). *Idéburet offentligt partnerskap (IOP) med Folkets Husby.* Dnr1.2.5.-276-2018, 5 May 2018.

Sassen, S. (2006). *Territory, Authority, Rights: From Medieval to Global Assemblages.* Princeton (NJ): Princeton University Press.

Schclarek Mulinari, L. (2020). *Race and Order. Critical Perspectives on Crime in Sweden.* Department of Criminology. Stockholm: Stockholm University.

Schierup, C.-U. (1991). "The ethnic tower of Babel: political marginality and beyond". In Ålund, A., Schierup C.U., and Neergaard A. (eds.) *Paradoxes of Multiculturalism: Essays on Swedish Society.* Aldership: Gower, 113–36.

Schierup, C.U., and A. Ålund (2011). "The end of Swedish exceptionalism? Citizenship, neoliberalism and the politics of exclusion". *Race & Class* 53 (1), 45–64.

Schierup, C.-U., and A. Ålund (2020). "The Enigma of Commoning in Precarious Times: A Critical Perspective on Social Transformation". *HighTech and Innovation Journal* 1 (2), 59–66.

Schierup, C.U., and S. Scarpa (2017). "How the Swedish Model Was (Almost) Lost. Migration, Welfare and the Politics of Solidarity". In Ålund, A., Schierup C.U., and Neergaard A. (eds.) *Reimagineering the Nation. Essays on Twenty First Century Sweden*, Political and Social Change. Frankfurt am Main and New York (NY): Peter Lang, 41–84.

Schierup, C.U., P. Hansen, and S. Castles (2006). *Migration, Citizenship and the European Welfare State. A European Dilemma.* Oxford: Oxford University Press.

Schierup, C.U., A. Ålund and L. Kings (2014). "Reading the Stockholm riots: A moment for social justice". *Race & Class* 55 (3), 1–21.

Schierup, C. U. and M. B. Jørgensen (eds. 2016). *Politics of Precarity: Migrant conditions, struggles and experiences.* Leiden & Boston (MA): Brill Academic Publishers.

Schierup, C. U., A. Ålund and A. Neergaard (2017). "'Race' and the upsurge of antagonistic popular movements in Sweden". *Ethnic and Racial Studies* 41 (10): 1837–54.

Schlarek Mulinari, L. and S. Wolgast (2020). *Folkets Husbys trygghetsundersökning 2020. Utsatthet och gemenskap i Järva.* Stockholm: Folkets Husby.

Scribd (2016). Stadgar Folkets Husby. Scribd. Available at: https://www.scribd.com/document/296837605/stadgar-folkets-husby.

Sernhede, O., R. León Rosales and J. Söderman (2019). *"När betongen rätar sin rygg". Ortenrörelsen och folkbildningens renässans.* Gothenburg: Daidalos.

Smith, A., B. Byrne, L. Garratt, and B. Harries (2021). "Everyday Aesthetics, Locality and Racialisation". *Cultural Sociology* 15 (1), 91–112.

Sommer-Houdeville, T. (2017). *Remaking Iraq: Neoliberalism and a System of Violence after the US Invasion, 2003–2011,* Doctoral Degree. Stockholm: Stockholm University.

Ståhl, M. (2005). *Möten och människor i Folkets hus och park.* Stockholm: Atlas.

Sunkara, B. (2019). *The Socialist Manifesto. The Case for Radical Politics in an Era of Extreme Inequality.* New York (NY): Basic Books.

Therborn, G. (2018). "Twilight of Swedish Social Democracy". *New Left Review.* 113, 1–14.

Unity & Cultivation (2021). Unity and Cultivation – Ideell Organisation, Unity & Cultivation, https://www.facebook.com/unitycultivation/.

Verwoert, J. (2009). "Back to the future". Catalogue article (Ed, Linz, Lentos Kunstmuseum) Lentos Kunstmuseum Linz: Linz.

Västerbro, M. (2018). *Svälten. Hungeråren som formade Sverige.* Stockholm: Albert Bonniers förlag.

Wettergård, A. (2019). "Region Stockholm vill lära av Folkets Husby". *Mitt i Kista/ Rinkeby/Tensta.* Available at: https://www.mitti.se/nyheter/region-stockholm-vill -lara-av-folkets-husby/repsjj!NQONHdP4eA@8i8C2V5x2kg/.

WFP (2020). "WFP Chief warns of hunger pandemic as COVID-19 spreads". *Statement to the UN Security Council.* World Food Programme: Rome.

Wikström, F., and T. Lundström (2002). *Den ideella sektorn: Organisationerna i det civila samhället.* Stockholm: Sober Förlag/European Civil Society Press.

Williams, J. E. (2013). "The Original Rainbow Coalition: An Example of Universal Identity Politics". *Tikkun.* 2016, 27 August. Available at: http://www.tikkun.org/next gen/the-original-rainbow-coalition-an-example-of-universal-identity-politics.

Yuval-Davis, N. (1999). "What is 'transversal politics'". *Soundings* (12), 94–98.

Ålund, A. and C. U. Schierup (1991). *Paradoxes of Multiculturalism. Essays on Swedish Society.* Aldershot: Avebury. Republished 2009 as E-Book on the REMESO home-page, Linköpings University. Available at: http://liu.diva-portal.org/smash/record .jsf?pid=diva2:213706.

Ålund, A. and R. León Rosales (2017). "Becoming an activist citizen; Individual experi-ences and learning processes within the Swedish suburban movement". *Journal of Education and Culture Studies* 1 (2), 123–40.

Ålund, A. and C. U. Schierup (2018). "Making or unmaking a movement? Challenges for civil society in the global governance of migration?" *Globalizations* 15 (6), 809–23.

CHAPTER 9

The Spatial Politics of Far-Right Populism

VOX, Antifascism and Neighborhood Solidarity in Madrid City

Ana Santamarina

Under a triumphant rhetoric of 'reconquest' and seeking to liberate Spain from all the enemies of the nation – migrants, feminists or separatists – the xenophobic populist party VOX has become the third political force in the Spanish Parliament after the 2019 national elections.[1] Thus, halfway between the ghost of Francoism and the global rise of anti-establishment right-wing populisms, the Spanish far-right has taken off its mask. The rise of VOX has taken place in a conjuncture of crisis of the traditional right – represented by the *Partido Popular* – and escalating authoritarianism in the face of increasing political upheavals over the last years, shaped by the conflict in Catalonia, the feminist movements and the post-indignados politics. The discursive strategies of VOX draw on three overlapping mainstays: ultranationalism, racism and anti-feminism. While national pride and xenophobia are recreated through imperial nostalgia, the historical racist myth of the Christian war against the Muslim or the nationalist enemy within (Catalonia), a neocolonial anti-feminist language attempts to protect the Spanish traditional family against the challenges raised by powerful contemporary feminist movements.

Through a spatial analysis of VOX's far-right politics in Spain, I aim to contribute to ongoing discussions on the spaces of xenophobic populism and antifascism. The first section situates some of the key theoretical debates crisscrossing my argument. Engaging with different literature on populism and the far-right, I discuss inputs that a spatial perspective can bring to current debates. Then, I analyze VOX's far-right populism in Spain, disclosing the key elements of its discourse and situating them in relation to the long-term histories of the Spanish Civil War, Francoism and the 'transition to democracy'. The last sections of the paper situate everyday politics related to xenophobic populism, both in terms of political reproduction and contestation. I explore VOX's everyday politics of hate focusing on Hortaleza, a neighborhood in the

---

1 An earlier version of this work has been published as an article in Critical Sociology: Santamarina, A. (2020). The Spatial Politics of Far-right Populism: VOX, Anti-fascism and Neighborhood Solidarity in Madrid City. *Critical Sociology*, 0896920520962562.

outskirts of Madrid, discussing how VOX exploits spatial inequalities linked to the urban dimension of border regimes, institutional racism and spaces of precarity. I argue that xenophobic populisms cannot be understood separately from the institutional architectures that induce fascism to grow and from the situated grievances that the far-right attempts to mobilize. Second, learning from neighbors' anti-racist responses in Hortaleza, I address the neighborhood as a key scale of articulation of anti-fascist politics. I finish with a discussion of silences and limitations of left-wing populism in building antifascist politics in the Spanish context. My argument draws on interviews and informal conversations with migrant activists in Madrid and participants of neighborhood movements and grassroots associations between December 2019 and June 2020 in Hortaleza, as well as discourse analyses of publicly available statements of VOX's representatives and the party's political programme.

1   Spaces of Far-Right Populism

The significant advance of the far-right during the last years has attracted a growing scholarly and popular attention. A vast literature has emerged exploring the rise of populist anti-establishment discourses in mainstreaming politics across the globe. Most of this academic work focuses on the nation-state and institutional politics as the *natural* objects of political analysis. Interest is placed in electoral processes yet missing the everyday spaces of sociopolitical reproduction. Such a perspective overlooks the generative role of space in producing political positions and feelings and the quotidian conditions, consequences and processes underpinning the politics of hate.

Addressed under different nomenclatures ('post-fascism', 'radical populist right', 'xenophobic populism', etc.), analyses of today's far-right underline its heterogeneity and its populist, anti-establishment and nativist dimensions (Mudde 2019; Rydgren 2007; Traverso 2018). Indeed, 'populism' has become one of the most resounding buzzwords addressing a wide range of political phenomenon in the current conjuncture. Intellectual debates have discussed some of its key features: the politicization of an antagonism between the 'people' and the 'elite' (De Cleen, et al. 2020), its anti-establishment character (Mudde 2019), its performative and mediatic dimensions (Moffit 2016) or the political role of affect and emotions in political discourse (Laclau 2005). However, the spatial and grounded dimensions of populist politics remain largely unexplored.

Through a spatial perspective, I suggest a hybrid understanding of populism as a political practice, which has demonstrated itself to be very effective in shaping and responding to the political cartographies of the crisis. This hybrid character entails a triple intervention in current debates. Firstly, I move beyond the excessive stress on discourse that characterizes the previous literature to emphasize the material practices of far-right populist politics. Second, this understanding allows shifting the focus from institutional and electoral politics to foreground their intertwining with the multiple spaces of the political. Finally, through this hybridity, I highlight the ways populism is not exclusive to 'populist actors'. It has rather become a resource used by many political agents, from traditional parties to other movements in their fight for hegemony. This challenges the rigid and formalist understandings of populisms through stressing its nuanced reality as a practice. Mobilized in multiple contexts in a conjuncture of the crisis of the hegemonic party consensus, established political parties and media are making use of a wide range of populist strategies. Populism emerges, accordingly, as a generalized and effective political practice in a conjuncture of political and ideological crisis – a situation that is not new, as evidenced by Stuart Hall's analyses of the 1980s crisis and the politics of Thatcherism (Hall 1982). This hybrid, mixed and heterogeneous nature of populism as a practice partly underlies the ambiguity with which this term is often used.

Valluvan (2019) argues that an excessive focus on 'populism' in current literature is obscuring the racist and nationalist dimensions of the European far-right. For Featherstone and Karaliotas (2019, 31), the "formalist account of the political" that characterizes most of the discussions on populism overlooks the "histories and geographies that shape political activity". From this perspective, more interest should be placed in the 'content' of the particular articulations mobilized through populist politics and how these respond to particular idealized constructions of place. Indeed, nationalism, xenophobia and anti-feminism – at the core of contemporary far-right populisms worldwide – never appear framed in abstract and universalist terms. Rather, their articulation is deeply contextual and subjected to historical and geographical specificity.

A comprehensive analysis of the spaces of xenophobic populisms demands moving beyond nation-centered and institutional accounts paying particular attention to "the everyday spaces and political infrastructures that make populism possible" (Featherstone and Karaliotas 2019, 35). Some leftist approaches to populism have certainly sought to overcome methodological nationalism by exploring transnational populist articulations (De Cleen, et al. 2020) or the local experiences of municipalism (García Agustín 2020). However, the ways in which populism builds its success through the politicization of everyday inequalities and the construction of situated imaginaries of the crisis remain unexplored. More interest needs to be placed in addressing how the 'interpellation' of the populist practice targets situated subjects and the ways in which it politicizes lived spaces of hardship. From neoliberalized urban spaces to deprived neighborhoods or forgotten rural areas, deeply embedded injustices are materialized in spaces; these become people's subjective levels of experience of the crisis. It is precisely the situatedness of the articulation of xenophobia, nationalism and anti-feminism that allows its subsequent abstraction as a structure of meaning that integrates the differently situated far-right stories of the crisis.

As the core element of far-right ideologies, hate is the driving force of its discourses, actions and strategies. A spatial approach on the politics of hate brings attention to the grounded and material dimensions of hatred discourses, highlighting the ways in which these are spatially framed and practiced. This allows foregrounding the relations between the abstract dimension of fascism and xenophobia as 'abstract' ideologies or discourses and the politics of the everyday life. Further, I argue a spatial approach sheds light on the question of how to challenge the 'politics of hate' from the lived spaces in which these are practiced.

Moreover, this spatial approach needs to grasp the intertwining of far-right narratives of place and the institutional architectures that induce racism and xenophobia to grow. Space is not an innocent backdrop: it cannot be dealt with as if it were merely a passive, abstract arena on which things happen. Through the materialization of politics and ideology, relations of power and discipline are inscribed – and negotiated – into the apparently innocent spatiality of social life (Soja 1989). Work on anarchist geographies highlights how 'imposed demarcations of space can buttress a shift towards fascism'. The epistemic dominance of sovereign powers 'blinds us to inherent authoritarianism and capacity for fascism' (Ince 2011). In this sense, the paper discusses how the spatial inequalities mobilized by right-wing populism are shaped by institutional racism and the direct production of everyday xenophobia and exclusion by sovereign powers. The urbanization of border regimes operates as a main trigger for racism reproducing the ontologies of postcolonial geographies. The emergence of the far-right is directly linked to institutional hegemonic practices and discourses inscribed in everyday spaces.

Finally, the extensive literature on xenophobic populism is essentially descriptive and depoliticizing, avoiding the question of anti-fascism. The last section of the paper discusses the implications of the previous analyses for anti-fascist politics, challenging positions that opt for a left-wing populist strategy (Mouffe 2018). A crisis of identity linked to processes like globalization or post- Fordism (Kinnvall 2015) interplaying with long-term histories of racialization and nationalist politics (Valluvan 2019) stands at the core of far-right

politics. In his analyses of fascism, Eric Fromm exposed how in circumstances of risk and uncertainty, the individual seeks subjection to overarching
imposed identities and authority in the exercise of their 'negative freedom',
or freedom from previous stable social arrangements. In this conjuncture,
I draw upon geographical work (Arampatzi 2017; Featherstone 2012) to evidence the potential of everyday solidarities in generating alternative projects
of belonging to those defined by the state and the far-right building spaces of
'positive freedom' (Fromm 2001). I argue that situating the neighborhood as a
key scale for intervention of anti-fascist politics becomes crucial particularly
in a moment in which left-wing populisms and electoral initiatives are failing
on this endeavor (Ince 2011).

2 VOX and the Rearticulation of the Far-Right in Spanish Politics: Ultranationalism, Racism and Anti-feminism as Mainstays of a Xenophobic Populism

The emergence of the far-right party VOX in Spain has been addressed as the
end of the 'Spanish exceptionalism', whereby Spain remained one of the few
European countries without any powerful far-right-wing movement (Urbán
2019). Furthermore, it has been argued that the eruption of *Podemos*-left-wing
populist party that emerged after the *Indignados* uprisings in the context
of the post2008 financial crisis left no space within the political arena for a
Spanish version of the populist neofascist organizations that were appearing
across Europe (Traverso 2018). However, as Rubio-Pueyo (2019) evidences, a
deeper genealogy of the Spanish far-right attests to the frailty of this narrative.
The far-right has always been a constitutive element of the political regime
that resulted from the 'Spanish transition to democracy' (1978) and the roots
of VOX are found in the continuities of many elements of the dictatorship, in
the 1978 regime and the persistence of a strong 'sociological Francoism'. This
term refers to the continuation of many features of Francoist society after the
dictatorship, from the normalization of authoritarianism to the politics of fear
and the enormous influence of Catholic morality.

Forty years after the death of the dictator, Spain is the second country in
the world with the largest number of mass graves and missing people that
remain in ditches. The Spanish 'transition to democracy' was a top-down process driven by the Francoist elites, who remained positioned within the different levels of the state administration and the security forces. They founded
their own party – *Alianza Popular*, which later became the *Partido Popular* – so
they never left the institutions. The 1977 Amnesty Law, known as the 'Pact of

Oblivion', set the legal ground for an absolute immunity, meaning the denial of any process of reparation to the victims of Francoism. Since then, the ubiquitous existence of a conservative far-right in the streets and the institutions has been a sort of taboo; no one was allowed to 'open old wounds'. This is what has changed with the arrival of VOX, a party that has sought to break what is considered 'politically correct' from an anti-establishment discourse.

The discursive strategies of VOX draw on three overlapping mainstays: ultra-nationalism, racism and anti-feminism. Recreating the Spanish Civil War with a 'national force' facing what they frame as 'anti-Spain', the construction of VOX is rooted in the historical development of Spanish authoritarian politics. The historical enemy, *los rojos* (the reds), is now represented by a heterogeneous amalgam of subjects and movements that are risking the unity of the nation and the purity of the Spanish Catholic family (the feminists, the migrants, the Catalans, the Muslims, the *'podemitas'* – a derogatory word used by the right to refer to the supporters of the left-wing populist party *Podemos*).

As the 15M Indignados Movement was the political ground for the emergence of *Podemos* in 2014 (García Agustín 2018), analysts situate the origins of VOX in what is popularly known as *la España de los Balcones* – 'the Spain of the balconies' (Urbán 2019). Against the democratic independent movement in Catalonia and in the middle of an anti-Catalan campaign in the media, people began to hang Spanish flags in their balconies. This created a public landscape that contributed to the mobilization of centralist, authoritarian and reactionary positions in the public opinion and buttressed the authoritarian reaction to the Catalan movement, shaping ideas of the Spanish nation in particularly antagonistic ways. The conservative and colonial connotations of the Spanish flag, heir of 40 years of cultural and ideological monopoly of the idea of the Nation by Franco's regime, set the perfect ground for VOX's populism to flourish giving political shape to the anti-Catalan discontent. In the age of the armistice of the separatist armed organization ETA and the decrease of the conflict in the Basque Country, the right had lost its 'enemy within'. Spanish nationalism was disoriented, and corruption plunged the traditional right into a crisis. The national question is intrinsic to Spanish politics where separatists are the classic resource used to reproduce nationalism and the militarization of the State, and to divert public attention from social problems.

VOX capitalized on the politics of hate towards Catalonia to build a broader national project recreating an *imagined* history of Spanish greatness (Anderson 2006). The national pride appears constantly adorned with nostalgic recreations of the colonial past and the time when the northern Catholic Kingdoms struck down Muslims in *Al Andalus* (Rubio-Pueyo 2019). After the Andalusian regional elections, VOX spread a public message: "The Reconquest started in Andalusia". Neocolonialism and the recreation of imperial power are indeed common elements structuring the proliferation of nationalisms in today's European politics (Valluvan 2019; Virdee and McGeever 2018).

With its roots in this ultranationalism, VOX aims to appear as the Spanish people's advocate. Appealing to *el Español que madruga* ('the Spaniard who wakes up early'), VOX's xenophobic populism seeks to reach not only the upper classes but also the national working classes. Despite their programme being deeply neoliberal (with privatizations, deregulation and 'fiscal revolution'), their discourse is often focused on what they call the 'everyday Spaniard', sometimes combined with traditionalism and nostalgia. Pucciarelli (2019) signals a common trend within recent far-right nationalist movements and leaders attempting to 'talk to the stomachs and the hearts of the people' in promoting nativist representations of the community. In particular, anti-immigration and racism have been core instruments mobilized by VOX to expand their influence amongst popular classes. *Policing the Crisis* (Hall, et al. 2013) demonstrates how racism is mobilized by the conservative elites to preserve hegemony in contexts of crisis and win consent for shifts to the right. VOX's racist discourse combines two elements. First, a rhetoric that directly targets the material conditions of the national popular classes and seeks to convince the workers that immigrants are the reason of their social agony (unemployment, precarity, crime ...). Second, a supremacist colonial discourse that pretends to essentialize the cultural and ideological basis of Spain and Europe in a context in which Islamophobia is a common constitutive element to European nationalisms.

Under the language of 'order', the wall becomes a central idiom in today's xenophobic populisms. The basic proposal in VOX's 'immigration, borders and security policy' is the construction of an 'unbreakable concrete wall' in Ceuta and Melilla. Despite studies confirming that VOX's voters belong mainly to upper classes, the electoral map shows that the 'populism of the wall' (Urbán 2019) has reached border areas (Ceuta, Andalusia) as well as working-class villages where migrant exploitation in the agricultural industry is a daily reality (e.g. El Ejido). A similar 'populism of the ports' has become the signature policy of Salvini's anti-immigration crusade in Italy (Pucciarelli 2019).

Alongside separatists and migrants, the third key enemy in VOX's antagonistic discourse are feminists. Indeed, misogyny and homophobia constitute an axis of the new reactionary far-right worldwide, combined with neocolonialist and Islamophobic elements (Farris 2012). In recent years, feminist mobilizations in the streets have gathered millions of people in Spain. With its roots in everyday emancipation and mutual care, it draws on a global

network of action (Cabezas González and Brochner 2019). Notwithstanding
the heterogeneity of the movement, it is politicizing a wide sector of society
and articulating a potential force for social change and transformation. This
is particularly challenging considering the weight of the Catholic Church and
the traditional family as basic social structures – both legacies of sociological
Francoism and constitutive elements of the national imaginary. Against the
subversive potential of feminist and LGBTQI movements in the streets, VOX
has sought to reverse feminist discourse as a way to promote racism and misogyny: 'Feminism is a cancer. Supremacist feminism wants to put a burka on all
women' (Rocío Monasterio head of VOX Madrid 20 November 2019).

VOX's anti-feminism emerges in a conjuncture where traditional conceptions of masculinity are deeply damaged in the wake of the precariousness
generated by austerity politics in Spain after the 2008 financial crisis. Women's
empowerment in both the streets and their private lives eroded the role of the
pater familias as the head of the traditional family. In the course of massive
mobilizations energetically contesting violence against women, VOX's most
famous slogan is that 'Violence has no gender'. It rather 'has race', as most of
the efforts have been focused on stressing that sexist violence is foreign to
Western culture and comes with the 'waves' of black and brown migrants.

Hence, VOX has sought to capitalize arenas of political rupture to promote
a far-right xenophobic populism that binds neoliberalism, colonialism and a
nostalgic traditionalism. What so far was a neoconservative trend within the
Partido Popular now emerges as an anti-establishment party that aims to liberate the nation from separatists, migrants and 'feminazis'. In what follows,
I demonstrate how the politicization of these elements is grounded in everyday life. A spatial approach enables an engagement with lived spaces as a terrain of dispute, where racism needs to be challenged from the grassroots on a
daily basis.

3   VOX and the Everyday Politics of Hate

Most of the discussion around the rise of xenophobic populisms in Europe
and beyond has focused on the nation state and electoral politics, missing the
everyday spaces of sociopolitical reproduction (Mudde 2019; Traverso 2018).
Looking at Hortaleza – a neighborhood in the Northeast of Madrid – this section aims to fill this gap exploring the dialectics between everyday politics of
hate, institutional racism and VOX's xenophobic populism. I engage with some
of the ways far-right populisms exploit specific narratives on space and place
in generating political positions and feelings. This move situates everyday

politics at the core of far-right politics, both in terms of political reproduction and contestation.

Some weeks after the Spanish national elections in November 2019 – after which VOX became the third national political force – an explosive device was found at the door of a center of reception of *migrant minors not accompanied by parents or guardians* (*MENAS*) in Hortaleza. Not by chance, these centers have been key spaces of political mobilization within VOX's electoral campaign. In Madrid and other cities, VOX – alongside neo-Nazi groups like *Hogar Social Madrid* – orchestrated demonstrations in these facilities arguing that they promote a 'pull effect' and the 'degradation of the neighborhood and its inhabitants'. Rather than mobilizing racism in abstract terms, the electoral strategies of the party focus on everyday spaces and 'ordinary people'. In the words of Rocío Monasterio (head of VOX in Madrid November 2019):

> VOX has the responsibility to protect the ordinary Spaniards that desire freedom and security in their neighborhood. Especially in the case of women of all ages that do not dare to walk alone during the night in certain neighborhoods (...) We came here to talk to the everyday Spanish people, who have the right to walk peacefully in their neighborhood without being assaulted by a *herd of MENAS*

The effects – and roots – of this mobilization strategy go far beyond the electoral success of the party. The attacks on *MENAS* reception centers have been widespread not only in Hortaleza but also in different localities where VOX has achieved electoral success (Andalusia, Murcia). Neighbors highlight that the explosive attack was the culmination of years of invisible unpunished violence against migrant children and teenagers. Although racist terrorism is not a new phenomenon, now it finds the coverage and legitimation of political discourses and the media (García López 2019). Since Hortaleza is in the spotlight of VOX's discourse, neighbors account a worrying normalization of everyday racism in the different spaces of the neighborhood:

> What happens is that since the arrival of *VOX*, people feel legitimized to speak in the language of racism. It feels like you are entitled to say all those stupidities and an extremely brutal discourse becomes normalized. In practice, that legitimation means: 'alright, anything goes', and from there they go huge and become organized and then is when we have the big problem: The discourse becomes facts and physical aggressions. What happens is that these people come to Hortaleza, give their speech and then return to their houses, leaving people here killing each other.

And the ones who are actually killing each other are the last one against
the second last.

Interview with JULIO, neighbor and member of *Raíces*, a grassroots association
working against hate in HORTALEZA 4 June 2020

The relationship between racist terrorism and the rise of xenophobic populism is complex and embedded in the spatial conditions of institutional racism. Indeed, the grounds where xenophobic populism thrives are produced
through structural racism, as the urbanization of a social, economic and political system of racial exploitation. Hence, institutions play a key role in the
reproduction of racist conflicts in the neighborhood, the urbanization of border regimes and the intertwining between political parties, neo-Nazi groups,
neighbors and the police in the politicization of everyday inequalities.

Hortaleza materializes the urbanization of some of the ways public
authorities generate and reproduce exclusion, racism and social marginality
in connection with border regimes. The neighborhood hosts two 'reception
centers' for unaccompanied minors, generally children from the Maghreb that
migrate alone. These centers are overcrowded, doubling their capacity, and
children there are subjected to abuse, police beatings, threats of deportation
and deprivation of liberty by the authorities. The result is that very often, the
same children that jumped the Melilla fence decide to jump the wall of these
centers and sleep in the park in between them, where institutions push them
to marginality and exclusion. Once these children 'escape' outside the center,
they lose their place within it and if they want food or a bed, the only way is
to go through police custody again. The soil of the *Claruji* – a popular name
given to the park – has become home to migrants between 10 and 17 years
old; at the same time, it is an area of racist assaults by young gangs and fascist demonstrations. Paradoxically, the same public institutions that are the
legal guardians of these children – *Comunidad de Madrid* – are the ones giving public permit to neo-Nazi groups like *Hogar Social Madrid* to demonstrate
against them in the park where they live. Further, police dawn raids are used to
beat the children sleeping in the park in the early mornings, taking away their
blankets and belongings 'as they are not supposed to be there' (Rubio Gómez
2018). Neighbors also denounce that sometimes it is the police themselves who
encourage people to act against the Moroccan children:

The police continuously sow hatred. The police hate the kids of the center. They hit them and do all they can do against them up to the limit of
not trespassing public opinion. The problem is that the police are generating a conflict in the neighborhood saying that they cannot do anything

because they are protected under the minors law, and if they arrest them, tomorrow they will be on the street (which is not true). They launch an indirect message that the neighborhood needs to become organized against them.

JULIO 4 June 2020

Through these dynamics, these minors have become the target of racist discourses that situate all the problems and fears of the neighborhood in the park and the reception centers. In addition to mainstream media, such representations are very often reproduced through digital spaces (Facebook groups, Twitter, etc.). Racialization here functions as a powerful mechanism for displacing social responsibility and containing social anxieties in a working-class neighborhood that is experiencing the problems of the neoliberal transformations in post-crisis Madrid: young people without expectations, commodification of the urban space, lack of affordable housing, progressive gentrification of the neighborhood, unemployment, distrust of the authorities, etc. Anti-Moroccan racism in the neighborhood, embedded in long-term colonial relations and imaginaries, is much more nuanced than a simple conflict between fascists and the Moroccan. Under a 'feeling of belonging' to the neighborhood, deprived groups and young gangs have been involved in beatings against the boys of the center. These are not only groups of 'white Spaniards' but also other groups and ethnic minorities living in the neighborhood. Through mechanisms of 'differential racialization' (Brah 1996) children of the center are often presented as 'racialized outsiders' (Virdee 2014), aiming to perpetuate the material and symbolic privileges of the insiders (Oliveri 2018):

> In Hortaleza there is a strong consciousness of 'the neighborhood'. The neighborhood is something really important. And what people are doing is repeating 'they have nothing to do with the neighborhood, they don't belong to the neighborhood, they don't belong to the neighborhood' (...) A speech of 'the neighborhood against the center is behind the attacks.
>
> AITOR, HORTALEZA 9 January 2020

Of course, this is not the only – or the main – way in which 'politics of belonging' to the neighborhood are mobilized, as the following section evidences. However, it shows how racialization operates as a key dividing force in everyday contexts and the ways it can be mobilized in multiple ways beyond the nation state.

All these tensions that spatialize embedded injustices, entangled with the urbanization of borders in the neighborhood, become the veins to spread

vox's propaganda. Therefore, xenophobic populisms can neither be understood apart from the everyday institutional production of the fertile ground
where racism emerges, nor can they be separated from the situated grievances
that the far- right discourse attempts to mobilize. Talking in the language of
barrios and *vecinos* (neighbors and neighborhoods), vox's strategy is deeply
spatial. The case of Hortaleza evidences the dialectics between the 'politics of
the street' and 'institutional politics'. The next section engages with some of
the ways Hortaleza's neighbors have effectively contested vox's far-right politics. From there, I discuss some of the contributions that a spatial analysis of
the far-right can bring to anti-fascist politics in connection to the potentialities
and limitations of the left politics that emerged in the aftermath of the crisis
in Spain.

4   On the Spatial Politics of Anti-fascism: Neighborhood Movements,
       Migrant Activism and the Limitations of Left-Wing Populism

A key emerging question that arises in the face of a conjuncture of proliferation
of xenophobic populisms is how to build anti-fascism in practice. However,
most of the analyses on far-right populisms are merely descriptive: either
they do not bring any proposal on anti-fascism or they do it in a vague and
ambiguous way (see Mudde 2019; Rydgren 2007; Traverso 2018). Debates on
anti-fascism, nevertheless, are crucial for politics on the ground. This section
focuses on some of the contributions that a spatial analysis of the far-right
can bring to anti-fascist politics. I draw on Anthony Ince's work on 'anti-fascist
geographies', which addresses the struggle against the far- right as a struggle
over the spatial articulation. Insofar 'communities are constituted and discursively contested through spatial practice', he advocates for an anti-fascist
politics articulated at the heart of the community that challenges the deterri-
torialization of anti-fascism that characterizes some forms of recent left-wing
electoral strategies. I look at the neighborhood movement in Hortaleza to
explore the essential role of neighbor solidarity in pushing forward anti-fascist
politics from the grassroots. Navigating the tensions around the spaces of the
political, I engage with migrant political movements in Madrid to discuss the
shortcomings of *Unidas Podemos'* left-wing populism and *Ahora Madrid*'s
municipalism in regard to anti-fascism and anti-racism, which never was a priority for these coalitions.

     The centrality of the neighborhood as the lived space of political socializa-
tion makes it a key scale of articulation of anti-fascist politics. This is strengthened by the 'neighborhood culture' that characterizes Spanish popular life,

where 'el barrio' is a strong source of territorial identity. Indeed, this 'neighborhood culture' has shown to be a ground for alternative projects of belonging, particularly strong in working-class areas (Narotzky 2014). Capturing this, Pedro Limón López (2015) uses the concept of *barrionalism* to refer to the 'cognitive framework shaping collective identifications amid the ideological element of the *barrio*'. He evidences the ways – in Hortaleza and in other working-class areas – *barrionalism* operates as a "primary political imaginary" constructed through "common practices of protest and contestation" that draw on a historical memory of solidarity and collective struggle assumed as 'patrimony' of the neighborhood. It is therefore in the streets of the neighborhood where the relationship between institutional racism and xenophobic populism could be most effectively contested. The *barrio* entails a potential to subvert the schemes of belonging and exclusion defined by the state and the different forms of structurally grounded exploitation. *Barrionalism* portrays the tension and negotiation between semi-autonomous *barrio* identities and institutional power. In Hortaleza, it inspires the creation of horizontal forms of identification and solidarity based on a common strong sense of place and origin, residency and quotidian practice (Limón López 2015).

Linked to Featherstone, et al.'s (2012) notion of progressive localisms, *barrionalisms* and the anti-fascist identities constructed at a neighborhood level are not 'merely defensive' or contestational. Rather, they are "expansive in their geographical reach" and productive of new relations between places and social groups reconfiguring existing communities. In a discussion of his memories of neighbor solidarity in Hortaleza, Julio Rubio Gómez – community activist – charts the progressive articulation of networks with places beyond the neighborhood. For example, he tells how the struggles against injustice in the neighborhood led to the construction of strong chains of support with Melilla. Rally cries like 'Africa and Europe united in Hortaleza' also exemplify the potentially expansive character of political identities constructed at the level of the *barrio*. After the explosive was found at the door of the reception center, over a thousand of neighbors came down warning "These kids are our brothers and if you touch them, you will find us in the street". Ahead of the latest neo-Nazi demonstrations, "what some people from the *Barrio* did was going to the park and staying with the kids" (Aitor and Miguel 9 January 2020). Furthermore, a *barrio sisterhood* or solidarity can also be witnessed across different working-class areas in Madrid.

Hortaleza exemplifies the relevance of the construction of anti-fascism in the neighborhood. The mechanisms of 'differential racialization' mentioned in the previous section evidence the "processual, often contradictory, constitution" of neighborhood communities (Arampatzi 2017) and the importance of recognizing grassroots activity as central to anti-fascism and as an alternative to state power (Ince 2019). This means that the potential of the *barrio* for the construction of alternative and progressive political identities and projects of belongings cannot be taken for granted. Rather, political identities are constructed through everyday relations (Featherstone 2012). In Hortaleza, despite the efforts of vox and neo-Nazi groups to mobilize racism and exclusionary imaginaries of the neighborhood, a number of individuals, neighbor associations, community projects, political organizations and NGOs have put together a 'platform for the coexistence' to articulate a collective response to racism in the neighborhood, contest the mediatic image of violence and fear and demand institutional responsibility on the situation in the center.

> The Platform publicly arises after Abascal [leader of vox] mentions the center in Hortaleza in the electoral debate five days before the national elections. The situation was becoming very serious and neighbors didn't want Hortaleza to be associated with vox. Before that, in times of the municipal elections, Javier Ortega Smith [vox general Secretary] also visited the center. Until that moment, any political party had ever directly used the center for their political propaganda. That day, we organized a 'escrache' blocking the entrance to the center. He couldn't pass, which was his intention. He took a photo and he left. We were a lot of neighbors there ... and this was just the first time this was being used as an electoral strategy.
>
> JUAN, one of the promoters of the platform 4 June 2020

Despite the platform emerging in light of the most recent events, anti-fascist grassroots work dates back to the times when Hortaleza was not in the news:

> When all this wasn't in the media, the kids were sleeping in the park, but people weren't aware about what was going on. In that time, we got organized to both give material support to the children and to publicly denounce the situation. All the neighborhood associations in the district signed together a Manifesto
>
> JUAN 4 June 2020

In addition to the awareness-raising and political work, community projects like Hortaleza Boxing Club emerged, seeking to build bonds among the youth in the neighborhood. Through the creation of common spaces, initiatives like this have broken with racist stereotypes allowing everyday encounters and the construction of an 'emotional cityzenry' (Askins 2016). This exemplifies the ways the *barrio* is a 'struggling community', a term coined by Arampatzi (2017) to re-center grassroots forms of everyday solidarity and social reproduction as a key site of struggle and a potential for building new spatial imaginaries.

> The boxing space has created a very healthy environment and through everyday interactions many children and teenagers in Hortaleza are starting to empathize with the kids of the park and understand the situation is terribly unjust. Many kids bring hatred discourses from home. But these discourses are theoretical, cognitive, it's something that is on peoples' minds. However, when you face this theory and get to know the other, the emotions and interactions radically change and that hatred discourse collapses from its own weight.
>
> JULIO, founder of Hortaleza Boxing Club 4 June 2020

The multiple practices of solidarity challenging the narrative mobilized by vox on public media in Hortaleza were articulated through a fabric of historical neighborhood forms of associationism, solidarity and struggle in connection with emerging youth anti-fascist movements. The *barrio* has been both the scenario and the collective subject of social and neighbor struggles over the years. Annexed to Madrid with the economic transformations of the 1950s, Hortaleza became the classic suburb that absorbed workers coming from rural exodus. The accelerated transformation of the original village and the lack of infrastructures accompanying a chaotic urban expansion led to a strong development of neighborhood movements during the 1960s and the 1970s (Tienda, et al. 2009). As the district grew, it became home to many migrants and inhabitants from slums areas in the outskirts of the city – mainly with Roma background –rehoused in the neighborhood, leading to a powerful culture of organizing and to a particular multi-ethnical 'barrio' identity. The gentrification of the neighborhood in the last years, with urban regeneration projects and middle class and wealthy people moving to new 'green residential areas' – including the leader of vox – is attempting to destroy those identities. This is where the far-right is focusing its battle and where the construction of anti-fascisms becomes crucial.

5   Local Solidarities and the Shortcomings of Left Populism

This advocacy for a community-based anti-fascist politics counters a generalized position in current left-wing politics that frames the struggle against the far-right in terms of electoral politics (Ince 2011). For Chantal Mouffe (2018), the 'populist moment' demands the construction of strong left-wing populisms able to win the struggle for hegemony. Voices like Mezzadra and Neuman (2019) or Enzo Traverso (2018) have argued that the emergence of *Podemos* avoided a strong European-style far-right populism in Spain. In the remainder of this section, I challenge this belief focusing on the silences, exclusions and shortcomings of the left-wing populist experience in Spain and its municipalist version in Madrid. To do so, I engage with the criticisms articulated by migrant political movements in the city and beyond.

In Madrid, the right-wing 'shift to the streets' (Ince 2011) finds its origin in the neoconservative turn of the *Partido Popular*, which after the failure of José María Aznar was embodied in Esperanza Aguirre and the Madrilenian PP (Rubio-Pueyo 2019). Madrid local and regional governments were used to launch and fund a strategy of right-wing and ultra-catholic social activism against the socialist government of Zapatero. In addition to this, neo-Nazi groups like *Hogar Social Madrid* squatted buildings and organized community support actions for Spanish people following the example of Casa Pound in Italy. Other fascist groups (*España 2000, Frente Nacional, Democracia Nacional, Fuerza Nueva*) were also focusing their action on the local scale in specific neighborhoods. Certainly, the 'Madrilenian exceptionalism' – as the only big city where VOX achieved a significant electoral success – has much to do with this local entrenchment of conservative lobbies and neofascist groups. On the other hand, the left-wing 'shift to the institutions' finds its local expression with Manuela Carmena's 'Council of Change'. The neoconservative experiment in Madrid was interrupted by the Indignados Movement in 2011 that was part of a local and nationwide cycle of urban protests and public occupations (Karaliotas and Swyngedouw 2019) and gained particular force in the capital. The clearance of the squares led to an unprecedented local – and national – cycle of mobilizations of networked struggles named as 'mareas' - tydes- (public health, housing, education, feminism, etc.). *Podemos* emerged in this moment, capitalizing on the mobilization cycle towards the institutions from a populist left-wing strategy. In the capital, *Ahora Madrid* appeared as a coalition between *Podemos* and the social movements allowing the first electoral defeat of the right in 15 years.

For many, Madrid's Council of Change represented a moment of opportunity. However, the 'institutionalization moment' led to a progressive relaxation of the movements in the streets, not only in Madrid but across the *indignados* geographies. Karaliotas (2019) analyses similar dynamics in Greece with the experience of Syriza after the 'politics of the square'. Nevertheless, anti- racism never was a priority for *Ahora Madrid*, who perpetuated institutional racism in the neighborhoods. Neighbor associations and grassroots organizations in Hortaleza account how the Council umpteen times ignored their complaints about migrant children being made homeless by public institutions – alleging lack of power on this issue or implementing simple patch measures (Rubio Gómez 2018). Further, against the demands of undocumented migrants in the city – organized in a Union of 'top-manta' workers, *Sindicato de Manteros y Lateros de Madrid* – the Council launched a public campaign of criminalization of street trade in 2017. During this time, the death of Mame Mbaye, an undocumented migrant who was running away from an identity control of the police, also occurred. 'Stop and search' practices not only continued to take place under Carmena's government, but also the Mayor stepped forward to endorse the police's conduct as 'doing their work' after this tragedy.

Broadly, the failures of *Podemos* as an alternative to xenophobic populism go beyond the example of *Ahora Madrid*. In general, the processes of institutionalization had a clear effect on the weakening of urban movements, provoking a shift regarding the spaces of anti-fascist struggles (Karaliotas 2019). The main strategy of the party against the rise of VOX took the shape of advocating 'voting against VOX' together with the Socialist Party (PSOE). Further, within this electoral strategy, *Podemos* has positioned itself as a guardian of the constitutional rule. With the 1978 Constitution on hand, the night of the electoral debate in November 2019, Pablo Iglesias defended the *supreme law* against the far and conservative right. This move, aligning the party with the 78 Regime, meant leaving all the 'anti-establishment' political space in the institutions to the far-right. This raises different questions regarding how long could left political parties present themselves as anti-establishment in their populist mode.

Furthermore, Featherstone and Karaliotas (2019) criticize how *Podemos'* discourse equates 'the people' they seek to represent with the nation which is a central element in *Podemos'* discursive strategies. This exclusionary framing of 'the people', devoid of any colonial analysis, has material consequences that reinforce institutional racism. *Podemos'* migration discourses, for example, address migrants as 'people who are about to arrive' rather than as a constitutive part of the society:

> Nobody talks about us as part of this society, but we are here, and we belong to this society. The Left needs to construct a very different imaginary ... One imaginary that emphasizes how we also make the city, how we build society and create culture, how we stand to defend public health and struggle for housing rights for all. No one wants to assume the political task of building imaginaries that could effectively challenge the far right. We have a very colonial Left that is still not willing to undertake any process of decolonization.
>
> YEISON GARCÍA LÓPEZ, afrocolombian activist 26 December 2019

These exclusions silence the ways migrants have been building solidarities and quotidian resistances and networks against precariousness in Spanish neighborhoods for years. In the course of the economic crisis, they played a key role in shaping oppositional cultures within Spain (Featherstone and Karaliotas 2019). The Platform of those Affected by Mortgage (PAH) was founded by Ecuadorians, who were the first to suffer the consequences of the bursting of the housing bubble: 'We were the first ones in denouncing the violence surrounding evictions, although the media did not arrive until Spanish nationals began to be evicted too' (Bosaho, et al. 2018). Migrants were also a key part of the movement advocating for a universal public health against the neoliberal logics of privatization of the common. Further, migrant feminist struggles preceded the last cycle of mobilization, with collectives such as *Territorio Doméstico* or *Migrantes Transgresores* working in the city from the intersection of transnational trajectories of migration, gender, class and sexuality (Santamarina and Cabezas 2019). Broadly, although migrants were a generative force within the mobilization cycle contesting the crisis, their role has often been overlooked and invisibilised, both by the media and the political left. Such exclusions have been perpetuated by the structures of *Podemos* as the lack of migrants in positions and spaces of power. Further, under VOX's fascist threat, the party has not been able to situate anti-fascism as a priority. Yeison García López, Afrocolombian activist and member of *Podemos*, sent a clear message to the party after the explosive attack in Hortaleza: "the tweets with 'antiracist flavoring' are useless if behind them there is no political work".

6   Conclusion

In a global conjuncture of growing nationalisms and xenophobic populisms, debates on anti-fascism become crucial. Contributing to ongoing discussions on "anti-fascist geographies" (Ince 2011), this paper has sought to deepen current debates on populism and far-right politics from a spatial perspective. Beyond traditional approaches that address the far-right through the lenses of the nation state and institutional politics, I looked at the operation of everyday politics of hate in urban environments to explore the socio-spatial context in which racism is grounded and reproduced. Focusing on a working-class area of Madrid (Hortaleza), I evidenced the ways VOX attempts to politicize situated inequalities that are deeply embedded in the institutional reproduction of racism. This perspective denies the position of 'externality' to the system that very often is granted to the far-right, situating it instead at the heart of its functioning. Furthermore, it shifts the comprehension of the extreme right from the 'deviant individual' to the quotidian workings of structural racism.

On the other hand, insofar the local scale becomes a main target of far-right production of political meanings, the paper has addressed the neighborhood as a key site for the articulation of anti- fascist struggle and alternative politics of belonging. Drawing on neighbor solidarities in Hortaleza, I highlighted the potential of these to build alternative imaginaries of place and politics of belonging (Arampatzi 2017; Featherstone, et al. 2012). Emphasizing the construction of transversal solidarities on a grassroots level, the paper has argued that the articulation of anti-fascist politics from below is now, and always a priority. Engaged with migrant's political criticisms evidences the shortcomings of the left-wing populist strategy in Madrid and Spain in the endeavor of challenging the far-right. These experiences of neighborhood movements in Hortaleza and migrant political activism in Spain shed light to crucial debates in the present political conjuncture that are relevant beyond the Spanish context.

References

Agustín, Ó.G. (2018). *Podemos and the New Political Cycle*. London: Palgrave Macmillan.

Agustín, Ó.G. (2020). "New municipalism as space for solidarity". *Soundings* 74(74): 54–67.

Anderson, B. (2006). *Imagined Communities: Reflections on the Origin and Spread of Nationalism*. London and New York, NY: Verso books.

Arampatzi, A. (2017). "Contentious spatialities in an era of austerity: everyday politics and 'struggle communities' in Athens, Greece". *Political Geography* 60: 47–56.

Askins, K. (2016). "Emotional citizenry: everyday geographies of befriending, belonging and intercultural encounter". *Transactions of the Institute of British Geographers* 41(4): 515–527.

Brah, A. (1996). *Cartographies of Diaspora: Contesting Identities*. Psychology Press.

Bosaho, R., Y. García López, L.B. Rojas Jaldín et al. (2018). "Una mirada diferente a las luchas migrantes". El Salto Diario.

Cabezas González, A., and G. Brochner (2019). "The new cycle of women's mobilizations between Latin America and Europe: a feminist geopolitical perspective on interregionalism". In: Cairo, H., Bringel, B. (eds.) *Critical Geopolitics and Regional (Re) Configurations*. New York, NY: Routledge, 178–196.

De Cleen, B., B. Moffitt, P. Panayotu et al. (2020). "The potentials and difficulties of transnational populism: the case of the Democracy in Europe Movement 2025 (DiEM25)". *Political Studies* 68(1): 146–166.

Farris, S. (2012). "Femonationalism and the 'Regular' army of labor called migrant women". *History of the Present* 2(2): 184–199.

Featherstone, D. (2012). *Solidarity: Hidden Histories and Geographies of Internationalism*. London: Zed Books Ltd.

Featherstone, D., and L. Karaliotas (2019). "Populism". *Soundings* 72(72): 31–47.

Featherstone, D., A. Ince, D. Mackinnon et al. (2012). "Progressive localism and the construction of political alternatives". *Transactions of the Institute of British Geographers* 37(2): 177–182.

Fromm, E. (2001). *The Fear of Freedom*. Sussex: Psychology Press.

García López, Y.F. (2019). "Sobre Hortaleza o por qué el antirracismo tiene que ir más allá del discurso". El Salto Diario.

Hall, S. (1982). *The Empire Strikes Back: Race and Racism in 70s Britain*. Centre for Contemporary Cultural Studies. London: Routledge.

Hall, S., C. Critcher, T. Jefferson et al. (2013). *Policing the Crisis: Mugging, the State and Law and Order*. London: Macmillan International Higher Education.

Ince, A. (2011). "Contesting the'authentic'community: far-right spatial strategy and everyday responses in an era of crisis". *Ephemera: Theory & Politics in Organization* 11(1): 6–26.

Ince, A. (2019). "Fragments of an anti-fascist geography: interrogating racism, nationalism, and state power". *Geography Compass* 13(3): e12420.

Karaliotas, L. (2019). "Geographies of politics and the police: post-democratization, SYRIZA, and the politics of the 'Greek debt crisis'". *Environment and Planning C: Politics and Space*.

Karaliotas, L., and E. Swyngedouw (2019). "Exploring insurgent urban mobilizations: from urban social movements to urban political movements?" In: Schwanen, T., and Kempem, R. (eds.) *Handbook of Urban Geography*. Cheltenham: Edward Elgar Publishing 369–382.

Kinnvall, C. (2015). "Borders and fear: insecurity, gender and the far right in Europe". *Journal of Contemporary European Studies* 23(4): 514–529.

Laclau, E. (2005). *On Populist Reason*. London and New York, NY: Verso.

Limón López, P. (2015). *Un barrio para gobernarlos a todos: gentrificación, producción de globalidad y barrionalismo en Hortaleza (Madrid) y Poblenou (Barcelona) (1992–2014)*. Doctoral dissertation, Universidad Complutense de Madrid.

Mezzadra, S., and M. Neumann (2019). *Clase y diversidad. Sin trampas*. Tafalla: Txalaparta.

Moffit, B. (2016). *The Global Rise of Populism: Performance, Political Style, and Representation*. California, CA: Standford University Press.

Mouffe, C. (2018). *For a Left Populism*. London and New York, NY: Verso Books.

Mudde, C. (2019). *The Far Right Today*. New Jersey, NJ: John Wiley & Sons.

Narotzky, S. (2014). "Structures without soul and immediate struggles: rethinking militant particularism in contemporary Spain". In: Kasmir, S., Carbonella, G. (eds.) *Blood and Fire: Toward a New Anthropology of Labour*. New York: Berghahn Books, 167–202.

Oliveri, F. (2018). "Racialization and counter-racialization in times of crisis: taking migrant struggles in Italy as a critical standpoint on race". *Ethnic and Racial Studies* 41(10): 1855–1873.

Pucciarelli, M. (2019). "Salvini ascendant". *New Left Review* 116(1): 9–30.

Rubio Gómez, J. (2018). *El Parque: La infancia entre cartones*. Madrid: Las Barricadas Ediciones.

Rubio-Pueyo, V. (2019). "VOX:¿ Una nueva extrema derecha en España?" Rosa Luxemburg Stiftung, New York Office.

Rydgren, J. (2007). "The sociology of the radical right". *Annual Review of Sociology* 33(1): 241–262.

Santamarina, A., and A. Cabezas (2019). "Urban resistances and migrant activism challenging border regimes in Madrid city". In: Teke Lloyd, A. (ed.), *Exclusion and Inclusion in International Migration*. London: Transnational Press 183–205.

Soja, E.W. (1989). *Postmodern Geographies: The Reassertion of Space in Critical Social Theory*. London and New York: Verso.

Tienda, T., R. Anula and D. Pereyra (2009). "Hortaleza (Madrid): crónica de un barrio indómito y sus desafíos al PP". *Viento sur: Por una izquierda alternativa* (102): 115–118.

Traverso, E. (2018). *Las nuevas caras de la derecha: Conversaciones con Régis Meyran*. Ciudad de México: Siglo XXI Editores.

Urbán, M. (2019). "La emergencia de Vox". *Las nuevas derechas radicales. Viento Sur*, n 166.

Valluvan, S. (2019). *The Clamour of Nationalism: Race and Nation in Twenty-First-Century Britain*. Manchester: Manchester University Press.

Virdee, S. (2014). *Racism, Class and the Racialized Outsider*. London: Macmillan International Higher Education.

Virdee, S., and B. McGeever (2018). "Racism, crisis, brexit". *Ethnic and Racial Studies* 41(10): 1802–1819.

CHAPTER 10

Sanctuary and Solidarity Cities in the Global South

A Review of Latin America

Margaret Godoy and Harald Bauder

Cities are the primary destination for migrants and refugees around the world (IOM 2020). In this context, urban municipalities are increasingly finding themselves positioned as critical actors at the forefront of integration and settlement efforts for international migrants and refugees. In the Global North, the solidarity city and sanctuary city movements have arisen at the crux of the tension between exclusionary national-level migration policies and realities faced by municipalities and civil society actors engaging with migrants and refugees at the local level. Although there is no universal template of what comprises a solidarity or sanctuary city, in the context of the Global North, these cities generally seek to include and protect vulnerable migrants and refugees, and provide access to essential municipal services for all inhabitants regardless of legal status. An abundance of literature examines the phenomenon of urban sanctuary and solidarity in the Global North (Ataç, et al. 2020; Bagelman 2013; Bauder 2016; Bauder and Gonzalez 2018; Darling and Bauder 2019; Hershkowitz, et al. 2020; Houston & Lawrence-Weilmann 2016; Hudson, et al. 2017; Manfredi-Sánchez 2020; McDonald 2012; Nyers 2010; Villegas 2018). However, there remains a gap in the literature about urban sanctuary and solidarity policies and practices in the Global South. Filling this gap offers an important contribution to the 'Southern perspective' of migration and development, with its focus on human rights, social justice, and the social, political, and economic inclusion of migrants and refugees.

In this article we review the literature on urban sanctuary and policies and practices of solidarity in the Global South, specifically in Latin America. This research complements recent work examining urban sanctuary and sanctuary in African and Asian cities (Bauder 2019; Kassa 2019; Missbach, et al. 2018). The following two research questions guide our investigation: (1) In which way do the concepts of urban sanctuary and solidarity apply in Latin America in reference to migrants and refugees? (2) What are possible differences between urban solidarity and sanctuary policies and practices enacted in the Global North and Latin America? In our review of the literature, we pay particular attention to the connection between top-down urban policies and bottom-up grassroots initiatives and practices of migrant and refugee solidarity and sanc-tuary. Recent research suggests that this connection is critical to the success of many sanctuary and solidarity cities, especially in the Global North (Bauder forthcoming; Bauder and Gonzalez 2018). At the same time, this connection has also been a main point of critique from radical perspectives of urban sanctuary and solidarity (Bagelman 2016; Dietrich 2019; Houston & Lawrence-Weilmann 2016).

Given the exploratory nature of our research, we conducted a scoping review using the following search parameters: grey literature (e.g. government docu-ments, community organization research reports, theses) and academic litera-ture (peer-reviewed) published between 1990 and 2020 in English and Spanish, and relevant to the Latin American context. For the purpose of this review, 'Latin America' refers to countries and territories in the Americas with Spanish, Portuguese, and French as the dominant languages (Bakewell 2004). Academic literature was identified through a search of online common electronic data-bases (JSTOR, ProQuest, Scholars Portal, SciELO, and Social Sciences Citation Index), while grey literature was found through hand-searching reference lists and conducting web searches using Google Scholar. We searched for the following main keywords in both Spanish and English: sanctuary, sanctuary cities, solidarity, solidarity cities, and urban sanctuary. To broaden the results, we also included the following Spanish keywords: Provincia(s) solidaria(s), Ciudad(es) refugio(s), Ciudad(es) inclusiva(s), crossed with Latin America(n), South America(n), Central America(n), Iberoamerica(n), migrant, immi-grant, migration, and immigration. Our scoping review resulted in 32 items of peer-reviewed and grey literature. We used the reference management soft-ware Zotero to organize the data and an Excel table to conduct data charting. Concept-mapping was employed to drive the analysis of findings and themes in both academic and grey literature results.

In the following sections we first summarize the literature on urban sanc-tuary and solidarity in the Global North considering our focus relating to the interconnection between top-down and bottom-up approaches. Thereafter, we describe the findings of our review of the Latin American literature. In the final section, we conclude with a brief discussion of the findings, limitations to the study, and implications for future research.

1 Urban Sanctuary and Solidarity in The Global North

The scholarly literature on urban sanctuary and solidarity theorizes the trans-formative potential of urban space and how it might impact migrants' and refugees' access to rights and their social, political, and economic inclusion at the urban level. This theorization is premised on Eurocentric and Western theoretical foundations, such as Henri Lefebvre's 'right to the city', that should not be uncritically applied to the Global South (Bauder 2019; Landau 2010). Drawing on Lefebvre (1996), Purcell (2002) explains that the right to the city is "earned by living out the routines of everyday life in the space of the city" (102). This point is particularly salient to the concept of sanctuary and solidarity cities, which seek to challenge exclusionary national policies and conceptions of who is and is not permitted to have access to the city. According to this perspective, illegalized migrants and refugees – i.e. inhabitants who are denied legal status by the nation state (Bauder 2013) – have a right to the city based upon their presence and domicile in the city, regardless of their national status (Varsanyi 2010). The transformative potential of sanctuary and solidarity cities lies in the ability to change the everyday interactions among all people residing in and using shared urban space and thereby reimagining the city as a space for all (Bauder 2016; Purcell 2014).

In the Global North, the transformative potential of sanctuary and solidarity cities is not associated with a radical reconfiguration of the urban society or urban political and institutional structures (Bagelman 2016; Houston and Lawrence-Weilmann 2016). Rather, sanctuary and solidarity cities mobilize existing municipal political structures and institutional infrastructure to advocate for and work towards the inclusion of inhabitants excluded by national migration policies and law (Bauder 2017a). Urban sanctuary and solidarity imply the engagement of local authorities and municipalities with civil society organizations and the individual members of the urban community. In this way, urban sanctuary and solidarity diverge from Lefebvre's original 'right to the city' as a radical and revolutionary idea.

Urban sanctuary and solidarity policies and practices differ widely between municipalities and according to factors such as local demographics, histories, and politics, or national and geopolitical contexts (Bauder 2017b; Walker and Leitner 2011). In Canada and the United States (US), sanctuary cities date back to the 1980s when San Francisco (California) passed a milestone 'City of Refuge' ordinance which prohibited the use of the municipal budget to be allocated towards federal immigration enforcement efforts (Mancina 2012). While initially this municipal response was garnered in reaction to an exclusionary stance assumed by the federal government towards refugee claimants from Central America, the sanctuary city movement that has since emerged and spread to dozens of cities across the US has broadened its focus to include illegalized migrants and refugees (Delgado 2018; Ridgley 2008). Across the US, sanctuary city initiatives range from policies to provide municipal services to illegalized inhabitants, to establishing local voting rights, and issuing municipal identification cards on the basis of residency rather than legal status (de Graauw 2014). In Canada, Toronto became the country's first sanctuary city in 2013 (Hudson, et al. 2017), followed by other municipalities that have since adopted sanctuary city policies (Hershkowitz, et al. 2020). Despite these local efforts, immigration in the US and Canada continues to be a federal responsibility, rendering urban sanctuary policies and practices unable to offer full protection from federal immigration authorities (Tramonte 2011).

In Europe, the term 'cities of sanctuary' is used in United Kingdom and Ireland referring to cities that focus not so much on the legal protection of migrants and refugees from national authorities but rather on creating a 'culture of hospitality' (Bagelman 2013, 14), actively reshaping the narrative and public discourse towards refugees and migrants, and reimagining the city as an inclusive space (Darling 2010). In Continental Europe, hundreds of cities have articulated other forms of urban solidarity and sanctuary, particularly after the arrival of large numbers of migrants and refugees from Africa and the Middle East during the summer of 2015 (Christof and Kron 2019; Dietrich 2019). In Germany, over a hundred municipalities have joined the Seebrücke (sea bridge) and 'safe harbors' initiatives, signaling their willingness to accept refugees who are rescued at sea or stranded in camps at Europe's periphery. In Italy and Spain major municipalities such as Naples and Barcelona have also joined a European 'Solidarity Cities' alliance in protest of the hostile national and European Union policies and practices towards migrant and refugee accommodation (Kron and Lebuhn 2020).

Previous research has examined the various urban sanctuary and solidarity policies and practices in the Global North and highlighted common components. Christof and Kron (2019) distinguish between policies and legal measures offering concrete protections at the municipal level, and discursive and symbolic strategies intended to shift dominant narratives and attitudes. Similarly, Bauder (2017) observes that there are four aspects that outline how top-down and bottom-up dimensions are both represented in urban sanctuary and solidarity initiatives: the legal aspect entail some level of official municipal legislative support that is typically driven by grass roots political activism; the discursive aspect refers to challenging and rescripting exclusionary migration and refugee narratives in municipal politics and civic society; the identity formative aspect involves municipal and civic city space to be reimagined as a place of equal belonging and participation; and finally, the scale aspect describes the mobilization of the local civic society resources and municipal social and political infrastructure for the purpose of migrant and refugee inclusion. This research has made clear that urban sanctuary policies are neither solely top-down initiatives led by municipalities or only grass-roots campaigns. Rather, they combine top-down and bottom-up approaches involving diverse stakeholders ranging from mayors and policy makers to service providers and activists (Bauder and Gonzalez 2018).

In the US, for example, the policies and practices put into place by the City of San Francisco under the leadership of Mayor Gavin Newsom created the space and political opportunity structure for faith-based and grassroots initiatives to engage with the city through legal strategies and mobilization processes (Freeland 2010). In an extensive study of San Francisco's non-profit sector, de Graauw (2016) reveals how civil society organizations have worked collaboratively with city and government officials to address migrant and refugee communities' needs. In Canada, Toronto has had a strong base of grass-roots organizations that has long organized and advocated various levels of government to stop deportations and make Toronto a sanctuary city (Villegas 2018; Hudson, et al. 2017). In these cities, bottom-up and top-down initiatives work in concert at the local level.

In Europe, the City of Barcelona enacted itself as a 'City of Refuge' which involved a City Council declaration in 2015 and the cooperation between urban institutions and civil society and activists (Agustín and Jørgensen 2019; Bauder and Gonzalez 2018). This enactment coincided with the rise of a global movement known by many names, including Fearless Cities, Rebel Cities, Cities of Change, and municipalism (Barcelona En Comú, Bookchin, and Colau 2019). 'Municipalism' is defined as "the democratic autonomy of municipalities (from town parishes to metropolitan boroughs to city-regions) over political and economic life vis-à-vis the nation-state" (Thompson 2020, 1). Though not specifically centered on the inclusion and protection of vulnerable migrants and refugees, municipalists around the world aim to transform cities to resist social inequalities and injustices. This effort includes working in alignment with sanctuary and solidarity cities to provide spaces of inclusion, integration, and welcome for all residents. In 2017, Barcelona hosted the first international Fearless Cities gathering of over 180 cities participating in the municipalist movement, a movement that is also characterized by its deliberate efforts to deepen participation between civil society actors and municipal institutions (Thompson 2020).

Other European cities like Vienna, Amsterdam, and Stockholm highlight the importance of horizontal relations between municipalities and civil society organizations and actors in strengthening local positions to resist exclusionary national migration and refugee policies (Ataç, et al. 2020). Lambert and Swerts (2019), however, caution against painting all forms of urban top-down and grass-roots collaboration as beneficial. Studying the 2017 Sanctuary City campaign in Liège, Belgium, they found that collaboration resulted in a discursive shift from 'sanctuary' to 'welcoming', which weakened the protection of illegalized migrants who were no longer represented in the campaign. Similar critiques have been articulated in relation to other cities across the Global North (Bagelman 2016; Houston and Lawrence-Weilmann 2016).

There are interesting connections between urban sanctuary and solidarity efforts in the Global North and Latin America. For example, the concept of 'sanctuary' has a longstanding religious association with Christianity, and the initial Sanctuary Movements of the US drew upon the moral authority and traditions of the church citing the biblical tradition of sanctuary (Ridgley 2011). According to Cunningham (1998), the principal theological influence on the movement was Latin American liberation theology, which at its core criticizes the social conditions that result in structural poverty and human suffering. To this day, the church holds a strong presence and plays an important role in enacting solidarity and sanctuary for migrants across Latin America. For example, the casas del migrante ('safe-houses') that offer shelter to migrants and refugees passing through Mexico are frequently run by religious organizations, such as the Scalabrini network of safe-houses (Guevara 2015).

However, the literature has not offered a systematic review or comparison of urban sanctuary and solidarity in the Global North and Latin America. While the literature on the Global North highlights and problematizes the top-down and bottom-up connections of urban sanctuary and solidarity, it is less clear whether and in which way this connection exists in Latin America. The below review of the literature will shed light on this issue.

2   Urban Sanctuary and Solidarity in Latin America

The realities of migration in the context of the Global South are unsurprisingly different from the Global North. A recent review of urban sanctuary and solidarity in Africa, for example, shows how unique migration, demographic, geopolitical, and economic context shape cities ability and willingness to accommodate migrants and refugees (Bauder 2019). Similarly, the nature of migration in Latin America is influenced by the continent's social, historical, political, and geographical nuances, marked by South-South and South-North migration as well as the Central American transit migration corridor. Urban sanctuary and solidarity are embedded in these circumstances.

There is a general scarcity of literature on the topic of urban sanctuary and solidarity in the Global South, including Latin America. We find that although there is substantial academic and grey literature on municipal responses to migration in terms of local integration practices in Latin America, most of this literature does not make an explicit connection to urban sanctuary or solidarity, or sanctuary or solidarity cities. We organized the literature that does exist on this topic and that we reviewed for this study along two themes: (1) Literature pertaining to the Solidarity Cities program, a top-down initiative established by the 2004 Mexico Declaration and Plan of Action, and (2) literature pertaining to bottom-up approaches towards urban migrant and refugee sanctuary and solidarity, in which an analysis of the involvement of municipal actors and structures is generally lacking.

2.1   *The Mexico Plan of Action and 'Solidarity Cities'*

There is some literature on the Ciudades Solidarias program (referred to as the 'Solidarity Cities' or 'Cities of Solidarity' program in English translations) that resulted from the 2004 Mexico Declaration and Plan of Action. The Mexico Plan of Action (MPA) gathered together governments from across Latin America to mark the twentieth anniversary of the 1984 Cartagena Declaration on Refugees and reinvigorate the region's tradition of asylum (Regional Refugee Instruments and Related 2004; Varoli 2010). The durable solutions that emerged from the 2004 MPA are articulated through the principles of solidarity, and regional solidarity in particular. The 2004 MPA emphasizes that "humanism and solidarity are fundamental principles that should continue to guide State policies on refugees in Latin America" (Regional Refugee Instruments and Related 2004, 1). The MPA employs the principle of solidarity alongside the principle of responsibility-sharing in the context of achieving effective durable solutions in the region for refugees. These principles were reaffirmed in 2014 with the Brazil Declaration and Plan of Action (Regional Refugee Instruments and Related 2014). This regional approach to cooperation articulated through the 2004 MPA is considered to be a break from the past. Although a tradition of solidarity and responsibility sharing was reflected in both the 1984 Cartagena Declaration on Refugees and 1994 San Jose Declaration, the MPA offered a tangible roadmap to implement a plan of regional solidarity (Barichello 2016). However, this regional solidarity approach in Latin America is largely state-led with support by supranational and regional institutions such as UNHCR and the Organization of American States (Kneebone 2016). This approach differs from the dynamics of protection frameworks in Europe, in which individual nation states have positioned themselves in opposition to the supranational regional entity, the European Union, and South East Asia, where nation states have not appeared to assume significant leadership with regard to the issue of refugee protection (Kneebone 2016).

The 2004 MPA was adopted by twenty Latin American countries and established three solidarity programs: (1) Borders of Solidarity, (2) Solidarity Resettlement, and (3) Solidarity Cities. The Solidarity Cities program is considered to be one of the most novel components of the 2004 MPA (Barichello 2016). By 2011, more than 50 formal and informal Solidarity Cities agreements had been established across Latin America (UNHCR 2011a). The initial mention of the program in the MPA cites several broad goals of the Solidarity Cities program, including:

Fostering the generation of sources of employment, in particular, the establishment of micro-credit systems;

Setting up mechanisms for the expedited issuance of documents and simplifying procedures for authentication and recognition of certificates and diplomas issued abroad; and

Contemplating mechanisms for the participation of civil society and UNHCR in designing, implementing, monitoring and improving integration projects. (Regional Refugee Instruments and Related 2004, 9)

The latter two goals mirror the urban sanctuary and solidarity initiatives that exist in the Global North. In addition, the last goal, referring to the 'participation of civil society,' affirms the intention to connect top-down and bottom-up urban solidarity efforts throughout Latin America.

As a whole, the literature we reviewed is mostly descriptive in nature, situating the Solidarity Cities program within the larger regional framework of the 1984 Cartagena Declaration (UNHCR 1984) and 2004 Mexico Plan of Action and citing a few case studies of cities that have signed on as examples (Mejía 2010; UNHCR 2018; Varoli 2010; Villena Del Carpio and Annoni 2015). Fischel de Andrade (2014) speaks more broadly to the MPA and does not delve into the Solidarity Cities program with any significance, choosing to focus instead of the Solidarity Resettlement program. Jubilut and Carneiro (2011) draw on all three components of the MPA to offer a case study of the Solidarity Resettlement program in Brazil. In this case, the authors note the massive involvement of civil society organizations that complemented efforts of local authorities and solidified the establishment of a network of solidarity. They attribute the success and rapid increase of refugee resettlement capacity in the region largely to the collaborative efforts of individuals, local governments, and various civil society organizations including churches and social clubs (Jubilut and Carneiro 2011). Vera Espinoza (2018) examines the limits and opportunities of regional approaches to solidarity through the cases of Chile and Brazil, focusing on Solidarity Resettlement more than the Solidarity Cities program.

The few studies that focus on cities that have engaged with the Solidarity Cities program do not explicitly frame this program in reference to urban sanctuary and solidarity. Nevertheless, there are similarities to urban sanctuary and solidarity as it is articulated in the Global North. Barichello (2016) refers to the transformative potential of solidarity at the local level. She notes: "The city is presented as an open space and a place for opportunities to be explored and experienced" (201). She further describes the Solidarity Cities program as a novel and positive approach given the strategies that it outlines for establishing new partnerships between local governments and civil society actors and fostering participation from and interaction between top-down and bottom-up initiatives. Harley (2014) dedicates an entire section to the Solidarity Cities program in his assessment how Latin American governments have developed and implemented a "south-south" regional approach to refugee protection. He notes that the Solidarity Cities program "recognizes that solidarity can be achieved not only through international diplomacy, but also through the active participation of lower level governments" (Harley 2014, 36), thus scaling solidarity with migrants and refugees to the local level. He further indicates that success of the program relies heavily on the political will of local governments to act on issues of forced migration and refugee protection. As a result, there have been varying levels of engagement with the cities that have so far participated in the Solidarity Cities program. Although the program is designed to actively engage NGOs and civil society actors, their levels of participation vary considerably (Harley 2014). This variability could be attributed to the lack of established criteria in the initial 2004 MPA for municipalities to become a Solidarity City, resulting in range of different levels of non-binding commitments. This problem was addressed in 2017, when the Regional Discussion on the Program 'Cities of Solidarity' in Quito, Ecuador, outlined a list of ten draft criteria for municipalities to receive the public award and designation of 'City of Solidarity', noting the potential of municipalities' good practices to positively influence migration and refugee policy and regulatory frameworks at the national level (UNHCR 2017).

Although the studies examining the local implementation of the MPA's Solidarity Cities program generally do not make comparisons to urban sanctuary and solidarity efforts in the Global North, a literature exists on municipal solidarity networks that offer such comparisons. For example, Kron & Lebuhn (2020) make the comparison between Europe's 'Solidarity Cities' alliance of municipalities and the Solidarity Cities program in Latin America, calling it a "similar network" (Kron and Lebuhn 2020, 100) of participating governments and administrations. Koellner (2019) presents the 2004 MPA's Solidarity Cities program as representative of Latin America's initiatives of urban sanctuary and solidarity towards migrants and refugees, and compares it to local refugee and migrant integration networks in the European Union. This comparison concludes that "promising results can be attributed especially to the local level" (42) and highlights that these results are especially linked with efforts made at the local level by NGOs, universities, or other civil society actors. Again, this work suggests that the Solidarity Cities program's success relies on top-down political will as well as the participation of the bottom-up initiatives and actors.

3   Urban Sanctuary and Solidarity: Bottom-Up and Top-Down
        Approaches

In addition to the literature related specifically to the Solidarity Cities program that emerged from the 2014 Mexico Plan of Action and that is coordinated by UNHCR, we also reviewed literature that suggests that the terminology of 'solidarity city' and 'sanctuary city' is too narrow in scope to capture the complexities of urban sanctuary and solidarity in the context of Latin America. The case of Mexico City presents an interesting example of how the application of the ideas of urban sanctuary and solidarity intersect and diverge between Latin America and the Global North. In 2017, purportedly in response to contemporary migratory processes and exclusionary immigration policies enacted by the Trump administration in the US, Miguel Mancera, the governor of Mexico City, declared the city to be a *Ciudad Santuario*, or 'Sanctuary City' (Alejo 2020; Chelius 2018; Marzorati and Marconi 2018). This declaration was accompanied by The Framework Agreement of Collaboration between the UNHCR and Mexico City, a formal agreement with UNHCR that aligned the city with its *Ciudades Solidarias* (Solidarity Cities) program (UNHCR 2018). There has been a strong grassroots movement on the part of civil society in Mexico City to accommodate migrants and refugees, and civic society organizations are acknowledged to have played a role in the Intercultural Law that preceded the Sanctuary City declaration in Mexico City (Marzorati 2017; Marzorati and Marconi 2018).

However, declaring itself a sanctuary city in parallel to the sanctuary city movement in the US does not necessarily imply that the city stands in solidarity with all international migrants and refugees residing in Mexico City. Rather, in Mexico City's official declaration, 'sanctuary' applies to Mexican nationals who are re-entering and being forcibly returned to country:

> [...] Mexico City – Capital of our Country – is a place where all people are welcome and, specifically, all Mexican migrant workers and their families on their return to the national territory, where the respect of their human

rights and dignity is ensured, providing them with the services that are
detailed in [...] this Agreement.

GOBIERNO DE LA CIUDAD DE MÉXICO 2017, 4

Although the same official declaration emphasizes that Mexico City is an
intercultural space that is enriched by national and international migrations
(Gobierno de la Ciudad de México 2017, 3), the application of 'sanctuary' in the
context of being a Sanctuary City is limited to Mexican nationals. Preceding the
2017 'Sanctuary City' declaration, Marzorati and Marconi (2018) offer an analysis of migration and urban diversity in Mexico City that focuses on the 2011 Ley
de interculturalidad, atención a migrantes y movilidad humana en el Distrito
Federal (Law of Interculturality, Attention to Migrants and Human Mobility in
the Federal District), a law that was the result of a political process that engaged
various government and organized civil society actors. The law puts forth that
"No human being will be identified or recognized as illegal because of their
immigration status" (Gobierno de la Ciudad de México 2011, Article 5) and
proposes various interventions including the creation of a padrón de hués-
pedes (guest register) in order to better serve and attend migrants (Gobierno
de la Ciudad de México 2011, Article 10). However, the authors problematize
the potential of importing a top-down discourse of 'interculturality' stemming
from the European context and international network of Intercultural Cities,
and applying it to the context of Mexico. Furthermore, a discourse of 'interculturality' implies that the problem at hand is a cultural one, absolving it from
any socio-political dimension (Marzorati and Marconi 2018). Though they recognize the symbolic value of Mexico City's Law of Interculturality, Marzorati
and Marconi (2018) ultimately question whether the label of 'intercultural city'
is too disconnected from the local context for the inclusion of all migrants.

The framing of the discourse of inclusion is an important theme in the literature we examined. Indeed, Jorge Morales Cardiel argues in his chapter in
this book that discussions of sanctuary cities in Mexico should begin with the
response and concept of migrant accompaniment to understand the emergence of alternate networks of common solidarity, such as sanctuary cities.
In a report for the civil society organization Sin Fronteras IAP, Chelius (2018)
makes the case for 'hospitable' cities in Mexico rather than 'sanctuary' cities.
According to Chelius, hospitality lays a structural foundation for universal
inclusion in a city – including migrants, refugees, asylum seekers, etc. – and distinguishes neither between nationals and 'foreigners' nor between residents of
a city and migrants who may be travelling through it. In this case, "Hospitality
is not decreed, it is practiced" (Chelius 2018, 10), which associates the concept
with a bottom-up rather than top-down approach. However, recent research

(not included in this review's original sample) asserts that the framing of sanctuary in the case of Mexico City raises an important question: why is sanctuary
needed for returning citizens when there is no risk of deportation or exclusion
based on citizenship? (Délano Alonso 2021). Délano Alonso (2021) aligns this
framing with 'freedom cities' in the United States that offer "expanded sanctuary" and argues that Mexico City's declaration of being a Sanctuary City was an
important step in acknowledging the systemic conditions of exclusion experienced by migrant populations in general, including those returning to their
countries of origin.

Nonetheless, in 2019, under the administration of a new mayor, Mexico
City's label of 'Sanctuary City' was replaced by the "City of Hospitality and
Human Mobility Program" (Délano Alonso 2021). 'Hospitality' as a concept of
migrant and refugee inclusion in Mexico also resonates in the some of the academic literature we reviewed. Mexico is a country of significant emigration
to the US, increasingly the recipient of (forcibly) repatriated Mexican nationals, and a transit site for migrants, primarily Central Americans, making their
way north to the US. Hundreds of thousands of migrants pass through this
'Mexican corridor' each year on a risky and dangerous journey. In response to
this situation, a network of dozens of Mexican faith-based and non-religious
NGOs and shelters have appeared along the corridor, offering hospitality in
the form of services and shelter to migrants in transit (Olayo-Méndez, et al.
2014). Though there are examples from the grey literature that do suggest that
there is collaboration between various levels of government and civil society
organizations, such as the Grupos Beta that operate with the support of three
levels of government agencies in Mexico to offer essential services and protect
migrants' human rights (Aguilera, et al. 2018), much of the academic literature
we reviewed positions churches, NGOs, and grassroots organizations as leading the humanitarian response along the Mexican corridor of hospitality.

In the context of hospitality towards migrants and refugees, the academic
literature generally frames solidarity as a bottom-up rather top-down practice.
Roses and Terrones (2019) describe the case of Doña Concepción, a resident
of a small town in Mexico who was arrested in 2005 for her individual acts of
solidarity, providing shelter and care to Central American migrants in transit.
Their analysis concludes that solidarity is enacted by the migrants themselves,
the inhabitants of the local towns and villages through which the migrants
travel; and within networks of civil and ecclesiastical organizations that assist
migrants along the transit corridor (Roses and Terrones 2019). The local level
government or municipalities are not identified as enacting either hospitality
or solidarity. In another example, Flores (2011) discusses the experiences that
Central American migrants and refugees who are in transit to the US make

in Veracruz, Tabasco, and in the State of Mexico. She examines the potential impact of local comunidades solidarias e informadas ('solidary and informed communities') and finds that these communities of solidarity shape a discourse from below that differs sharply from the top-down narrative of the state, which seeks to criminalize and portray migration as a national security threat (Flores 2011). Flores focuses on the grassroots, bottom-up responses of community members, organized civil society, NGOs, and religious institutions.

Turning to the case of Chile, the term 'solidarity city' can be found in grey literature sources such as reports from UNHCR pertaining to the Solidarity Cities program (Gobierno de Chile 2014; UNHCR 2011b; Varoli 2010). Moving beyond the terminology "solidarity city", Bauder and Gonzalez (2018) present the case of the Municipality of Quilicura in Santiago RM, which employs the local label of Comuna de Acogida ('Commune of Reception'). Their analysis of Quilicura's migration policies and local practices are framed within the four dimensions of a solidarity city: Legality; Discourse; Identity Formation; and Scale. Bauder and Gonzalez's (2018) research suggests that there are similarities between Quilicura's urban policies and those of solidarity and sanctuary cities in the Global North in the way top-down and bottom-up efforts converge to address migrant and refugee inclusion at the urban scale.

As per Correa, et al. (2020) there is sparse academic literature on the subject of local governments in Chile and migration policies and practices, inclusive or otherwise. The existing studies tend to offer analyses of the current status of municipal policies and actions directed towards migrants, detail the demographic trends of specific neighborhoods to understand how local policies align with their local populations, or present case studies of municipalities within Santiago RM (Carvahal Gamonal 2018; Mangini 2019; Matus, et al. 2012; Segura and Abde 2014; Torres and Garcés 2013). More recently, Correa, et al. (2020) have provided an analysis of municipal activities of integration throughout the Province of Santiago, Chile. The authors' findings, though not framed in terms of urban sanctuary or solidarity, indicate that these local governments' actions prioritize the legal incorporation of migrants into their communities rather than "the creation of solidarity ties" amongst all residents of the community (Correa, et al. 2020, 191). However, several municipalities in the Province of Santiago, such as Quilicura, Recoleta, and Independencia, have explicitly included in their policies intentions to coordinate and formally incorporate the participation of civil society in the ongoing work and programming related to migrants and refugees, including those with precarious national status (Godoy 2020). These intentions indicate a concerted effort on the part of municipalities to coordinate top-down and bottom-up approaches to the local integration of migrants and refugees.

4 Discussion and Conclusions

Our research confirms that the concepts of urban sanctuary and solidarity play important roles in the accommodation of migrants and refugees in Latin America, as evidenced in the 2004 MPA Solidarity Cities program. Although this program is often framed as a top-down initiative by governments across the region (Barichello 2016; Harley 2014; Regional Refugee Instruments and Related 2004), the literature affirms the importance of engaging the participation of bottom-up civil society organizations to ensure the success of the program (Harley 2014; Koellner 2019; UNHCR 2017). This connection between top-down and bottom-approaches echoes the enactment of urban sanctuary and solidarity movements in the Global North.

However, when reviewing the academic and grey literatures beyond the theme of the 2004 MPA's Solidarity Cities program, we observed a difference regarding a connection between top-down and bottom-up efforts in the enactment of urban sanctuary and solidarity and treatment of these concepts. Grey literature sources such as NGO reports and policy documents pertaining to local government initiatives on migrant and refugee integration and inclusion indicate the active and intended engagement between civil society actors and local governments. However, in the academic literature we reviewed, there remains a gap in terms of an explicit analysis of connections and synergies between the top-down municipal and bottom-up grassroots urban sanctuary and solidarity initiatives.

Our literature review further revealed that the terminology of 'sanctuary' and 'solidarity' city is used only sparingly in Latin America. Furthermore, our review showed that the label 'solidarity city' is mostly applied in reference to UNHCR's Solidarity City program. Beyond this program, other labels, such as 'intercultural city' (Chelius 2018), 'refuge city' (Marzorati and Marconi 2018), or 'commune of reception' tend to be applied to policies and practices that resemble urban sanctuary and solidarity. The case studies of municipal initiatives addressing migration in our sample usually do not align with the concepts urban sanctuary and solidarity (Mangini 2019; Matus, et al. 2012; Torres and Garcés 2013). Interestingly, the concept of hospitality resonates with local initiatives in Latin America that resemble urban sanctuary and solidarity. This term is also used in the Global North in reference to such initiatives (Darling 2014). When the terminology used in Latin America align with urban sanctuary as conceived of in the Global North, the meaning of this terminology may differ. For example, Dahbura's (2018) research on a "sanctuary city regime" (p. 130) that was implemented in El Salvador in 2013 was concerned with mitigating and reducing gang violence rather than migrant and refugee inclusion.

Interestingly, the idea of urban solidarity is often not limited to migrant and refugee accommodation but is extended to other groups that are vulnerable due to their ethnicity, class, gender, sexuality, as well as their migratory status, as evidenced by the initiative *Bogotá mejor para todos* ('Bogotá, better for everyone') in Colombia and (Alcaldía Mayor de Bogotá D.C. 2016) and Quito ciudad inclusiva ('Quito, inclusive city') in Ecuador (El Municipio del Distrito Metropolitano de Quito 2019). This inclusive approach towards urban solidarity beyond migrants and refugees mirrors urban solidarity approaches in some cities of the Global North, such as Berlin (Bauder 2020).

Additional research is needed to further explore the policies and practices of urban sanctuary and solidarity in Latin America. The region is diverse and expansive, and an exhaustive review was beyond the scope of this article. For instance, this review excluded academic and grey literature in Portuguese (and French), which may provide additional insights. Including labels and concepts beyond urban 'sanctuary' and 'solidarity', such as 'hospitality' and 'interculturality' in future research would allow widening the scope of the investigation to policies and practices that may mirror those of urban sanctuary and solidarity in the Global North under a different name. Additionally, by dint of focusing on the concepts of urban sanctuary and solidarity, this review may paint an overly positive picture of migrant hospitality, inclusion, and integration in Latin America. Empirical research that seeks to capture the lived experiences of migrants themselves may reveal shortcomings and gaps between the intended policies and implementation of solidary practices that have been discussed in this chapter. Future research might also explore the different types of mobility that exist in Latin America and develop an understanding of how the different models of solidarity across the region address the diverse forms of migration. Finally, empirical research is needed to address the gap in the academic literature that exists regarding the role of civil society organizations and municipalities working together in Latin American to create inclusive urban spaces of sanctuary and solidarity for all.

References

Aguilera, S.A., A.C. Gómez del Campo, E.C. Márquez, C.F. Vega, T.G. López, M.D. París Pombo, G. Pérez Duperou, and L. Velasco Ortíz (2018). "Migrantes Haitianos y CentroAmericanos en Tijuana, Baja California, 2016–2017. Políticas Gubernamentales y Acciones de la Sociedad Civil". Informe Especial. Mexico: CNDH México y El Colegio de la Frontera Norte.

Agustín, Ó.G., and M.B. Jørgensen (2019). *Solidarity and the "Refugee Crisis" in Europe.* Cham, Switzerland: Springer.

Alcaldía Mayor de Bogotá D.C. (2016). "Bogotá Mejor Para Todos". Planes de Desarrollo y Fortalecimiento Local. Secretaría Distrital de Planeación. 2016.

Alejo, A. (2020). "Foreign Policy and Sanctuary City in Light of a Denationalization Process. The Case of Mexico City". *Colombia Internacional*, no. 102 (April): 165–89.

Ataç, I., T. Schütze, and V. Reitter (2020). "Local Responses in Restrictive National Policy Contexts: Welfare Provisions for Non-Removed Rejected Asylum Seekers in Amsterdam, Stockholm and Vienna". *Ethnic and Racial Studies* 43 (16): 115–34.

Bagelman, J. (2013). "Sanctuary: A Politics of Ease?" *Alternatives* 38 (1): 49–62.

Bagelman, J. (2016). *Sanctuary City: A Suspended State.* New York: Palgrave Macmillan.

Bakewell, P. (2004). "Preface to the First Edition". In A History of Latin America, 2nd ed., 613. United Kingdom: Blackwell Publishing Ltd.

Barcelona En Comú, D. Bookchin, and A. Colau (2019). *Fearless Cities: A Guide to the Global Municipalist Movement.* Oxford: New Internationalist Publications Ltd.

Barichello, S.E. (2016). "Refugee Protection and Responsibility Sharing in Latin America: Solidarity Programmes and the Mexico Plan of Action". *The International Journal of Human Rights* 20 (2): 191–207.

Bauder, H. (2013). "El porqué debemos utilizar el término inmigrante ilegalizado". 2013/1 (Spanish). *RCIS Research Briefs.* Toronto.

Bauder, H. (2016). "Possibilities of Urban Belonging". *Antipode* 48 (2): 252–71.

Bauder, H. (2017a). *Migration Borders Freedom.* London, UK: Routledge.

Bauder, H. (2017b). "Sanctuary Cities: Policies and Practices in International Perspective". *International Migration* 55 (2): 174–87.

Bauder, H. (2019). "Urban Sanctuary and Solidarity in a Global Context: How Does Africa Contribute to the Debate?" *MIASA Working Paper* 2019(1). Accra: University of Ghana. https://www.ug.edu.gh/mias-africa/sites/mias-africa/files/images/MIASA %20WP_2019%281%29%20Bauder_0.pdf.

Bauder, H. (2020). "Urban Solidarity: Perspectives of Migration and Refugee Accommodation and Inclusion". *Critical Sociology*, no. Early view. https://journals .sagepub.com/doi/abs/10.1177/0896920520936332.

Bauder, H. (n.d.). "Urban Migrant and Refugee Solidarity Beyond City Limits". *Urban Studies.*

Bauder, H., and D.A. Gonzalez (2018). "Municipal Responses to 'Illegality': Urban Sanctuary across National Contexts". *Social Inclusion* 6 (1): 124–34.

Carvahal Gamonal, I. (2018). "Acciones de Participación que Las Comunas de Recoleta, Quilicura y Santiago Realizan para la Inclusión de los Migrantes". Santiago, Chile: Universidad Alberto Hurtado.

Chelius, L.C. (2018). "La Hospitalidad Imaginada o Cómo Podemos Construir Una Ciudad Hospitalaria Sin Exaltar Los Mitos Que Nos Dieron Patria". Mexico City: Sin Fronteras I.A.P.

Christof, W., and S. Kron (2019). "Solidarische Städte in Europa: Urbane Politik Zwischen Charity Und Citizenship". In *Solidarische Städte in Europa: Urbane Politik Zwischen*

Charity Und Citizenship, edited by Christof, W., and Kron, S. 5–16. Berlin: Rosa-Luxemburg Stiftung.

Correa, L.E.T., M.F. Stang, and C.D. Rodríguez (2020). "La política del estado de ánimo. La debilidad de las políticas migratorias locales en Santiago de Chile". *Perfiles latinoamericanos: revista de la Facultad Latinoamericana de Ciencias Sociales, Sede México* 28 (55): 171–201.

Cunningham, H. (1998). "Sanctuary and Sovereignty: Church and State Along the U.S.-Mexico Border". *Journal of Church and State* 40 (2): 371–86.

Dahbura Nelson Martínez, J. (2018). "The Short-Term Impact of Crime on School Enrollment and School Choice: Evidence from El Salvador". *Economía* 18 (2): 121–45.

Darling, J. (2010). "A City of Sanctuary: The Relational Re-Imagining of Sheffield's Asylum Politics". *Transactions of the Institute of British Geographers* 35 (1): 125–40.

Darling, J. (2014). "From Hospitality to Presence". *Peace Review* 26 (2): 162–69.

Darling, J., and H. Bauder (2019). *Sanctuary Cities and Urban Struggles: Rescaling Migration, Citizenship, and Rights.* Manchester, UK: Manchester University Press.

de Graauw, E. (2014). "Municipal ID Cards for Undocumented Immigrants: Local Bureaucratic Membership in a Federal System". *Politics & Society* 42 (3): 309–30.

de Graauw, E. (2016). *Making Immigrant Rights Real: Nonprofits and the Politics of Integration in San Francisco.* Ithaca, NY: Cornell University Press.

Del Carpio, V., D.F. Santiago, and D. Annoni (2015). "El reasentamiento solidario en América Latina: un ejemplo de solidaridad con los refugiados". In *Direitos Humanos nas Américas*, 1st ed. Curitiba.

Délano Alonso, A. (2021). "Sanctuary in Countries of Origin: A Transnational Perspective". *Migration and Society: Advances in Research* 4: 84–98.

Delgado, M. (2018). *Sanctuary Cities, Communities, and Organizations: A Nation at a Crossroads.* Oxford University Press.

Dietrich, A. (2019). *Solidarity Cities: Lokale Strategien Gegen Rassismus Und Neoliberalismus.* Münster: Unrast Verlag.

El Municipio del Distrito Metropolitano de Quito (2019). "Quito Ciudad Inclusiva". 2019. http://gobiernoabierto.quito.gob.ec/?page_id=6734.

Fischel de Andrade, J.H. (2014). "Forced Migration in South America". In *The Oxford Handbook of Refugee and Forced Migration Studies*, 651–63. Oxford, United Kingdom: Oxford University Press.

Flores, M. (2011). "Experiencias Positivas de La Migración Centroamericana En Tránsito Por México En Las Localidades de Veracruz, Tabasco y Estado de México". Lecture presented at the IV Congreso de la Red Internacional de Migración y Desarrollo. Crisis Global y Estrategias Migratorias: hacia la redefinición de las políticas de movilidad., Flacso-Quito, Ecuador, May. http://rimd.reduaz.mx/ponencias_flacso/PonenciaMarianaFlores.pdf.

Freeland, G. (2010). "Negotiating Place, Space and Borders: The New Sanctuary Movement". *Latino Studies* 8 (4): 485–508.

Gobierno de Chile (2014). "Quilicura es declarada Ciudad Solidaria por Naciones Unidas". Ministerio de Desarrollo Social. December 14, 2014. http://www.desarroll osocialyfamilia.gob.cl/noticias/quilicura-es-declarada-ciudad-solidaria-por-nacio nes-unidas.

Gobierno de la Ciudad de México (2011). "Ley de Interculturalidad, Atención a Migrantes y Movilidad Humana En El Distrito Federal". Mexico: CONSEJERÍA JURÍDICA Y DE SERVICIOS LEGALES.

Gobierno de la Ciudad de México (2017). "Gaceta Oficial de la Ciudad de México No. 43 Bis". Órgano de Difusión del Gobierno de la Ciudad de México. http://data.metro bus.cdmx.gob.mx/transparencia/documentos/art14/I/LL_DPersonasAdultasMayo resDF040417.pdf.

Godoy, M. (2020). "Solidarity Cities in Santiago de Chile and Civil Society Participation During COVID-19". Master of Arts Major Research Paper, Toronto, ON, Canada: Ryerson University.

Guevara, Y. (2015). "Migración de tránsito y ayuda humanitaria: Apuntes sobre las casas de migrantes en la ruta migratoria del pacífico sur en México". *The Forum for Inter-American Studies (FIAR)* 8 (1): 63–83.

Harley, T. (2014). "Regional Cooperation and Refugee Protection in Latin America: A 'South-South' Approach". *International Journal of Refugee Law* 26 (1): 22–47.

Hershkowitz, M., G. Hudson, and H. Bauder (2020). "Rescaling the Sanctuary City: Police and Non-Status Migrants in Ontario, Canada". *International Migration*, April.

Houston, S.D., and O. Lawrence-Weilmann (2016). "The Model Migrant and Multiculturalism: Analyzing Neoliberal Logics in US Sanctuary Legislation". In *Migration Policy and Practice*, edited by Bauder, H., and Matheis, C. 1st ed., 101–26. New York, United States: Palgrave Macmillan.

Hudson, G., I. Atak, M. Manocchi, and C.A. Hannan (2017). "(No) Access T.O.: A Pilot Study on Sanctuary City Policy in Toronto, Canada". *RCIS Working Paper 1.* Toronto: Ryerson Centre for Immigration and Settlement. https://www.ssrn.com/ abstract=2897016.

International Organization for Migration (IOM) (2020). "World Migration Report 2020". Geneva, Switzerland. https://www.un.org/sites/un2.un.org/files/wmr_2020.pdf.

Jubilut, L.L., and W.P. Carneiro (2011). "Resettlement in Solidarity: A New Regional Approach Towards a More Humane Durable Solution". *Refugee Survey Quarterly* 30 (3): 63–86.

Kassa, D.G. (2019). *Refugee Spaces and Urban Citizenship in Nairobi: Africa's Sanctuary City*. Lanham: Lexington Books.

Kneebone, S. (2016). "Comparative Regional Protection Frameworks for Refugees: Norms and Norm Entrepreneurs". *The International Journal of Human Rights* 20 (2): 153–72.

Koellner, F. (2019). *Refugee Integration in Solidarity Cities in Latin America & the EU: A regional comparative analysis*. AV Akademikerverlag.

Kron, S., and H. Lebuhn (2020). "Building Solidarity Cities: From Protest to Policy". In *Fostering Pluralism Through Solidarity Activism in Europe: Everyday Encounters with Newcomers*, edited by Baban, F., and Rygiel, K. 81–105. Cham, SWITZERLAND: Springer International Publishing AG.

Lambert, S., and T. Swerts (2019). "'From Sanctuary to Welcoming Cities': Negotiating the Social Inclusion of Undocumented Migrants in Liège, Belgium". *Social Inclusion*; Lisbon 7 (4): 90–99.

Landau, L. (2010). "Inclusion in Shifting Sands: Rethinking Mobility and Belonging in African Cities". In *Urban Diversity: Space, Culture, and Inclusive Pluralism in Cities Worldwide*, edited by Wanjiku Kihato, C., Massoumi, M., and Ruble, B.A. 169–86. Washington, D.C. : Baltimore: Johns Hopkins Univ Pr.

Lefebvre, H. (1996). *Writings on Cities*. Translated by Eleonore Kofman and Elizabeth Lebas. Massachusetts: Blackwell Publishers Ltd.

Mancina, P. (2012). "The Birth of a Sanctuary-City: A History of Governmental Sanctuary in San Francisco". In *Sanctuary Practices in International Perspectives: Migration, Citizenship and Social Movements*, edited by Lippert, R.K., and Rehaag, S. 205–18. Abingdon: Routledge.

Manfredi-Sánchez, J.L. (2020). "Sanctuary Cities: What Global Migration Means for Local Governments". *Social Sciences* 9 (8): 146.

Mangini, J.P.G. (2019). "Transformar Desde El Territorio. Hacia Una Política Pública Comunal de Migraciones. El Caso de Estudio de La Comuna de La Pintana, Santiago de Chile". *CUHSO*, July, 13–32.

Marzorati, R. (2017). "La Sociedad Civil Organizada En El Ámbito Migratorio En La Ciudad de México: Tipología, Funciones y Retos (2006 – 2016)". Mexico: Observatorio de Legislación y Politica Migratoria. http://observatoriocolef.org/boletin/la-socie dad-civil-organizada-en-el-ambito-migratorio-en-la-ciudad-de-mexico-tipologia -funciones-y-retos-2006-2016/.

Marzorati, R., and G. Marconi (2018). "Governing Migration and Urban Diversity in Mexico City. A Critical Reflection Starting from the Ley de Interculturalidad". *REMHU, Rev. Interdiscip. Mobil. Hum. (Impr.)* 26 (52): 149–66.

Matus, T., F. Sabatini, F. Cortez-Monroy, P. Hermansen, and C. Silva (2012). "Migración y Municipios. Construcción de Una Propuesta de Política Pública de Gestión Municipal Para La Población Inmigrante". In *Propuestas Para Chile. Concurso Políticas Públicas*, 323–62. Santiago: Centro de Políticas Públicas UC.

McDonald, J. (2012). "Building a Sanctuary City: Municipal Migrant Rights in the City of Toronto". In *Citizenship, Migrant Activism and the Politics of Movement*, edited by Nyers, P. and K. Rygiel, 1st ed., 129–45. New York, NY: Routledge.

Mejía, D. (2010). "Políticas públicas que mejoran la convivencia en la frontera, construyen Fronteras Solidarias". Programa Estudios de la Ciudad. FLACSO Sede Ecuador.

Missbach, A., Y. Adiputera, and A. Prabandari (2018). "Is Makassar a 'Sanctuary City'? Migration Governance in Indonesia After the 'Local Turn'". *Austrian Journal of South-East Asian Studies* 11 (2): 199–216.

Nyers, P. (2010). "No One Is Illegal Between City and Nation". *Studies in Social Justice* 4 (2): 127–43.

Olayo-Méndez, A., S.N. Haymes, and M.V. de Haymes (2014). "Mexican Migration-Corridor Hospitality". *Peace Review* 26 (2): 209–17.

Purcell, M. (2002). "Excavating Lefebvre: The Right to the City and Its Urban Politics of the Inhabitant". *GeoJournal* 58 (2/3): 99–108.

Purcell, M. (2014). "Possible Worlds: Henri Lefebvre and the Right to the City". *Journal of Urban Affairs* 36 (1): 141–54.

Regional Refugee Instruments and Related. (2004a). "Mexico Declaration and Plan of Action to Strengthen the International Protection of Refugees in Latin America". https://www.refworld.org/docid/424bf6914.html.

Regional Refugee Instruments and Related. (2014). "Brazil Declaration and Plan of Action". https://www.refworld.org/docid/5487065b4.html.

Ridgley, J. (2008). "Cities of Refuge: Immigration Enforcement, Police, and the Insurgent Genealogies of Citizenship in U.S. Sanctuary Cities". *Urban Geography* 29 (1): 53–77.

Ridgley, J. (2011). "Refuge, Refusal, and Acts of Holy Contagion: The City as a Sanctuary for Soldiers Resisting the Vietnam War". *ACME: An International Journal for Critical Geographies* 10 (2): 189–214.

Roses, R.P., and L. Alquisiras Terrones (2019). "Desplazamientos discursivos y transformaciones institucionales en las prácticas de solidaridad hacia migrantes centroamericanos en México". *Migraciones Internacionales* 10 (36).

Segura, D.M., and K.B. Abde (2014). "Barrios y población inmigrantes: el caso de la comuna de Santiago". *Revista INVI* 29 (81): 19–77.

Thompson, M. (2020). "What's so New about New Municipalism?" *Progress in Human Geography*, March, 0309132520909480.

Torres, O., and A. Garcés (2013). "Representaciones Sociales de Migrantes Peruanos Sobre Su Proceso de Integración En La Ciudad de Santiago de Chile". *Polis (Santiago)* 12 (35): 309–34. https://doi.org/10.4067/S0718-65682013000200014.

Tramonte, L. (2011). "Debunking the Myth of 'Sanctuary Cities': Community Policing Policies Protect American Communities". Washington DC: American Immigration

Council. https://www.immigrationresearch.org/report/immigration-policy-center/debunking-myth-sanctuary-cities-community-policing-policies-protect.

UNHCR (1984) 1984 Cartagena Declaration

UNHCR (2011a). "Los Beneficios de Pertenecer: Opciones y oportunidades de integración local para países y comunidades de acogida y para refugiados". https://www.refworld.org.es/docid/4e844a072.html.

UNHCR (2011b). "Arica, primera 'Ciudad Solidaria' con los refugiados en el norte de Chile". Noticias | ACNUR. UNHCR. August 26, 2011. https://www.acnur.org/noticias/noticia/2011/8/5b0c1b891/arica-primera-ciudad-solidaria-con-los-refugiados-en-el-norte-de-chile.html.

UNHCR (2017). "Regional Discussion on the Program 'Cities of Solidarity.'" UNHCR. https://www.acnur.org/fileadmin/Documentos/BDL/2018/11488.pdf?file=filead min/Documentos/BDL/2018/11488.

UNHCR (2018). "UNHCR: Brazil Plan of Action. First Triennial Progress Report. 2015–2017". Alto Comisionado de las Naciones Unidas para los Refugiados (ACNUR). https://www.refworld.org.es/docid/5c883e844.html.

Varoli, F. (2010). "Ciudades Solidarias: la integración local en Latinoamérica". *Migraciones Forzadas Revista*, 2010.

Varsanyi, M. (2010). *Taking Local Control: Immigration Policy Activism in U.S. Cities and States*. Stanford University Press.

Vera Espinoza, M. (2018). "The Limits and Opportunities of Regional Solidarity: Exploring Refugee Resettlement in Brazil and Chile". *Global Policy* 9 (1): 85–94.

Villegas, F.J. (2018). "'Don't Ask, Don't Tell': Examining the Illegalization of Undocumented Students in Toronto, Canada". *British Journal of Sociology of Education* 39 (8): 1111–25.

Walker, K.E., and H. Leitner (2011). "The Variegated Landscape of Local Immigration Policies in the United States". *Urban Geography* 32 (2): 156–78.

CHAPTER 11

Solidarity Cities in Santiago de Chile and Civil Society Participation during COVID-19

Margaret Godoy and Harald Bauder

The solidarity city movement has emerged internationally at the crux of the tension between exclusionary national-level migration policy and municipal practices of local integration (Bauder 2017; Foerster 2019). Solidarity city policies and practices vary significantly and are highly contextual based upon the local and national political and geopolitical circumstances. They typically seek to offer protection to migrants in vulnerable situations, who lack legal documentation or experience heightened vulnerability due to other structural and individual circumstances, while they may also address the precarious situation of non-migrant populations (Bauder 2021). 'Solidarity city', a term that is employed sporadically across Latin America (Godoy & Bauder this volume), encompasses various urban solidarity and sanctuary policies and practices in relation to local migrant and refugee accommodation. In addition, solidarity city policies and practices tend to involve a blend of bottom-up grassroots initiatives as well as top-down policies and practices, led by municipalities (Bauder and Gonzalez 2018). These horizontal relations between civil society actors and municipalities are "crucial for strengthening the local position" of cities in resisting exclusionary government policy at the national level (Ataç, et al. 2020, 129).

Much of the current academic research on solidarity cities is centered on the Global North (Bauder 2017; Darling and Bauder 2019); only recently has some research on the Global South emerged (Bauder 2019; Kassa 2019; Missbach, et al. 2018). In this chapter, we contribute to this emerging literature by focusing on municipal policies and practices of local integration of migrants in Latin America. Specifically, we explore the role of civil society actors – i.e. the third sector beyond public and private sectors (Jezard 2018) that encompasses foundations, NGOs, and faith-based organizations as well as individual actors such as activists, volunteers, and local community members – in engaging with municipal policies and practices of solidarity in Chile's Santiago Metropolitan Region (RM). Santiago RM, consisting of 52 *comunas* (communes) each of which is governed by its own municipality (Garreton 2017), is not to be confused with the Municipality of Santiago (sometimes referred to as Santiago, or Santiago Centro), which is the capital city of Chile. Several municipalities located in Santiago RM participate in the 'Solidarity Cities' program administered by UNHCR (Regional Refugee Instruments & Related 2004). In addition, our study is embedded in the greater context of the COVID-19 global pandemic. It thus makes a three-fold contribution: it expands existing solidarity city literature beyond the current geographic focus on North America and Europe; it contributes to our understanding of civil society actors in offering protection to vulnerable migrants and refugees at the local level; and it offer insights into developments related to the COVID-19 pandemic which have not yet been addressed robustly in academic literature.

As such, our chapter is guided by several research questions beginning with: how does the participation of civil society actors relate to solidarity city policies and practices, in the context of Chile? More specifically, how does the participation of local civil society actors impact municipalities' ability to enact solidarity city policies and practices? Finally, our research explores how recent measures to combat the COVID-19 pandemic affect solidarity policies and the lived experiences of migrants.

To answer the above research questions, we used the Municipalities of Independencia, Recoleta and Quilicura in Santiago RM as illustrative cases of how civil society actors in relation to solidarity city policies in Chile impact migrants in vulnerable situations, especially during the COVID-19 pandemic. The study's primary source of data is key informant interviews. These interviews are contextualized through a document review of relevant municipalities' policies pertaining to migrants and refugees, which we analyzed for any direct reference to the role and participation of civil society actors. We applied purposive sampling (Bryman 2012) and selected potential interviewees based on the insight they could provide into municipal policies and practices of solidarity related to migration and the relationships between the local and national levels, and between local government and civil society actors. The final sample of ten key informants included: three senior municipal employees (from Independencia, Quilicura, and Recoleta) with in-depth knowledge of their respective municipalities' Migrant and Refugee Offices and Programs; two former, senior policy-makers in Chile's national Department of Foreign Affairs and Migration (*Departamento de Extranjería y Migración*); a researcher at one of Chile's national associations of municipalities; and four civil society actors (NGO staff, volunteers, and activists) (see Table 11.1). There are several limitations to this study: first, we conducted the interviews between May 20 and August 2, 2020 before the pandemic ended and before we may have fully seen the full impacts of COVID-19 on communities in Chile. Secondly, it was beyond the scope of this project to interview migrants and thus examine

TABLE 11.1   Description of key informants

Interviewee

A – Researcher for a national association of municipalities
B – Activist, part of a national network of migrant organizations
C – NGO staff member
D – Municipal government employee
E – Former national government employee
F – Former national government employee
G – Municipal government employee
H – NGO staff member
I – Municipal government employee
J – Volunteer for NGO

For reasons of confidentiality, we cannot offer more detailed descriptions of the participants' roles

their lived experiences. Finally, we warn against romanticizing municipal policies and practices of solidarity of migrant inclusion in Santiago RM. Racism
remains pervasive in Chilean society (Segovia and Lufin 2013; Tijoux 2016;
Tijoux and Ambiado 2019; Tijoux and Córdova Rivera 2015).

1   Emergent Spaces of Transformation: Potentials and Limitations

Solidarity cities address an inherent tension between immigration policy and
citizenship law that are typically the responsibility of national governments,
and migrants' lived experiences that occur at a local level. Solidarity cities represent an innovative municipal approach towards the accommodation and
inclusion of migrants in light of exclusionary national policies (Darling and
Bauder 2019). However, the phenomenon escapes a set definition, demanding
instead a multi-dimensional approach to encompass its complexities (Bauder
2017; Kuge 2019). The concept of 'solidarity' (Agustín and Jørgensen 2016, 2019;
Featherstone 2012) is contested and has been applied inconsistently in the general migrant and refugee academic literature (Bauder and Juffs 2019) as well as
among urban activists, municipal administrators, and community leaders who
support migrants in vulnerable situations (Bauder 2021). Perhaps due to the
complexity of the solidarity concept, solidarity cities engage in a wide variety

of practices and strategies that focus on soliciting official municipal legislative support of sanctuary city initiatives; challenging exclusionary migrant
and refugee discourses at the local level; reimagining the city as a space of
co-belonging in which all inhabitants can participate equally; and asserting
the rescaling of migration policies from the national level to municipal level
(Bauder 2017). These urban sanctuary practices and strategies apply specifically
in the Municipality of Quilicura in Santiago RM (Bauder and Gonzalez 2018).

The literature has connected solidarity city approaches to Henri Lefebvre's
concept of the 'right to the city,' which relies on two critical rights for all urban
inhabitants: "The right [...] to participation and appropriation (clearly distinct
from the right to property)" (Lefebvre 1996, 174). The right to the city is enacted
through active participation of all urban inhabitants in the everyday routines
of life that are played out in the city. It is also a core principle of the solidarity
city movement, which renegotiates inclusion, belonging, and citizenship in the
urban context as premised upon one's presence and participation in the city
space (Nyers 2010). The sanctuary city movement's transformative potential
lies in the way that it changes everyday interactions between different actors
within the city: mayors and municipal officials, activists, service workers, and
migrants in vulnerable situations (Darling 2010). The nature of such participation may be political, social, cultural, yet what matters is that the everyday
interactions are such that all urban actors that comprise civil society, regardless of migratory status, are enabled and empowered to participate within the
context of the city. In this way, sanctuary cities often "blend bottom-up and
top-down approaches" (Bauder and Gonzalez 2018, 130).

Criticisms centering on the theme of participation have focused especially on urban 'sanctuary' policies and practices, which can be understood
as closely related to urban solidarity. Bagelman (2013, 55) critiques sanctuary
practices in Glasgow for facilitating a 'politics of ease', which offers hope for
migrants in vulnerable situations while obscuring and normalizing the pas-
siveness and liminality that urban sanctuary demands of migrants. This politics of ease brings into question the transformative potential of the sanctuary
city. Similarly, Foerster (2019) remarks that the narrative of 'protection' that
is engrained in urban sanctuary politics has failed to empower migrants in
vulnerable situations. Furthermore, Houston and Lawrence-Weilmann (2016)
criticize sanctuary city policies in the United States for ultimately safeguarding a capitalist economy that relies on migrant exclusion. They instead suggest
that equity and justice concerns should be addressed through "intentional and
sustained collaboration between policymakers, grassroots community organizations and residents who are directly affected by sanctuary legislation or
the lack thereof" (Houston and Lawrence-Weilmann 2016, 122). Walia (2014)

assumes a similar position when she says: "zones of sanctuary are actively constituted not by politicians but by us – as service providers, educators, healthcare professionals, and neighbors – on the basis of solidarity and mutual aid"
(Walia 2014, para. 13). These authors emphasize the importance of a bottom-
up, grassroots and collaborative approach to imagining the city as a space of
belonging and participation. In this sense, civil society is crucial to achieving
the transformative potential of solidarity cities.

The classical understanding of civil society traces back to ancient Greece.
Aristotle conceptualized civil society as a part of governance, with the groups
and communities that comprise civil society participating in governance and
working towards the common good (Mclean 1997). The classical understanding of civil society as a "politically organized commonwealth" (Ehrenberg
1999, xii) changed in the early nineteenth century through Georg Wilhelm
Friedrich Hegel who separated civil society from the state and political authority (Kervegan, et al. 2018). Building on Hegel, Karl Marx theorized civil society
as separate from the political state but was also critical of the state and emphasized the importance of social practice for structural transformation and sub-
lation of both political state and civil society (Chitty 2011; Rockmore 2018).
Antonio Gramsci further developed the Marxist approach, conceptualizing
civil society as a conflicting realm in which hegemony is organized (Ehrenberg
1999). Agustín and Jørgensen (2016) leverage Gramsci's ideas to explore emerging solidarities between civil society and refugees in Europe. They argue that
spaces and scales of resistance provide the opportunity to account for diverse
actors (political and civil) as well as diverse struggles that co-exist and interact
within civil societies. From this position, it is possible to explore the potential
of spaces of resistance within civil society in Chile's solidarity cities, as well as
the limitations that might exist or have been imposed by national government
responses to the COVID-19 pandemic.

A neoliberal perspective, however, emphasizes the role civil society plays in
improving efficiency in government and the market, and as a source to deliver
social services that otherwise are the responsibility of the state (Dagnino 2010;
Koppelman 2017). Ataç, et al. (2020) add a multi-level governance perspective
in the contexts of municipal policies and practices of migrant inclusion. In
particular, they stress the importance of both vertical and horizontal relations: the local incorporation of civil society actors (e.g. NGOs) strengthen a
municipality's ability to deliver services and it strengthens the municipality's
position to contest exclusionary national policies.

Turning to Latin America, the political and theoretical concept of 'civil society' fully materialized to take root in the early 1980s (Avritzer 1997). Due to
the geographical, political, economic, and social diversity of Latin America,

a Brazilian model, Southern Cone model (Argentina and Chile), Mexican model, and Andean model of civil society can be identified (Avritzer 2006). In Chile, the Pinochet regime targeted political institutions by outlawing communists and socialists, leaving civil society as the only space where political action could take place (Avritzer 2006, 42). Between 1990 and the early 2000s, the participation of civil society was enshrined in the constitutions of at least nineteen Latin American countries, with various legal-institutional frameworks and mechanisms providing space for civil society's engagement with the state and democracy (Dagnino 2010). In 2004, a bill was brought to Chile's National Congress seeking to secure the right of civil society participation. After years of legislative proceedings, *Ley 20.500 Sobre Asociaciones y Participación Ciudadana en la Gestión Pública* [Law 20.500 on Associations and Citizen Participation in Public Management] was passed in 2011, addressing the specific and formal mechanisms that state institutions must implement to ensure the inclusion and participation of civil society, including a facilitated pathway for the legal recognition of associations formed by citizens (Ministerio del Interior y Seguridad Pública 2011; Muñoz Aravena 2018). However, barriers remain to public participation of civil society, for instance, Law 20.500 failed to put into place the systems to ensure the law's implementation. As a result, civil society participation has significantly declined in recent years (Sanfuentes and Garreton 2018).

2   Immigration to Chile and the Role of Municipalities

The history of Chile is indelibly marked by immigration and settlement. In the 16th century the Spanish conquistadors invaded the Americas and in 1540 Pedro de Valdivia arrived in Chile to found Santiago, beginning the colonial project of settling the region (Galeano 1997; Valdes 2018). There have subsequently been several waves of immigration from Europe (Valdes 2018; Doña & Levinson 2004). In the 1970s, following General Augusto Pinochet's violent military coup (Williamson 1992), Chile became a country of emigration (Doña and Levinson 2004). As Pinochet's regime came to its end, in the 1990s, new immigrants arrived (Staab and Maher 2006). Since the 1990s, immigration to Chile has continued to increase exponentially, with economic migrants arriving mostly from countries such as Peru, Bolivia, and Argentina (Cabieses, et al. 2015). By the end of 2019, the number of international migrants living in Chile had jumped to nearly 1.5 million, an increase of 19% from 2018 (Instituto Nacional de Estadísticas 2020). The Government of Chile has reported that approximately 30% of all international migrants residing in Chile have irregular legal status (Tumba 2018). Chile has received approximately 10% of the four million Venezuelans who have left their country, representing the largest (30%) demographic of international migrants in the country (OEA 2020). In addition, following a devastating earthquake in 2010, the number of Haitian migrants to Chile has increased steadily. As of December 2018, there were over 179,000 Haitians in Chile (Instituto Nacional de Estadísticas 2019) and the majority of these migrants are racialized men between the ages of 30–44 (Rojas Pedemonte, et al. 2019). Despite its rapidly changing landscape, Chile has long practiced a 'policy of no policy' in terms of migration (Reveco 2018). Even in the 1990s, as immigration to Chile began to increase, the government did not react proactively to immigration with any coherent policy or integration strategy. Subsequently, there were several unsuccessful attempts to develop comprehensive national immigration legislation and in 2018 Chile declined to sign the UN's Global Compact on Migration (Laing 2018).

At the same time, there had been important regional developments that affect the accommodation of migrants in Chilean cities. In 2004, Latin American governments, including Chile, gathered in Mexico City to celebrate the 20th Anniversary of the 1984 Cartagena Declaration on Refugees – a non-binding regional protection instrument that was adopted expanded the classic definition of a 'refugee' to include individuals who have been forced to leave their country of origin due to war, massive violations of human rights or because of other causes that severely disturb public order (UNHCR 2013b). The 2004 Mexico Declaration and Plan of Action (MPA) was the outcome of this meeting: a regional framework for the protection of forced migrants, based upon the principle of solidarity (Jubilut and Carneiro 2011), which includes the "Solidarity Cities" program, which "is to provide effective protection which encompasses enjoyment of social, economic and cultural rights and observance of the obligations of refugees" (Regional Refugee Instruments & Related 2004, 10). The program seeks to mitigate 'irregular' migration, through protecting and ensuring the ability of urban refugees and migrants in vulnerable situations to achieve self-sufficiency. Furthermore, the program seeks to shift negative discourses and attitudes, framing migration in the context of the urban space as an opportunity to be explored (Barichello 2016). The Solidarity Cities program, which is administered by UNHCR, was reaffirmed in 2014 with the Brazil Declaration and Plan of Action (Regional Refugee Instruments & Related 2004), and again in 2017 with a Regional Discussion on the Program "Solidarity Cities" in Quito, Ecuador (UNHCR 2017). By 2011, more than 50 formal and informal Solidarity Cities agreements have been established across Latin America (UNHCR 2011a), including the Chilean municipalities Quilicura, Arica, La Calera, and San Felipe (Gobierno de Chile 2014; UNHCR 2011b, 2013a).

Nevertheless, there is scant literature on the implementation of the Solidarity City program, although some research highlights the activities of various participating cities while emphasizing the lack of a systemic approach to defining what constitutes a Solidarity City (Harley 2014). A comparative analysis of the Solidarity Cities program in Europe and the Solidarity Cities program in Latin America found that successful urban sanctuary policies and practices are often associated with a strong "supportive anchor" be it a partnership with a university or NGO (Koellner 2019, 42). In the case of Chile, the term 'solidarity city' is only explicitly used in grey literature and limited to reports related to UNHCR and the Solidarity Cities program (Gobierno de Chile 2014; UNHCR 2011b; Varoli 2010). There is little academic literature that directly addresses the subject of local governments and migration policies in Chile (Correa, et al. 2020).

Despite this sparse scholarly attention, Santiago RM's municipalities are key institutions that impact the everyday lives of their local community members. Approximately 60% of Chile's international migrants live in Santiago RM (AMUCH 2016) and, as of 2017, the municipalities with the highest proportion of migrants living in them were Santiago, Las Condes, Independencia, Recoleta, and Ñuñoa (OIM 2018). Five municipalities have been particularly active in implementing policies and practices to protect vulnerable migrants Santiago, Quilicura, Recoleta, Independencia, and La Pintana (OIM 2018). The political efforts in these municipalities were disrupted by COVID-19. Chilean President Sebastien Piñera declared a 90-day "State of Constitutional Exception and Catastrophe" on March 18, 2020, which offered expanded power to the country's armed forces to maintain 'public order' and protect the country's 'national security' (Gobierno de Chile 2020c). Over 70% of Chile's confirmed COVID-19 cases occurred in Santiago RM (Ministerio de Salud – Gobierno de Chile 2020) and, in response, a strict physical distancing directive was put into place on May 13, 2020 when the Ministry of Health announced a state of total quarantine for 32 of Santiago RM's *comunas* (Gobierno de Chile 2020d). In this state of total quarantine no one is permitted to leave their house without an official permit, which can only be obtained online by submitting one's personal identification information (national ID card, a passport, etc.) to a website that is hosted by Chile's national police (Carabineros de Chile 2020). Other than in the case of essential workers, residents can only obtain a maximum of two three-hour permits per week; those who violate either the permit's time-limit or who do not have a permit face steep fines and potential detainment by authorities (Gobierno de Chile 2020b).

Very few studies detail the current status of municipal policies and actions directed towards migrants. A 2012 study of Santiago RM analyzed six municipalities with high levels of international migrant populations (Santiago,

Estación Central, Independencia, Recoleta, Quilicura, and La Pintana) to propose a policy for municipalities to better manage the increasingly diverse populations that they serve (Matus, et al. 2012). Another study examined the social
representations constructed by Peruvian migrants through their interactions
with municipal public services in the municipality of Santiago (Torres and
Garcés 2013). A socio-territorial profile of neighborhoods in the municipality
of Santiago showcases the different groups (Segura and Abde 2014). Individual
case studies of specific municipalities in Santiago RM examine the development of a public policy serving international migrants in the Municipality
of La Pintana (Mangini 2019), the lack of consistent policies on the inclusion
of immigration in the municipalities of Santiago, Quilicura, and Recoleta
(Carvahal Gamonal 2018), and the recognition of migrants by municipalities
throughout the Province of Santiago (Correa, et al. 2020).

3   Spaces of Resistance in Santiago RM

To begin with, none of the interviewees used the label of 'solidarity city'.
Instead, all three of the municipalities included in this study use different
terminology in reference to their municipal policies and practices of solidarity. The Municipality of Quilicura uses the term 'Commune of Reception'
(*Comuna de Acogida*) (Bauder and Gonzalez 2018; Correa, et al. 2014). The
Municipality of Recoleta uses a different slogan: 'We are all Recoleta' (*Recoleta
somos todos*) (Municipalidad de Recoleta 2020a), which, according to
Interviewee I, reflects the mayor's understanding that access to rights should
be determined by one's residency in a community rather than legal status in
a country. The Municipality of Independencia uses the labels 'intercultural
comuna' and 'inclusive *comuna*' in official communications (Municipalidad de
Independencia 2020a), which "addresses not only the inclusion of migrants
but of the entire population" (Interviewee G). Regardless of the terminology
or label used, each municipality included in this study has incorporated solidarity policies and practices that are intended to ensure the participation of
all community members, including migrants, and that involves the inclusion
of civil society actors.

4   Participation and Municipal Coordination with Civil Society Actors

Each of the three municipalities, Independencia, Recoleta, and Quilicura, have
taken explicit steps to coordinate and formally incorporate the participation

of civil society in the ongoing work and programming related to migrants and refugees.

4.1   *Independencia*

The Municipality of Independencia passed Decree 3634 in 2016, which outlines the objectives, guidelines, and programs for the municipality's Office of Migration. The general objective for the Office is the "Coordination of the Communal Immigration Policy of Independencia" (Municipalidad de Independencia 2016, para. 2); a more specific objectives is to "include, spread, and promote the focuses of Human Rights, Anti-discrimination, Interculturality and Social Inclusion in diverse local organizations and institutions in the *comuna*" (Municipalidad de Independencia 2016, para. 6). Furthermore, the municipality's application package for the "Migrant Seal" program – a national-level program launched in 2015 by Chile's Department of Foreign Affairs and Migration (*Departamento de Extranjería y Migración*) to recognize and incentivize municipalities that develop plans, programs, and actions to include migrant populations with a focus on human rights (Gobierno de Chile 2019) – details a three-pronged approach to promoting the participation of the migrant community in Independencia: (1) The participation of the migrant community in municipal management, through Independencia's civil society advisory board, (2) promoting the organization of migrant community groups themselves, e.g., the 'Organization of United Haitians of Independencia', as well as the creation of the 'Group of Entrepreneurial Women Entertainment and Gastronomy', and (3) exercising the rights of citizens, and ensuring political participation through education campaigns (Municipalidad de Independencia 2018). Therefore, embedded within the Municipality of Independencia's policies is the explicit intention to include a variety of civil society actors in the Office of Migration's work.

The policies' explicit inclusion of civil society participation is echoed by a senior municipal employee of Independencia's Office of Migration, who reiterated the office's horizontal relations with a variety of civil society actors:

> One of the first things we [the Office of Migration] did in 2015 was to install in the commune – to diagnose critical issues, mainly because almost everything had to do with living together at the neighborhood level – we created a "table of intercultural coexistence" (*mesa de convivencia intercultural*), where there are national leaders and migrants from organizations, neighborhood councils, NGOs of different types, where regularly [...] it is a "table" (*mesa*) where we are detecting problems and

looking for solutions, but with all the actors, public and private. It is a "table" that we coordinate and that we schedule. We review issues of all kinds, security, integration problems, overcrowded housing, cultural activities.

Interviewee G

Although the municipality is fostering the participation of civil society, the Office of Migration is careful to ensure a level of autonomy in the role that civil society plays. The same interview continues:

What we want is that organizations make proposals [for activities] and we collaborate in the things that they organize. Because we also realized that there were organizations that did nothing if we did not organize, finance, and execute any activity. Therefore, we stopped doing it so that they would initiate. Obviously, we gave them tools, training, aids, we also helped them in applying for public funds to generate some activities, but now we are not organizing them ourselves. The idea is that organizations can generate autonomous processes and become empowered with respect to their role in the community. That it is not the public body that mediates everything.

Interviewee G

This attempt to empower civil society actors was framed as a form of 'solidarity' with civil society and migrants, distinguishing Independencia from other municipalities: "In other *comunas* it has to do with a more welfare issue. In some *comunas*, where the authorities are more religious, it has more to do with charity. We [Independencia's Office of Migration] have tried to be something different" (Interviewee G, municipal employee).

4.2   *Recoleta*

The Municipality of Recoleta has actively incorporated civil society in its activities since the inception of its Migrants and Refugees Program. The diagnostic report on the migrant situation in Recoleta documented the consultatory and participatory process by which the municipality's Migrants and Refugees Program was developed and that included local civil society organizations to address migrant-related issues of housing, education, health, and discrimination (Huerta and Martinez 2015). Recoleta's various mechanisms of participation for civil society include 'Neighborhood Tables' (*Mesas Barriales*) (Municipalidad de Recoleta 2020b). These 'Neighborhood Tables' are

an occasion of participation and exchange between different actors with
an integral approach that is participatory and systemic, in order to see the
comuna's structural problems and seek collaborative solutions to communal and neighborhood problems. They are spaces of participation and
territorial planning that seek consensus on common actions that aim to
improve the quality of life in the neighborhood.

MUNICIPALIDAD DE RECOLETA 2020b, l. 6

Recoleta organizes a special 'Table' (*mesa*) with the migrant community to
include their voices and ensure their participation (Aninat and Vergara 2019,
58). An activist in one of Chile's national coordinating network of migrant
organizations said that Recoleta

has generated certain instances of participation for the migrant population. I understand that as foreigners [to Chile] we have limited civil and
political rights, so, for example, in the case of Recoleta the municipality
itself created, from its Office of Migrants, the Recoleta 'Migrant Table'
where different organizations participated as a migrant council, following up on the municipality's policy, right? Follow-up and implementation
of municipal policies, this is no small thing – but recognizing that civil
and political rights are also rights to participate in public policy, in other
municipalities this would not even be considered as a theme.

Interviewee B

A senior municipal employee suggests that the municipality has established
vertical ties with civil society when they said: "I have no problem working with
institutions. Right now, we are working with the IOM" (Interviewee I). This
same participant emphasized that the municipality also worked to establish
horizontal ties with civil society:

We have always tended to work with the organized community. ... In our
case it's been better to work together or join others than to be direct and
each on their own. This time of pandemic, this situation, this very specific situation has shown that where we were proposing to work with the
community, that was the most correct thing to do.

Interviewee I

This interviewee affirms the importance including civil society in the development and implementation of Recoleta's policies and practices, especially
during the time of COVID-19.

4.3   *Quilicura*

Quilicura's Reception Plan outlines the approach to establish the municipality's policy for its Office of Migrants and Refugees. In the Plan and its various recommendations, "the perspective of migrants and refugees as well as the local society's institutional actors were actively incorporated, though the pending task was to incorporate local civil society members in the definition of the policies" (Correa, et al. 2014, 18). The Plan further emphasizes the critical role that the municipality's native-born population plays in the success of what it calls "reception and recognition policies" and recommends the implementation of a neighborhood program (Correa, et al. 2014, 48). Quilicura's Office of Migrants and Refugees regularly holds meetings with leaders and migrant organizations to consult on local issues and to promote the participation of civil society (Aninat and Vergara 2019).

In 2010, the Office was created with the direct support of local civil society institutions and members. A municipal employee described how the vertical and horizontal resources were mobilized to create the Office:

> I knocked on the IOM's door, I called on UNHCR, UNDP, and they told me they were not going to give me money. I told them, 'No, do not give me money, but do give me training, give me human resources because I am alone.' It was me and my computer, nobody else, I didn't even have an office. I went from office to office until I got to a place where I was a little bit more established. What I did to start was get outside, and with UNHCR we began to observe, and they gave me some information about the people living here in Quilicura. I held a meeting where I invited refugees and migrants, and about 300 people came.
>
>   Interviewee D

Vertical institutional participation was critical to the municipal employee in terms of providing apolitical support: "I tried to work a lot with international organizations because international organizations are neutral, and that helps to bring everyone all together at the table" (Interviewee D). Quilicura's Office of Migrants and Refugees has also widely encouraged the participation of volunteers and other local civil society actors in its various activities:

> I first created a group of 25 people, and then another group of young people from the Raúl Silva Henríquez University arrived, who were psychologists and had to do a community practicum. I said, "look, here you have 25 people, give me a consolidated platform of migrants that will last over time" [...] what I need is people who support me in the activities of

the community so that I don't have to be the only one picking up chairs, tables, questions [...].

Interviewee D

The success of Quilicura's Office of Migrants and Refugees can in part be attributed to the horizontal relations that it was able to create with civil society actors as well as municipalities across Chile:

I do feel that this office grew because we had a great capacity to network, network at the national level, network at the international level. We were, I say this with great pride, we were the ones who put together the first network of municipal offices that addressed the issue of migrants and refugees in Chile. We had a network that worked heavily with UNHCR and IOM.

Interviewee D

Overall, civil society has been consulted and included for meaningful participation in Quilicura's Office of Migrants and Refugees' activities in a variety of ways.

Each of the three municipalities included in this study have developed and maintained horizontal relations with a variety of civil society actors, including local NGOs and the international migrant community. Interviewees I and E noted that the loss of a key municipal staff member would result in a negative change in the office's actions or programming for migrants. However, the strong horizontal relations between the municipality and civil society actors will facilitate the continuity of inclusive municipal programming and services for migrants. An interviewee remarked:

Civil society has been more belligerent, more of a warrior with the state, than the municipality. The Municipal Office for Migrants is not belligerent, it fights the little things. The mayor may fight, he may be against the government and fight, but here the voice of migrant associations, the voice of NGOs, has been quite critical.

Interviewee F

Civil society actors have more freedom to make demands and pressure the state and, in doing so, through horizontal ties can strengthen the position of municipalities to resist exclusionary national policies and practices.

Furthermore, in 2014 the Municipalities of Independencia, Recoleta, and Quilicura were the first *comunas*, alongside Santiago Centro, to participate in the Inter-Municipal Table for Migrations (*Mesa Intermunicipal para las Migraciones*), organized by IOM Chile (IOM Chile 2017). Ataç, et al. (2020) argue that the incorporation of civil society actors and organizations will strengthen each city's local position not only with regard to service delivery but also in their ability to contest and resist exclusionary national policies. Having established the horizontal relations of these three municipalities in Santiago RM – Independencia, Recoleta, and Quilicura – the following section explores this thesis in the context of local and national responses to COVID-19.

5   Solidarity and Municipal Responses to COVID-19

To mitigate the spread of COVID-19, the national government enforced a mandated total quarantine which has severely restricted mobility for a significant portion of Santiago RM's population. These restrictions on mobility have had devastating economic impacts on migrant communities, particularly those that have irregular status. A participant explains that "the emergency, has – let's say – sharpened the structural problems that the migrant population already faced. And in Chile, one of the most important elements is irregularity" (Interviewee B).

The Chilean national government has initiated emergency financial relief programs in response to COVID-19 (Gobierno de Chile 2020a, 2020e; Ministerio de Desarrollo Social y Familia 2020). These programs have been largely administered through the Chilean national identification number for individuals, the RUN (Rol Único Nacional), also referred to as a RUT (Rol Único Tributerio). The unique identification number is assigned to all Chilean nationals as well as foreigners residing in Chile, whether temporarily or permanently. Migrants with irregular status, or who are in the process of regularization, are excluded from access to emergency relief funds by dint of not having a RUN/RUT:

> The only national policy that was made was the delivery of the COVID Bonus, a COVID subsidy, which is money that is paid to the most vulnerable families. But they require [...] you to have a *cédula* [national identification card]. If you do not have a *cédula*, if you do not have a Social Household Registry, you have no possibility of help.
>
> Interviewee B

Another interviewee comments on the divide created by the national financial relief program between Chilean nationals and migrants:

> The State's resources are not reaching migrants because they do not have a RUT, because they're not inside the group to which aid is being directed and because it is also being announced this way, "Aid for Chileans", not "for human beings". We are still in this division between those who come from here and those from outside, we have these boundaries.
>
> Interviewee C

Prior to COVID-19, many migrants in Chile already lived in a state of heightened precarity related to their irregular status or being in the process of regularization. COVID-19 created an 'impossible' situation for migrants who lack regular status, and correspondingly, state-level support during the pandemic:

> Many people have been left without work, among them the migrant community. Imagine, if before I had difficulty, because of the blessed RUT I had no access, now I have even less. Most of them, since they were in the process [of regularization], in order to be able to subsist in the meantime had to become street vendors, sell on the street, offer any product on the street. They were doing alright. Not now. Now we are in quarantine and it is impossible [...] they do not receive any help from the State.
>
> Interviewee I

The exclusion of migrants with irregular status from national COVID-19 emergency relief programs, coupled with mandatory total quarantine measures, has resulted in situations of increased vulnerability, as an NGO employee explains:

> There is a very high number of entire families in confinement because they are in quarantine, but with nothing to eat at home and the State has not given any help to anyone who is not a national – even for nationals State aid has been greatly reduced and limited to certain populations, even less to migrants.
>
> Interviewee H

For many migrants, this situation of irregular status and heightened precarity during COVID-19 has resulted in food insecurity, as an activist explains:

> The sectors that are most affected by the emergency and therefore by layoffs, are the sectors where the majority of the unemployed are the migrant population. The services, in construction, domestic workers in private homes, agriculture and where the majority have been fired, well the first to be dismissed is the foreigner who has no contract, and

therefore they don't have to pay any compensation for this dismissal. This has been a critical situation and the migrant population is going hungry, which is exacerbated because they do not have contracts, they do not have papers [...] And today, the municipalities are trying to face the emergency not only in terms of health but also, if not in economic terms, then in food, which is a very serious issue in Chile.

Interviewee B

Indeed, despite the strict fines and consequences for breaking the quarantine, there have been demonstrations in protest of the food insecurity created by the mandatory lockdown in Santiago RM:

A total quarantine in the Metropolitan Region. But well, in general, they are not respecting it, because the people, not only the migrant population, Chileans too, we have seen protests these days [...] people these weeks have already been demonstrating and confronting the police out of hunger, if not for anything else, but out of hunger. And in this too [the demonstrations] the migrant population is present.

Interviewee B

Several participants emphasized the economic challenges faced by municipalities that lack the resources to respond:

Currently the municipalities in Chile [...] we find ourselves highly dependent on the municipal common fund, and that is what often affects the provision of quality services to the general population, without making this division of a migrant or a non-migrant.

Interviewee A

This interviewee emphasizes that the need for municipalities to prioritize quality service delivery for all migrants is constrained due to their limited resources. Another participant further elaborates upon the unequal distribution of municipal resources and off-loading of responsibilities by the national government:

In the case of Chile, which is a very centralized country and where there is a very unequal distribution of municipal income, that is, the poor or vulnerable *comunas*, they have very few resources but are also the ones receiving the migrant population. Well, I believe that in the case of Chile, the state has delegated a large part of the competencies, or a large part of

the key elements for immigration, such as the case of integration, has delegated them to the municipalities, to the municipalities at the local level, without delivering them more money, without giving them more money.
Interviewee B

In this situation, certain municipalities have few resources to respond to the pandemic and the hunger crisis: "Everything that the municipality gives – at this moment, the municipality doesn't have anything to give to the people" (Interviewee D).

In response to the hunger crisis being faced by community members – not just migrants but all residents – the municipalities of Independencia, Recoleta, and Quilicura have coordinated with civil society actors to support networks of *ollas comunes* (literally translated as 'communal pots' but referred to as 'community kitchens' for the remainder of this paper). There is a strong history of *ollas comunes* as organized actions and manifestations of solidarity in Latin America:

> Our people in Latin America have been very creative. Before these neoliberal models were applied, our people were highly organized; unions, neighborhood organizations, students. A very solidary way of sharing actions in the struggle was not only to strike but also installing an *olla común* where people were asked for support. There was a class solidarity, supplies were obtained and a committee was formed that was in charge of preparing food for all those who were there participating in the struggle, because, obviously, they are not going to go home, saying "Wait everybody, I have to go home to cook".
> Interviewee I

For over a century, *ollas comunes* in Chile have appeared alongside working class strikes to support unions, families out of work, and land squatters in the late 1940s and throughout the 1960s (Gallardo 1985). Unlike *ollas del pobre* (*ollas* for the poor), in which the church or the state deliver food to lower income neighborhoods to relieve hunger (Gallardo 1985), *ollas communes* are not acts of charity but of solidarity. These community kitchens are civil society not government initiatives; they are organized and run by local volunteers with contributions from the larger community. A municipal employee explains:

> It is a process of resistance against poverty to be able to contain the hunger. Because I might have a bag of rice but nothing else. I don't have gas, I don't have other supplies, I don't have oil. And then another one might

have a pot, another one a bit of gas. So, we gather it all, we meet in a place, cook together for everyone and then distribute what we can, whatever there is. It is shared out and afterwards we agree to gather supplies, ask for donations, gather from what we have, come back again to prepare a lunch and call people again to congregate.

Interviewee I

Notably, municipalities are working directly with civil society actors to facilitate these community kitchens. In Recoleta, the employees of the municipality's Migrants and Refugees Program are working at community kitchens that were started during the pandemic:

In the *olla* where we are, where specifically I am working, it's part of a unit where there is an 80% migrant population. There, an *olla común* was formed. Now another is going to be formed. There will be two, then, in this neighborhood. Sure, there are plenty of people, but it's starting with 100 servings, 150 servings [...] The mother who goes to sell on the street because she has to get daily bread for her son knows that at least that she is going to have a ration for her and her son. Now if she is able to give CLP 100 or CLP 1,000, she can do it. The important thing is solidarity; not charity, but solidarity.

Interviewee I

The same participant emphasized that the solidarity manifested at *ollas comunes* extends to both migrants and national-born Chileans equally:

It is not that this *olla* is only for foreigners and no one else can enter, or this is one is for Chileans and no foreigner can come close. No, it doesn't work like that. Solidarity does not measure [...] "You, yes, and you, no". No, it is with everyone and above all with all the workers who live in the *comuna*.

Interviewee I

Access to the *olla común* is inclusive and established based on residency in the *comuna*, rather than national citizenship or legal status.

The Municipality of Independencia is also directly involved in the coordination and support of community kitchens during COVID-19. On its website, it has announced its support of community kitchens, praising the local organizations that have taken on the planning of *ollas comunes* and encouraging other neighborhoods to follow suit:

Community kitchens are a collaborative network between neighbors and the Municipality. Go for it, cook in your neighborhood with and for the community, and if you are not from the community but want to contribute food to this initiative, you can do so by writing to cocinascomunitarias@independencia.cl.

MUNICIPALIDAD DE INDEPENDENCIA 2020b

The mayors of both Quilicura and Recoleta have issued directives for their municipal staff to participate in the community kitchens. In Quilicura, the mayor requested that his staff support the *ollas comunes* through coordinating resources amongst the various sites of the *ollas*. A municipal employee reports:

All these initiatives began to emerge from civil society [...] *Ollas comunes* began to emerge. Everyone, and I mean everyone wanted to do something without having anything themselves ... The mayor asked me to install a little order and see what we could do to help and what we could not help with, and divide the aid that came. For example, if 10 kilos of rice arrived, one kilo of rice for each one [*olla*]. To those who did not have rice, we gave them beans and so on.

Interviewee D

Similarly, in Recoleta the collaboration between civil society and the municipality has been direct and explicitly requested by the mayor, as indicated by a municipal employee:

The mayor is asking for donations and channeling donations to deliver resources to all the *ollas comunes* that appear. The government has understood [...] it has understood that it cannot go against the mobility of people who are going to organize a community kitchen either, because basically people have to eat. It authorizes, or delegates to the municipalities the authorization to be able to operate the *ollas comunes* and not persecute them, ensure that the *carabineros* [national police] don't go.

Interviewee I

When prompted further, the interviewee confirmed that indeed the municipality was able to mitigate police enforcement of the nationally mandated total quarantine for the purposes of community members attending *ollas comunes*:

Yes. You have to ask the police for permission, but [...] it is enough that the mayor or the municipality grant permission to the volunteers and to the people who come to collect their food too. When mentioning, "I'm going to the *olla común* X," obviously you have to go and come back with your lunch.

Interviewee I

Municipalities in Santiago RM are working closely with diverse civil society actors to provide a space of solidarity where all members of the community, regardless of their legal status, are able to access essential support and resist the negative outcomes of national responses to the COVID-19 pandemic.

6   The Evolution of Solidarity Cities in Santiago RM

There has been a 'local turn' in which municipal governments have taken more initiative in developing and implementing policies for the reception and accommodation of migrants (Penninx and Garcés-Mascareñas 2019). In this context, local policies and practices of inclusion are sometimes in conflict with national level policy and seek to ensure that migrants with irregular or precarious legal status can access essential municipal services (Spencer and Delvino 2019). In Chile, where there is no explicit national integration policy for migrants (Torres Matus 2019), municipalities are in a position where they are required to react and respond to the realities of migration in their communities. Indeed, our research shows that in the context of COVID-19, the horizontal ties between municipalities and civil society actors in Santiago RM have facilitated solidarity policies and practices and access to spaces of inclusion, participation, and resistance for the benefit of all community members, including migrants with precarious legal status. These ties also strengthen the city's ability to resist exclusionary national government responses to the COVID-19 pandemic.

The municipalities of Independencia, Recoleta, and Quilicura all exhibit dimensions of solidarity cities although none of these municipalities officially use this label. In particular, these municipalities' policies and practices of solidarity are facilitating access and claims to rights for migrants with precarious legal status, and redefining belonging and integration at a local scale. Furthermore, Independencia, Recoleta, and Quilicura have actively promoted the participation of diverse civil society actors in the development of policy, the delivery of services and programs, ongoing consultations with community members, and the planning of neighborhood events.

The emphasis that these municipalities place on solidarity and the participation of civil society may mark a shift in municipal service delivery practice. The Observatorio de Políticas Migratorias (2016) found that municipalities in the Province of Santiago are delivering the vast majority of services to their migrant populations either without participation by another public or private institution or in conjunction with other public institutions (e.g. the Ministry of Interior, Ministry of Social Development) or universities. Only a relatively small share of the actions taken by municipalities involve local community organizations, or religious organizations and foundations. In addition, Correa, et al. (2020) reported that municipal offices in the Province of Santiago that are working actively to address issues faced by migrants, are prioritizing the legal inclusion of migrants and the incorporation of migrants into local institutions; less action is taken by municipalities to promote the "creation of solidarity ties" (191) within the local community. Conversely, the key informants we interviewed emphasized the importance of the inclusion of civil society actors to deliver programs for migrants. This result indicates a transformation towards local solidarity practices in Santiago RM that shift responsibility towards civic society.

The COVID-19 pandemic has deepened the precarity of irregular-status migrants who are excluded from national emergency relief funds and programs, and unable to obtain official permission to be on the street during the total quarantine in Santiago RM. Although *ollas comunes* are not specifically organized to benefit the migrant population of Santiago RM, migrants are included as members in community which the *ollas* serve. These *ollas* are sites of solidarity where belonging and participation are premised on residency rather than legal status, and where social bridges between migrants and non-migrants form (Strang and Ager 2010). These practices are the premise of solidarity cities.

By leveraging the horizontal relations with civil society, municipalities in Santiago RM are able to strengthen their local position in terms of delivering services to migrants in vulnerable situations. Furthermore, civil society participation in the *ollas comunes* has bolstered the position of the municipality to push back, to a degree, against the exclusionary practices put in place by the national government. Finally, the municipalities' roles in organizing *ollas comunes* illustrates accordingly how solidarity cities are blending bottom-up, grassroots and top-down, municipal-led approaches in the form of establishing horizontal ties of interaction, collaboration, and participation. Through such efforts, Independencia, Recoleta, and Quilicura have effectively become solidarity cities with transformative potential.

Acknowledgements

We thank Dr. Judith Bernhard for her generous commitment of time and insightful comments in reviewing this chapter, and Dr. Luis Eduardo Thayer

Correa for the early guidance offered regarding the existing municipal landscape in Santiago, Chile.

References

Agustín, Ó.G., and M.B. Jørgensen (2016). "Solidarity without Borders: Gramscian Perspectives on Migration and Civil Society Alliances". In *Solidarity without Borders: Gramscian Perspectives on Migration and Civil Society Alliances*, edited by Agustín, Ó.G., and Jørgensen, M.B. 3–20. London: Pluto Press.

Agustín, Ó.G., and M.B. Jørgensen (2019). *Solidarity and the "Refugee Crisis" in Europe.* Cham, Switzerland: Springer.

AMUCH. 2016. "Impacto de La Migración a Nivel Local: ¿Qué Han Hecho Los Municipios al Respecto?" Dirección de Estudios AMUCH. Chile: Asocioación de Municipalidades de Chile.

Aninat, I., and R. Vergara (eds.) (2019). *Inmigración en Chile: Una mirada multidimensional.* 1st ed. Santiago, Chile: Centro de Estudios Públicos.

Ataç, I., T. Schütze, and V. Reitter (2020). "Local Responses in Restrictive National Policy Contexts: Welfare Provisions for Non-Removed Rejected Asylum Seekers in Amsterdam, Stockholm and Vienna". *Ethnic and Racial Studies* 43 (16): 115–34.

Avritzer, L. (1997). "Introduction: The Meaning and Employment of 'Civil Society' in Latin America". *Constellations* 4 (1): 88–93.

Avritzer, L. (2006). "Civil Society in Latin America in the Twenty-First Century: Between Democratic Deepening, Social Fragmentation, and State Crisis". In *Civil Society and Democracy in Latin America*, edited by Feinberg, R., Waisman, C., and Zamosc, L. 34–57. New York, UNITED STATES: Palgrave Macmillan.

Bagelman, J. (2013). "Sanctuary: A Politics of Ease?" *Alternatives* 38 (1): 49–62.

Bauder, H. (2017). "Sanctuary Cities: Policies and Practices in International Perspective". *International Migration* 55 (2): 174–87.

Bauder, H. (2019). "Urban Sanctuary and Solidarity in a Global Context: How Does Africa Contribute to the Debate?" In *MIASA Working Papers on Migration, Mobility, and Forced Displacement.* Accra, Ghana: MIASA. https://www.ug.edu.gh/mias-afr ica/miasa-working-papers-migration-mobility-and-forced-displacement.

Bauder, H. (2021). "Urban Solidarity: Perspectives of Migration and Refugee Accommodation and Inclusion" *Critical Sociology*, 47(6): 875–889.

Bauder, H., and D.A. Gonzalez (2018). "Municipal Responses to 'Illegality': Urban Sanctuary across National Contexts". *Social Inclusion* 6 (1): 124–34.

Bauder, H., and L. Juffs (2019). "'Solidarity' in the Migration and Refugee Literature: Analysis of a Concept". *Journal of Ethnic and Migration Studies* 46 (1): 45–65.

Barichello, S. E. (2016). Refugee protection and responsibility sharing in Latin America: solidarity programmes and the Mexico Plan of Action. *The International Journal of Human Rights*, 20(2), 191–207.

Bryman, A. (2012). *Social Research Methods*. 4th ed. New York, NY: Oxford University Press.

Cabieses, B., H. Tunstall, and K. Pickett (2015). "Understanding the Socioeconomic Status of International Immigrants in Chile Through Hierarchical Cluster Analysis: A Population-Based Study". *International Migration* 53 (2): 303–20.

Carabineros de Chile (2020). "Información General Sobre Permisos y Salvoconductos". Comisaría Virtual. 2020. https://comisariavirtual.cl/.

Carvahal Gamonal, I. (2018). "Acciones de Participación que Las Comunas de Recoleta, Quilicura y Santiago Realizan para la Inclusión de los Migrantes". Santiago, Chile: Universidad Alberto Hurtado.

Chitty, A. (2011). "Hegel and Marx". In *A Companion to Hegel*, edited by Houlgate, S., and Baur, M. 477–500. Hoboken, UNITED KINGDOM: John Wiley & Sons, Incorporated.

Correa, L., S. Correa, and T. Novoa (2014). *Plan de Acogida y Reconocimiento de Migrantes y Refugiados de la Comuna de Quilicura*. 1st ed. Santiago, Chile: Municipalidad de Quilicura.

Correa, L., E. Thayer, M.F. Stang, and C.D. Rodríguez (2020). "La política del estado de ánimo. La debilidad de las políticas migratorias locales en Santiago de Chile". *Perfiles latinoamericanos: revista de la Facultad Latinoamericana de Ciencias Sociales, Sede México* 28 (55): 171–201.

Dagnino, E. (2010). "Civil Society in Latin America : Participatory Citizens or Service Providers?" In *Outlook on Civil Society*, 23–39. Uppsala University. h.

Darling, J. (2010). "A City of Sanctuary: The Relational Re-Imagining of Sheffield's Asylum Politics". *Transactions of the Institute of British Geographers* 35 (1): 125–40.

Darling, J., and H. Bauder (eds.) (2019). *Sanctuary Cities and Urban Struggles: Rescaling Migration, Citizenship, and Rights*. Manchester, UK: Manchester University Press.

Doña, C., and A. Levinson (2004). "Chile: Moving Towards a Migration Policy". Migration Policy Institute. February 1, 2004. https://www.migrationpolicy.org/article/chile-moving-towards-migration-policy.

Ehrenberg, J. (1999). *Civil Society: The Critical History of an Idea*. New York and London: New York University Press.

Featherstone, D. (2012). *Solidarity: Hidden Histories and Geographies of Internationalism*. London: Z Books.

Foerster, A. (2019). "Solidarity or Sanctuary? A Global Strategy for Migrant Rights". *Humanity & Society* 43 (1): 19–42.

Galeano, E. (1997). *Open Veins of Latin America: Five Centuries of the Pillage of a Continent*. NYU Press.

Gallardo, B. (1985). "El Redescubrimiento del Caracter Social del Problema del Hambre: Las Ollas Comunes". Documento de Trabajo 247. Santiago de Chile: FLACSO Chile. http://flacsochile.org/biblioteca/pub/memoria/1985/000931.pdf.

Garreton, M. (2017). "City Profile: Actually Existing Neoliberalism in Greater Santiago". Cities 65 (Complete): 32–50. https://doi.org/10.1016/j.cities.2017.02.005.

Gobierno de Chile (2014). "Quilicura es declarada Ciudad Solidaria por Naciones Unidas". Ministerio de Desarrollo Social. December 14, 2014. http://www.desarroll osocialyfamilia.gob.cl/noticias/quilicura-es-declarada-ciudad-solidaria-por-nacio nes-unidas.

Gobierno de Chile (2019). "Sello Migrante". Departamento de Extranjería y Migración | Gobierno de Chile. 2019. /sello-migrante/.

Gobierno de Chile (2020a). "Bono COVID". Chile Atiende. Bono COVID. 2020. http:// bonocovid.cl.

Gobierno de Chile (2020b). "Preguntas Frecuentes – Cuarentena". Plan de Acción Coronavirus. 2020. https://www.gob.cl/coronavirus/cuarentena/.

Gobierno de Chile (2020c). "Presidente Declara Estado De Excepción Constitucional De Catástrofe En Todo El Territorio Nacional". Noticias. Gobierno de Chile. March 18, 2020. https://www.gob.cl/noticias/presidente-declara-estado-de-excepcion-con stitucional-de-catastrofe-en-todo-el-territorio-nacional/.

Gobierno de Chile (2020d). "Ministerio de Salud Decreta Cuarentena Total Para La Ciudad de Santiago y Seis Comunas Aledañas". Ministerio de Salud – Gobierno de Chile. May 13, 2020. https://www.minsal.cl/ministerio-de-salud-decreta-cuarent ena-total-para-la-ciudad-de-santiago-y-seis-comunas-aledanas/.

Gobierno de Chile (2020e). "Plan Solidario de Conectividad". Chile Atiende. July 9, 2020. https://www.chileatiende.gob.cl/fichas/77607-plan-solidario-de-conectividad.

Harley, T. (2014). "Regional Cooperation and Refugee Protection in Latin America: A 'South-South' Approach". International Journal of Refugee Law 26 (1): 22–47.

Houston, S.D., and O. Lawrence-Weilmann (2016). "The Model Migrant and Multiculturalism: Analyzing Neoliberal Logics in US Sanctuary Legislation". In Migration Policy and Practice, edited by Bauder, H., and Matheis, C. 1st ed., 101–26. New York, United States: Palgrave Macmillan.

Huerta, D.C., and L. Martinez (2015). "Diagnóstico de La Situación Migrante En Recoleta". Programa Migrantes y Refugiados de Recoleta.

Instituto Nacional de Estadísticas (2019). "Estimación de Personas Extranjeras Residentes En Chile". Santiago, Chile: Gobierno de Chile.

Instituto Nacional de Estadísticas (2020). "Según Estimaciones, La Cantidad de Personas Extranjeras Residentes Habituales En Chile Bordea Los 1,5 Millones al 31 de Diciembre de 2019". Default. March 12, 2020. http://www.ine.cl/prensa/2020/03/ 12/según-estimaciones-la-cantidad-de-personas-extranjeras-residentes-habitua les-en-chile-bordea-los-1-5-millones-al-31-de-diciembre-de-2019.

IOM Chile (2017). "Sistematización de La Mesa Intermunicipal: Los Migrantes y Las Ciudades (2014–2016). CHILE". Organización Internacional para las Migraciones (OIM) Misión Chile. https://reliefweb.int/sites/reliefweb.int/files/resources/OIM%20Chile%20Sist.%20Migrantes%20y%20Ciudades.pdf.

Jezard, A. (2018). "Who and What Is 'Civil Society?'" Blog. World Economic Forum. April 23, 2018. https://www.weforum.org/agenda/2018/04/what-is-civil-society/.

Jubilut, L.L., and W. Pereira Carneiro (2011). "Resettlement in Solidarity: A New Regional Approach Towards a More Humane Durable Solution". *Refugee Survey Quarterly* 30 (3): 63–86.

Kassa, D.G. (2019). *Refugee Spaces and Urban Citizenship in Nairobi: Africa's Sanctuary City*. Lanham: Lexington Books.

Kervegan, J.F., D. Ginsburg, and M. Shuster (2018). "Law: Its Concept and Actualizations". In *The Actual and the Rational: Hegel and Objective Spirit*, 15–54. Chicago, UNITED STATES: University of Chicago Press.

Koellner, F. (2019). *Refugee Integration in Solidarity Cities in Latin America & the EU: A regional comparative analysis*. AV Akademikerverlag. https://www.bookdepository.com/Refugee-Integration-Solidarity-Cities-Latin-America-EU-Francy-Koellner/9786202218801.

Koppelman, C.M. (2017). "Deepening Demobilization: The State's Transformation of Civil Society in the Poblaciones of Santiago, Chile". *Latin American Perspectives* 44 (3): 46–63.

Kuge, J. (2019). "Uncovering Sanctuary Cities: Between Policy, Practice, and Politics". In *Sanctuary Cities and Urban Struggles: Rescaling Migration, Citizenship, and Rights*, edited by Darling, J., and Bauder, H. 49–76. Manchester: Manchester University Press.

Laing, A. (2018). "Chile Declines to Sign U.N. Pact, Says Migration Not a Human Right: Report". *Reuters*, December 9, 2018. https://www.reuters.com/article/us-chile-migration-idUSKBN1O80QT.

Lefebvre, H. (1996). *Writings on Cities*. Translated by Eleonore Kofman and Elizabeth Lebas. Massachusetts: Blackwell Publishers Ltd.

Mangini, J.P.G. (2019). "Transformar Desde El Territorio. Hacia Una Política Pública Comunal de Migraciones. El Caso de Estudio de La Comuna de La Pintana, Santiago de Chile". *CUHSO*, July, 13–32.

Matus, T., F. Sabatini, F. Cortez-Monroy, P. Hermansen, and C. Silva (2012). "Migración y Municipios. Construcción de Una Propuesta de Política Pública de Gestión Municipal Para La Población Inmigrante". In *Propuestas Para Chile. Concurso Políticas Públicas*, 323–62. Santiago: Centro de Políticas Públicas UC.

Mclean, G.F. (1997). "Philosophy and Civil Society: Its Nature, Its Past and Its Future". In *Civil Society and Social Reconstruction*, edited by Mclean, G.F.16:7–82. Culture and Values 1. Washington, D.C.: The Council for Research in Values and Philosophy.

Ministerio de Desarrollo Social y Familia (2020). "Ingreso Familiar de Emergencia (IFE)". Chile Atiende. July 21, 2020. https://www.chileatiende.gob.cl/fichas/78385 -ingreso-familiar-de-emergencia.

Ministerio de Salud – Gobierno de Chile (2020). "Casos Confirmados En Chile COVID-19". Plan de Acción Coronavirus. April 8, 2020. https://www.minsal.cl/nuevo-coro navirus-2019-ncov/casos-confirmados-en-chile-covid-19/.

Ministerio del Interior y Seguridad Pública (2011). "Ley 20.500". Participación Ciudadana. 2011. http://participacionciudadana.subdere.gov.cl/ley-20–500.

Missbach, A., Y. Adiputera, and A. Prabandari (2018). "Is Makassar a 'Sanctuary City'? Migration Governance in Indonesia After the 'Local Turn'". *Austrian Journal of South-East Asian Studies* 11 (2): 199–216. https://doi.org/10.14764/10.ASEAS-0003.

Municipalidad de Independencia (2016). "Aprueba Objetivos, Lineamientos y Programas Que Componen la Oficina de Migración de Independencia". Secretaria Municipal.

Municipalidad de Independencia (2018). "Informe Postulación Sello Migrante".

Municipalidad de Independencia (2020a). "Oficina de Migración e Interculturalidad". 2020. https://www.independencia.cl/oficina-de-migracion-e-interculturalidad/.

Municipalidad de Independencia (2020b). "Las cocinas comunitarias se levantan en Independencia como espacios organizados de ayuda territorial". Municipalidad de Independencia. May 22, 2020. https://www.independencia.cl/las-ollas-comunes -se-levantan-en-independencia-como-espacios-organizados-de-ayuda-territorial/.

Municipalidad de Recoleta (2020a). "Recoleta Somos Todos". Municipalidad De Recoleta. 2020. https://www.recoleta.cl/?op=pcv.

Municipalidad de Recoleta (2020b). "Recoleta Transparente: Ley N° 20.285 – Sobre Acceso a La Información Pública". 2020. http://www.recoletatransparente.cl/web/.

Muñoz Aravena, W.T. (2018). "La Participación Ciudadana En Chile. El Caso de Los Consejos Comunales de La Sociedad Civil En La Región Del Biobío". *Estudios Sobre Estado y Sociedad* XXV (73): 203–31.

Nyers, P. (2010). "No One Is Illegal Between City and Nation". *Studies in Social Justice* 4 (2): 127–43.

Observatorio de Políticas Migratorias (2016). "Una Mirada a La Provincia de Santiago". FONDECYT Proyecto 1140679 1. Chile: Universidad Central.

OEA (2020). "Situación de Los Migrantes y Refugiados Venezolanos En Chile". Chile: Oficina de la Secretaría General para la Crisis de Migrantes y Refugiados Venezolanos.

OIM (2018). "Programa Los Migrantes y Las Ciudades: Sistematización 2014–2017 Chile". 1. Migrantes y Las Ciudades. Santiago de Chile: Organización Internacional para las Migraciones (OIM) Chile. https://chile.iom.int/sites/default/files/pubica cion_1_los_migrantes_y_las_ciudades_oim_sistematizacion.pdf.

Penninx, R., and B. Garcés-Mascareñas (2019). "The Concept of Integration as an Analytical Tool and as a Policy Concept". In *Integration Processes and Policies in Europe*, 11–29.

Regional Refugee Instruments & Related (2004). "Mexico Declaration and Plan of Action to Strengthen the International Protection of Refugees in Latin America". https://www.refworld.org/docid/424bf6914.html.

Reveco, C.D. (2018). "Amid Record Numbers of Arrivals, Chile Turns Rightward on Immigration". Feature. Migration Policy Institute. January 17, 2018. https://www.migrationpolicy.org/article/amid-record-numbers-arrivals-chile-turns-rightward-immigration.

Rockmore, T. (2018). "On Marx's Theory of Practice". In *Marx's Dream: From Capitalism to Communism*, 7–71. Chicago: University of Chicago Press.

Rojas Pedemonte, N., C. Silva, N. Amode, J. Vásquez, and C. Orrego (2019). "Boletín Informativo: Migración Haitiana En Chile". 1. Departamento de Extranjería y Migración.

Sanfuentes, M., and M. Garreton (2018). "Renegotiating Roles in Local Governments: Facing Resistances to Citizen Participation in Chile". *Action Research*, September, 1476750318801470.

Segovia, J.S., and M. Lufin (2013). "Approaches to the Afro-Colombian Experience in Chile: South-South Immigration Toward the Northern Regions". *Journal of Black Studies* 44 (3): 231–51.

Segura, D.M., and K.B. Abde (2014). "Barrios y población inmigrantes: el caso de la comuna de Santiago". *Revista INVI* 29 (81): 19–77.

Spencer, S., and N. Delvino (2019). "Municipal Activism on Irregular Migrants: The Framing of Inclusive Approaches at the Local Level". *Journal of Immigrant & Refugee Studies* 17 (1): 27–43.

Staab, S., and K. Hill Maher (2006). "The Dual Discourse About Peruvian Domestic Workers in Santiago de Chile: Class, Race, and a Nationalist Project". *Latin American Politics and Society* 48 (1): 87–116.

Strang, A., and A. Ager (2010). "Refugee Integration: Emerging Trends and Remaining Agendas". *Journal of Refugee Studies* 23 (4): 589–607.

Tijoux, M.E. (2016). *Racismo En Chile: La Piel Como Marca de La Inmigración*. Santiago de Chile: Editorial Universitaria.

Tijoux, M.E., and C. Ambiado (eds.) (2019). "Informe Alternativo Para El Comité Para La Eliminación de La Discriminación Racial (CERD): Racismos y Migración Contemporánea En Chile". Universidad de Chile.

Tijoux, M.E., and M.G. Córdova Rivera (2015). "Racismo en Chile: colonialismo, nacionalismo, capitalismo". *Polis. Revista Latinoamericana*, no. 42 (December).

Torres Matus, L.R. (2019). "La Integración de Los Migrantes En Chile. Asimilación y Retórica Multiculturalista". *Migraciones Internacionales* 10 (4): 1–20.

Torres, O., and A. Garcés (2013). "Representaciones Sociales de Migrantes Peruanos Sobre Su Proceso de Integración En La Ciudad de Santiago de Chile". *Polis (Santiago)* 12 (35): 309–34.

Tumba, E. (2018). "¿Cuántos inmigrantes irregulares hay en Chile?" *El Mostrador*, September 24, 2018, sec. Blogs y Opinión. https://www.elmostrador.cl/noticias/opin ion/2018/09/24/cuantos-inmigrantes-irregulares-hay-en-chile/.

UNHCR (2011a). "Los Beneficios de Pertenecer: Opciones y oportunidades de integración local para países y comunidades de acogida y para refugiados". https:// www.refworld.org.es/docid/4e844a072.html.

UNHCR (2011b). "Arica, primera 'Ciudad Solidaria' con los refugiados en el norte de Chile". Noticias | ACNUR. UNHCR. August 26, 2011. https://www.acnur.org/noticias/ noticia/2011/8/5b0c1b891/arica-primera-ciudad-solidaria-con-los-refugiados-en-el -norte-de-chile.html.

UNHCR (2013a). "Base de Datos de Buenas Prácticas de Medios de Vida e Integración Local en América Latina". 2013. http://livelihoods.acnur.org/buscar-por-categoria/ cat/ciudades-solidarias/.

UNHCR (2013b). "Summary Conclusions on the Interpretation of the Extended Refugee Definition in the 1984 Cartagena Declaration". https://www.unhcr.org/protection/ expert/53bd4dcc9/summary-conclusions-interpretation-extended-refugee-definit ion-1984-cartagena.html.

UNHCR (2017). "Regional Discussion on the Program 'Cities of Solidarity'". UNHCR. https://www.acnur.org/fileadmin/Documentos/BDL/2018/11488.pdf?file=filead min/Documentos/BDL/2018/11488.

Valdes, C. (2018). "The Changing Demographic Landscape of Chile, Crime, and Recent Immigration Patterns". *Revista Encrucijada Americana* 10 (2): 47–54.

Varoli, F. (2010). "Ciudades Solidarias: la integración local en Latinoamérica". *Migraciones Forzadas Revista*, 2010.

Walia, H. (2014). "Sanctuary City from Below: Dismantling the City of Vancouver". *The Mainlander* (blog). June 2, 2014. http://themainlander.com/2014/06/02/sanctuary -city-from-below-dismantling-the-city-of-vancouver/.

Williamson, E. (1992). "Discovery and Conquest". In *The Penguin History of Latin America*, 3–36. London, England: Penguin Books.

CHAPTER 12

Nascent Solidarity and Community Emergency

Forced Migration and Accompaniment

Jorge Morales Cardiel

Mexico plays a changing role in the context of international migration dynamics. Its shift from being a country of high emigration to becoming, increasingly, a country of transit, has given the country a new regional function. This includes a border security policy targeted at containing irregular and/or forced migration. Border control mechanisms under the pretext of stopping this migration have left organized crime groups operate with impunity in Mexico without control, trafficking and smuggling of migrants along traditional transit routes, and generating in turn precarious forms of settlement. All of this should become exacerbated in connection with the first so called 'caravans' of transit migrants trough México; an intensified wave of forced migration taking off from Central America in 2018. Consequences for the migrants included a marked rise of xenophobia in local Mexican communities. On this background new initiatives by civil society organizations have seen the day, involving practices and mechanisms of solidarity.

Faced with this reality, the present chapter scrutinizes prospects for the development of 'sanctuary cities' in Mexico. I set off by a discussion of the concept of 'accompaniment' (*acompañamiento*), encapsulating solidarity and recognition of human rights with a potential impact on Mexican society and state. I discuss, conveyed by the principle of accompaniment, efforts of CSOs to involve the local population and governments at different levels, especially government in migrant receiving local communities. Thus, the process of accompaniment is seen by involved CSOs as a 'community emergency' facing violence by criminal syndicates and by the state. Seen from this perspective the idea of the 'Sanctuary City' is pertinent to the analysis.

It is an idea and concept derived from North American and Western European social and political contexts, but its adaptation to the Mexican context appears pertinent in confrontation with the grave situation of forced migration and the plight of transit migrants in the country. The involved CSOs, regardless of their political and ideological profile, their social or religious background and their location throughout the vast Mexican geography, have managed to establish a political dialogue with the Mexican State and with the most prominent international organizations on migration policy, which appears to harbor prospects for a changing governance of migration and a new reality that may eventually favor the constitution of sanctuary cities.

I set off in the following from a discussion of historical-structural causes generating forced migration in the communities of origin of migrants, located in the Northern Triangle of Central America: Honduras, Guatemala and El Salvador. I trace the meaning and opportunities that Sanctuary Cities may harbor in the Mexican context, which, even though they are still nascent, is considered a basic long-term perspective of the work that csos implement through their practices of accompaniment. On this background I go on to scrutiny the idea and articulation of the concept of 'accompaniment' relating to its varying ideopolitical content and orientation; be it confessional and civil. I describe two specific cases, represented by respectively the shelter of *Casa de migrantes de Saltillo* and the *Casa de migrantes de Aguascalientes*. This is based on fieldwork, performed mainly by participant observation and interviews with volunteers, reflecting concrete practices and results of processes of accompaniment.

1   Ground Causes and Conditionality of Forced Migration from Central America

Ground causes of the current forced migration of Central Americans, and their transit through Mexico needs to be discussed in the wider context of imperialism and dynamics of capital accumulation in the Central American region and of politics of precarization embedded in inter- and intra-state power relations. It has generated a social fabric marked by extreme inequality, social expulsion, and a huge 'surplus population' with little alternative to emigration.

Deep seated political conflicts and criminal violence affecting the proliferation of forced migration are linked to geopolitical and geoeconomic ground causes and to a lack of institutional capacity for facing sociopolitical conflicts or containing organized crime (Delgado 2006); a complex mix triggering variable forms of forced migration (López 2013). Thus, the current migration from the region reflects a transformation of agrarian societies subjected to local political authoritarianism, combined with subordination to the exploitative dynamics of transnational capital accumulation (Morales 2007).

Contemporary circuits of social reproduction, subjected to politics of securitization and contemporary forms of imperialism, have redefined, and deepened the precariousness of growing parts of the population; urban workers and small agricultural producers especially (Delgado 2006; Castles 2003). The deepening integration of this Central American region in the macroeconomic context of US imperialism is articulated with local power relations; an excluding multipolar scheme (Morales 2007).

A set of discriminatory industrial, financial and commercial capital networks have expanded, emplaced through a broad program of structural adjustment programs, policies and instruments (Delgado and Márquez 2012). Free trade agreements have created special economic zones and promoted the construction of megaprojects that take the form of new enclave economies. This is encompassed by the privatization of public goods and services at a grand scale. In turn, security and geostrategic cooperation programs have been implemented, which has resulted in the militarization of borders throughout the extended region of Central and North America. One of the most conspicuous products of this development throughout the region pertains to selectivity, disciplining and containment of migrant workers from Central America seeking employment and a better future in the United States (Delgado and Marquez 2012).

Added to this, is forced displacement of people, who were not necessarily subjected to socio-economic precarity but suffered effects of violence derived from social segregation and exclusion. They became victims of constant extortion by the criminal gangs known as "Maras", which made them join the massive exodus of workers fleeing the most pernicious consequences of poverty. We are talking about sections of the middle class who supposedly would provide the vertebral column for a more stable economy; a fact affirming that an urban middle class has become a superfluous luxury in the social composition of these Central American states.

Finally, a series of natural disasters has left serious damage and subsequent economic and material consequences behind them, especially for small agricultural producers. This relates to Hurricane Cesar-Douglas in 1996, Hurricane Mitch, two years later in 1998 (leaving behind three million victims), and Storm Stan in 2005. Since 2006 the El Niño phenomenon has caused consecutive droughts triggering new forced displacements. Thus, a new wave of forced migration is related to global climate change with particularly grave consequences for the entire so-called 'Dry Corridor' (*Corredor seco*) of Central America (ECLAC 2019).

In sum, a massive displacement has taken place; an exodus tormented, in turn, by criminalization and persecution when crossing the borders and entering the Mexican transit route to the United States. It counts a large contingent of uprooted in forced migration, who do not have the possibility of accessing political asylum on legal terms. As a consequence, they are exposed, at any time, to arbitrary detentions and deportations back to where they were trying to escape.

This Mexican route of transit is where all dangers of irregularity stand out, in terms of a crude humanitarian crisis. An incremental militarization of borders is dovetailed by the trafficking and smuggling of persons by criminal groups. It generates, altogether, a migratory 'state of exception' with exposure to the violation of basic human rights. Migrants are forced to travel defenseless through a territory plagued by violence, persecution, criminalization, xenophobia, and extreme vulnerability, along the different migratory routes that cross the rugged Mexican terrain, exposed to kidnappings, robberies, super-exploitation and violent death.

The convergence of the Mexican state's immigration policy with the security policy of the United States, has tended to further violate Central American migrants, in particular from the imposition of Mexico as a 'safe third country' through the Migrant Protection Protocol (MPP), the so-called *Quédate en Mexico* program, launched in 2019. It permits the implementation of the same political standards of illegitimate tax and persecution that has been standard for decades, relating to irregular Central American migrants in transit. But today migrants are being kept settled in Mexico awaiting their political asylum resolution there, which has turned the focus onto the major Mexican cities south of the US border.

2   Sanctuary Cities: A Real Utopia?

Sanctuary cities are, as summarized by Suárez (2017), cities that protect migrants, especially the undocumented and/or irregular, safeguarding them through data protection and laws and politics at the city or municipal level. This relates to violations of their basic rights and possible deportations, many times in confrontation with current national immigration laws. The 'Sanctuary City' is a category of biblical origin widely used today politically, especially in Europe and North America, and it is a key term for UNESCO (2016). It encompasses a combination of welcoming, protection and civil disobedience; a city of refuge posited against the anti-immigrant policies of mass arrests and deportations, relating to political refugees and irregular migrants.

There is still no legal definition of the term, nor are there any geographic neighborhood relations between these cities of refuge (with the exception of Oakland-Berkeley and San Francisco in the Bay Area of the state of California). Also, there are no specific demographic similarities, less legal certainty. These cities pose a varying jurisdiction confronting federal authorities on matters of forced migration and deportation (Suárez 2017). Altogether, this denotes a lack of collaboration on the part of the local authorities, where these sanctuary cities have been established against federal or national immigration laws. For example, when a government official wants to know about the immigration status of one or more persons, it is the obligation of the local authorities to pass on this information. This is generally the case when federal or national administrations have openly anti-immigrant positions. Non-compliance of local authorities, in turn tends to unleash restrictive measures.

Overall, sanctuary or refuge cities are supposed to be ones where migrants can feel free from the violence and persecution generated by expulsion and persecution, related to restrictive institutional policies and practices of governments. At the same time, they represent spaces attempting to be a welcoming cultural site for migrants arriving under conditions of vulnerability, persecution and risk of being deported. Recently, they have become a political action space of local governments practicing non-cooperation. The best example is that of San Francisco, developing a project of legal self-determination with the purpose of granting refugee status and protection of human rights to irregular migrants. It follows the Ordinance Law of the City and Convicted of San Francisco adopted in 1989 (Suárez 2017). However, this did not happen overnight. It has materialized as the product of activism within established migrant communities, their information of transversal solidarities with other CSOs and with trade unions, strongly positioned in frameworks of local governance (Graauw and Shannon 2020).

But this seems to be one more utopia today when it is moved to a migratory transit context in México, as it comes up to challenging an exclusivist global order from a position of political and economic submission. In effect sanctuary cities are still and mostly imaginary spaces. Contributing to this actual fragility is what was launched in 2008 by George W. Bush, in Harris County, Texas under the deceptive label of 'Secure Communities'. It was targeted at, in cooperation with local and state authorities, identifying migrants with some type of criminal history, or without legal residence permit, in order to proceed with their removal and deportation. This is done by collecting fingerprints and biometric data to be processed into the databases of institutions such as the FBI. Obviously, this goes beyond the investigation of the immigration status of the individual in question. It has also led to the classification of more crimes related to immigration and allowed judges to limit and to suspend citizenship or political asylum process through the removal of the applicants (Meissner 2013, cited in Canales and Rojas 2018).

This has however, been met with local resistance, for example in the case of Harris County that went from allowing local agencies to collaborate with the

US Immigration and Customs Enforcement to declaring itself a 'Welcoming City' in 2017 (Graauw and Gleeson 2020). In reality, sanctuary cities or safe communities can become inclusive or exclusive, dependent on the extent to which they are exposed to the arrival of forcibly displaced and pressured by discriminatory public policies. These communities have, in effect, with reference to Bauman's (2013, 119) critical verdict become "the dump of the problems generated and gestated globally". They profess to find local solutions to global problems, generating what Boaventura de Souza (2014) calls 'localized globalisms'.

2.1 The Context and Conditions in Mexico

Sanctuary or refuge cities have become a relevant theme in Mexico, given a moral impetus among CSOs to develop solidarity and community hospitality towards irregular migrations. However, in the Mexican case, these sanctuary cities are still embryonic. This does not exclude that the notion has a potential analytical impact with concern to the development of alternatives targeted at combating the humanitarian crisis of forced transit migration. Potentially it could be a new response for engaging the local population, government institutions at different levels, and the migrants themselves, in a broad solidarity within the host communities of newly arriving migrants. Yet in Mexico, most local communities are still very far from being in such a position. It is also hampered by the stance of the Mexican state on irregular migration and by its collusion with the United States.

Seen from that perspective the prime agents for a potential development of sanctuary cities in Mexico would be networks of CSOs. It implicates, that sanctuary cities in Mexico would, if at all, foremost come about related to strategies of networks of civil organizations that have been accompanying the migrants, targeted at their inclusion into the host communities. It would thus be a measure built from below, from the level of accompaniment, driven by the actors most committed to this process, themselves exposed to all the vicissitudes of the humanitarian crisis, whether involving stalking by organized crime or punitive government policies.

The reformulation in terms of 'sanctuary cities' was actualized immediately before the curtailment of the institutional capacities of the Mexican state concerning migratory security, and thus, inability to guarantee the human and legal rights of irregular migrants (Canales and Rojas 2018). This relates especially to new petitioners for political asylum in Mexican cities, waiting for resolution concerning political asylum. But it concerns, as well, those who already have an asylum status. Their fate is not much different since they suffer from a similar situation of rejection and xenophobia on the part of the local population.

It is a situation that has become influenced by anti-immigrant policies and by symbolic violence channeled by the prevalent media discourse.

Consequently, there is a turnaround concerning the nascent sanctuary cities in Mexico, related to the robust rejection of newly arrived forced migrants, as in the case of the migrant caravans in 2018. This includes community organizations endorsed by political councils, which were close to managing a kind of 'safe communities' copying the American example in México. The development of sanctuary cities in Mexico may thus seem to be an unrealizable utopia, but it is useful to deepen the understanding of the potentialities for the development of transversal solidarity related to the idea of sanctuary cities. For this reason, the concept of 'accompaniment' holds central importance, as a theory and practice of organized civil society, which could help to produce conditions for the formation of sanctuary or solidarity cities from the ground up, even in México.

Accompaniment emerges as the counterpart to the violent face of crime and the persecutory policies of the Mexican State. It is the community emergency staged by organized local actors, who little by little ventured into the field of irregular migration. They are both secular and confessional CSOs, generated from below. They have, with increasing impact, demonstrated a capacity to process claims, alternatives and strategies in the sphere of human rights, even with implications beyond the limits of the Mexican State. The role played by these organizations, starting from the concept of accompaniment, demonstrates recognition and respect for the rights of Central American migrants, and that they have managed to articulate a trajectory among themselves. However, as I will address in the following, the accompaniment needs to further involve the wider population and local governments, with respect to support and social integration of migrants.

2.2   Concept, Context, Practices, and Potentialities of Accompaniment

Following the definition of the Royal Spanish Academy, the RAE (*Real Académica Española*), the concept of accompaniment corresponds to the action or effect of accompanying, or to the people who are accompanying someone, and it refers to a harmonic support or aid. This support or harmonious assistance in the process of accompaniment of vulnerable groups, such as forced and/or irregular migrants, represents thus a humanitarian assistance service. The institutions that provide these accompaniment services, voluntary non-governmental organizations, which are part of civil society or ecclesiastical organizations, endeavor to go beyond the mere provision of care services, in offering a broadly defined, and much-needed, company and solidarity.

They have an important role in creating encounters and meeting places marked by respect for the human dignity of migrants. Over the years, they have acquired significant experience in defending human rights through documentation and dissemination of the abuses suffered by migrants during their transit. This includes public and legal denunciation of attacks on migrants and strategic litigation in paradigmatic cases before national and international authorities (Tavera, et al. 2014), as is the case of legal support with requests for political refuge in Mexico. By offering these services, these organizations have a special scope that prioritizes accompaniment at a personal level. This assistance, in addition to the services provided, represents a set of attitudes, principles and values congruent with the reality of the migrant, with hospitality and solidarity as the most outstanding qualities (Tavera, et al. 2014).

Pedagogically, accompaniment embodies different perspectives and can be approached from an alternative ethnography of activism. For example, Sepulveda (2011) argues that it is generated through different techniques and actions connected to the living reality of migrants, and their suffering in transit and, above all, related to their precarious situation in being far from their place of origin. Consequently, accompaniment is a practice and action that symbolizes a state of honor towards the human being. It includes not only 'being with the other' but 'feeling and doing with the other'.

In other words, it is walking with and relating to the dispossessed, such as the forced migrant. Therefore, accompaniment implies the possibility of meeting the dispossessed, and being participants in dialogue and interaction under equal conditions (Goizueta 2001, cited in Sepulveda 2011). As a liberating project towards forced migrations, accompaniment can generate mutual commitments, ideally, without goals or objectives that seek to instrumentalist migrants. (Sepulveda 2011). Ventura (2008), mentions that facing the task of accompaniment implies first an understanding the nature of interaction between the parties, given the special relationship between the actors involved, as well as respecting diversity and at the same time unity. In the process, when the power to take charge of specific situations comes about, the repercussions of central problems can be approached. The United Nations High Commissioner for Refugees (UNHCR 2016), recommends taking into account certain specific circumstances, such as gender perspectives or the life course related to specific ethnic groups, in order to define forms of accompaniment that avoid inapt generalizations in the understanding of specific cases.

For the Christian Church it is, as Pontin (1992) points out, more a function of faith-based doctrines that prioritize charity for the unprotected. However, despite the differences that may exist between secular and confessional humanitarianism, it is important to recognize the strengths of faith-based organizations. In general, confessional organizations may have access to the community that other civil organizations hardly command, thereby, argues Thomson (2014), they play a cardinal role in recovery and adaptation of irregular migrants, refugees and asylum seekers from Central America in transit.

Confessional organizations may indeed have an advantage over secular-civil organizations, in relation to humanitarian work and psychosocial accompaniment with migrants. They may generate a greater impact on local communities, helping to raise awareness of the basic rights of the irregular migrant, given that faith-based accompaniment promotes a generous spirit towards the dispossessed. James (2009), in his study on the distinctive role and operation of faith-based organizations (FBOs), mentions that the most important challenge that faith-based organizations have regarding humanitarian assistance, is knowing how to properly handle how their humanitarian aid should be provided, but at the same time maintaining the identity of the different actors involved, with a clear focus on true needs.

2.3   A Positive Agent for Change

In general, the focus of mainstream humanitarian CSOs may have made it difficult to see the role that religious communities play for irregular migrants. In recent years we have indeed seen a renewed interest in how religion can be a positive agent for change has surfaced. However, Kidwait, Moore, and FitzGibbon (2014) hold that it may still be early to fully assess the positive or negative roles that confessional organizations can play in the case of forced migrations.

Nevertheless, there are indeed noteworthy cases of Christian confessional agency along the route of forced migration in transit through Mexico, representing 'migration governance' based on faith. As Vidal and Martínez (2006) point out, they represent places of worship for new migrant communities, from which empowerment opportunities can be built and managed, by alternative projects for social mobility, including ideological foundations for resistance.

The ideational ground for such Christian movements of confessional accompaniment in Mexico stems from the Theology of Liberation in Central America. Its main precursors can be traced to El Salvador and Guatemala (places from where most irregular migrants in Mexico come) in the 1970s and 1980s. These societies have long suffered and continue to suffer serious conflicts and violence that have aggravated economic and social instability. The quandaries deepened when the United States government in the late 1980s targeted armed support for El Salvador and Nicaragua from the Soviet Union, Cuba and North Vietnam.

This includes, for example growing fears stemming from the victory of the Sandinista insurgency in Nicaragua, with the supposed intention of forging a strategic communist bloc throughout the Latin American region (Gettleman, et al. 1981). It motivated paramilitary interventions, instigated by the United States with the support of local oligarchies, encompassing repression that has shaped an entire spectrum of violence and population displacement.

Since the years of repression, the celebrated Archbishop Oscar Romero, should become the standard bearer of a liberation theology, denouncing the excesses of the military dictatorship that had brought the Salvadoran community to the brink of collapse. Romero denounced an unscrupulous US military intervention, calling on the Democratic Party that governed El Salvador to stop covering up the repression. Unfortunately, Oscar Romero was assassinated by the paramilitary forces of the local extreme right during a massive repressive action (Gettleman, et al. 1981).

The baggage of this Christian Liberation Theology movement was part of a counter-vailing movement in Central America, opposing a prevalent obscurantism that dominated the Catholic Church. It emerged thus from the shadows as a kind of 'Christian social doctrine' or 'social doctrine of the church'. It was, so to speak, a striving to Christianize social structures (Escontrilla 2009) that inspired Archbishop Oscar Romero's revolutionary struggle (Gettleman, et al. 1981).

Struggles for social justice amid the context of Guatemalan violence, but also in neighboring El Salvador, were led by Catholic priests. In Guatemala, due to the situation of ethnic groups permanently repressed by state violence and corporate mafia rule, the army sparked large-scale massacres in the rural areas. The massacres were part of a counterinsurgency campaign, with the alleged pretext that guerrillas were domiciled in those areas and that the local population was considered an enemy as well, supposedly sympathetic to the guerrillas (Amnesty International 2002). In the process, an environment inducing struggles for social justice emerged from this counter-vailing transformation of the Central American Catholic Church, yet often with serious personal consequences for its protagonists. For example Bishop Juan José Girardi, a staunch defender of Mayan languages, who led an investigation into the abuses committed in the years of the conflict, was beaten to death by members of the Guatemalan armed forces (Amnesty International 2002).

Originally, this position of the Catholic Church was inspired by and had as a platform the Second Conference of Bishops in Latin America, held in Medellin, Colombia, in 1968. It grounded a radicalized position of the Church relating to social injustice and poverty, common across Latin America. This meeting in 1968 was inspired by the experience of liberation theology and the work carried out by radical ecclesial communities on the ground (Escontrilla 2009). In the 21st century, liberation theology has grown in importance also in Mexico, and has found a special mission in accompaniment and defense of displaced persons and irregular migrants from Central America caught in dire humanitarian crisis. Likewise, it became concerned with the violence experienced by migrants during their transit to the United States, carried up by ecclesial communities, endeavoring to systematize the evangelizing potential relating to the poor and uprooted (Escontrilla 2009). Their trajectory was described as "community emergency" by Father Pedro Pantoja from the Casa de Migrantes "Camino con Justicia A.C" in the city of Saltillo; together with Father Alejandro Solalinde; both emblematic figures in the defense of Central American transit migrants.

Therefore, when analyzing networks of accompaniment it is important to recognize the alternative represented by these ecclesial communities, and their importance relating to the humanitarian crisis of forced migration. Seen from this perspective, confessional accompaniment represents a principle that seeks to strengthen the capacities of migrants, trying to restore self-confidence, responsibility, and autonomy, once they have been victims of the violations of practically all their basic rights (Vidal and Martínez 2006).

This is vital for the Central American migrants, as it lends them the power to understand and claim changes regarding their condition of extreme vulnerability. Confessional accompaniment, in extension, encompasses empowerment in terms of assets: resilience, relationships, rights and representations. Highlighting the principle of recognition is central, here, relating to the dynamics of solidarity in receiving societies. Thus, the empowerment process, carried forth by radical religious communities, foreshadows the veracity and honesty of the role that public security institutions should have in the task of defending the human rights of forced migrants (Vidal and Martínez 2006).

The most important thing concerning this empowerment is above all that it highlights a true lack of political and social action in facing the humanitarian crisis connected with contemporary transit r migration. This, as in the case of Mexico, is not just a consequence of the absence of laws or formal regulations in favor of human rights, but a result the lack of will and capacity, and of systemic corruption. Mitigate the power void on the part of government institutions, Hanson, et al. (2014) argue, means that to become substantial in a position as key actor confessional accompaniment it is necessary to forge strong ties with local host communities, which will allow to implement the values of hospitality and solidarity. Thus, the local population is key for the accompaniment to be substantial. The local population is to start with those who make it difficult to open and operate the shelters and immigrant houses, but through awareness-raising work, in the end they are also the ones who can become actors that make possible the permanence and maintenance of these refuges.

Based on this conceptualization of accompaniment, we can discern strengthened forms of commitment that represent the support and defense of the rights of migrants in transit. It means enhancing the ability to move forward, to have the courage to defend values and principles recovering the most fundamental emotional aspects of the life of a human being. This, in turn, helps to draw a line in relation to restrictive public policies to contain borders and to xenophobic social practices.

3   Community Emergency as a Real Utopia: Two Cases

I carried out the documentation on the accompaniment process for irregular migrants in transit through Mexico for seven years, embedded within a network of civil, confessional, and secular organizations. At present (2020) there are at least 62 organizations throughout the Mexican territory, which provide some type of service or assistance to irregular migrants related to the accompaniment process. This includes an infrastructure of dining rooms, shelters, and points of medical, psychological and legal assistance. Some of these organizations have an important background in being the product of the experience and the territorial roots that resistance through the years has given them. But some other organizations have strong disadvantages relating to a continuity in their operations and in serving undocumented immigrants.

This is not least due to the risks they suffer from being in the focus of organized crime and exposed to the rejection by the bulk of Mexican society. Documenting accompaniment practices in these shelters must therefore be on the lookout for factors that make the accompaniment process possible or difficult. This includes models and strategies, awareness-raising actions relating to the local community, intervention plans and possible solutions to the problems of violation that human rights of migrants present; all to explore the leeway these organizations have as key local actors.

The two organizations selected for reference here are the Saltillo Migrant House *Frontera con Justicia* and the *Camino a la Vida* migrant house in Aguascalientes. Both cases illustrate that despite the existence of an entire spectrum of violence, there are on the Mexican side important attempts to generate refuge or sanctuary cities. These are also two places that have experienced problems connected with forced migration in transit, and for the same reason, places in which organizations that accompany migrants have been better established.

The case of the city of Aguascalientes represents the instrumentalization of the city ordinance of immigration regulatory frameworks, the so-called

"Hospitality Law for the State of Aguascalientes". The city is also an example of how the community work carried out by the Saltillo migrant shelter, materializes in the transformation of this space into a place of coexistence and social encounters based on the approach of confessional accompaniment, endeavoring to achieve a so-called 'social shield'.

These places, both illustrate ways in contending violence and criminalization that stalks irregular migrants throughout their forced transit, without the intervention of the security forces and organized crime, which are often in collusion. They both, in varying ways demonstrate examples of good practice. They illustrate ways in which existing political and institutional frameworks and traditional ways of doing politics, as well as making decisions, can be dislocated and contended.

3.1   Research Methodology

Based on my experience obtained through field work in several migrant shelters in Mexico, I have observed that it is possible to achieve a change among the local population with respect to a widespread lack of trust in migrants. This has been achieved through building solidarity and support networks for migrants in awareness-raising spaces located in homes and shelters founded on the side of the freight train tracks, along which most of the Central American irregular migrants travel, or a few meters from the border.

A methodological strategy of conducting participatory fieldwork rested on the accessibility of sites, in this case migrant shelters open for the engagement of volunteers. Between 2015 and 2020, I served as a volunteer in seven separate shelters in five states (Aguascalientes, Chihuahua, Coahuila, Tamaulipas and San Luis Potosi) along the transit route through Mexico. At each site, I used ethnographic research tools grounded in participant observation.

While my experiences and observations at all seven sites has informed my understanding and analysis, I focus in the following on my work at the two sites mentioned; the one in Saltillo and the other in Aguascalientes. Here, I conducted a series of semi-structured interviews with staff and with irregular migrants, mostly from Central America, who were in transit to the United States, some of them political asylum seekers. I was embedded in the shelter at Saltillo for three months and passed through the shelter at Aguascalientes for brief intervals over the course of four years.

Ethnographic tools are valuable in the documentation of forced migration processes, because they allow for, as Pachirat (2009) argues, an active participation that makes it possible to sustain a direct dialogue with the investigated. Likewise, Gluckman (1968, cited in Schierup and Alund 1987) observes that when studying the behavior of the community, the physical environment and the lives of the community members are intimately connected. Life stories are of particular use, being one of the most informative forms of expression of human experience of key informants, communicating their lived experience (Bertaux 2005).

This helps to counter what Bertaux (2005) refers to as the double plane of subjectivity, or the researcher initiating interaction with his specific interests acting as a filter for data collection and, consequently an instrument for the development of the facts and the narrative as a whole. This is coupled with the interpretation of the subjects interviewed, who, while agreeing to narrate their migratory experience, will always tend to be selective, in interpreting social situations, forming a vision reaching beyond their direct experience.

3.2   The Case of the Saltillo Migrant Shelter: Social Shielding

Saltillo is the capital of the state of Coahuila. It is one of the most industrialized cities in the north of Mexico, being a hub of the automotive industry. It is divided by the train tracks that lead from the border town of Piedras Negras to the neighboring city of Monterrey. When it was founded, in 2002, the shelter in Saltillo provided humanitarian assistance at a different location from where it is currently located. Soon, the founder, Priest Pedro Pantoja, received a warehouse donated by a charitable religious organization. At first, the residents of the neighborhood in which the shelter is located were reluctant to share space and resources with the migrant population. At the time the shelter received support from the Food Bank, significant discounts, as well as donations from nearby farming collectives, which decided to support the shelter based on the founder Pantoja's charisma (Tavera 2014).

The concept of community emergency was suggested by Pantoja, whom I interviewed on site. At the time, he characterized the shelter's inner workings as an attempt to transform the space into a meeting place for locals and migrant communities, in order to 'live together', or coexist, based on the confessional approach, where the norms of coexistence and collaboration in solidarity serve as protective mechanisms to achieve 'social shielding' of displaced persons by the host community. Father Pantoja argued that local popular movements can be strategic collective actors for the foundation a 'social subjectivity'. He described this as a qualitative force that can create places of refuge, where violence and criminalization stalking irregular migrants throughout their transit can be contended without the involvement of security forces, which are often in collusion with organized crime. Pantoja also maintained the local population must be a key player, not only in the accompaniment as confessional approach, but in the eventual foundation of genuine sanctuary cities in Mexico.

The church's accompaniment of migrants has generated ties of 'belonging' between the migrants and the community surrounding the shelter. These social networks, rooted in religious practice, emerge as a valuable element for the migrants' integration into the host community. Another critical element is the information about fundamental rights that the shelter provides, including legal advice relating to asylum and political refuge.

I observed cases of migrants who decided to return to their home countries based on the confessional form of accompaniment at the shelter. Evidently, when people decide to return to their communities of origin, they do so with mixed feelings. On the one hand, there is the joy of returning home to reunite with the family after months of absence and uncertainty, to feel free of the threat of arrest, extortion, daunting legal procedures, and deportation. On the other hand, however, there are strong feelings of discouragement and demotivation, related to not having achieved their original goal, the long-awaited American dream that ended up becoming a Mexican nightmare.

Before the war on drug trafficking began in Mexico, in 2006, The Migrant House of Saltillo received an average of 300 migrants from Central America per week. Since then, an unusually severe wave of violence was unleashed against irregular migrants, and the number of migrants received by the shelter fluctuated significantly. It settled at an average of around 200 people per month, and remained on this level since mid-2014. This is connected with the implementation of the "Programa Frontera Sur" (Southern Border Program) by which the Federal Government has curbed the transit of migrants from Central America through militarization of Mexico's southern border.

The shelter has long since stopped receiving financial aid through any of the three levels of government in Mexico. When the shelter was consolidated as *Frontera con Justicia A. c* (Border with justice, A.c) in 2004, it received up to 20,000 pesos per month (about 1,000 euros), but donations were suspended due to Father Pantoja's public criticism of the government's migration policy (Tavera 2014). Since 2012, an international donor, the Canada Fund for Local Initiatives (FCIL), has supported the staff working within the shelter. The FCIL is a Canadian government program administered by the Canadian embassy in Mexico. It aims to promote and implement projects designed by civil society organizations and has been present in Mexico for 30 years. Its official objective is to support small projects in priority areas by providing financial resources to initiatives of civil society or other non-profit institutions.

3.3   The Case for Hospitality and Human Mobility for Migrants in the State of Aguascalientes

The migrant shelter in Aguascalientes is an organization distinguished by its defense of the human rights of people in transit through the State of Aguascalientes. It promotes actively the principles of non-discrimination and inclusion, and its motto 'No human being is illegal' reflects these principles. The objective of the organization is to achieve dignified and fair treatment of migrants with respect for their human rights and constitutional entitlements through promotion of humanitarian aid, institutional connections, societal engagement, academic research, sensitization of the host community, and awareness of the conditions of migration.

Aguascalientes has a privileged location for the study of migration as it is located exactly in the geographical center of the country, at one of the nodal points of transit migration towards the United States. It is at the center of the three traditional migration routes in Mexico: The Center Route, the Western Route and the Gulf of Mexico Route. These routes align with rail corridors, starting from the southern border and heading towards the northern border of the country along the primary transport route used by migrants. For decades, the city of Aguascalientes was itself the place of origin and return for many Mexican migrants, but in the first decades of this century it became a transit hub for migrants displaced from Central America. The current character of migration to the northern border and the increase in deportations of Mexican nationals has generated a greater interest on the part of the *Camino a la Vida* shelter to adequately address this issue, and the needs of the migrant population. An initiative to promote a Law of Hospitality for Migrants in the State of Aguascalientes arose, given the urgent need for precautionary measures to protect the human rights of migrants.

In 2016, I drafted an initial version of the Law on Hospitality in my capacity of a volunteer at the migrant shelter of Aguascalientes. At that time, the coordinator of the shelter was Xicontecatl Cardona, a local political activist and Mexican ex-emigrant. Cardona had a strong political position in the city; hence the organization's interest in drafting the initiative. The draft law was passed by the state congress in 2017 but was rejected by the local congress. A revised version of the proposed law was, at the time of writing, being prepared for submission under a new city administration instituted in 2021. The new proposal goes further in expanding and standardizing initiatives for constitutional reforms through federal and local law, in that is prohibits reference to a person's legal status, in particular any reference to nation of origin or immigration status, in any constitutional text. It is considered a good opportunity to resume the progress made towards international protection standards for migrants in transit.

This initiative coincides with others across México at the state as well as federal levels, and in varying stages of development. The draft law of Aguascalientes is in line with the changes and modifications that have been taking place at the federal level with the creation of the Migration Law of 2011. Similar proposals at the local level, include the Hospitality Law of the FM4 Collective of Guadalajara that was presented in the Jalisco state congress, Mexico City's "Law of Interculturality, Migrant Care and Human Mobility", and related examples in Sonora, Michoacán, Durango, Tlaxcala and Hidalgo.

4   Conclusion

As argued in the preceding the discussion on the emergence of sanctuary cities in Mexico should start from the accompaniment process. This is due to the extent that engaged civil society, confessional and secular organizations are committed to assisting forced migrants in transit, by articulating networks of solidarity encompassing local communities, through which they can contribute to the recognition of the human rights of forced migrants in a broader context. To this comes their perspective of transcending public policy decisions and of counteracting the widespread criminality across Mexico.

Processes of accompaniment are fundamental, in turn, for understanding the need for an alternative trajectory of development; that is a process building on the joint and active participation of local communities, public institutions, and international organizations relating to forced migration, including the migrants themselves as actors. This implies promoting social practices with a scope that can affect decision-making, so that forced migrants and organizations that accompany them are emplaced as transversal solidarities, and the shelters they coordinate as social arenas for reforming the governance of migration. Hence, emerging sanctuary cities, could found new forms of governance of irregular and forced migrations as a viable answer to the humanitarian crisis.

Seen through the lens of 'accompaniment' it can be concluded that all actors involved in migratory processes should endeavor to focus their humanitarian assistance on the genuine needs and concerns of the individual, helping migrants regain their dignity and hope in the face of the uncertain future that they face. The networks of civil organizations that assist forced migrants in Mexico have achieved social mobilization through community work as a way of social shielding in refuge spaces, emplaced in the different 'houses' or shelters of migrants. Positioning defense of migrants in transit against organized crime and state violence, new strategic groups of committed citizens will continue to be formed and emplace social spaces for contending violence and persecution, in solidarity with vulnerable minorities, such as Central American migrants in transit through Mexico. It is important to take advantage of the basic knowledge they possess. The shelters that they manage cover practically the entire Mexican forced transit route, which make them truly strategic places for catapulting sanctuary cities as a next step, whose emergence is, however, still embryonic. As related to in the discussion of confessional accompaniment above, it is essential 'to be with the other, to feel, to walk and to do with the other', being closely related to the most vulnerable and dispossessed.

Seen through this lens nascent sanctuary cities in Mexico can be derived from accompaniment relating to acute community emergency. Sanctuary cities emerging from the practice of accompaniment may become the new commitment of international organizations, including the UNHCR. This would also make it possible to revalue processes around transit migration in Mexico in defense of human rights, endeavoring to counteract restrictive state policies, xenophobia and criminal violence yet not revaluated as 'sanctuary cities', properly speaking, but as spaces under conditions of community emergency emplaced in solidarity spaces for the mediation of forced migration, such as migrant houses.

In Mexico, for now, it is still unrealistic to talk about this type of initiatives in terms of sanctuary cities. In other parts of the World, it took decades to develop consolidated and moderately viable solidarity cities, such as San Francisco. The embryonic Mexican sanctuary cities still require a more specific instrumental approach, coordinated with public policies to achieve a truly powerful and alternative development. It is no easy task. Its realization would demand a changing commitment at relevant institutional levels.

References

Bauman, Z. (2013). *Tiempos líquidos. Vivir en una época de incertidumbre.* México: Tusquets.

Bertaux, D. (2005). *Los relatos de vida. Perspectiva etnosociológica.* España: Ediciones Bellaterra.

Canales, I. A., and M. Rojas (2018). Panorama de la migración internacional en México y Centroamérica. *Serie población y desarrollo.* CELADE-CEPAL.

Castles, S. (2003). "Towards a sociology of forced migration and social transformation". *Sociology* 37: 13–24.

Delgado, R., and H. Márquez (2012). *Desarrollo desigual y migración forzada. Una mirada desde el sur global.* Universidad Autónoma de Zacatecas: Miguel Ángel Porrúa.

Delgado R. (2016). *Migration and development in Latin America. The emergence of a southern perspective.* Researchgate.net. pdf.

De Sousa Santos, B. (2014). *Si Dios fuese activista de los derechos humanos.* Madrid: Trotta.

El legado mortal de Guatemala: el pasado impune y las nuevas violaciones a los derechos humanos. Amnistía Internacional (2002): https://www.amnesty.org/es/documents/AMR34/001/2002/es/.

Gettleman, E. (ed.) (1981). *El Salvador: Central America in the new cold war.* Grove Press. New York.

Graauw, E., and G. Shannon (2020). "Labor Unions and Undocumented Immigrants: Local Perspectives on Transversal Solidarity During DACA and DAPA". *Critical Sociology:* 1–15.

Hanson, J., T. Mcrea, R. Calvo, and F. Álvarez (2014). "El valor del acompañamiento. La fe y las respuestas al desplazamiento". *Revista Migraciones forzadas (48):* 7–8.

James, R. (2009). *What is distinctive about FBOs: how european FBOs define and operationalize their faith.* Praxis Paper (22).

Kidwai, S., L. Moore, and A. Fitz Gibbon (2014). "El papel de la religión en la formación de relaciones entre comunidades". *Revista Migraciones Forzadas (48):* 10–13.

López, V. (2013). "Desarrollo, migración y seguridad: el caso de la migración hondureña hacia los Estados Unidos". *Migración y desarrollo (21):* 65–104.

Morales, A. (2007). *La diáspora de la posguerra. Regionalismos de los migrantes y dinámicas territoriales en América Central.* Costa Rica: FLACSO.

Pachirat, T. (2009). "The political in political ethnography: dispatches from the kill floor". In Edward S. (ed.). *Political ethnography. What immersion contributes to the study of power.* The University of Chicago Press.

Pontin, M. (1992). "Iglesia y migraciones latinoamericanas". *CEPAM CIM.* pdf.

Sepulveda, E. (2011) "Acompañamiento: mexican migrant youth writing from undersite of modernity". *Harvard Educational Review 81 (3).*

Schierup, C., and A. Alund (1987). *Why they still be dancing? Integration and ethnic transformation among Yugoslav inmigrants in Scandinavia.* Sweden: Almqvist & Wiksell International.

Suárez, P. (2017). "Ciudades santuario de California: la acción política de los gobiernos locales en la política pública migratoria contemporánea de los Estados Unidos". *Migración y Desarrollo 29 (15):* 51–71.

Tavera, P., M. and Pérez (2014). *Solidaridad en el camino. Atlas de organizaciones de apoyo a personas migrantes centroamericanas.* México: Propuesta cívica.

Thomson, J. (2014). "Los actores religiosos locales y la protección en entornos comple-jos e inseguros," *Revista Migraciones Forzadas (48):* 5–7.

UNESCO (2016). "Welcoming Cities Refugges and Migrants". *Inclusive and Sustainable CITIES series.*

UNHCR (2016). *Tendencias globales. Desplazamiento forzado en 2015: forzados a huir.* Alto Comisionado de las Naciones Unidas para los Refugiados: España.

Valdez, E. and H. Armando (2009) El catolicismo social en la Iglesia mexicana, *Política y Cultura,* Spring (No. 31): 139–59

Ventura, M. (2008). "Asesor es acompañar". *Revista de Curriculum y Formación de Profesorado 12 (1):* 1–14.

Vidal, F., and J. Martínez (2006). *Religión e integración social de los inmigrantes: la prueba del ángel.* España: Universidad Pontificia de Comillas.

CHAPTER 13

Migrant Solidarities and Spaces of Encounter in European Cities

Ilker Ataç, Kim Rygiel and Maurice Stierl

Over the past several years, we have seen a rise in political mobilizations in EUrope,[1] and elsewhere, by and in solidarity with migrants.[2] We have described these mobilizations previously as "forms of contentious politics with transformative potential" that are both transnational and trans-categorical in that "they are disruptive, not just of territorial borders of the nation-state and regional regimes of control, but also of the very ontological and political borders upon which notions of traditional citizenship as both a legal status and a political identity are based" (Ataç, et al. 2016, 539).[3] Building on our earlier work, and in view of the rise of migrant solidarity activism and social movements (della Porta 2018; Mezzadra 2018; Agustín and Jørgensen 2019; Heller, et al. 2019; Bauder 2019), particularly since 2015's "long summer of migration" (Kasparek and Speer 2015), this article focuses our attention on specific examples of what we understand and conceptualize as *transversal solidarities* by and with migrants, and rooted in the city.

The examples we explore in this article include: *Trampoline House*, a civil society organization in Copenhagen which provides support and a home to migrant newcomers in Copenhagen; *Queer Base*, an activist organization in Vienna providing support and shelter for LGBTIQ (Lesbian, Gay, Bisexual, Transgender, Intersex and Queer) migrants; and finally, a coalition of diverse

---

1   This article speaks of 'EUrope' to problematize frequently employed usages that equate the EU with Europe and Europe with the EU and suggests, at the same time, that EUrope is not reducible to the institutions of the EU.

2   We use the term migrant (or migrant newcomer) as an expansive term to include mobile groups of people who are often classified as irregular and regular migrants, refugees, asylum seekers, and rejected asylum seekers. We do so to problematise the refugee/migrant binary, which not only fails to recognise the complex realities behind the reasons, conditions and ways that people leave their countries of origin or second or third countries, but also to problematise the bureaucratic management of peoples in 'managing migration' (e.g. Crawley and Skleparis, [2018]; Zetter, [2007]).

3   A version of this article appeared in *Critical Sociology*, Jan. 4, 2021: https://doi.org/10.1177/0896920520980522.

groups coming together under the name of the *Palermo Charter Process*, a coalition of diverse groups seeking to create safe harbors and 'corridors of solidarity', from the Mediterranean to cities throughout EUrope. While these examples are situated in and across different cities and urban spaces, they share a common grounding in building solidarity through spaces of encounters related to ideas of *home, community,* and *harbor*. By exploring these three distinct solidarity initiatives in tandem, we examine on the one hand, how the production of spaces of encounters is linked to building transversal solidarities and, on the other, how transversal solidarities also connect different spaces of solidarity across different political scales – from the home, or even the sea, to the city, and to cities across EUropean spaces.

Engaging our examples in this way enables us to explore the question of how migrants transform city spaces into home, or what Blunt and Sheringham (2019) call "home-city geographies". This is an approach to "examine the interplay between lived experiences of urban homes and the contested domestication of urban space" and "the ways in which urban homes and the ability to feel at home in the city are shaped by different migrations and mobilities" (Blunt and Sheringham 2019, 815). We understand their collective impact as performing a subversive form to what Walters (2004) calls "domopolitics", that is a rationality of governing fusing paradigms of national security and social security through appeals to the home and the home front. Through their work, these initiatives create spaces of encounters based on identifying gaps in service provision and outrage at asylum policies and violent border practices, fostering models of shared living between locals and newcomers as well as 'corridors of solidarity', not in a sort of prescriptive way, but more as a call to collectively generate 'infrastructures of freedom of movement' that can support the 'autonomous' movements of migrants. In our discussion, we underscore the importance of space and spatial strategies in political mobilizations (Martin and Miller 2003; Bauder 2021), through which the city *may* be created as a progressive space (rather than assuming it to necessarily be so), noting how "struggles for and around rights to movement emerge in response to strategies and spaces of control and containment, but they also provide a means to reconnect sites and scales of politics with the potentiality of creating alternative citizenship geographies and political community" (Ataç, et al. 2016, 540). We examine how *transversal solidarities* are built through these spaces of encounters, teasing out different understandings of solidarity as well as their limits.

In thinking about transversal solidarities, we build on others, such as Featherstone (2012), Bauder (2019; 2021), Schwiertz and Schwenken (2020), who use the term transversal solidarity to reflect collective political struggles against oppression and injustices across differences, positionalities and hierarchies, with the potential to create new forms of spaces, subjectivities and social relations. In their discussion of "solidarity citizenship", Schwiertz and Schwenken (2020, 408) correctly note that transversal solidarity struggles are always an unfinished business, requiring "an infinite process of solidary practice".

Recently, Agustín and Jørgensen (2019) have provided a typology that outlines three types of solidarity: autonomous, civic, and institutional solidarity. In this typology, autonomous solidarity is viewed as the practice of producing horizontal relations and practices "in self-organized (mainly urban) spaces", civic solidarity as initiatives of civil society actors seeking "to include refugees", and institutional solidarity as the process of formalizing solidarity by connecting "the civil society arena with the one of policy-making". While each of the three examples discussed in this article might demonstrate one or more of the types of solidarity, our desire here is to extend the analysis to emphasize the transversal nature of solidarity and its disruptive potential of ways of thinking about solidarity in the city. This disruptive potential might work across the different types, following della Porta and Steinhilper (2020, 1), who argue for putting "solidarities in motion" by considering "hybridization" of forms of solidarity that have "blurred the lines between contentious and non-contentious forms of civil society engagement", but also in terms of reflecting on the limits of solidarity. Critical reflection on limits is a reminder that progressive politics in urban space is not predetermined by the essence of urbanism and processes of urbanization but, instead, derives from processes of place and space-making, and the forms of relations and relationships we make (whether economic, political, social, cultural, and other) in the space of the city and which, in turn, make the city.

For us, spaces of encounters in the city are created through social relations and networks in ways disruptive of borders and boundaries of enclosure, whether they be territorial, ontological, or political (including across different types of solidarity). Recent scholarship highlights diverse ways in which these spaces of encounters have been built. In their analysis of emerging refugee organizations in Vienna, for example, de Jong and Ataç (2017) show how organizations manage to occupy a middle space between service provision and political mobilization by creating spaces of encounters between migrants and non-migrants. By creating spaces of encounter, these organizations challenge the intentional isolation of migrants with precarious status and foster new political belongings that form bonds of solidarity which transcend borders and strengthen struggles against injustices.

Drawing from our case studies, this article explores the notion and enactment of solidarity but also, in keeping with contentious politics, points of tension, constraints, and conflicts. We do so in order to call attention to nuancing a discussion on how to avoid potential pitfalls in approaches to solidarity in city spaces. Some of these pitfalls include romanticizing the city as a space of progressive politics (especially in counter to more xenophobic national politics), downplaying the precarity of position of groups of newcomers and their legal status, or over-emphasizing the city as a place of permanent settlement. In the following section, we highlight the fact that cities are also places of increasing polarization, racialized inequality and violent displacement, which may offer, if at all, merely temporary shelter to those 'on the move'. All of this impacts the possibilities and limits of transversal solidarities in urban settings and emphasizes that enactments of solidarity are ultimately experimental and "without guarantees" (Featherstone 2012, 244).

Our article is organized into three main sections. We first review some key aspects of the EUropean border regime in order to illustrate Walter's (2004) concept of domopolitics. We then provide a review of some recent literature on migrant solidarity struggles centered in and around the city, noting how the city comes into focus as a site of political struggle. In the second section, we explore three transversal solidarity initiatives, illustrating how they advance our understanding of providing a counter-domopolitics, and elaborate on how spaces of encounter and transversal solidarity is understood within these initiatives. In the last section, we tease out both the transversal aspects of this counter-domopolitics more collectively but then also outline considerations for thinking about the potential limits or constraints of transversal solidarity in the city.

1   The EU Border Regime as Domopolitics and Its Contestation

1.1   *The EU Border Regime as Domopolitics*
Recent figures put the number of forcibly displaced persons at a record high of 79.5 million individuals (UNHCR, n.d.). At the same time, governments – in particular those of the 'global north' – are investing in more restrictive border and migration policies and are creating a "non-entrée regime" (Hathaway and Gammeltoft-Hansen 2015). Regularly, governments evoke a certain rationality towards governing through security that brings together the 'diagrams' of national security with those of political economy and social security – a rationality that Walters (2004, 241, emphasis in original) describes as "domopolitics", and which "refers to the government of the state (but, crucially, other political spaces as well) as a *home*". This trope of home "implies a reconfiguring of the relations between citizenship, state, and territory" (Walters 2004,

241), as might be found in notions such as Homeland Security in the US or the UK's 2002 White Paper called *Secure Borders, Safe Haven*. As Walters (2004, 232) notes, domopolitics, as its name suggests, relates also to "domo as conquest, taming, subduing; a will to domesticate the forces which threaten the sanctity of home". He (2004, 242) adds that, frequently, domopolitics reveals a "tendency which takes it outwards, beyond the home, beyond even its own 'backyard' and quite often into its neighbors' homes, ghettos, jungles, bases, slums. Once domopolitics extends its reach, once it begins to take the region or even the globe as its strategic field of intervention, then the homeland becomes the home front, one amongst many sites in a multifaceted struggle". While Walter's article focuses on the ways in which domopolitics plays out in the UK, we seek to develop the idea of domopolitics in the EUropean context.

In EUrope, domopolitics has long translated into attempts to turn the union into an "area of freedom, security and justice without internal frontiers" (European Union 2012). In order to create European communalization through this area in which EU citizens, finances, goods, as well as services could move and flow freely, a complex security and surveillance landscape – or regime – has emerged to govern such movements and flows to and within the union. The EU border regime seeks to filter out unwanted or threatening mobilities and subjectivities, commonly thought to be emanating from the outside, to secure and purify the 'homey' inside. The COVID-19 pandemic serves as a useful example of Europe's supra-national domopolitical rationality. Although the World Health Organization (2020) advised "against the application of travel or trade restrictions to countries experiencing COVID-19 outbreaks", the European Commission (2020) recommended the introduction of travel restrictions, aiming at "drastically reducing incoming people flows at the external borders of the Union". Though admitting that the EU had become the "epicenter of the pandemic", the external borders, described by the European Commission as "a security perimeter for all Schengen States", would need to be reinforced. Further securitizing the external border was suggested not only to prevent the 'import' of the Coronavirus but also to return to freedom of movement within the Schengen Area. The consequences of such external border reinforcements were dire, with deterrence practices escalating particularly in the Mediterranean Sea, and leading to systematic, and at times fatal, forms of abandonment and push-back of migrant boats.

Securing EUrope's 'inside' by securing its 'external dimension' and preventing border crossings has prompted not merely interventions in its immediate neighborhood – for example through migrant containment agreements with third countries – but also forms of violence that are spatially displaced. To maintain the EUropean homeland, or to defend the home front, this

EUropean border regime had to indeed "extend its reach outward" , as Walters has noted. Deterring and containing unauthorized movements has coalesced with a (necropolitical) violence that, to a large degree, occurs 'elsewhere', in the rather inaccessible terrains of the Mediterranean Sea or the Saharan desert, and that rarely returns 'home'. And yet, the home front cannot be exhaustively secured given that migrant movements continue to manifest across EUropean borders. For those who have reached EUropean space and are deemed as not rightfully belonging, diffused forms of border enforcement have been designed to ensure that the EUropean homeland does not turn into 'their' home.

EUropean domopolitics is enforced through "hostile environment" policies with EUropean member states seeking to actively render spaces unlivable for migrants. These "hostile environments exist", Pezzani (2020) writes, "at the intersection of two sets of laws: one aiming to contain and restrict people's movement to their respective nation-states, and the other seeking to govern their social (dis-)integration". The Dublin regulation and its 'first country of entry' principle which, in theory, prevents migrant newcomers from moving across EUrope's internal borders to 'asylum shop', as derogatively phrased, has produced a regime of containment *and* forced displacement within the union where member states deport irregularized migrants to the ostensible first country of entry. Social (dis-)integration and deterrence measures are pursued, moreover, through an ever-more restrictive asylum system in which grounds for receiving asylum are narrowed, worker and welfare rights are restricted, access to independent and qualified counselling services is limited, spaces of forcible confinement are extended and turned increasingly disciplinary and punitive (Ataç and Rosenberger 2019; Hamlin 2012).

Securing the EUropean inside has thus coalesced with a proliferation of bordering mechanisms that, frequently, rely on racialized imaginaries of who belongs and who does not. Intruding into urban spaces, for example through acts of policing based on racial profiling, de-localized border control has turned the city into a bordered space. Indeed, as De Genova (2015, 3) has shown, we can witness "the extension of borders deep into the putative 'interior' of nation-state space through immigration law enforcement that increasingly saturates the spaces of everyday life". Seeking to evade controls and deportations has meant that those without regular status often seek to remain under the radar, which in turn further impedes access to vital resources, including access to healthcare, education, social welfare, and employment. At the same time, a range of solidarity initiatives have emerged that seek to counter the EU's domopolitics from above, a politics that, in the name of 'homey-ness', has militarized borders and produced mass encampments for EUrope's *other*.

1.2   Building a Counter- 'Domo'- Politics

Since 2015, forms of solidarity have surged in the EUropean context, many of which have appealed to welcoming migrant newcomers into new 'homes.' In contrast to the top-down governmentality of domopolitics described by Walters (2004, 232), which operates by locking down borders on the home front and "taming" or "subduing [...] the forces which threaten the sanctity of home", these solidarities are built around the concept of home to politicize the presence of those seeking asylum and other migrants with precarious status and to introduce practices against the exclusionary logic and border politics of EUropean domopolitics. In looking collectively at such solidarity movements, we suggest that they provide a counter-politics contesting the logics of domopolitics, one which often focuses on opening local spaces within the city as a way of countering more restrictive national or EUropean border policies.

Examples of such solidarity movements include various mobilizations of non-citizens, mostly in urban spaces, who engage in political struggles and campaigns for the right to stay, to housing, work, education, medical care, food and clothes, and family reunification as well as to fight against border controls, asylum policy, detention and deportation (De Genova 2017; Rosenberger, et al. 2018; Fontanari 2019; Dadusc, et al. 2019; Stierl 2019). We have also seen an upsurge in mobilizations of citizens in solidarity with newcomers and their struggles for rights and resources, ranging from service provisions and everyday support (Siim, et al. 2018; Baban and Rygiel 2020), including 'welcoming' campaigns (Karakayali and Kleist 2016), rescue operations in the Mediterranean (Stierl 2018; Schwarz and Stierl 2019); anti-deportation struggles, language classes, legal support, housing and food provision, and so forth (Kirchhoff 2020). In the European context, many of these solidarity mobilizations have more recently come under attack, becoming the object of de-legitimization campaigns or criminal investigations as 'crimes of solidarity' (Duarte 2020; Taylor 2018; Schack and Witcher 2020; Tazzioli 2018).

The city becomes an important location for building transversal solidarity struggles by migrants and citizens to counter the EUropean border regime. As long observed by critical citizenship, migration (including the autonomy of migration), social movement and urban geography literatures, the city is an important site of struggle for "rights to the city" and forms of "urban citizenship" (e.g. Isin 2000 and 2002; Staeheli 2003; Lefebvre 2009; Mitchell 2003; Purcell 2014; and Holston 2009). The city has, moreover, been regarded as a "migrant metropolis", the product of transnational human mobilities that form "a central and constitutive dynamic in the contemporary social production (and transformation) of urban space" (De Genova 2015, 4). Such bodies of literature point to the importance of cities: as spaces of place-making through the appropriation of space and rights-claiming, as sites of everyday living through settlement, employment and belonging, as hubs where newcomer services are concentrated, and as centers of heterogeneity, networks and exchange. Particularly within the current political climate in Europe and elsewhere, as national governments pursue more restrictive immigration and refugee policies (Schwiertz and Schwenken 2020), cities have become important strategic sites for circumventing or contesting restrictive border policies. Here, as Stefan Kipfer (2009, 68) observes, "The urban functions as a level of analysis mediating between macro- and micro levels of reality and possibility. In other words, the urban leads not only to analysis of the macrorealities of the state, capital and empire but also to a differential and dialectical critique of everyday life". The turn towards the city level of governance, to circumvent more restrictive federal or national border policies, can be seen in such social movements such as sanctuary and solidarity city movements (Kron and Lebruhn 2020; Paik, et al. 2019; Darling and Bauder 2019). Building on a historical trajectory of the city's association with progressive politics,[4] scholars have recently looked to cities as progressive spaces from which to fight against the unequalizing forces of capitalism, globalization and the "neoliberal city" (Mayer 2013), while noting the importance of not romanticizing the city as necessarily a place of a more progressive politics.

While the city thus provides an important site of building a counter-politics to EUropean domopolitics, it is also important not to romanticize the city as necessarily a place of a more progressive politics (Misra 2017), that is as a welcome retreat from the divisionary and undemocratic trends at the national, transnational, or global levels. Though cities provide potential for building progressive struggles, cities are also places of (anti-migrant) violence, injustice, "austerity urbanism" (Mayer 2013) and growing economic polarization (Rolnik 2019; Caldeira 1999). Urban spaces have become increasingly segregated, as noted by Skop (2006, 394), reinforcing social inequality by limiting access of some to important resources, including "economic rewards, social networks, cultural capital, political power, physical safety, quality schools, social status, and so on". Not least, due to the often excessive and racialized policing of disadvantaged neighborhoods, the fact of urban inequalities in Western countries is highlighted in the eruptions of protest and violence, such as in Paris in 2005, London in 2011, or Ferguson in 2014 (Fassin 2013). Most recently, protests have erupted across US cities such as Portland, Oregon and Louisville, Kentucky,

---

4   The city has historically been identified as a place of progressive politics because of its association with liberalism, heterogeneity and anonymity (e.g. Wirth 1995; Sandercock 2004).

decrying racial and economic injustice, police brutality, and the racist killings of African-American citizens such as George Floyd and Breonna Taylor. The ongoing COVID-19 health crisis has further crystallized urban inequalities, with marginalized populations and neighborhoods being particularly affected by the pandemic and governmental lockdown measures.

Wary of both pitfalls, that of idealizing cities as sites of progressive politics or dystopian spaces of violence and inequality, we draw attention to the importance of cities through the concept of spaces of encounters, which enables us to inquire into their, as of yet, settled potential as spaces in which to build transversal solidarities. De Genova (2015, 3) has argued that "migration studies research tends to be disproportionately urban in its empirical orientation, but commonly leaves the urban question profoundly under-theorized". Taking up his (2015, 3) invitation to think not just empirically but also theoretically about "the intersections of transnational migration and urban space" and "how migrants become involved in the production of distinct urban spaces", we look to the types of spaces that are created through solidarity struggles, reflecting on both the potential and limits to generate progressive politics around and in solidarity with migrant newcomers. We do so in the next section by focusing on three examples of transversal solidarity: *Trampoline House* in Copenhagen, *Queer Base* in Vienna, and the *Palermo Charter Process*, stretching from the Mediterranean Sea to cities throughout EUrope.

2   From Home and Safe Shelter to Open Harbors

The three examples we explore in this section are connected in their focus on building relationships between newcomers and locals through practices and ideas of home, building communities and harboring within urban spaces, but in ways that also connect cities to create solidarities that extend and disrupt city limits and territorial boundaries. As Bauder (2019, 1075) points out: "solidarity is closely connected to a politics of place that, on the one hand, focuses on local belonging; on the other hand, it is relational, connecting places at national and transnational scales. With its transformative and productive nature, solidarity has a 'place-making character' (Oosterlynck, et al. 2017, 10)". As we detail below, they reveal how solidarity mobilizations challenge a domopolitical rationality by building spaces of encounters in the city that connect people across different positionalities and legal statuses, traverse across different types of solidarities, and link different spaces and scales of governing that work to open community and borders to newcomers.

2.1   Trampoline House: "This Is My House, It Is Your House, It Is Our House, We Share This Space"

Trampoline House is an example of solidarity mobilizations with migrants that take housing as a core issue along two fronts. First, the example of housing highlights the fact that, rather than romanticizing the city, transversal solidarity often builds from seeing cities as spaces of growing polarization, poverty, and inequity, with the right to affordable and adequate housing being a key issue. The OECD (2020) estimates that 1.9 million people are homeless in OECD countries, in addition to those without proper access to adequate housing. Moreover, compounding urban growth and lack of housing is the fact that there has been an increased "financialization of housing" (Aalbers 2016; Balakrishnan, et al. 2016), whereby corporate finance (e.g. banks, hedge funds, global real estate companies etc.) are investing in housing as a commodity, transforming cities into "hedge cities", driving housing prices up, decreasing affordable housing and buying up affordable or foreclosed properties for investment (UN Human Rights Council 2017, 7–8). As the former UN Special Rapporteur on the Right to Housing, Leilani Farhani (n.d), has importantly and repeatedly remarked: "Housing is a human rights issue – it makes or breaks us. It is the difference between life and death".

Housing is particularly important to migrant newcomers in the city for, as Damaris Rose (2016) explains, "affordable housing is the scaffolding refugees need to rebuild and feel settled". Housing is the "anchor point for a new start". Housing provides a foundation from which newcomers develop a sense of belonging and access health, education, and employment. Housing initiatives are important, then, not only for materializing rights to the city and fighting the commodification of housing, but because these initiatives provide platforms for linking "home-making in the city" to thinking about "the city as home" (Blunt and Sheringham 2019, 815). Housing initiatives, like *Trampoline House* in Copenhagen, create spaces of encounters that encourage newcomers and locals to live and create together, a key element in pre-emptively fighting against xenophobia and fostering pluralism more broadly (Baban and Rygiel 2020).

Housing solidarity initiatives with migrant newcomers across EUropean cities take a variety of forms. These include more activist models of migrant squatting (Dadusc, et al. 2019; Mudu and Chattopadhyay 2016), with one of the better-known examples being the now closed (as of July 2019) Hotel City Plaza initiative in Athens (Raimondi 2019; Squire 2018). City Plaza was a self-organizing housing initiative based on the occupation of an unoccupied hotel (closed since 2010), that provided accommodation for some 400 asylum seekers and refugees. Agustín and Jørgensen (2019, 40) describe City Plaza as an example of autonomous solidarity as it is self-organized, based on horizontal forms of participation and relations of equality, rather than charity or government support, and engages in creating "infrastructures of dissent". The squat's goals included: "to create, on the one hand, a space of safety and dignity in which to house refugees in the center of the city and, on the other, to create a center of struggle against racism, borders, and social exclusion; for the freedom of movement and for the right to stay" (Socialist Project 2019).

In contrast to migrant squatting, "civic solidarity" models (Agustín and Jørgensen 2019, 41) are based on civil society actors organizing with migrant newcomers independent from the state. Examples include more charitable initiatives, such as the Christian-based Sharehaus Refugio in Berlin, to the more entrepreneurial models like the Refugees Welcome international network (Baban and Rygiel 2017). Trampoline House in Copenhagen is an initiative that traverses both housing models and typologies of solidarity, following somewhere in between civic and autonomous typologies of solidarity, or what Siim and Meret (2020a, 4) describe this as a "hybrid" form, combining "the provision of practical support for migrants with transformative activism". Housing initiatives are important here not only for materializing rights to the city but because they provide platforms for linking "home-making in the city" to thinking about "the city as home" (Blunt and Sheringham, 2019, 815).

Trampoline House is an independent and self-governing initiative that operates as both a support center for refugees and asylum seekers and accommodation for newcomers alongside locals. It was formed in 2010 by a group of asylum seekers, artists, students, and professionals in reaction to the Danish government's restrictive asylum policies and punitive approaches to newcomers and to the conditions within asylum centers. Trampoline House's original intention was "to create a reversed space of exception to the camp's space of exception: a reversed space in which asylum seekers would temporarily be re-equipped with their basic civil rights that they are deprived of in the camps" as well as "encourage 'the meeting between Danes and asylum seekers'", thereby "showing to integration authorities that a 'non-profit, user-driven cultural space could function'", and could promote "'integration, learning, and an exchange of knowledge, creating networks and mutual respect'" (Siim and Meret 2020b, 41–42). Today, *Trampoline House* offers many types of activities some of which include: asylum advocacy and support in navigating the system; job training and educational support; developing strategic partnerships with other NGOs, companies etc.; helping newcomers and locals develop social networks with one another; and finally, democratic practice "because active citizenship entails understanding the social contract, your rights and duties and last but not least, the Danish democratic tradition and system" (Trampoline

House. n.d.). As co-founder and Director, Morten Goll further explains, although *Trampoline House* is an organization that assists migrant newcomers with advocacy and accessing their rights to the city, the idea of solidarity differs from providing charity. As Goll explains, "we have expelled, abandoned charity. We have prohibited charity in this house. Because charity sets up a relation of inequality" (Interview with Baban and Rygiel, Copenhagen, March 20, 2018).[5]

In addition to supporting migrant newcomers' rights and daily needs, *Trampoline House* is a grassroots housing project designed to create a space of encounter based on facilitating a politics of connectivity and exchange but one that does not depend on finding common ground so much as it builds connection through what Said (1993) calls "contrapuntality". With respect to the idea of living together, contrapuntality requires "processes of translation, whereby people give up their old selves in order to become something else. That something else comes from encountering others, who are different and who, in return, also become something else, such that what becomes common is something anew to both parties" (Baban and Rygiel 2020, 6). As such, *Trampoline House*'s creation of a living space, is designed to create a space of encounters through which transversal solidarity is built. This includes building relations with people across very different walks of life, different positionalities, and statuses (citizen and newcomer). *Trampoline House*'s co-founder, Tone Olaf Nielsen, explains the thinking behind the project as follows:

> Trampoline House as a concept was developed in collaboration with asylum seekers and migration activists during a series of workshops that Morten, me and another artist organized in 2009. Trampoline House, and our use of the house as a model [and] the family as a model was a way to combine self-empowerment platforms, notions of agency, co-ownership [...] It is really this idea that because people feel that 'this is my house, it is your house, it is our house, we share this space', they are also able to put aside extremist positions and are willing to negotiate, unlearn and de-program. That's my experience here.
>
> Interview with BABAN and RYGIEL, COPENHAGEN, March 20, 2018

This idea described here by Nielsen, of *Trampoline House* as shared space is not one that romanticizes the experiences of living together and the process

---

5   Interviews referred to in this section were conducted as part of a 5-year project funded by the Social Sciences and Humanities Research Council of Canada [435-2015-0140] "Living with others: Fostering cultural pluralism through citizenship politics" (Kim Rygiel and Feyzi Baban).

of building transversal solidarity. Rather, as Nielsen explains, it is by engaging
with others who are different that one is forced to "negotiate, unlearn and de-
program", that is to confront and challenge one's own prejudices through the
process of living together. This includes both locals and newcomers, equally
challenging their prejudices to find new ways of relating to one another. Nielsen
explains that the starting point is by establishing certain "ground rules". In
order to live at the house, one must agree to adhere to the "ground rules" of "No
racism, no sexism, no discriminations of religious, political whatever, no hard
liquor, and no violence" (Interview with Baban and Rygiel, Copenhagen, March
20, 2018). The hope is that over time, and through co-ownership of the space,
that the house becomes a home to locals and newcomers and by providing a
safe space in which to encounter one another and to learn to work through
differences to build relations of solidarity between locals and newcomers that
are supportive of both providing rights to housing beyond the camp, and assist
with other rights to the city such as employment and education, that come
with first having a place in which to safely settle. The hope is that this then
enables newcomers to find a sense, through homemaking, of belonging in the
city, and thinking of the city as home.

3   *Queer Base* in Vienna[6]

Queer Base was founded in 2015, just before the 'long summer of migration', as
a reaction to the increasing number of queer migrants who faced systematic
failures in the asylum system as well as homophobia and transphobia more
broadly (Interview with Ataç, Vienna, September 30, 2020). The organization
was founded in the space of the *Türkis Rosa Lila Villa* which was established
in 1982 as a political and social space for queer activism. *Queer Base* has an
activist background with organic relations to the LGBTIQ movement and
developed an independent organizational structure. The initiative emphasizes
both service delivery as well as advocacy for the rights of queer refugees. They
offer legal counselling, support in processes of social inclusion and 'coming
out', as well as medical and psychological support, provides a system of buddies (Queer Base. n.d.). The support offered also includes the translation of
everyday stories and vulnerabilities into legal claims and the search for shelter
and housing facilities. They also offer a system of buddies who are there "to

6   Interviews referred to in this section were conducted by Ilker Ataç and Sara de Jong as part
    of a collaborative project on refugee organisations in Vienna from 2015–2018. Interviews in
    2020 are conducted by Ilker Ataç.

listen, to be tandem partners [...] Buddies are part of the community who help through sharing their knowledge and abilities" (Queer Base 2020).

In addition, they provide support in finding shelter and housing facilities for queer refugees. On the one hand, they arrange housing for LGBTQI asylum seekers to cover their needs in collaboration with other established service organizations. Housing poses a challenge for LGBTIQ refugees as the heteronormative conditions in the refugee accommodation centers make it difficult to live openly, revealing their sexual and gender identity. In precarious housing situations, the danger is great of being pushed 'back into the closet' again (Interview with Ataç, Vienna, September 30, 2020). On the other hand, they support refugees by searching for affordable housing against the backdrop of increasing rent prices in larger cities such as Vienna. A voluntary subgroup called Housing Buddies supports refugees in their search for affordable housing, helping with applications for community housing or looking for financial means for paying the deposit. By mobilizing resources to include newcomers in different societal fields, these examples show that *Queer Base* contributes towards a civic model of solidarity (Agustín and Jørgensen 2019).

Queer Base creates spaces of encounters between migrants and supporters, in particular those provided by the Türkis Rosa Lilla Villa, which forms the basis for social encounters of care and solidarity and led to the development of strong ties between activists and migrants that crossed borders and enabled new forms of identification and belonging, by becoming part of the queer community (Interview with Ataç, Vienna, September 30, 2020). As one activist highlights, "I don't believe that someone says to Caritas after a consultation or recognition: 'You are my family'. And I think that is the big difference to the established welfare organizations [...], who do not have this aspect of community work, and not the aspect of activism" (ibid). In all interviews (2016, 2018 and 2020), activists from *Queer Base* described how refugees and supporters 'become family', how they themselves feel like 'part of the family'. The metaphor of 'family' is used in the queer movement "to revise the criteria of membership in the family" (Gamson 1995, 396), defining a common identity on the fringe. Queer scholar-activists emphasize the role of collective identities in the construction of new communities and the specific role of emotions and challenges that come with it during protest movements (Jasper 2010).

Queer Base actively creates transversal spaces for encounters and performs extended community work (de Jong and Ataç 2017). By focusing on the specific needs of queer migrants, *Queer Base* responds to an emerging demand and a gap in the provision of existing services. They deal with special needs at the intersection of being a refugee, being queer, and arriving in a new city. As they write on their homepage, they "aim to create intersectional settings in all areas of service. This enables the consideration of specific vulnerabilities and activates participation" (Queer Base, n.d.).

The activists emphasize the racist bias in the asylum procedure and point out that street-level bureaucrats and courts rarely believe the specific experiences of LGBTIQ migrants. To overcome this, they build infrastructures for migrants "to access and participate in queer life in Vienna in whatever way the queer refugees wish for" (Interview with Ataç, Vienna, September 30, 2020). This helps them to ensure their credibility assessment in the asylum procedure. The city makes it possible to "have access to the gay community in comparison to being isolated somewhere in the country [...] For many people, the networks they come across are easier to establish in a queer or, let's say, more friendly environment" (ibid).

Queer Base acts also as a political actor, thinking transversally and contributing to community building by dealing with everyday problems of queer migrants in forms of infrastructure of solidarity (Schilliger 2020). They conduct awareness-raising activities in the community and intervene also in political debates and policymaking by making political claims and protesting for a change in the asylum and border regime. For their work they are well recognized in the LGBTIQ community and beyond (Falch 2020). This mixture of community work and activism, intertwining knowledge, not only offering consulting hours but also organizing community life, constitutes the unique character of *Queer Base.* In this way, *Queer Base* constitutes also an example of autonomous solidarity as they place value on forms of self-organization, horizontal participation and equality between citizens and non-citizens, and produce dissent in the political sphere (Agustín and Jørgensen 2019). As in the example of Hotel City Plaza, they want to serve as a micro-example on how community work can provide a practical alternative to established forms of support.

On their way from a social movement to an established organization, their interaction with the city of Vienna was an important milestone. The organization has been subsidized by the city since 2016, which helped them improve the quality of support; especially housing, mental health, and legal advice is now much more advanced than in the early days of the organization. The funding enables them to remunerate activists for their work and to build an infrastructure which leads to more professionalization. In effect, *Queer Base* has become a more recognized voice in Viennese and in Austrian politics. And yet, are there some pitfalls to such shift toward a professionalized organization? As Nicholls and Uitermark (2016, 32) emphasize, local governments are selective in their relations with NGOs and prioritize those with whom they can build reliable relations: "ignoring questionable groups, driving wedges between good and bad actors, and stigmatizing deviants are normal parts of governing the trenches of urban civil societies" (ibid, 32). Through effective policing, civil society should serve as an extension of the local government and become part of a web of governance "rather than an uncontrollable and tangled site that nourishes multiple resistances" (ibid). Recognizing such danger, *Queer Base* aims to stay independent and reflexive of potential co-optation and the threat of being swallowed by the city and established NGOs, by focusing on the fight for basic rights and actively working against turning into agents that police queer migrants.

Queer Base can be considered not only a case of autonomous and civic solidarity but also one of institutional solidarity, since they connect the civil society arena with the arena of policymaking and intervene for establishing the human rights of queer migrants in the institutions of policy making (Agustín and Jørgensen 2019). They have been recognized and are cooperating with all relevant refugee support organizations, such as Diakonie, Caritas and the social department of the city of Vienna, which has led to a change in perspective on the position of LGBTIQ migrants within these organizations. *Queer Base* started to use this power to develop an impact on institutions, for example by offering training opportunities for organizations involved in the asylum system, such as the federal administrative court, or by engaging in a civil society dialogue with the Ministry of Internal Affairs to raise the quality standards in initial interviews and interpreter training. In doing so, *Queer Base* seeks to foster alliances and networks to challenge exclusionary and fragmented asylum policies that are underwritten by hetero-normative societal norms and aim for a transformation of the state's legal framework and practices towards a more inclusive approach.

4   The *Palermo Charter Process*: From the Sea to the Cities

In Rome in late May 2018, the right-wing Italian government coalition was formed between the League and the Five Star Movement, among whose first orders of business it was to declare Italy's harbors closed for migrants rescued in the Mediterranean Sea. At the same time, in Palermo, a coalition of a different sort came together, composed of migrant rights and community activists, sea rescuers, church groups, NGOs, and members of progressive municipalities.[7]

---

7   Maurice Stierl is a participant in the *Palermo Charter Process* and involved in drafting some of its statements referred to in this section.

Hosted by the mayor Leoluca Orlando, this diverse group gathered to call for the creation of safe harbors and "corridors of solidarity", stretching from the Mediterranean Sea to cities throughout EUrope. Under the collective name *Palermo Charter Process*, inspired by the Charter of Palermo – a manifesto published in 2015 declaring the right to mobility as an inalienable human right – the participants concluded after the first meeting:

> We will enact our disobedience by building a new transnational alliance, an additional counter-pole based on practical solidarity. From the external borders to the inner cities, we see contested spaces and undeterred daily struggles therein. By inventing and multiplying practices of solidarity, we want to intervene, all over Europe and beyond.
>
> ALARM PHONE 2018a

After gathering in the Sicilian capital city, this emergent alliance met again over the following two years in cities that had declared themselves as solidarity or sanctuary cities – Barcelona, Naples, and Bologna – and later online, during the first months of the 'Covid era'.

The central aim of the *Palermo Charter Process* was not per se to invent entirely novel means of intervention but, rather, to strengthen and connect already-existing migrant solidarity networks *from the sea to the cities*, as its slogan went. Since 2015, these networks had multiplied but also become subject to ever-more draconian state measures seeking to delegitimize or even criminalize solidarity and humanitarian engagement. In view of "the racist and authoritarian drift carried by many governments, national parties and movements across Europe" (Alarm Phone 2018b), with right-wing parties and governments gaining more influence on the production of ever-more restrictive migration policies, the *Palermo Charter Process* saw the need to tighten a transnational web of solidarity. Members of this alliance were already concretely involved in solidarity work, including through the assistance of people escaping across the Mediterranean (actors of the civil fleet), the attempt to turn places of disembarkation into 'safe harbors' (progressive Italian municipalities), the production of info-guides and other underground knowledge economies for precarious journeys across EUrope (exemplified by *Welcome2Europe*), the creation of 'welcoming structures' in transit and places of arrival (squat and church shelter projects), the campaigning for quick relocations and evacuations from hotspot and detention camps (such as Seebrücke and German municipalities), as well as through the building of legal support structures in cases of looming detention and deportations.

> We are active in municipalities and church groups, we belong to migrant communities, non-governmental organizations and human rights initiatives, we are lawyers, researchers and activists, we are self-organized and supporters. We all build and spread novel structures of disobedience and solidarity. From sea rescue to solidarity cities, from access to housing to medical care and fair working conditions, from legal counselling to protection against deportation: we prefigure and enact our vision of a society, in which we want to live. And we ask the civil society to join this process: to create corridors, spaces and projects of solidarity, crisscrossing and subverting all internal and external borders of Europe.
>
> ALARM PHONE 2018a

Through the *Palermo Charter Process*, these different actors and political practices were meant to be stitched together more tightly, in order both to counter the increasingly proliferating bordering practices reaching deep into the everyday and to adapt to migratory mobilities to and throughout EUrope.

The aim to reinforce corridors of solidarity was underpinned by a particular conception of solidarity, informed not so much by the intention to shape migratory realities but, instead, to be shaped by them and to build spaces of encounter. The aim to collectively foster "infrastructures of the freedom of movement", rested on the acknowledgement of already-existing webs and structures of migratory solidarity (Stierl 2019). Such solidarity, best conceptualized as "mobile commons" (Papadopoulos and Tsianos 2013) and constituted through an "invisible knowledge of mobility that circulates between people on the move", forms a decisive, even if commonly under-acknowledged, factor in unauthorized migration. Instead of simply demanding that "migrants out to be escorted by us to safety", the emphasis in the *Palermo Charter Process* was thus placed on 'mobile commoning' – supporting and enlarging existing migratory and solidarity infrastructures 'along the way'. Though related to the autonomous, civic, and institutional types of solidarity outlined by Agustín and Jørgensen (2019), mobile commoning thus engenders a practice of transversal solidarity that is cognizant of the many migratory infrastructures of solidarity 'beyond (public) recognition' and which manifest on different scales.

Adapting to migratory realities means viewing urban spaces as pivotal for unauthorized migration projects but not necessarily as static spaces of arrival and settlement. Rather, they often form transitory hubs of encounter where those passing through can find temporary shelter and places of rest, hiding, anonymity, (re-)orientation, knowledge exchanges, and possibly new identities. While, certainly, such "erratic presence of migrants" (Tazzioli 2015, 10) is considerably impacted by the geographical conditions inscribed in EUropean migration policies, such as the Dublin regulation, as well as by neoliberal market forces, it is also the expression of migratory dynamics that exceed governmental regulation. Indeed, the desire to reunite with families and friends, to join diasporas, or to find particular linguistic and cultural environments are often crucial factors in movements that continue to zigzag throughout EUrope without authorization. Adapting to, and being shaped by, migratory realities mean, moreover, acknowledging what Asef Bayat (2010, 15) has termed migratory 'encroachment', the ways in which urban spaces are shaped by assertions of "physical, social and cultural presence in the host societies".

Instead of reducing expressions of solidarity to acts of welcoming 'others' into 'one's city', the practice of mobile commoning recognizes these assertions through which migrant mobility and presence continuously shape "distinct urban spaces", even create "the migrant metropolis [through] the disruptive and incorrigible force of migrant struggles that dislocate borders and instigate a rescaling of border struggles as urban struggles" (De Genova 2015, 3). And rather than downplaying the ability of these constitutive migratory struggles to "make and open up spaces (of livability, of refuge, etc.) and generate unusual collective formations" (Tazzioli 2020, 2), the *Palermo Charter Process'* conception of solidarity was tied to a practice of strengthening, rather than streamlining, infrastructures of disobedient migrant mobility (Heller, et al. 2019). Whether the creation of such transversal solidarities has been successful or not, is difficult to estimate at this stage. What can be said for certain is that the many exchanges between actors struggling in distinct spaces, including at sea, places of disembarkation and in urban centers, and on different scales, including at grassroots and institutional levels, have connected actors present along migratory pathways to build and strengthen forms of solidarity and encounter 'along the way'.

5   Building Transversal Solidarities in and across EUropean Cities

EUropean domopolitics operates by governing movements "in the name of a particular conception of home" (Walters 2004, 241). Through the "fateful conjunction of home, land and security" (241), governments have securitized borders and societies, often with disastrous consequences for those considered as not rightfully belonging. Above, we have explored initiatives that also appeal to ideas around home, whether through the open and welcoming house, shelter, or harbors. *Trampoline House, Queer Base* and the *Palermo Charter Process* are each unique examples of solidarity initiatives, located across EUrope in different city-spaces, and beyond.

Focusing on homemaking in the city and/or the turning of the city into a home, they enact a different understanding of "domo"-politics, one that similarly appeals to "powerful affinities with family, intimacy, place" (Walters 2004, 241) but in ways that undermine the domopolitical rationality of governing through securitization by enclosure and the perpetuation of a hostile environment for 'others.' Rather, in these counter-mobilizations, the appeal is of transversal nature, calling to open up home, city, and EUropean space to others and to creating more inclusive spatial concepts such as "mobile commons" and "corridors of solidarity". In these migrant solidarity initiatives, welcoming newcomers through 'home-making' in the city is a way of opening spaces to newcomers – spaces which have the potential to be places in which to build transversal solidarities. They enact such solidarities in the city in several ways.

First, they illustrate *a commitment to building transversal politics by transgressing ontological borders, based on bringing together people across positionalities and hierarchies.* In the case of *Trampoline House*, this can be bringing locals and migrant newcomers together with individuals who are positioned differently within the city of Copenhagen not only due to status of being newly arrived and long-term residents – migrant newcomers or local Danish citizens – but also because of their various intersectionalities such as gender, class, race, and sexuality. *Trampoline House* then provides a space of encounter in which to work through learning about these differences and challenging the limits that come with understanding other people who are different by committing to a common struggle for improved migrants' rights to the city.

For *Queer Base*, the organization approaches the multiple difficulties facing queer refugees in the asylum procedure, in their experiences of homophobia and racism in everyday life, as well as in the overpriced housing market of a larger city by combining system critique with a response to newcomers' needs. They create spaces for encounters and focus on community work, which enables the consideration of specific vulnerabilities and activates participation. Through extending the idea of family in a community with activist background, migrant and non-migrant queer persons interact towards transgressing forms of solidarity by sharing joy, life, troubles, and political activism.

Finally, in the case of the *Palermo Charter Process*, the emphasis is placed on building and strengthening urban infrastructures for the freedom of movement that enable encounters between locals and those who might want to stay only for a short while and move on. Instead of viewing such initiative simply as bringing (or even integrating) others into one's home and building a collective identity, the activists understood that transgressing ontological borders would also mean accepting the divergent realities and positionalities of those encountering one another. For many migrant newcomers, homemaking does not begin in the first urban space they reach, even if they encounter those who are willing to welcome them. Frequently it means moving on disobediently to reach those – often relatives, communities, friends – who signify home, regardless of where they reside.

Second, *the examples are reflective of building solidarity networks that are politically transgressive of typologies of civic, institutional and autonomous forms of solidarity.* In the case of *Trampoline House*, from one perspective, the organization provides a form of civic solidarity, organized by a civil society organization that seeks to assist migrant newcomers with rights related to asylum but also rights to the city such as finding a job or job training. However, *Trampoline House* is more than this for it also provides a space that is potentially transformative of the very way people think and understand one another, not by eradicating differences but by living with and learning from them.

In the case of *Queer Base,* the organization contributes to all three different forms of solidarity outlined by Agustín and Jørgensen (2019). They contribute to civic solidarity by mobilizing resources to include newcomers and developing an active framework based on collaboration with authorities such as municipalities and established welfare organizations. They contribute to autonomous solidarity by placing great value on forms of self-organization, horizontal forms of participation and equality between citizens and noncitizens as well as producing dissent in the societal sphere. As in the example of Hotel City Plaza, they want to serve as a micro-example on how community work can provide a practical alternative to established forms of housing. Finally, they foster institutional solidarity by connecting the civil society arena with one of policymaking and by and by intervening for the establishment of human rights of queer refugees in the institutions of the state. Through these actions, they aim for a transformation of the state's legal framework and practices towards a more inclusive approach.

Finally, regarding the *Palermo Charter Process*, the often-unrecognized solidarity that is expressed through mobile commoning, that is the way in which unauthorized migration is often realized through the support among those on the move, is considered central. Being politically transgressive means acknowledging, and seeking to support, the migratory underground railroads without which migratory transgressions of violent borders would often not materialize in the first place.

Third, *the examples are reflective of building solidarity networks that are transgressive of territorial borders, political spaces and scales of governing.* In this sense they challenge domopolitics by creating transversal solidarities that also work to 'reconfigure relations between citizenship, state, and territory' by building networks that transgress and link up people and places from the home to the city to building networks between cities, and sea and across EUropean spaces. In the case of *Trampoline House*, the organization's model challenges distinctions between civil societies operating more in the public space of the city with the idea of the private spaces of the home. As Blunt and Sheringham (2019, 817) note, the focus on "home-city geographies" enables us to challenge the distinction that feminist scholars have noted privileges public space as the space of citizenship and political activism, drawing attention to the ways in which politics and political activism also draws from more interior spaces of home and homemaking. Moreover, as these scholars note, "The widely held discursive separation between 'city life' and 'home life' rested upon the distinction between the public and the private which was a defining feature of understandings of home in western bourgeois societies". *Trampoline House* challenges this distinction between public and private space not only in defining the space of politics and who can be political but also the definition of home, offering a type of platform that at once provides home but also a platform for newcomer rights within the city but also beyond at the national and EUropean levels calling for more just asylum processes and rights to movement across EUropean spaces.

In contrast, *Queer Base* provides safe spaces for sexual expression in antiracist settings. By identifying gaps in existing service provision, providing spaces of encounters, and developing a political critique, they act in through different scales. Through this, they challenge explicitly the way border regimes channel migrants into 'bare life' and build relations between community, city, and activist networks.

Finally, in the case of the *Palermo Charter Process*, the building of corridors of solidarity 'from the sea to the cities' was understood as a political necessity to counteract EUropean forms of domopolitical governance which has connected seemingly unconnected spaces and scales. EUropean interventions in third countries to halt transiting migrants, systematic interception, and pushback operations at sea, as well as the detention and deportation of those who have reached EUrope's nominal space have meant that migration governance has reached both deeply outward and inward. The *Palermo Charter Process* thus sought to foster relationalities between the Mediterranean Sea, spaces of migrant arrival along EUropean coasts, and urban centers, conscious that transversal solidarity would be required to both struggle against EUrope's diffused border regime and to assist migratory dynamics that often 'make the road while walking' instead of following prescribed paths.

However, as noted earlier, while these examples offer the hope for creating transversal solidarities, the enactments of solidarity are ultimately experimental and "without guarantees" (Featherstone 2012, 244). Given the very real inequities and violence of city spaces, such initiatives also face obstacles and structural constraints. These limits include a lack of resources to be able to self-organize, with some financial (and other) independence from more institutionalized actors, such as governments at the municipal, national and federal levels. When city governments and other established welfare organizations are involved, they may define the boundaries of autonomy within which such civil society actors and initiatives operate. Moreover, because these are small-scale interventions, which create changes and opportunities for better life in an organizational context, their transformative political intervention on a larger scale is always precarious. The capacities of these organizations are limited and therefore they can offer services only for a limited number of migrants with precarious status. This leads to the question whether these organizations act selectively under the conditions of scarce resources. For the cases of *Trampoline House* and *Queer Base*, building of transversal solidarities through networks and spaces of encounters work much more effectively at the small scale and in ways that try to circumvent the more restrictive migration and asylum policies at the national and EU levels.

6   Conclusion

In this article, we have explored three very different migrant solidarity initiatives – *Trampoline House, Queer Base,* and the *Palermo Charter Process* – taking place across, and in resistance to, EUropean spaces and the EUropean border regime. We have sought to tease out how ideas around transversal solidarity are understood within each of these initiatives, noting some of the ways in which by linking ideas around, home, shelter, harbor in, through and beyond the city, these initiatives build spaces of encounters, in which transversal solidarities are forged. We have also pointed to some of the very real limitations of such initiatives, in part because of the scale and the need for resources. Yet, integral to our focus, here, is the putting of seemingly disparate examples into conversation with one another to press us to think transversally about the motivations and spaces in which these initiatives operate.

In her work on "transversal alliances and the temporality of solidarity", Tazzioli (2020, 143) has pointed out that thinking about transversal solidarity frequently focuses on the spatial dimension, such as how "social movements and solidarity practices have travelled across spaces". This focus on space, which has admittedly also been much of our focus here, leaves the temporal dimensions of migrant struggles under-theorized. The result is that more attention is paid to "hearable claims and punctual moments of bodily exposure and irruption in the public spaces", which "get center stage in these analyses". This diverts attention from quieter spaces and forms of struggle. Our approach employed here of "home-city" geographies, addresses in part Tazzioli's concerns, in that it enables us to connect forms of solidarity across different types of spaces, linking smaller and quieter struggles in the space of the home to more public spaces of activism in the city and beyond. Yet, Tazzioli also prompts us to think about temporal aspects in that they enable us to understand individual struggles within a much broader context in connection to past and future histories of struggles to which they contribute. She notes that migrant struggles are not just about the visible and present struggle but are also about "a sedimentation of practical knowledges and memory of the struggles that have been reactivated in the present in support of the migrants in transit" (Tazzioli 2020, 143, 148). In this sense, while the examples discussed in this article may be smaller and more local in scale, their impact is much larger if we consider this temporal dimension, seeing the connection between individual initiatives to this larger history of struggle and the ways in which they, too, are part of the creation of corridors of solidarity, building collective memory through 'a sedimentation of knowledge', and the sharing of practical experiences and know-how of moving and navigating through, as well as contesting, EUropean domopolitics.

When viewed together, the examples that we have highlighted in this article challenge EUrope's domopolitics by creating solidarities that work to 'reconfigure relations between citizenship, state, and territory' by building networks that transgress and link up people and places from the home to the city to building networks between cities, the sea and across EUropean spaces. Putting these seemingly disparate examples into conversation with one another presses us to think transversally about the motivations and spaces in which these initiatives operate. They offer a glimpse into what could be conceived as a counter-politics to EUropean domopolitics, thus transversal solidarities that are built around the concept of home but where home constitutes a space and relation that facilitates encounters, not separations

Acknowledgements

We would like to thank the reviewers and the editors, Martin Bak Jørgensen and Carl-Ulrik Schierup for their comments on an earlier version of this article. Maurice Stierl would also like to thank the Leverhulme Trust. Kim Rygiel would like to thank her coinvestigator, Feyzi Baban, and the Social Sciences and Humanities Research Council of Canada for their support on the "Living with others" project, research from which informs part of this article.

References

Aalbers, M. (2016) *The Financialization of Housing: A Political Economy Approach*. London and New York: Routledge.

Agustín, Ó.G., and M.B. Jørgensen (2019). *Solidarity and the Refugee Crisis in Europe*. Basingstoke: Palgrave Macmillan.

Alarm Phone (2018a). "Toward a Coalition of Solidarity". Retrieved November 18, 2020 from: https://alarmphone.org/en/2018/06/17/toward-a-coalition-of-solidarity-for-the-right-to-mobility-and-equal-rights-for-all/.

Alarm Phone (2018b). "Call for Safe and Open Harbours!". Retrieved November 18, 2020 from: https://alarmphone.org/en/2018/06/17/call-for-safe-and-open-harbours/.

Ataç I., and S. Rosenberger (2019). "Social Policies as a Tool of Migration Control". *Journal of Immigrant and Refugee Studies* 17 (1): 1–10. DOI: 10.1080/15562948.2018.1539802.

Ataç I., K. Rygiel, and M. Stierl (2016). "Introduction: The contentious politics of refugee and migrant protest and solidarity movements: remaking citizenship from the margins". *Citizenship Studies* 20 (5): 527–544.

Baban F., and K. Rygiel (eds.) (2020). *Fostering Pluralism through Solidarity Activism in Europe: Everyday Encounters with Newcomers*. Basingstoke: Palgrave Macmillan.

Baban F., and K. Rygiel (2017). "Living with others: fostering radical cosmopolitanism through citizenship politics in Berlin". *Ethics & Global Politics* 10 (1): 98–116.

Balakrishnan R., J. Heintz, and D. Elson (2016). *Rethinking Economic Policy for Social Justice: The radical potential of human rights*. London and New York: Routledge.

Bauder, H. (2021). "Urban Solidarity: Perspectives of Migration and Refugee Accommodation and Inclusion". *Critical Sociology*. 47(6): 875–889. DOI: 10.1177/0896920520936332.

Bauder, H. (2019). "Migrant solidarities and the politics of place". *Progresses in Human Geography* 1: 1–15.

Bayat, A. (2010). *Life as Politics*. Amsterdam: Amsterdam University Press.

Blunt, A., and O. Sheringham (2019). "Home-city geographies: urban dwelling and mobility". *Progress in Human Geography* 43 (95):815–834.

Caldeira, T. (1999). "Fortified Enclaves: The New Urban Segregation". In: Holston, J. (ed) *Cities and Citizenship*. Durham and London: Duke University Press: 115–138.

Crawley, H., and D. Skleparis (2018). "Refugees, migrants, neither, both: categorical fetishism and the politics of bounding in Europe's 'migration crisis'". *Journal of Ethnic and Migration Studies*, 44 (1): 48–64, DOI: 10.1080/1369183X.2017.1348224.

Dadusc, D., M. Grazioli, and M.A. Martínez (2019). "Introduction: Citizenship as Inhabitance? Migrant Housing Squats Versus Institutional Accommodation". *Citizenship Studies* 23 (6): 521–539.

Darling, J., and H. Bauder (eds.) (2019). *Sanctuary cities and urban struggles: Rescaling migration, citizenship, and rights*. Manchester: Manchester University Press.

De Genova, N. (2015). "Border Struggles in the Migrant Metropolis". *Nordic Journal of Migration Research* 5 (1): 3–10.

De Genova, N. (ed.) (2017). *The Borders of 'EUrope': Autonomy of Migration, Tactics of Bordering*. Durham and London: Duke University Press.

de Jong, S., and I. Ataç (2017). "Demand and Deliver: Refugee Support Organisations in Austria". *Social Inclusion* 5 (3): 28–37. DOI: 10.17645/si.v5i3.1003.

della Porta, D. (ed) (2018). *Solidarity Mobilizations in the 'Refugee Crisis': Contentious Moves*. Cham, Switzerland: Palgrave MacMillan.

della Porta, D., and E. Steinhilper (2020). "Introduction: Solidarities in Motion: Hybridity and Change in Migrant Support Practices". *Critical Sociology*. August 26, 1–11 Online first; https://journals.sagepub.com/doi/10.1177/0896920520952143.

Duarte, M. (2020). "The Ethical Consequences of Criminalizing Solidarity in the EU". *Theoria* 86: 28–53.

European Commission (2020). "COVID-19: Temporary Restriction on Non-Essential Travel to the EU". Retrieved September 7, 2020 from: https://eur-lex.europa.eu/legal-content/EN/TXT/HTML/?uri=CELEX:52020DC0115&from=EN.

European Union (2012). "Consolidated version of the treaty on European Union". Retrieved November 15, 2020 from: https://eur-lex.europa.eu/resource.html?uri=cellar:2bf140bf-a3f8-4ab2-b506-fd71826e6da6.0023.02/DOC_1&format=PDF.

Falch, B. (2020).*Queer Refugees. Sexuelle Identität und repressive Heteronormativität als Fluchtgrund*. Wiesbaden: Springer vs.

Farhani, L. (No Date). "UN Special Rapporteur on the Right to Housing". Retrieved November 5, 2020 from: http://www.unhousingrapp.org/.

Fassin, D. (2013). *Enforcing Order: An Ethnography of Urban Policing*. Oxford: Polity.

Featherstone, D. (2012). *Solidarity: Hidden Histories and Geographies of Internationalism*. London: Zed Books.

Fontanari, E. (2019). *Lives in Transit*. London: Routledge.

Gamson, J. (1995). "Must Identity Movements Self-Destruct? A Queer Dilemma". *Social Problems* 42: 390–407.

Hathaway, J.C., and T. Gammeltoft-Hansen (2015). "Non-Refoulement in a World of Cooperative Deterrence". *Columbia Journal of Transnational Law* 53 (2): 235–284.

Hamlin, R. (2012). "Illegal Refugees: Competing Policy Ideas and the Rise of the Regime of Deterrence in American Asylum Politics". *Refugee Survey Quarterly* 31 (2): 33–53.

Heller, C., L. Pezzani, and M. Stierl (2019). "Toward a Politics of Freedom of Movement". In.

Holston, J. (2009). "Insurgent Citizenship in an Era of Global Urban Peripheries". *City & Society* 21 (2): 245–267.

Isin, E.F. (2002). *Being Political: Genealogies of Citizenship*. Minneapolis: University of Minnesota Press.

Isin, E.F. (ed.) (2000). *Democracy, citizenship and the global city*. Abingdon, Oxon and New York: Routledge.

Jasper, J.M. (2010). "Social Movement Theory Today: Toward a Theory of Action?". *Sociology Compass* 4 (11): 965–976. DOI: 10.1111/j.1751-9020.2010.00329.x.

Karakayali, S., and J.O. Kleist (2016). "Volunteers and asylum seekers". *Forced Migration Review* 51: January. https://www.fmreview.org/destination-europe/karakayali-kleist.

Kasparek, B., and M. Speer (2015). "Of Hope. Hungary and the Long Summer of Migration". Translation by Elena Buck. *Border Monitoring*. http://bordermonitoring.eu/ungarn/2015/09/of-hope-en/.

Kipfer, S. (2009). "Why the urban question still matters: Reflections on rescaling and the promise of the urban". In: Keil, R. and Mahon, R. (eds.) *Leviathan undone? Towards a political economy of scale*. Vancouver: UBC Press: 67–86.

Kirchhoff, M. (2020). "Differential solidarity: protests against deportations as structured contestations over citizenship". *Citizenship Studies* 24 (4): 568–586.

Kron, S., and H. Lebruhn (2020). "Building Solidarity Cities: From Protest to Policy". In: Baban, F., and Rygiel K. (eds.) *Fostering Pluralism through Solidarity Activism in Europe: Everyday Encounters with Newcomers*. Basingstoke: Palgrave Macmillan: 81–106.

Lefebvre, H. (2009). *Le droit à la ville*. 3e édition. Paris: Economica/Anthropos.

Martin, D., and B. Miller (2003). "Space as Contentious Politics". *Mobilization: An International Journal* 8 (2): 135–156.

Mayer, M. (2013). "First world urban activism: Beyond austerity urbanism and creative city politics". *City* 1 (1): 5–19, DOI: 10.1080/13604813.2013.757417.

Mezzadra, S. (2018). "In the Wake of the Greek Spring and the Summer of Migration". *South Atlantic Quarterly* 117 (4): 925–933.

Misra, T. (2017). "We have to be careful not to romanticize cities". *City-Lab*, October 24. Retrieved November 15, 2020, from https://www.citylab.com/equity/2017/10/we-have-to-be-careful-not-to-romanticize-cities/543789.

Mitchell, D. (2003). *The Right to the City: Social Justice and the Fight for Public Space*. New York: Guilford.

Mudu, P., and S. Chattopadhyay (2016). *Migration, Squatting and Radical Autonomy*. New York: Routledge.

Nicholls, W.J., and J. Uitermark (2016). *Cities and social movements: Immigrant rights activism in the US, France, and the Netherlands, 1970–2015*. Chichester: Wiley Blackwell.

OECD (2020). *Social Policy Division – Directorate of Employment, Labour and Social Affairs*. https://www.oecd.org/els/family/HC3-1-Homeless-population.pdf.

Oosterlynck, S., N. Schuermans, and M. Loopmans (2017). "Beyond social capital: Place, diversity and solidarity". In: Oosterlynck, S., Schuermans N., and Loopmans M. (eds.) *Place, Diversity and Solidarity*. Abingdon: Routledge:1–18.

Paik, A.N., J. Ruiz, and R. Schreiber (2019). *Radical Histories of Sanctuary*. Durham: Duke University Press.

Papadopoulos, D., and V. Tsianos (2013). "After citizenship: autonomy of migration, organisational ontology and mobile commons". *Citizenship Studies* 17 (2): 178–196.

Pezzani, L. (2020). "Hostile environments". *E-Flux*. Retrieved August 28, 2020 from: https://www.e-flux.com/architecture/at-the-border/325761/hostile-environments/.

Purcell, M. (2014). "Possible Worlds: Henri Lefebvre and the Right to the City". *Journal of Urban Affairs* 36 (1): 141–154.

Queer Base (2020). "Buddy" Retrieved November 13, 2020 from: https://queerbase.at/buddy/.

Queer Base (n,d.). Retrieved November 13, 2020 from: https://queerbase.at/.

Raimondi, V. (2019). "For 'Common Struggles of Migrants and Locals'. Migrant Activism and Squatting in Athens". *Citizenship Studies* 23 (6): 559–576.

Rolnik, R. (2019). *Urban Warfare: Housing under the Empire of Finance*. London: Verso.

Rose, D. (2016). "Affordable Housing for Refugees is a Major Challenge". *Policy Options*, 20 May. Retrieved December 6, 2019 from: https://policyoptions.irpp.org/magazines/may-2016/affordable-housing-for-refugees-is-a-major-challenge/.

Rosenberger, S., V. Stern, and N. Merhaut (eds.) (2018). *Protest Movements in Asylum and Deportation*. Cham, Switzerland: Springer.

Said, E. (1993). *Culture and Imperialism*. New York: Knopf.

Sandercock, L. (2004). *Cosmopolis II: Mongrel Cities*. London: Continuum.

Schack, L., and A. Witcher (2020). "Hostile hospitality and the criminalization of civil society actors aiding border crossers in Greece". *Environment and Planning D: Society and Space*. Online first 20 September. https://doi.org/10.1177/0263775820958709.

Schilliger, S. (2020). "Challenging Who Counts as a Citizen. The Infrastructure of Solidarity Contesting Racial Profiling in Switzerland". *Citizenship Studies* 24 (4): 530–547.

Schwarz, N., and M. Stierl (2019). "Amplifying Migrant Voices and Struggles at Sea as a Radical Practice". *South Atlantic Quarterly* 118 (3): 661–669.

Schwiertz, H., and H. Schwenken (2020). "Introduction: inclusive solidarity and citizenshipalong migratory routes in Europe and the Americas". *Citizenship Studies* 24 (4): 405–423.

Siim, B., A. Saarinen, and A. Krasteva (eds.) (2018). *Citizens' Activism and Solidarity Movements: Contending with Populism*. Basingstoke: Palgrave MacMillan.

Siim, B., and S. Meret (2020a). "Migrant Resistance in Copenhagen and Berlin". *Critical Sociology*. Online first: 28 July: https://doi.org/10.1177/0896920520944517.

Siim, B., and S. Meret (2020b). "The Politics and Art of Solidarity: The Case of Trampoline House in Copenhagen". In: Baban, F., and Rygiel K. (eds.) *Fostering Pluralism through Solidarity Activism in Europe: Everyday Encounters with Newcomers.* Basingstoke: Palgrave Macmillan: 31–58.

Skop, E. (2006). "Introduction – Urban Space: The Shape of Inequality". *Urban Geography* 27 (5): 393–396.

Socialist Project (2019). "Greece: 39 Months at City Plaza for Refugees Ends". July 15. *Socialist Project.* https://socialistproject.ca/2019/07/greece-39-months-city-plaza/.

Squire, V. (2018). "Mobile solidarities and precariousness at City Plaza: Beyond Vulnerable and Disposable Lives". *Studies in Social Justice* 12 (1): 111–132.

Staeheli, L.A. (2003). "Cities and Citizenship". *Urban Geography* 24 (2): 97–102.

Stierl, M. (2019). *Migrant Resistance in Contemporary Europe.* London: Routledge.

Stierl, M. (2018). "A Fleet of Mediterranean Border Humanitarians". *Antipode* 50 (3): 704–724.

Taylor, A. (2018). "'Crimes of Solidarity': France's contemporary crisis of hospitality". In Maazaoui, A. (ed.) *Making Strangers: Outsiders, Aliens and Foreigners.* Delaware and Malaga: Vernon Press: 39–53.

Tazzioli, M. (2020). "What is left of migrants' spaces?: Transversal alliances and the temporality of solidarity". *Political Anthropology Research on International Social Sciences* 1: 137–161.

Tazzioli, M. (2018). "Crimes of solidarity: Migration and containment through rescue". *Radical Philosophy* 2 (1). Retrieved June 23, 2021 from: https://www.radicalphiloso phy.com/commentary/crimes-of-solidarity.

Tazzioli, M. (2015). "Which Europe? Migrants' Uneven Geographies and Counter-mapping at the Limits of Representation". *movements. Journal for Critical Migration and Border Regime Studies* 1 (2): Retrieved June 23, 2021 from:https://movements -journal.org/issues/02.kaempfe/04.tazzioli--europe-migrants-geographies-coun ter-mapping-representation.html.

Trampoline House. (n.d.). "About Trampoline House". Retrieved November 12, 2020 from: https://www.trampolinehouse.dk/about-trampoline-house.

UN Human Rights Council (2017). *Report of the Special Rapporteur on adequate housing as a component of the right to an adequate standard of living, and on the right to non-discrimination in this context.* Human Rights Council Thirty-fourth session, Agenda item 3 (A/HRC/34/51), 27 February-24 March.

UNHCR (n.d.). "Figures at a Glance". Retrieved November 12, 2020 from: https://www .unhcr.org/figures-at-a-glance.html.

Walter, W. (2004). "Secure borders, safe haven, domopolitics". *Citizenship Studies* 8 (3): 237–260, DOI: 10.1080/1362102042000256989.

Wirth, L. (1995). "Urbanism as a Way of Life". In Kasinitz, P. (ed.) *Metropolis.* New York: NYU Press: 156–172.

World Health Organization (2020). "Updated WHO recommendations for international traffic in relation to COVID-19 outbreak". Retrieved from September 10, 2020 from: https://www.who.int/news-room/articles-detail/updated-who-recommendations -for-international-traffic-in-relation-to-covid-19-outbreak.

Zetter, R. (2007). "More Labels, Fewer Refugees: Remaking the Refugee Label in an Era of Globalization". *Journal of Refugee Studies* 20 (2): 172–192.

CHAPTER 14

Civil Society Organizations Engaged with Illegalized Migrants in Bern and Vienna

Co-production of Urban Citizenship

Ilker Ataç and Sarah Schilliger

In recent years, several studies have shown that, within Europe, innovative approaches towards migration emerge at the local level against the back-drop of increasingly restrictive and polarizing national and EU immigration policies (Agustín and Jørgensen 2019; Ataç, et al. 2020; Bauder 2019; Darling 2017; Spencer and Delvino 2019). The political space of the city has thereby become a "dynamic battleground" (Hajer and Ambrosini 2020) and a field of experimentation not only around the future of migration regimes but also for a fundamental democratization of urban life in the sense of a general right to the city for all. Looking at this 'local turn' specifically in the field of illegalized migration, we observe a growing activism by both municipalities and local civil society actors calling for the inclusion of migrants without legal status in public service provision, for formal rights protections, and for democratic participation.

Various comparative studies indicate that policies and practices of solidarity towards illegalized migrants vary greatly, depending not only on place-particular circumstances and factors such as national and regional legal frameworks; varying institutional competences of cities; the constellation of political parties in power; the ethnic diversity of the electorate; as well as the financial wealth of the municipality but also on the presence and strength of civil society actors (Ataç, et al. 2020; Bauder 2021; De Graauw 2016; Kaufmann and Strebel 2019; Kron and Lebuhn 2020). In recent years, several researchers (such as Kreichauf and Mayer 2021; Lambert and Swerts 2019; Hajer and Ambrosini 2020; de Graauw 2021; Holm and Lebuhn 2020) have identified civil society actors as crucial in improving the precarious situation of illegalized migrants. Nevertheless, there is often little investigation and theorizing about the variety of civil society actors engaged in urban citizenship practices and their interplay with formal politics and municipal bureaucracies.

We argue that, for a more nuanced understanding of urban citizenship, we must take a closer look at the role of CSOs in urban contexts in relation to the provision of inclusionary services for illegalized migrants and the construction of urban infrastructures of solidarity. Drawing on empirical data from two cities (Vienna and Bern), we therefore engage in an in-depth analysis of the variety of actors co-producing and negotiating local welfare arrangements for illegalized migrants within urban settings. We thereby examine the organizational structures and practices of CSOs who support illegalized migrants and how they differ in their relation towards the city and urban authorities. To do so, we use Agustín and Jørgensen's (2019) typology of three types of solidarity (institutional solidarity, civic solidarity, and autonomous solidarity) and refine it in relation to CSOs in the field of illegalized migration.

The article proceeds as follows: We first present our theoretical framework (2.) and our methodological approach as well as the context of our empirical fields (3.). We then analyze the practices of multiple CSOs working with illegalized migrants and highlight some commonalities and challenges they face on the ground (4.). To draw a more precise picture of the landscape of CSOs in this field, we differentiate between three types of CSOs and discuss their organizational structures and their relations to municipal authorities (5.). In the concluding section, we summarize the results and discuss the relevance of our empirical findings for debates on urban citizenship (6.).

1   Theoretical Framework

To elucidate the role of civil society actors in urban contexts, we refer to the theoretical debates around urban citizenship. The concept of urban citizenship highlights the socio-spatial dimension of solidarity and conceives the city "as both a context for struggles over citizenship, and a political actor to whom, and for whom, claims are made" (Darling 2017, 719). Its focus is on the engagement at the municipal level regarding the inclusion of migrants and the capacity of cities to challenge restrictive national citizenship regimes. One common characteristic of urban citizenship policies and practices is that access to rights and resources is derived from 'presence' (place of residence) rather than 'legality' (national immigration status). By linking membership in the urban community to being an inhabitant of the city, citizenship is derived from a relational perspective and is seen not only as a legal status but also as "a social process through which individuals and social groups engage in claiming, expanding and losing rights" (Isin and Turner 2002, 4).

Accordingly, not only institutional actors but also a multiplicity of civil society actors are involved in the negotiation and realization of urban citizenship practices. The civil society category includes a broad spectrum of bodies, ranging from formal, pro-migrant NGOs to religious institutions, trade unions, migrant organizations, grassroots initiatives, and antiracist/urban social move-ments. Local CSOs not only represent migrants' collective interests and engage in political advocacy but they also establish offers of support and legal advice centers, provide expertise to city governments, create safe spaces, and develop relations of care and "transversal solidarities" (Ataç, et. al. 2021; Bauder 2021).

Scholars identify different urban citizenship practices in relation to the situation of illegalized migrants by both municipal actors as well as urban civil society organizations (Holm and Lebuhn 2020; Bauder 2019; Darling and Squire 2012; Delvino and Spencer 2019):

The *first* way of fostering urban citizenship includes initiatives and policy innovations of municipal governments and administrations to respond to the needs of people with irregular status. Through this "municipal activism on irregular migration" (Spencer and Delvino 2019), municipalities set up parallel structures to provide illegalized migrants with access to healthcare, or they treat people with precarious status as equal to co-inhabitants of the city and give them full access to local welfare services and/or subsidies (ibid; Schweitzer 2019). In some cases, cities issue municipal ID cards that allow illegalized migrants to identify themselves to frontline city officials, the police and other important local actors (de Graauw 2016; Kaufmann and Strebel 2020). More often, cities use their room to maneuver for modifying and weakening control strategies (Delvino and Spencer 2019; Schilliger 2019) or refuse to fully trans-late national requirements into official actions (Bauder 2019; de Graauw 2021). While some local authorities avoid political conflicts by keeping visibility of their pro-migrant actions low, other city officials go on the offensive and claim to be a "solidarity city" (Kreichauf and Mayer 2021; Kron and Lebuhn 2020).

A *second* way of expanding urban citizenship are those processes through which urban social movements and migrant's rights organizations claim from urban governments and administrations the expansion of social rights for ille-galized migrants. In most cases, the engagement of municipalities in inclusive policies towards illegalized migrants is initiated and claimed from the bottom up by civil society actors (including illegalized migrants themselves). In fact, inclusive migration policies in many cases "are put onto cities' agendas only by social movement actors and through strong bottom-up mobilizations" (Kron and Lebuhn 2020, 92; also Nyers 2019; Bauder 2021; Schilliger 2019; Nicholls and Uitermark 2016).

Not all CSO's strategies and initiatives are directed towards city administra-tions and legal frameworks, and not all are visible "acts of solidarity" (Schwiertz and Schwenken 2020, 407). As a *third* way of fostering urban citizenship, we identify CSOs engaged in organising practical support to realize the basic rights of illegalized migrants (Holm and Lebuhn 2020, 82). These practices by

CSOs furthermore create opportunities for everyday encounters and relations of solidarity that are crucial for navigating life as an illegalized migrant within the city (Darling and Squire 2012, 191; Ataç, et. al. 2021; Hajer and Ambrosini 2020). These kinds of urban citizenship practices can be captured with the concept of "urban infrastructures of solidarity" (Schilliger 2020), which encompasses "solidarity work and alliance-building, the creation of (counter-) spaces on different scales, the production and sharing of (counter-)knowledge, and the formation of social relations of solidarity and mutual care" (ibid, 532). Infrastructures of solidarity are to be understood as a process through which practices may become sedimented in time and space and by which "ties are built between groups of people that are structurally located in very distinct social positions" (ibid.), such as between supporters with a legal status and illegalized, often racialized, migrants.

Based on this description of the three different ways of "strengthening urban citizenship" (Holm and Lebuhn 2020), we would like to emphasize that a simplistic dichotomization between urban citizenship 'from above' (by municipal governments) and 'from below' (by urban civil society actors/movements) is not helpful. On the contrary, various empirical studies on solidarity cities show that a successful expansion of urban citizenship is rather achieved through a (cooperative as well as conflictive) interplay between the city administration and the manifold civil society organizations (Christoph and Kron 2019; Agustín and Jørgensen 2019; Lambert and Swerts 2019; de Graauw 2016; Kreichauf and Mayer 2021; Holm and Lebuhn 2020). This requires a more process-oriented and relational perspective in which the different solidarity practices and actors are not analyzed in isolation but rather in their complex interplay. Inspired by the relational field approach by Bourdieu (1989), who avoids a dichotomous distinction of the state and civil society, we see urban migrant politics as a localized field in which various state and non-state actors influence one another. In order to obtain a nuanced understanding of urban citizenship and to analyse extensively the quality and scope of inclusive practices towards illegalized migrants in local settings, we must ask how inclusive policies and practices in urban settings are negotiated, contested, and co-produced between a wide variety of state/municipal and civil society actors. With our empirical analysis, we would therefore like to follow Holm and Lebuhn (2020, 97), who invite "scholars of urban citizenship (...) to open this 'black box' (...) and think about formats and processes of cooperation and co-production".

The progressive potential of the concept of 'co-production' is stressed particularly in urban studies (Mitlin 2008; Mitlin and Bartlett 2018) and has recently been used by scholars studying civil society participation in the support of refugees (Gesemann, et. al. 2019; Kreichauf and Mayer 2021). It discusses how horizontal collaborations between civil society actors and municipal actors can make cities more democratic and inclusive. Researchers thereby address the fact that civil society actors are always moving in a field of tension while engaging in 'co-production': On the one hand, there is the emancipatory potential to advance transformative policies and practices through, among other things, a general change of consciousness within urban institutions; the mobilization of structural resources in favor of the work of CSOs; influencing public discourse and, if possible, legal adaptations at the city level. On the other hand, there exists the danger that collaborations may only serve to 'fill the gap' left by neo-liberal mechanisms of outsourcing welfare services to private and non-profit partners – and not bring about the structural change needed (van Dyk and Misbach 2016).

To capture the practices and rationalities of the multiplicity of actors involved in urban citizenship struggles, we turn to Agustín and Jørgensen's (2019) actor-centered typology of solidarity practices. The authors differentiate between "autonomous solidarity", that is, relations and practices produced in self-organized (mainly urban) spaces; "civic solidarity" as activities by civil society initiatives to include (irregular) migrants; and "institutional solidarity" or the formalization of solidarity, connecting the civil society arena with institutional policy arenas (Agustín and Jørgensen 2019, 39–42). We use this typology, which refers in particular to solidarity practices with refugees, and adapt and refine it in our empirical analysis (section 5) in relation to solidarity practices of CSOs engaged in supporting illegalized migrants.

2   Methodological Approach

We examine the practices of CSOs in support of illegalized migrants in the two capital cities Vienna and Bern. Bern has 143.000 (official) inhabitants, 24 percent without Swiss citizenship. Vienna has 1.9 million (official) inhabitants, 30 percent without Austrian citizenship. Although both cities lack reliable estimations of the number of illegalized migrants, our CSO interviews show that their services are widely used.

Both cities engage in policy activities in support of illegalized migrants. The city of Bern claims to be a 'City for all' and, within this framing, views illegalized migrants as a target group. Since 2017, the city of Bern has been in the process of a project to introduce a municipal ID Card (Hürlimann 2021). The municipality of Vienna, by contrast, does not claim a public policy towards illegalized migrants. However, the city calls itself a 'City of Human Rights' and passed in 2014 a declaration aiming to establish a human rights approach in all the city's levels of government. It supports policies and CSOs enabling rejected asylum seekers access to welfare services in the form of shadow politics, meaning that it does not actively enhance the visibility of services. In both cities, we find an array of CSOs and social initiatives supporting illegalized migrants and advocating for their rights.

We selected our interview partners through a mix of theoretical sampling, following the typology developed by Agustín and Jørgensen (2019), and an inductive approach that enabled us to gain a broad overview of the field through expert interviews. Agustín and Jørgensen (2019) outline three types of solidarity movements (civic, institutional, and autonomous). Although our focus is not on solidarity movements but rather on practices of civil society organizations, their analytical differentiation and categories offer us a valuable lens for distinguishing "different ways of practicing, organizing, and articulating solidarity" (ibid, 39). In addition, the target group for practices is more limited in our case: We are concerned with migrants and refugees who do not have a regular residence status in the country in which they are residing, either because they have lost it (e.g., through a rejection of the asylum application) or because they never had a legal status in the first place (Triandafyllidou and Bartolini 2020).

In Bern, we draw on empirical material collected by the second author in the context of a study commissioned by the City of Bern in 2020 on the in-/exclusion of illegalized migrants from municipal services. While this study included semi-structured interviews with both municipal officials as well as CSO representatives, we selected for this article three CSOs to analyze in detail. In Vienna, the first field study was done in the context of the research project "Inside the Deportation Gap. Social Membership for Non-Deported Persons" supported by the Austrian Science Fund (FWF) between 2016 and 2018. In 2020 and 2021, the first author made further interviews as well as follow-up interviews with the CSOs.

For our analysis, we employ a "thick comparison" approach (Niewöhner and Scheffer 2010), relating distinct research sites and actors to one another as a means of improving analytical clarity rather than of extracting generalizations. This allows us to identify similarities and convergences as well as to point out situated particularities. By employing a "comparative optics", patterns identified in one research site can serve as "a sensor for identifying and mapping (equivalent, analogue, conflicting) patterns in the other" (Knorr-Cetina 1999, 4).

3   Varieties of CSO Solidarity Practices in Support of Illegalized
         Migrants

The CSOs engaged in supporting illegalized migrants are confronted with a
group whose precarity is particularly grounded in irregular migration status
but also often intersectionally linked to their socioeconomic status and their
position as a racialized minority. While many challenges faced by illegalized
migrants are similar to those faced by all migrants irrespective of migration
status (such as discrimination at work, language barriers, or everyday racism),
there exist specific vulnerabilities related to illegalized migrants' irregular status: Compared to refugees still in the asylum process or whose refugee status
is recognized, this group is excluded from access to a wide range of social services and from the formal labor market. Furthermore, illegalized migrants live
in a condition of "deportability" (de Genova 2002) and are confronted with the
constant risk and fear of being removed if detected by migration authorities.
Accordingly, CSOs engaged in solidarity with illegalized migrants face specific
challenges: They have fewer institutional/formal margins and move within a
limited "room de maneuver", compared to refugee solidarity. Additionally, the
particular situation of illegalized migrants implies that the highest discretion
is required. In the following, we elaborate on some characteristics and commonalities that characterize the solidarity work of CSOs in this field. While this
section primarily concerns the practical work of CSOs, in section 5 we discuss
their varying organizational structures, their form of political engagement and
the way they relate to municipal authorities.

3.1   "Getting the Basic Human Needs Met": Offering Services at Low
           Threshold and in a Trustful Environment

A substantial component of the CSO support on which we focused involves
their central role in enabling illegalized migrants access to basic services.
CSOs included in our study support illegalized migrants in "getting their basic
human needs met" (*Ute Bock*) by "humanizing their everyday life" (*Advice
Centre for Sans-Papiers*) and "trying to enable a decent life" (*Medina*). They
deliver services for illegalized migrants in diverse areas and settings, offering
support in accessing health care, accommodation, legal advocacy, language
courses, financial support, and in-kind contributions such as food and clothes.

   Some CSOs aim to provide structural and long-term support, such as *Ute
Bock* in Vienna, which supports – free of charge and in a fairly professional
manner – migrants in finding accommodation, gaining access to educational
services as well as legal and social advocacy. *Ute Bock* seeks to provide homeless

migrants with "a home in order to start a new life free from fear" or to provide education "as a cornerstone to build a new life" (Ute Bock). With the similar aim of granting illegalized migrants a longer-term perspective, organizations such as the *Advice Centre for Sans-Papiers* in Bern or the *Desserterursberatung* in Vienna offer legal support regarding regularization of residence status.

These CSOs attempt to reach a broad range of illegalized migrants and offer services at a low threshold. For this purpose, all organizations offer drop-in consultations for everyone, and migrants are not required to announce their impending arrival or register in advance. To ensure migrants can access their services without fear, they are given the opportunity to seek counselling anonymously. Furthermore, illegalized migrants face the "fear that the alien police are waiting for them around the corner" (*AmberMed*). In this respect, most of the CSO representatives interviewed did not report police raids – despite the lack of direct agreements between the CSO and the police.

All CSOs included in the study have in common that they unbureaucratically provide practical offers, thus building a parallel infrastructure through which the precarious situation of illegalized migrants is addressed. CSOs set up as few eligibility criteria as possible and thereby distinguish themselves from other established institutions in terms of their rationalities. As a representative of *Ute Bock* explains, "need" is the only criterion that counts: "Everyone gets food here. No matter whether they have an income or not. The main thing is that they need this food or donations in kind". The interviewees involved in health care refer to their professional ethos and emphasize that they "want to provide adequate health care to all people as professionally as possible – regardless of their status" (*Neunerhaus*). The *Caritas* interviewee emphasized: "That is our mandate as Caritas: That we somehow organize a place where people can sleep in an emergency. Or that we talk to a person for longer and try to find a solution" (*Caritas*).

Other CSOs with less established structures respond more to acute needs in the short term. The community center *Medina,* for example, was confronted during the lockdown in spring 2020 with the situation that various welfare institutions closed their doors. With the help of volunteers (both residents and illegalized migrants themselves), *Medina* set up a meal service and erected a gift fence where people in need could get clothes and food bags. During the corona pandemic, they also created opportunities for illegalized migrants to get financial support by establishing a catering service: The migrants cooked the meals in the kitchen of a closed restaurant (whose owners sympathize with the project) and delivered it to homes of their "customers" within the city.

3.2 *"It Is Not Enough to Close the Wound of a Patient": Practicing an Interdisciplinary and Holistic Approach*

An important characteristic of the CSOs we studied is their all-round approach towards persons and the interdisciplinary way through which they deliver their services. Given the combined exclusion of illegalized migrants from both the formal labor market and many social entitlements, CSOs encounter people with vital and complex issues who are in difficult situations in various social fields. This becomes evident, for example, in the practices of medical drop-in centers such as those of *AmberMed* and *Neunerhaus* in Vienna or the *Health Care for Sans-Papiers* in Bern: "There are not only medical problems or only social problems. The whole thing is a holistic construct. [...] So the most sensible thing is simply to look at it from several perspectives at the same time". (Neunerhaus) and "Our nurses make medical consultations but at the same time, they also take care of social issues". (Health Care for Sans-Papiers).

Often migrants come with a clearly identifiable, urgent concern but behind this lies a series of other social problems that also need to be addressed in order to bring about a sustainable improvement in the living situation of the people with whom they interact. For this reason, many CSOs work with social workers whose role it is to obtain an initial impression of a person, including information about their housing situation, income, and mental health. This is impressively described by the social worker from the *Neunerhaus*:

> It is not enough for me to close the wound of a patient if he still lives socially isolated on the street. With no income and poor food. Or if he has a psychiatric illness that is untreated. Then it's not enough to close the wound. The wound will rupture again. [...] And I believe that the motivation is also very strongly anchored in this interdisciplinary approach. To learn from each other.
> NEUNERHAUS

Cultivating an "interdisciplinary approach" to the needs of illegalized migrants requires working together in a collaborative process and developing a holistic response that relies on knowledge and skills of various persons involved. This integrated service is a relief for illegalized migrants, as it allows them to address multiple needs in one place and thus reduces the risks they face in public spaces. CSOs like *AmberMed, Neunerhaus* and the *Health Care for Sans-Papiers* therefore try to establish access to a comprehensive health system. *AmberMed* not only offers lab tests or x-rays free of charge but has also established a collaboration with a pharmacy in the same building where medical donations are delivered. The representative of the *Health Care for Sans-Papiers* "realized that dentistry is a huge issue and that we need to be able to offer help in this regard". Within the scope of their activities, they respond to individual needs and take on new tasks during the process. When migrant receive high hospital bills, they "try to intervene" by "writing off the claims" (*AmberMed*). *Neunerhaus* also offers debt counselling.

Another good example of this interdisciplinary and holistic approach is the *Advice Centre for Sans-Papiers* in Bern. In a network of professionals and volunteers, the center not only provides legal counselling regarding residency status and legalization but also offers support in cases of labour rights issues (especially for domestic workers), helps migrants to obtain health insurance, accompanies them in the process of getting married, and helps enroll children in elementary school. This coordinated action enables illegalized migrants to access basic services and meet their needs in an unbureaucratic way.

Despite this all-round approach through which CSOs offer broad-based services, they also set certain priorities and focus on some specific services. This contributes to the professionalization of services they offer and to a reasonable division of labor between the individual CSOs: In Vienna for example, *AmberMed* focuses on gynecology, hypertension patients and patients with chronic illnesses, while *Neunerhaus* is the only institution that runs a dental clinic for uninsured persons.

3.3   *"Try to Triage into Regular Systems": Creating Pathways to Social Services*

CSOs simultaneously build a parallel infrastructure for illegalized migrants while seeking to facilitate access to regular systems. Whenever possible, they attempt to explore possibilities for including illegalized migrants into existing public social services and welfare institutions:

> If possible, we always triage to regular services – that is one of our core ideas. We don't want to build a hospital next to the regular supply system, because we say that everything already exists. It's about access and admission, that's our main problem.
> Health Care for Sans-Papiers

According to this interviewee, illegalized migrants face various challenges in obtaining access to health insurance and public subsidies as well as in accessing medical services". They have many hurdles to overcome when dealing with authorities", also explains the representative of *Ute Bock*. In addition to language barriers, illegalized migrants face complex administrative procedures due to the lack of valid residency documents. CSOs help migrants to navigate the tricky terrains of bureaucracy, which consists not only of public officials and service providers but also of private companies and welfare institutions. The representative of the *Advice Centre for Sans-Papiers* reports that "such procedures are very time-consuming and can sometimes keep us busy for months". In fact, as many interviewees underlined, navigating the bureaucracy is a very labor-intensive process that cannot be accomplished without specialist knowledge.

CSOs thus take on an essential intermediary role in actualizing the rights of illegalized migrants. On the one hand, CSOs seek to establish trusting relationships and an openness towards the situation of precarious migrants within the local street-level bureaucracies by constantly negotiating with authorities and institutions, as the social worker of the *Health Care for Sans-Papiers* reports: "Very much has to be looked at on a case-by-case basis and doesn't work smoothly". This is also stressed by the interviewee of *Neunerhaus*:

> Our aim is not simply to mediate. We try to clarify things well. Possibly with a telephone call beforehand with an appointment. Because our experience is that very often people come to us who have already been sent back and forth three times. And when we refer people to other institutions, [...] we just want to make sure that they are in the right place.
> NEUNERHAUS

CSOs often facilitate connections between non-citizens and various state agencies, sometimes allowing for personalized relationships that would be impossible in direct interactions between state agents and illegalized migrants. As the social worker employed at the *AmberMed* in Vienna and the nurse working for *Health Care for Sans-Papiers* in Bern emphasize, they invest a lot in personal contacts to doctors, administrative persons at hospitals, and insurance employees – to build up awareness, to promote goodwill and to create relationships of trust: "When hospital entries are necessary, we act as intermediaries, making referrals to trusted medical professionals in hospitals when possible and guaranteeing funding". (Health Care for Sans-Papiers) The latter is needed because hospital administrations, which are increasingly driven by a business logic, often react with suspicion if they do not have a cost guarantee. For complex and expensive treatments, *AmberMed* liaise with mainstream hospitals and make deals to provide services to migrants, e.g., for women with a limited budget to give birth at a clinic. This shows that the CSO representatives must consider the different organizational cultures, norms and logics that guide the work of both local government officials and professionals in public institutions, such as doctors, social workers, or teachers. With their extensive experience, the CSOs know the rationales and moral frames of certain officials and perform a work of translation between the people on the ground and the cultures of different bureaucracies, whose logics and rules are far from obvious.

3.4   *"Because Relationships Are Essential": Caring and Creating Social Relations*

We argue that facilitating access to regular systems for illegalized migrants not only involves specific knowledge and information but is also a process of building social relations and of (often invisible) care work. One important but often invisible aspect of CSO work is the creation of social and affective relations and the provision of care. This form of work is an important part of the solidarity practices of all the CSOs interviewed, although it takes different forms of relationships depending on the institutional context and the self-perception of the organizations.

It is thanks to long-established relationships that illegalized migrants build trust to CSO staff and turn to them in the first place. Often, because of fear of being noticed by the immigrant authorities, illegalized migrants would not dare to go to a hospital or enroll a child in school. CSOs encourage illegalized migrants to do so and even travel with them to the offices and institutions, as the representative of *Medina* reports: "When we do triage, we accompany people all the way to the door. Because the distrust is huge, especially toward the authorities". (Medina) This close companionship and the establishment of trusting relationships is also essential for the preparation of a regularization application, as the legal advisor of the *Advice Centre for Sans-Papiers* explains. She emphasizes that it should not be the case "that a sans-papiers feels like he or she is being interrogated as part of an asylum procedure by the immigrant office". Rather, as an advisor of the *Ute Bock* explains, they are claiming rights on behalf of the migrants and, accordingly, are clearly taking sides with them.

In addition to practical matters such as medical and administrative support and basic service delivery, the CSOs offer psychosocial support and provide illegalized migrants the opportunity to talk about the difficulties (e.g., fear of deportation, lacking perspectives for the future, or issues such as caring about a family left behind) that directly stem from their irregular residency status. They engage in "the so-called atmosphere management [...] to make people arrive well", as the interviewee of *Neunerhaus* explains:

> It is also about helping illegalized persons who actually have no prospects and where there is not much you can do. What you can always do is offer the relationship and the conversation. That doesn't sound like much. But sometimes it can be a lot.
>
> NEUNERHAUS

A member of the *Advice Centre for Sans-Papiers* reports that the opportunity to "speak out" is already a great relief for many migrants: "It is central for the people who often have to live as hidden as possible, that there is a place for a 'coming-out', and that they finally can tell their story to somebody, without fear". (Advice Centre for Sans-Papiers) This emphasis on active listening and showing compassion is evident in all interviews with CSOs. At the same time, the nature and intensity of interpersonal encounters differs by CSO. Organizations that work in a more institutionalized setting often tend to maintain more professional and less personal and intimate relationships with migrants.

4   The Landscape of Civil Society Organizations Engaged with Illegalized Migrants in Vienna and Bern

In the following analysis, we discuss for each type of CSO (civic, institutional, and autonomous, Agustín and Jørgensen 2019) the organizational structures, the human and financial resources they can mobilize, their form of political engagement and the way they relate to municipal authorities (see Table 14.1). We thereby also address the potential, challenges and limits that arise in the respective organizations in terms of building an urban infrastructure of solidarity and fostering urban citizenship.

4.1   *Civic CSOs*
The organizations we conceptualize as examples of civic CSOs are *Health Care for Sans-Papiers* in Bern, *AmberMed* in Vienna and the refugee project *Ute Bock* in Vienna. What characterizes these three CSOs is that they are "receptive to the idea that the vulnerabilities, which prevent people from participating on equal terms, must be eliminated" (Agustín and Jørgensen 2019, 41). The vulnerabilities that CSOs address through their engagement are rooted in the restrictive migration regime that excludes people without residency status from basic rights. In the case of the three CSOs portrayed here, the right to health care (*AmberMed* and *Health Care for Sans-Papiers*) and the right to housing (*Ute Bock*) are addressed. With their commitment, the CSOs set up a parallel infrastructure outside the institutions of the welfare state to guarantee a substitute to regular structures of the social system. In this sense, they mobilize resources to mitigate the social consequences of denied rights.

The three organizations have in common that their creation as well as their current practice is rooted in a charitable logic. *Health Care for Sans-Papiers* was founded in 2007 and is part of a large, established welfare organization, the Red Cross Switzerland. At their drop-in center located on the outskirts of Bern,

TABLE 14.1   Types of different civil society organizations in support of illegalized migrants

	Civic CSO	Institutional CSO	Autonomous CSO
Main activities	Medical support, shelter, educational services, provision of basic assistance	Welfare services as well as juridical and social support	Provision of legal and social advice, sharing resources and knowledge, creating a space for encounter
Formalisation	Middle to high (in close relation with welfare associations; embedded or independent)	High (some commissioned by the city)	Low (self-organisation), participative in a non-hierarchical way
Human resources	Professionals and volunteers	Mainly professionals, volunteers as supplementary	Mainly volunteers
Financial basis	Mix of donations and support by municipal institutions, precarious financial base	Support by public institutions, donations, stable financial base	Only by donations – no funding from state/city
Political engagement	Humanitarian orientation and advocacy for illegalised migrants	Advocacy for illegalised migrants, campaigns	Protest, claim-making, empowerment, transformative orientation
Relations to municipality	claim-making towards municipalities for getting more resources	Rather cooperative, acting as intermediaries to expand outreach, claim-making directed to the municipality	No/selective relations

they currently provide health services to 300 patients a year, a number that is growing annually. About half of the patients are rejected asylum seekers, the other half consists of illegalized migrants who are not known to the authorities. *AmberMed* was established in 2004 and consists of a volunteer team of doctors, therapists, interpreters and assistants providing medical care "to all people who, for whatever reason, do not have health insurance". They also face growing demand and currently treat around 3.300 patients per year, a large proportion of which are people with uncertain or irregular status. *Ute Bock* has its origins in the humanitarian commitment of a retired social worker named Ute Bock, who began in 2002 organizing housing and support for refugees in need. In the meantime, numerous employees, social workers and volunteers keep Ute Bock's vision alive. They offer accommodation for about 300 people, 90 of which reside in the *Ute Bock* facilities and about 200 of which live in separate flats supervised by the *Ute Bock* staff. Most of the migrants supported by *Ute Bock* are illegalized persons who don't have legal access to housing and who are at risk of becoming homeless.

The work of civic CSOs is characterized by a simultaneous reliance on and contribution to "collaborative relations within and between different social groups" (Agustín and Jørgensen 2019, 41). The involvement of volunteers plays a major role in this. In *AmberMed* and in the *Health Care for Sans-Papiers*, the health care services are provided by volunteer doctors who work unpaid during certain days of the month. As the interviewee from *AmberMed* explains, in addition to "loving their job" and "finding meaningful activity", volunteers are motivated by the opportunity to "immerse themselves in a world of life they wouldn't otherwise know". The representative of *Health Care for Sans-Papiers* emphasizes that the doctors appreciate the rare opportunity to work outside the highly rationalized health care system.

At the same time, this arrangement with volunteers also brings with it various challenges, as reflected in statements made by our interviewees. One limitation is the reliability and sustainability of their service-provision due to voluntarism, which may have a negative impact especially on the quality of health care services: As most of the doctors are volunteering during their spare time, the CSOs are dependent on their limited availabilities. The result for patients is that they are usually treated by a different doctor each time. In addition, their commitments may not always be very binding, as the interviewee from *Health Care for Sans-Papiers* problematizes:

> A big challenge for us is to maintain the offer, and to be able to provide our services as constantly as possible, despite the fluctuating volunteers. Because suddenly a volunteer doctor jumps off again. [...] With some it

takes very little and then they are already gone. This can happen even if the parking space in front of the house is not ready for them.

Health Care for Sans-Papiers

In addition, during the Corona pandemic, limits also emerged regarding the sustainability of the services through volunteering, as many of the volunteer doctors were no longer able to offer their services on the spot due to their age (which placed them into a risk group).

Another difficulty emerges in terms of the nature of the relationships between volunteers and migrants: Even though the interviewees emphasize the value of these interpersonal encounters between people in very different life situations, doctors seem not always to have the sensitive diversity-conscious attitude the organizer of the clinic would wish:

> These doctors don't necessarily bring with them transcultural sensitivity – which is quite a challenge. After all, the doctors are not necessarily people who are easily trainable. Sometimes they assume that they can just do everything.
>
> Health Care Sans-Papiers

Thus, it can be an obstacle that the service providers are not sufficiently sensitive to the asymmetrical power relations that shape the encounters between patients as aid-receivers and volunteers as aid-providers. Despite efforts of volunteers to provide non-discriminatory care, questions of deservingness may shape a patient's performance in the humanitarian space of migrant health care (Huschke 2014).

A further challenge to the work of civic CSOs – and which results in limited resources – is their dependence on financial donations. *AmberMed* relies on donations from individuals and institutions for half of the funding of its services and mobilizes the other half through a mix of official subsidies, such as health insurance, state and municipal funds, as well as through cooperation with established welfare institutions. *Ute Bock* also relies heavily on donations, especially for services for illegalized migrants, while those for asylum seekers are funded by the City of Vienna. The *Health Care for Sans-Papiers* is fully financed by the Swiss Red Cross, which in turn relies heavily on donations. Thereby, fundraising for illegalized migrants seems to be more challenging than for other people in need of aid.

For the CSOs, these limited financial resources mean they lack the funds to facilitate the full range of services they wish they could (and should) provide. For example, all CSOs interviewed report having too little money to work with trained interpreters. Therefore, they must overcome the difficulties of communication and lack of language skills with the support of volunteers and migrants' family members. The CSOs must also cut back on their offerings in other areas: The two medical drop-in centers report that severe and expensive diseases like cancer are a big challenge to treat, which shows that the parallel health system they put up necessarily lags behind the one accessible to legal residents. Thereby, for uninsured patients, examinations and treatments are limited to the strictly necessary, unless some professionals and donators are willing to enable more. *Ute Bock* also faces a capacity bottleneck: Although the organization offers accommodation for 300 people, they have so many requests that they cannot accommodate them all.

To sum up, our analysis of the civic CSOs shows that, while they are making every possible effort to include illegalized migrants, inclusion remains partial and precarious, and exclusion is an ever-present threat. The civic CSOs we studied compensate for the absence of regular health care and accommodation by developing structures in which the services take place outside the regular system. In this sense, their "engagement is not transformative of the state's legal framework but can rather be seen as a necessary supplement or alternative social framework based on the collaboration with the authorities, municipalities, and schools as well as diverse range of voluntary activities" (Agustín and Jørgensen 2019, 73). CSOs compensate for a structural inappropriateness that can be observed within public systems. This makes these CSOs equally actors of inclusion and exclusion: they maintain a parallel structure and, through this, relieve the mainstream health or accommodation system. Leerkes (2016) discussed such arrangements as "poor house policies": He argues that in "the shadow of the Western welfare states, we now find elementary and, in many cases, rather archaic practices of poor relief and anti-pauperism measures for certain categories of unauthorized immigrants" (ibid, 140). From this point of view, CSOs do not tackle structural inequalities nor the roots of these inequalities. The result of their practices is thus far from realizing any form of universal citizenship right with the possibility of participation by the migrants themselves.

We support to some extent this critical assessment of the role of civic CSOs: Our analysis of the practices of civic CSOs shows that they alone cannot compensate for the lack of social infrastructure for illegalized migrants and cannot guarantee universal rights. The risk is high that illegalized migrants turn into passive recipients of charitable aid and are dependent on there being people "with a good heart". This aspect has also been discussed in the literature in relation to volunteering for the newcomers: van Dyk and Misbach (2016, 209) argue that volunteers are called upon to take care of refugees and thereby assume a "gap-filler" function in the context of austerity policies. According to them, this goes hand in hand with "a reinterpretation of the social question into one of a caring community" (ibid, 210), whereby "social rights are replaced by a culture of charitable helping" (ibid, 222).

In line with these considerations, in our case civic CSOs perform a 'gap-filler' function, whereby illegalized migrants, compared to recognized refugees or asylum-seekers, can hardly claim services from the state. As the representative of the *Health Care for Sans-Papiers* says herself: "I would say that we are taking quite a burden off the hospitals and especially the emergency services. And, of course, we're thereby also relieving the welfare state". This shows that CSO actors are aware of these structural gaps and their role therein. In this sense, we argue that civic CSOs cannot be reduced to the role of simple 'charitable helpers', as they simultaneously struggle with this role in various ways and are involved in a form of work that points beyond the status quo (as we presented in section 4):

First, in contrast to a restrictive governmental approach, civic CSOs unconditionally recognize migrants as being entitled to services and as being de-facto part of the society. Although the activities of the CSOs are often described primarily as practical support, both the intentions and implications of CSOs' engagement in our examples transgress a humanitarian-only approach. For example, although the interviewee from the *Health Care for Sans-Papiers* states that they are not engaged in "political activism" and "are clearly doing humanitarian work", she argues at the same time for an "unconditional right to good health care, regardless of residence status", aiming to produce better conditions for illegalized migrants by means of their concrete actions.

Second, through their dedicated way of collaboration with professionals and through awareness raising about the situation of illegalized migrants, civic CSOs participate in building an urban infrastructure of solidarity. The example of *AmberMed* is instructive in this regard: As a humanitarian organization, they do not claim to be 'neutral' but rather demonstrate a political stance by pointing out its budgetary limitations and the political responsibility of the municipality to mobilize more resources to provide sustainable services. They argue that, by providing basic health services to so many people without health insurance, they are making an essential contribution to the city's well-being. In this regard, they ask the municipality to fund them more generously and cover their entire budget. However, since the municipality did not respond to their request for an appointment, they recently launched a public campaign to reach the politicians and build up public pressure to bring them into negotiations.

4.2   *Institutional CSOs*

The organisations we see as manifestations of institutional solidarity are the *Advice Centre for Sans-Papiers* in Bern and *Caritas* in Vienna. Institutional solidarity refers, according to Agustín and Jørgensen (2019, 42), to "the formalization of solidarity relations" and describes "the capacity of enabling (infra) structures" to connect the civil society arena with the arena of policymaking. CSOs that perform this type of institutional solidarity try to use their power, networks, and alliances to develop an impact on public institutions on different scales (municipal, federal, international). Based on collaboration with authorities such as municipalities and established welfare organizations, institutional CSOs aim to challenge exclusionary policies and practices and advocate for a more inclusive approach.

We see two different organizational characteristics of institutional CSOs in our field: While some, like *Caritas* in Vienna, are directly commissioned by the city, others like the *Advice Centre for Sans-Papiers* in Bern do not have a direct mandate but maintain close relations to the municipal authorities. The two CSOs have in common that they act as intermediaries to expand outreach: CSOs enjoy a higher level of trust from illegalized migrants than the authorities, and they are able to mediate between migrants and local social or migration authorities. Of significance in this regard in Switzerland is the fact that CSOs (in contrast to most municipal authorities) are not subjected to the "duty to transmission" (Meldepflicht), a federal law that requires that information about 'illegal residents' be shared with national migration authorities.

In Vienna, The *Caritas Asylum Centre* is an operative partner on behalf of the welfare department of the municipality (Vienna Social Fund FSW) in providing services such as accommodation and social counselling both for asylum seekers and rejected asylum seekers (Ataç 2019). At the central service point, the counsellors from *Caritas* meet with migrants, including with those holding no or only precarious legal status. Although the *Caritas Asylum Centre* is not commissioned by the municipality nor officially responsible for supporting illegalized migrants, they have other service points such as *Caritas Sozialberatung Wien,* where they consult persons who are not eligible for social benefits. At this service point, the organization uses its knowledge and networks to provide services to people who would otherwise fall through the net. In some cases, the counsellors may act as gatekeepers when they are pushing hardship cases to influence local administrative decisions. In other cases, they use their limited budget, derived from donations, and their links to the church to offer services. In this example of institutional solidarity, *Caritas* uses its infrastructure acquired through providing services on behalf of the municipality to expand the services to illegalized migrants.

The *Advice Centre for Sans-Papiers* in Bern was created in 2005 in the wake of a series of church occupations by illegalized migrants. It is an independent association, supported by churches, humanitarian organizations, trade unions and engaged individuals. Although the *Advice Centre for Sans-Papiers* has no contractual relationship with the city, it maintains close – but not always conflict-free – relations with different municipal authorities. This is manifested, for example, in its geographical location: the *Advice Centre for Sans-Papiers* has its office and meeting rooms in a municipal building, where the city's *Office for issues of migration and racism* is located. The *Advice Centre for Sans-Papiers* benefits from 'short routes' to authorities with whom they are in contact for their support of illegalized migrants.

Institutional CSOs orchestrate complex interactions between various actors in order to facilitate access for illegalized migrants to social resources and municipal services. The professionals of these organizations are not only familiar with the various legal frameworks but also know who in the city might be receptive to which issue and can "pick up the phone and discuss the concern directly", as a representative of the *Advice Centre for Sans-Papiers* puts it. In both organizations, counsellors find ways of traversing the gaps between officials and (non-)citizens and translate complex life circumstances into persuasive cases framed in terms of legal definitions. They try to establish a culture of mutual trust between legal advisers and local authorities – although, as the counsellor of the *Advice Centre for Sans-Papiers* points out, this does not work equally well in every department and office of the city administration. Therefore, they try to sensitize urban authorities to the fact that they have leeway and can mitigate the control strategies derived from national policies in their concrete practice. From the perspective of the counsellors at *Caritas*, their influence on the municipalities' decisions exists on a more informal level and they can use their position and knowledge to push cases of hardship to influence administrative decisions: "It's always a case-by-case decision, it's a point of argument" (*Caritas*).

We also consider organizations as institutional CSOs that offer services for a specific category of 'vulnerable persons', including migrants who are not legally entitled to these services. *Neunerhaus* is a social organization in Vienna that offers services such as medical care, housing, and counselling to homeless people and people at risk of poverty. *House Frida* is a housing project for homeless migrant women and their children in Vienna. Financed by the *Caritas*, it offers a mother-child residence and acute places that provide accommodation for mothers in distress and their children. Both organizations allow non-status people in cooperation with the municipality to 'slip in' and find ways to give them access to their services. The same is the case with the *Women's Shelter* in Bern, where women affected by domestic violence and their children receive protection, counselling, and temporary shelter. This organization, which is partly financed by public funds, makes no distinction regarding the residence status of women and their children seeking refuge. However, it is important to mention that not all these organizations have the capacity to offer sustainable services for vulnerable illegalized migrants.

Institutional CSOs such as the *Advice Centre for Sans-Papiers, Neunerhaus* or *Caritas* use their status as established NGOs with expertise to draw the attention of policymakers and the public to the situation of illegalized migrants. The *Advice Centre for Sans-Papiers* in Bern, for example, has designed a public city tour that leads to various places and institutions in which illegalized migrants experience exclusion or danger, such as medical emergency centers, public places, prisons, or schools. Illegalized persons themselves participated in the design of this city tour and give testimonies about the internal borders they experience in their everyday life. Furthermore, the *Neunerhaus* as well as the *Advice Centre for Sans-Papiers* address various issues in the lives of illegalized migrants at the political level, making political campaigns in order to raise social awareness among urban residents. An effective strategy in this sense is the annual 'sponsor run' organized by the *Advice Centre for Sans-Papiers*. At this fundraising event, illegalized migrants run through the city together with city council members or local celebrities. In this sense, it is also powerful in terms of channeling urban solidarity.

One goal of institutional CSOs is to formalize both discretionary practices within the municipal bureaucracy as well as collaborations between civil society and municipalities. In this respect, the initiative for the introduction of a municipal identity card (ID) in Bern is an illustrative example in which the *Advice Centre for Sans-Papiers* took a leading role: They organized workshops with illegalized migrants and other civil society actors on their visions for a municipal identity card and then approached the city government and municipal parliamentarians. As a consequence of these mobilizations, the concept of a municipal ID was introduced into the city's 'Integration Priority Plan 2018–2021' (City of Bern 2018). Since then, a movement to campaign for the municipal ID has emerged under the slogan "We are all Bern". A working group including various municipal officials as well as representatives of the *Advice Centre for Sans-Papiers* set up by the city is currently concretizing the project of a municipal ID. In addition to their involvement in this municipal working group, representatives from the *Advice Centre for Sans-Papiers* collaborate with activists from Bern "We are all Bern in forming an alliance of migrant organizations and urban social movements to advocate for a 'City for all'".

Through both their dedicated way of collaborating with city officials and their efforts to build a common political terrain within civil society, the institutional CSOs we studied are crucial actors that co-produce an urban infrastructure of solidarity (Holm and Lebuhn 2019; Kreichauf and Mayer 2021).

However, there is often much more focus on the municipal representatives of cities where inclusive policies towards illegalized migrants are established, while the work of institutional CSOs is less visible and often also less recognized. The municipality is enabled to act beyond its formal role and expand its outreach and impact through its collaboration with CSOs that act as intermediaries between local authorities and illegalized migrants (Delvino and Spencer 2019). Urban authorities are thereby dependent on the CSOs; on their skills, networks as well as the outcome of their work.

However, the power hierarchies in which these collaborations between institutional CSOs and the municipality take place should not be overlooked. Indeed, the relationship between municipality and CSOs is shaped by an asymmetrical power balance. As Nicholls and Uitermark (2016, 32) emphasize, local governments are selective in their relations with CSOs and prioritize those with whom they can build reliable relations. Some municipalities aspire to have civil society acting as an extension of local government and becoming part of a web of governance "rather than an uncontrollable and tangled site that nourishes multiple resistances" (ibid). This makes institutional CSOs dependent of the decisions of urban authorities. A change in policy may decrease their sphere of impact as gatekeepers, as the example of Vienna shows: In our interviews in 2015 and 2016, counsellors of *Caritas* were more optimistic and brought many examples of how they can bring back into basic services migrants who are not eligible. During follow-up interviews in 2020, they reported that this had become much more difficult due to a change in policy, through which the criteria for accessing basic services became much narrower and the number of positive responses from the municipal welfare actors became fewer. In Bern, too, much about openness towards CSOs and about illegalized migrants' fate in the city depends on the political power relations in the municipal government and on some progressive leaders, who may also at some point be replaced.

4.3   *Autonomous CSOs*

The organizations we describe as autonomous CSOs are the Deserteur's and Refugee's Counselling Centre (*Deserteursberatung*) in Vienna and the mobile community center called *Medina* in Bern. According to Agustín and Jørgensen (2019, 40), autonomous solidarity "is based in forms of horizontal participation such as direct democracy and assemblies" to enable equality between citizens and non-citizens in self-organized (mainly urban) spaces. In line with the understanding of autonomous solidarity, our examples take more activist rather than charitable forms and aim to create community spaces that are potentially transformative, providing an alternative to established forms of support.

In Vienna, there exist several organizations such as *Asyl in Not*, *Helping Hands* and *Deserteursberatung,* which offer independent legal counselling, especially for illegalized migrants who are otherwise not entitled. The *Deserteursberatung* was founded in 1992 and offers free legal counselling made possible through volunteers and donations. The organization consists of a young team of mostly students or graduates of law, social work, and social sciences, as well as of recognized refugees. *Medina* was founded in 2019 and is committed to "low-threshold inclusion of people in the city who find themselves in difficult circumstances". Both organizations are self-organized and focus on building horizontal relationships within these self-organized structures. The activities are aimed at people who fall through the gaps of the social system. Rather than simply stepping into the gap, however, they are instead engaged in creating "infrastructures of dissent", aiming to work against exclusion and injustice, as well as producing dissent (Agustín and Jørgensen 2019, 40).

Collaboration at eye-level between illegalized migrants and citizens is considered by the representatives of the *Deserteursberatung* the best way to challenge the precarious position of illegalized migrants in society. Establishing trust with them and treating each legal case confidently is a foundational principle of the *Deserteursberatung*. They offer counselling for persons "who are sent away by other organizations", "who are labelled as illegal", asylum seekers with a negative decision, people in detention pending deportation, as well as people in "hopeless procedures" (*Deserteursberatung*). As reported by the counsellor of *Deserteursberatung*, migrants often do not know what legal status they have during the procedure, nor what may be the consequences of certain steps in their legal procedure. Rather than simply instructing migrants on what to do, *Deserteursberatung* has an inclusive approach and seeks to incorporate an empowerment perspective. Their aim is:

> [to] give the people as much knowledge as possible about their own situation or about the procedure or further steps and strategies. So that the people are as self-determined as possible [...]. They should be able to decide for themselves what paths they want to take. That is the basic idea behind it [...], to let them decide. We only consult. Or we try to show the consequences of different decisions.

The counselling takes place according to the "four-eyes-principle", which means they "never conduct counselling sessions alone but always in teams of two counsellors – which distinguishes us from other organizations" (*Deserteursberatung*). The idea is to share responsibility and knowledge but also to counterbalance the disadvantages of volunteering, such as lack of professionalism or reliance on a single person. With this collaborative way of working, they contribute to sustainable commitment, improve performance, and strengthen relationships of trust.

The mobile community center *Medina* in Bern, which involves Swiss citizens, refugees and EU migrants, places a strong emphasis on the creation of an environment for personal exchange and even friendships. They have created a self-organized space within the city, where everyday encounters can take place. According to the representative of *Medina*, it is important that "we do not simply hand out food for people who are hungry but cook together". She continues:

> What else we do with people: Go hiking, take a walk. Cut each other's hair, have movie nights. We also have a party together quite often. It's about us doing something together. Because relationships are essential.
> MEDINA

The shared "off-topic" time and the creation of "a home for those who do not belong" (*Medina*) is not only a side effect but a central goal of *Medina's* activities. Thereby, they are helping "to undo dichotomous categorizations" between citizen and non-citizen, as they "define their members by doing, like in the idea of 'activist citizens'" (Agustín and Jørgensen 2019, 40). By doing so, they aim to enable empowerment processes and to facilitate the autonomous agency of illegalized migrants.

For the development of interpersonal affiliations and caring relations, Medina stresses the importance of their "presence on the square". Since there are frequent controls by the cantonal police on this central square, suggesting it is a 'safe space' misrepresents the reality. However, the activists of *Medina* try to counter the police authorities with civil disobedience, for example with collective actions like encircling the police officers and attentively observing the controls assessed as racial profiling. Another strategy, according to the interviewee of *Medina*, is "to involve the cops in a conversation, until the people the [illegalized migrants] could disappear". *Medina* also has an additional safe space in a more protected setting where volunteers and migrants can retreat for consultation sessions.

Both organizations aim to produce a new imaginary and a practical alternative as a micro-example on how solidarity work can provide alternatives (Agustín and Jørgensen 2019). Instead of "taking or challenging power, new forms of communities are created as a strategy to slip away from power" (ibid, 40). *Medina* and *Deserteursberatung* take decisions on a grassroots level in weekly plenary sessions and aim to work with as little hierarchy as possible. As the interviewee of *Deserteursberatung* mentions, they also question their own privileges from a perspective of critical whiteness:

> But most of our counsellors are white people. Many of them are academ-
> ics and we are in this class-knowledge-structure. For this reason, we are
> not in a hierarchy-free space. At least we try: If it is not possible to make it
> hierarchy-free during the counselling, then we try it in our internal struc-
> ture, through decision making on a grassroots level.
> DESERTEURSBERATUNG

Another commonality among both autonomous CSOs we studied is that they explicitly see themselves as anti-racist organizations and not as charitable institutions. As activists from the *Deserteursberatung* emphasise, their main principle is economic, political, and organizational independence. The inter-viewee of *Medina* explains that they have a clear political commitment: "We are anti-capitalist, anti-racist, we criticize our society". At the same time, they distance themselves from political organizations that are merely "verbally anti-racist": "We do political work but on a practical level". By creating a self-organized space, they "try to change structures and thereby make a difference in the everyday of migrants' realities" (*Medina*).

Zamponi's (2017) concept of "direct social action" describes these rather 'in-between' actions, that is, "actions that do not primarily focus upon claiming something from the state or other power-holders but that instead focus upon directly transforming some specific aspects of society by means of the action itself" (97). Direct social actions can be political and humanitarian at the same time. Given the amount of hands-on support, however, some CSOs regret that they often have limited time resources for political work. The interviewee of the *Deserteursberatung* reports:

> It comes up again every other month, I'm sure, in our plenary sessions:
> 'We should do more and could do more. What is there right now (at the
> policy level) that can be supported?' But independently, it's often difficult
> for us.
> DESERTEURSBERATUNG

Autonomous CSOs insist on their independence from the city, even though they sometimes interact with the local government and cooperate with munic-ipal agencies beyond their efforts to push the local setting for more inclusive policies. Although they are outside of municipal governance mechanisms, they are an important part of the city's infrastructure of solidarity for illegalized migrants and are engaged in what Belloni (2016) calls "welfare from below".

5   Conclusion

In this article, we highlight the importance of the practices of CSOs engaged with illegalized migrants in urban settings. Our interviews with representatives of local CSOs in Vienna and Bern have brought to light a diversity of more and less visible solidarity practices towards illegalized migrants. CSOs are central actors in building-up an urban "infrastructure of solidarity" (Schilliger 2020). They are well connected, work collaboratively, and have an interdisciplinary approach to meeting the vital and complex needs of people without legal status. They not only establish offers of everyday support, provide legal advice to migrants as well as expertise to city governments, but they also engage in political advocacy, create safe spaces, and develop relations of care. Given the scope of the CSO's solidarity practices towards illegalized migrants, we can confirm what other researchers have analyzed regarding support initiatives for refugees: The boundaries between humanitarian volunteerism, often described as 'apolitical', and self-organized projects by activists critical of the state, are shifting and contested (Kreichauf and Mayer 2021: 10, della Porta/Steinhilper 2021). The organizations we examined seek a middle ground between providing social services ('deliver') and political mobilization ('demand'), fostering forms of solidarity that aim to strengthen communities against injustice (de Jong and Ataç 2017). We argue that, in light of the particular context in which illegalized migrants are mainly produced and governed through political decisions of actors of the nation-states, CSOs and their solidarity practices are inevitably linked to political dissent, even if they are mainly engaged with humanitarian reasons (which aligns with what Vandevoordt 2019 terms "subversive humanitarianism").

In our in-depth analysis of the multifaceted landscape of CSOs, we identified differences between the organizations in terms of their organizational form, the funding structures, the composition of the staff, their (political) self-conception as well as their relationships to the municipalities. Agustín and Jørgensen's (2019) typology, which has been developed in the context of solidarity practices towards a broader category of refugees, is also valuable to specify the in-/visible politics of solidarity towards illegalized migrants and to analyze the CSO's connections to the arena of urban institutional politics. While most CSOs are engaged in some forms of negotiation with urban authorities and municipal bureaucracies, we find diverging practices of their entanglements with urban governments: Institutional CSOs establish a collaborative interplay with city officials to formalize solidarity practices; civic CSOs, in contrast, engage more in (often invisible) advocacy and awareness-raising within the municipal bureaucracy. Autonomous CSOs, in turn, aim to provide self-organized alternatives to institutional forms of support and prefer to establish limited/no direct relations with the municipality.

In contrast to the context of Agustín and Jørgensen's research on refugee solidarity initiatives, the civil society organizations we studied operate in an even more restrictive political context that structures the conditions under which they work: often they have few public resources at their disposal, which results in requiring a lot of energy for mobilizing financial resources in order to be able to act at all. Since the group of illegalized migrants has fewer social entitlements than asylum seekers, it is necessary to simultaneously build a parallel infrastructure to cover basic needs and promote access to the regular system. Consequently, the relationships with municipal departments are multi-layered and marked by tensions, as CSOs are to varying degrees dependent on the decisions of the city government. At the same time, CSOs are not simply passive objects. They find ways to realize their aims and broaden their impact by developing alternative sources of funding, campaigning and politicizing the issue, as well as using and constantly deepening their networks of solidarity within the city. The latter – the capacity to network and build political alliances among civil society actors – is, according to our analysis, a crucial component of a productive and sustainable interplay between municipalities and civil society actors.

The solidarity practices of CSOs we have analyzed are often less spectacular and far more invisible than city official's public declarations of inclusive migration policies or political claims by grassroots movements. We argue that the CSO's contribution and role has thus far not been sufficiently explored and recognized in debates on urban citizenship, as their practices are not adequately conceptualized in a simplistic dichotomization between urban citizenship 'from above' versus 'from below'. In our view, the perspective of "co-production" is promising here, as it enables a deeper examination of negotiation processes between different actors on the municipal level. Co-production can thereby be understood as a political process that strives not only for a material improvement in terms of meeting the basic needs of all city residents but that also builds knowledge and relationships. These conflictual but also consensual relations between local actors form the dynamics in which the conditions of urban citizenship emerges and transversal solidarity unfolds.

Acknowledgements

We would like to thank our interview partners in Bern and Vienna for their willingness and time to tell us about their work. We are also thankful to Hannah Kentouche for her support in the research and to Martin Bak Jørgensen and Carl-Ulrik Schierup for helpful comments.

References

Agustín, Ó. G., and M. B. Jørgensen (2019). *Solidarity and the 'Refugee Crisis' in Europe.* Palgrave Macmillan.

Ataç, I. (2019). "Deserving Shelter: Conditional Access to Accommodation for Rejected Asylum Seekers in Austria, the Netherlands, and Sweden". *Journal of Immigrant & Refugee Studies* 17.1: 44–60.

Ataç, I., T. Schütze, and V. Reitter (2020). "Local responses in restrictive national policy contexts: welfare provisions for non-removed rejected asylum seekers in Amsterdam, Stockholm and Vienna". *Ethnic and Racial Studies* 43.16: 115–134.

Ataç, I., K. Rygiel, and M. Stierl (2021). "Building Transversal Solidarities in European Cities: Open Harbours, Safe Communities, Home". *Critical Sociology* 47.6: 923–939.

Bauder, H. (2019). "Urban Sanctuary in Context". In Darling, J., and H. Bauder (eds.) *Sanctuary cities and urban struggles: Rescaling migration, citizenship, and rights.* Manchester University Press: 25–49.

Bauder H. (2021). "Urban migrant and refugee solidarity beyond city limits". *Urban Studies* (2021). Pre-print. https://doi:10.1177/0042098020976308.

Belloni, M. (2016). "Learning How to Squat: Cooperation and Conflict between Refugees and Natives in Rome". *Journal of Refugee Studies* 29.4: 506–527.

Bourdieu, P. (1989). "Social Space and Symbolic Power". *Sociological Theory* 7.1: 12–25.

Christoph, W., and S. Kron (eds.) (2019). *Solidarity Cities in Europe: Charity or Pathsways to Citizenship – A New Urban Policy Approach.* Rosa Luxemburg Stiftung.

City of Bern (2018). *Schwerpunkteplan 2018–2021 zur Umsetzung des Leitbildes zur Integrationspolitik.* Online: https://www.bern.ch/mediencenter/medienmitteilungen/aktuell_ptk/stadt-fuer-alle-mit-fokus-migration-die-ziele-sind-definiert/dokumente/schwerpunkteplan-2018-2021.pdf/download.

Darling, J. (2017). "Acts, ambiguities, and the labour of contesting citizenship". *Citizenship Studies* 21.6: 727–736.

Darling, J., and V. Squire (2012). Everyday enactments of sanctuary. The UK City of Sanctuary movement. In Lippert, R., and S. Rehaag (eds.) *Sanctuary Practices in International Perspective. Migration, Citizenship and Social Movements.* Routledge: 191–204.

de Genova, N. (2002). "Migrant 'illegality' and deportability in everyday life". *Annual Review of Anthropology* vol. 31: 419–447.

de Graauw, E. (2016). *Making immigrant rights real: Non-profits and the politics of integration in San Francisco.* Cornell University.

de Graauw, E. (2021). "City Government Activists and the Rights of Undocumented Immigrants: Fostering Urban Citizenship within the Confines of US Federalism". *Antipode* 53.2: 379–398.

de Jong, S., and I. Ataç (2017). "Demand and Deliver: Refugee Support Organisations in Austria". *Social Inclusion* 5.3: 28–37.

della Porta D., and E. Steinhilper (2021). "Introduction: Solidarities in Motion: Hybridity and Change in Migrant Support Practices". *Critical Sociology* 47.2: 175–185.

Delvino, N., and S. Spencer (2019). *Migrants with Irregular Status in Europe: Guidance for municipalities.* Oxford: COMPAS. URL: https://www.compas.ox.ac.uk/2019/migrants-with-.

Gesemann, F., A. Seidel, and M. Mayer (2019). *Entwicklung und Nachhaltigkeit von Willkommensinitiativen.* vhw (Bundesverband für Wohnen und Stadtentwicklung).

Hajer, M., and M. Ambrosini (2020). "Who help illegalized migrants? Supporters of illegalized migrants in Amsterdam and Turin". *REMHU: Revista Interdisciplinar da Mobilidade Humana* 28.59: 199–216.

Holm, A., and H. Lebuhn (2020). "Strengthening Citizenship in Berlin. Three Modes of Claiming and Expanding Rights and Resources at the Local Level". In Turner, B., H. Wolf, G. Fitzi, and J. Mackert (eds.) *Urban Change and Citizenship in Times of Crisis. Vol. 3: Figurations of Conflict and Resistance.* Routledge: 81–101.

Hürlimann, B. (2021). "Ein Ausweis für die Unsichtbaren". *Republik* 31.08.2021, https://www.republik.ch/2021/08/31/ein-ausweis-fuer-die-unsichtbaren.

Huschke, S. (2014). "Performing deservingness: humanitarian health care provision for migrants in Germany". *Social Science & Medicine* 120: 352–359.

Isin, E. F., and B.S. Turner (2002). "Citizenship Studies: An Introduction". In Isin, E. F. and B. S. Turner (eds.) *Handbook of Citizenship Studies.* SAGE Publishing: 1–10.

Kaufmann, D., and D. Strebel (2020). "Urbanising migration policy-making: Urban policies in support of illegalized migrants in Geneva and Zürich". *Urban Studies.* Pre-print. https://doi:10.1177/0042098020969342.

Knorr-Cetina, K. (1999). *Epistemic Cultures: How the Sciences Make Knowledge.* Harvard University Press.

Kreichauf, R., and M. Mayer (2021). "Negotiating urban solidarities: multiple agencies and contested meanings in the making of solidarity cities". *Urban Geography* 2021. Pre-print. https://doi.org/10.1080/02723638.2021.1890953.

Kron, S., and H. Lebuhn (2020). "Building solidarity cities. From protest to policy". In Feyzi B., and K. Rygiel (eds.) *Living with others. Fostering cultural pluralism through citizenship politics.* Routledge: 81–105.

Lambert, S., and T. Swerts (2019). "'From sanctuary to welcoming cities': Negotiating the social inclusion of illegalized migrants in Liège, Belgium". *Social Inclusion* 7.4: 90–99.

Leerkes A. (2016). "Back to the poorhouse? Social protection and social control of unauthorised immigrants in the shadow of the welfare state". *Journal of European Social Policy* 26.2: 140–154.

Mitlin, D. (2008). "With and beyond the state – Co-production as a route to political influence, power and transformation for grassroots organizations". *Environment and Urbanization* 20.2: 339–360.

Mitlin, D., and Bartlett, S. (2018). "Editorial: Co-production – key ideas". *Environment and Urbanization* 30–2: 355–366.

Nicholls, W., and J. Uitermark (2016). *Cities and social movements: Immigrant rights activism in the US, France, and the Netherlands, 1970–2015.* Wiley-Blackwell.

Niewöhner, J., and T. Scheffer (2010). "Introduction: Thickening Comparison: On The Multiple Facets Of Comparability". Scheffer, T., and J. Niewöhner (eds.) *Thick Comparison. Reviving the Ethnographic Aspiration.* Brill: 1–15.

Nyers, P. (2019). *Irregular Citizenhip, Immigration, and Deportation.* Routledge.

Schilliger, S. (2019). "Ambivalences of a Sanctuary City". In Christoph, W., and S. Kron (eds.) *Solidarity Cities in Europe.* Rosa Luxemburg Foundation: 95–110.

Schilliger, S. (2020). "Challenging who counts as a citizen. The infrastructure of solidarity contesting racial profiling in Switzerland". *Citizenship Studies* 24.4: 530–547.

Schweitzer, R. (2019). "Health Care Versus Border Care: Justification and Hypocrisy in the Multilevel Negotiation of Illegalized migrants' Access to Fundamental Rights and Services". *Journal of Immigrant & Refugee Studies* 17.1: 61–76.

Schwiertz, H., and H. Schwenken (2020). "Introduction: Inclusive solidarity and citizenship along migratory routes in Europe and the Americas". *Citizenship Studies* 24.4: 405–423.

Spencer, S., and N. Delvino (2019). "Municipal Activism on Illegalized migrants: The Framing of Inclusive Approaches at the Local Level". *Journal of Immigrant & Refugee Studies* 17.1: 27–43.

Triandafyllidou, A., and L. Bartolini (2020). "Understanding Irregularity". In Spencer, S., and A. Triandafyllidou (eds.) *Migrants with Irregular Status in Europe. Evolving Conceptual and Policy Challenges.* Springer: 11–31.

van Dyk, S., and E. Misbach (2016). "Zur politischen Ökonomie des Helfens. Flüchtlingspolitik und Engagement im flexiblen Kapitalismus". *PROKLA. Zeitschrift für Kritische Sozialwissenschaft* 46.183: 205–227.

Vandevoordt, R. (2019). "Subversive Humanitarianism: Rethinking Refugee Solidarity through Grass-Roots Initiatives". *Refugee Survey Quarterly* 38.3: 245–265.

Zamponi, L. (2017). "Practices of Solidarity: Direct Social Action, Politicisation and Refugee Solidarity Activism in Italy". *Mondi Migranti* 11.3: 97–117.

Index

www.ingramcontent.com/pod-product-compliance
Lightning Source LLC
Chambersburg PA
CBHW070052030426
42335CB00016B/1866